KANJI F ZERO! 2

First Edition 初版

George Trombley
Yukari Takenaka
Kanako Hatanaka
Justin McGowan

Kanji From Zero! Book 2
Proven Methods to Learn Kanji with Integrated Workbook

PREFACE

Kanji From Zero! is a Japanese kanji book series built on the idea that learning kanji shouldn't be mechanical and shouldn't only be about learning the readings of each kanji. The relationship to Japanese culture and the way kanji is integrated into Japanese life is key in establishing a strong foothold in integrating kanji into your Japanese fluency!

DEDICATION

This book is dedicated to and made for those who want to truly learn Japanese: Japanese culture lovers, Japanese language learners, Japanese drama watchers, Japanese beginners, JPOP music fans, Japanese anime watchers, Japanese manga readers, people of Japanese heritage connecting to their history, and, last but not least, anyone planning travel to Japan!

This began as a project to create a better book to learn kanji. It's not enough to merely learn how to read kanji. Kanji, like the members of a JPOP group or the characters of an anime, have unique personalities and quirks to be explored.

So many kanji books are merely reference materials listing every kanji, their readings, and maybe a few words. This barely scratches the surface of the amazing discoveries awaiting you when you fully grasp the connection kanji has with Japan and its culture. The entire Kanji From Zero! team wishes you success.

COPYRIGHT

Printed in USA / England / Australia
ISBN-13: 978-0996786348

1st edition: May 2022

DISTRIBUTION

Distributed in the USA, Canada, Others by:
From Zero LLC.
10624 S. Eastern Ave. #A769
Henderson, NV 89052, USA
sales@fromzero.com

Distributed in the UK & Europe by:
Bay Language Books Ltd.
Unit 4, Kingsmead, Park Farm,
Folkestone, Kent. CT19 5EU, Great Britain
sales@baylanguagebooks.co.uk

Thanks for the nice comments! We love feedback!

I'm grateful for your work... wouldn't have gotten as far as I have if I hadn't found Japanese From Zero
Jack Haveman – JFZ Discord Server

I'm definitely a fan of your teaching and your books I have all of them JFZ 1-4 and Kanji from Zero.
Hat_On_A_Fox – Discord PM

These books and this website remain my nihongo bible!
Ray_San – YesJapan.com

The books are great! I like the way everything is explained, the examples, the lessons and the reviews.
Eijioo – YesJapan.com

Japanese From Zero Book 1 and 2 are amazing books for beginners! Having tried other ways of learning Japanese from the beginning, I find that the Japanese from Zero series are incredibly user friendly.
Kurisuti.Chan – YesJapan.com

I love JFZ, because it's so so so easy to use compared to others I've tried! It's clear you put a lot of work into it and I'm very grateful. Even though I lead a busy life and can't find too much time to learn, JFZ makes it easy for me to pick up where I left off and revise what I might have forgotten. THANKS!! ☺
J. Brooks – Facebook

THANK-YOU JFZ!!!!!! I think Everything JFZ does is wonderful! It is the most helpful book I've come across!
Rukia Kuchiki – YesJapan.com

Keep up the great work and the video series on YouTube, Love the series and the books they've been a great help in my studies with my one on one teacher and I will be getting books 4&5 to complete my set.
>>GameHacKeR<< – JFZ Discord

Thank you for your videos! I'm really enjoying learning Japanese and I'm using your resources the most at the moment.
cornwagon – Discord PM

Thank you, I just finished the 2nd book and can't wait to start with the 3rd! Soon am getting my hands on the 4th!
religionflag – YesJapan.com

JFZ! is perfect. If you're a complete beginner, this book takes you through the bare basics and really helps you progress quickly. I highly recommend it.
F. Morgan – Good Reads review

The perfect Japanese textbook for young learners. One of the benefits of this book, which also slows it down, are the tangents it takes to explain the nuances of Japanese that a beginner might encounter.
Michael Richey – Tofugu.com

You really learn Japanese from zero – no prior knowledge at all required. The grammar is easy to understand.
Karl Andersson - karlandersson.se

As someone who owns the first three books, I can say the books are great.
Mastema – YesJapan.com

feedback@fromzero.com

Kanji From Zero! ②

– CONTENTS –

❑ **THE BASICS A: KANJI BASICS** **11**

❑ **KANJI LESSON 1: 悪安暗温暑寒** **20**

UNDERSTANDING KANJI PARTS 漢字部分の理解

● 1-1. This, that, that over there in the olden days 23
● 1-2. Some kanji parts are "inferior" to others 亜 23

KANJI USAGE 漢字の使い方

● 1-3. Talk is cheap (安) 24
● 1-4. The bad part of kanji (悪) 25
● 1-5. Mid-winter (寒中) 26
● 1-6. い adjectives from the kanji 27

❑ **KANJI LESSON 2: 苦速重軽深短** **33**

UNDERSTANDING KANJI PARTS 漢字部分の理解

● 2-1. How long is, and what is 里 (Chinese mile) 36

KANJI USAGE 漢字の使い方

● 2-2. Don't be too fast when choosing kanji (速) 36
● 2-3. A short note about "short" (短) 36
● 2-4. More い adjectives from the kanji 37
● 2-5. Compound kanji words vs phrases 38

❑ **KANJI LESSON 3: 悲美幸曲助消** **45**

UNDERSTANDING KANJI PARTS 漢字部分の理解

● 3-1. 日 (reason) and 日 (day, sun) look similar 48

KANJI USAGE 漢字の使い方

● 3-2. Same sound, different words 48
● 3-3. The beauty of Japan (美) 49
● 3-4. The luck of the Japanese 49
● 3-5. More than one way to help (助) 50

❑ **KANJI LESSON 4: 申乗植育飲泳** **56**

UNDERSTANDING KANJI PARTS 漢字部分の理解

● 4-1. The upside-down baby radical 59
● 4-2. The "flesh" radical にくづき (肉、月、月) 59

KANJI USAGE 漢字の使い方

● 4-3. "Raising" things in Japan requires more than just 育 60
● 4-4. 十二支 (12 signs of the Chinese zodiac) 61
● 4-5. The difference between 言う and 申す 62

❑ **KANJI LESSON 5: 運開決想死感** **68**

Understanding Kanji Parts 漢字部分の理解

- 5-1. The road to 辶 71

Kanji Usage 漢字の使い方

- 5-2. Kanji is killing you「死」 71
- 5-3. Same sound, different kanji あける 72
- 5-4. Various feelings using 感 72

❑ **KANJI LESSONS 1-5: SUPER REVIEW 1 .... 79**

❑ **KANJI LESSON 6: 起使始終写守 83**

Understanding Kanji Parts 漢字部分の理解

- 6-1. How long is, and what is 寸 (measurement) 86
- 6-2. The "person" radical にんべん (HYPERLINK "https://dictionar) 86

Kanji Usage 漢字の使い方

- 6-3. The beginning and the end 始、終 87

❑ **KANJI LESSON 7: 取受拾持習集 94**

Understanding Kanji Parts 漢字部分の理解

- 7-1. Kanji Part: "again" 又 97

Kanji Usage 漢字の使い方

- 7-2. Obtaining and Acquisition (取) 97
- 7-3. Subtle Difference, Big Changes 98
- 7-4. The difference between 習う、勉強する and 学ぶ 99
- 7-5. Different types of learning 習 100

❑ **KANJI LESSON 8: 住向急去進整 106**

Understanding Kanji Parts 漢字部分の理解

- 8-1. The "movement" radical しんにょう (辶) 109

Kanji Usage 漢字の使い方

- 8-2. Japanese Proverbs using 住・急・去 110

❑ **KANJI LESSON 9: 送打待代着調 117**

Kanji Usage 漢字の使い方

- 9-1. Kinds of Clothing 着 120
- 9-2. Same sound, different words「ととのえる」 121
- 9-3. How many can you hit? 打 121

❑ **KANJI LESSON 10: 追定転投登動 129**

Kanji Usage 漢字の使い方

- 10-1. Compound words using 定 132
- 10-2. 定食 (set meals) 133
- 10-3. Japanese proverbs with 投 134

❑ **KANJI LESSONS 6-10: SUPER REVIEW 2 .... 141**

❑ **KANJI LESSON 11: 配表勝負返放** **145**

Kanji Usage 漢字の使い方

● 11-1. Same sound, different kanji「はなす」 148
● 11-2. The visible and hidden parts of kanji 表と裏 148
● 11-3. Winning and losing in kanji 勝・負 149
● 11-4. The origin of the term 負け犬 (loser) 150

❑ **KANJI LESSON 12: 問有遊落流練** **156**

Understanding Kanji Parts 漢字部分の理解

● 12-1. The "gate" radical もんがまえ (門) 159

Kanji Usage 漢字の使い方

● 12-2. Go with the "kanji" flow 流 160
● 12-3. Flowing sounds with 流 161

❑ **KANJI LESSON 13: 君者主相客係** **167**

Kanji Usage 漢字の使い方

● 13-1. The relationships of kanji 関係 170
● 13-2. Describing many kinds of people using 者 (person) 171
● 13-3. Affectionate name additions 君 and ちゃん 172

❑ **KANJI LESSON 14: 族他役童神様** **178**

Kanji Usage 漢字の使い方

● 14-1. Gods, Lords, and people coming home late 様 181
● 14-2. Phrases that use 様 181
● 14-3. The many roles kanji can play 役 182

❑ **KANJI LESSON 15: 医院駅屋館宿** **189**

Kanji Usage 漢字の使い方

● 15-1. Something about train stations 駅 192
● 15-2. Shops and people 屋 192
● 15-3. Building with kanji 院・館 193

❑ **KANJI LESSONS 10-15: SUPER REVIEW 3** **200**

❑ **KANJI LESSON 16: 宮局所州県区** **204**

Understanding Kanji Parts 漢字部分の理解

● 16-1. X marks the spot 207

Kanji Usage 漢字の使い方

● 16-2. The states of kanji 州 207
● 16-3. Tokyo divided by 区 208
● 16-4. The royal kanji 宮 209

❑ **KANJI LESSON 17: 岸橋湖港庭畑** **216**

Understanding Kanji Parts 漢字部分の理解

● 17-1. The "field" radical た (田) 219
● 17-2. To split or not to split... 220
● 17-3. The ten heavenly stems... 壬 is weird (a rant against kanji) 220

Kanji Usage 漢字の使い方

● 17-4. Famous landmarks in Japan 湖 橋 港 畑 庭 221

❑ **KANJI LESSON 18: 都島坂路庫式 228**

Understanding Kanji Parts 漢字部分の理解

● 18-1. The "dotted cliff" radical まだれ (广) 231
● 18-2. Where you place the village is important こざとへん 232

Kanji Usage 漢字の使い方

● 18-3. When and why 大坂 changed to 大阪 232
● 18-4. There are more than just prefectures in Japan 233
● 18-5. Small differences, different meanings 鳥 234

❑ **KANJI LESSON 19: 度等倍秒部列 241**

Kanji Usage 漢字の使い方

● 19-1. Every minute and second counts with kanji 度・秒 244
● 19-2. An interesting thing about 倍 and 二倍 244
● 19-3. Doing more than others with 人一倍 245
● 19-4. Company Departments 部 245
● 19-5. The many clubs of kanji 部 246
● 19-6. How can something mean "next time" and "this time" 今度 247

❑ **KANJI LESSON 20: 階級期号章丁 254**

Kanji Usage 漢字の使い方

● 20-1. The Japan Kanji Aptitude Test「漢検」 257
● 20-2. Same sound, different kanji「さいご」 258
● 20-3. Counting ships... 号 258
● 20-4. Japanese addresses 259
● 20-5. PROVERB: "One time one meeting" 一期一会 259

❑ **KANJI LESSONS 16-20: SUPER REVIEW 4 .... 266**

❑ **KANJI LESSON 21: 仕事委員研究 270**

Understanding Kanji Parts 漢字部分の理解

● 21-1. How kanji is made 273
● 21-2. The problem with kanji dictionary kanji breakdowns 277
● 21-3. A cheat code to guessing a kanji's おんよみ 278

Kanji Usage 漢字の使い方

● 21-4. Same kanji word, different reading and meaning 大事 279
● 21-5. Origin story of 事 280
● 21-6. Why do you "polish" rice?（研ぐ） 281

❑ **KANJI LESSON 22: 炭柱笛板筆皿 288**

UNDERSTANDING KANJI PARTS 漢字部分の理解

● 22-1. The "bamboo" radical たけかんむり (竹) 291

KANJI USAGE 漢字の使い方

● 22-2. Good fortune from upright-floating tea stalks? 柱 292

● 22-3. Useful set phrases using 板 292

❑ **KANJI LESSON 23: 品服物薬箱帳..299**

KANJI USAGE 漢字の使い方

● 23-1. Same kanji, different reading/meaning 品 302

● 23-2. People in the box 箱 303

● 23-3. Compound words using 物 304

❑ **KANJI LESSON 24: 詩漢題予勉礼..311**

UNDERSTANDING KANJI PARTS 漢字部分の理解

● 24-1. The "speech" radical ごんべん (言) 314

KANJI USAGE 漢字の使い方

● 24-2. Japanese Manners 礼 315

● 24-3. Bad and, not-so-bad manners in Japan 日本の礼儀 316

❑ **KANJI LESSON 25: 農羊緑豆葉根..323**

UNDERSTANDING KANJI PARTS 漢字部分の理解

● 25-1. More kanji with the "thread" radical, いとへん (糸) 326

KANJI USAGE 漢字の使い方

● 25-2. Food and seasonings made with soybean 大豆 327

● 25-3. What's wrong with 大根 (Japanese radish)? 328

❑ **KANJI LESSONS 21-25: SUPER REVIEW 5..335**

❑ **KANJI LESSON 26: 商業世界実球..339**

KANJI USAGE 漢字の使い方

● 26-1. The difference between 玉 and 球 342

● 26-2. Kanji industries 業 343

❑ **KANJI LESSON 27: 反対全両面命..350**

KANJI USAGE 漢字の使い方

● 27-1. Subtle Differences, Big Changes 353

● 27-2. Japanese proverbs using 両 and 面 353

● 27-3. Completely and not at all 全 354

● 27-4. A pair of Japanese words 一対 354

● 27-5. More words with 対 355

● 27-6. Best of both worlds 両 355

❑ **KANJI LESSON 28: 旅荷味具由発..362**

KANJI USAGE 漢字の使い方

● 28-1. "Departure" and "Origin" 発 365
● 28-2. Kinds of taste using 味 365
● 28-3. Useful set phrases using 荷 and 由 366
❑ KANJI LESSON 29: 酒祭昔福昭和 373
UNDERSTANDING KANJI PARTS 漢字部分の理解
● 29-1. A better breakdown of 祭 and 福 376
● 29-2. The "mouth" radical くち (口) 377
KANJI USAGE 漢字の使い方
● 29-3. Which one do you like, Japanese or Western? (和 and 洋) 378
● 29-4. Famous Japanese festivals 祭 378
● 29-5. Japanese eras 379
❑ KANJI LESSON 30: 氷波湯油注洋 386
KANJI USAGE 漢字の使い方
● 30-1. Useful set phrases using 波 and 油 389
● 30-2. Subtle Differences, Big Changes (Part 1) 390
● 30-3. Subtle Differences, Big Changes (Part 2) 390
● 30-4. Modern Japanese words with 洋 391
❑ KANJI LESSONS 26-30: SUPER REVIEW 6 398
❑ KANJI LESSON 31: 真意銀鉄第陽 402
KANJI USAGE 漢字の使い方
● 31-1. The Yin-Yang of kanji 陽 405
● 31-2. Useful set phrases using 真 405
● 31-3. Describing one's state of mind using 意 406
● 31-4. Your Japanese level is up to you! ～次第 406
❑ KANJI LESSON 32: 血指歯身鼻皮息 414
KANJI USAGE 漢字の使い方
● 32-1. Names of fingers 指 417
● 32-2. Useful set phrases using 歯, 鼻 and 息 418
● 32-3. Kinds of teeth using 歯 419
❑ KANJI LESSON 33: 横次化央病平談 426
KANJI USAGE 漢字の使い方
● 33-1. The "-ization" of things 化 429
● 33-2. Japanese proverbs using 化 and 病 430
● 33-3. Types of illness 病 430
❑ KANJI LESSONS 31-33: SUPER REVIEW 7 437
❑ GLOSSARY A: SEARCH BY READING 441
❑ GLOSSARY B: SEARCH BY ENGLISH MEANING 447

❑ GLOSSARY C: SEARCH BY PARTS 453
❑ GLOSSARY D: SEARCH BY STROKE COUNT 463
❑ OTHER "FROM ZERO!" BOOKS 466

We love book reviews!

Review on the seller's site

Your reviews help make new books and website additions possible! Not only do they help spread the word, but they also help us to improve our books and website. Please visit any of the major book seller websites and post a review of *Kanji From Zero!*

Send us direct feedback

If you love, hate, or are confused about anything in this book, please email us at **feedback@fromzero.com**. With your feedback we can improve future editions.

Videos and website

Check out FromZero.com!

All our books (Japanese, Korean, Chinese, German etc!) also have interactive versions at http://FromZero.com.

Check out our videos!

Watch the HUNDREDS of videos available at our YouTube channel:
http://www.youtube.com/yesjapan

Other social media!

TikTok	@japanese.from.zero
Instagram	@japanesefromzero
Facebook	@JapaneseFromZero
Discord	http://learnFZ.com/JFZDiscord

A Kanji Basics 漢字の基礎

● A-1. Should I learn to write the kanji?

The answer is YES, and NO. Nowadays it might be more valuable to be able to recognize a character than being able to write it. In the internet world, you will most likely be typing kanji on a computer or punching it into your smartphone rather than physically writing it.

That being said, writing helps you learn faster, and makes distinguishing similar kanji easier. So, we recommend you spend time writing each kanji at least 5-10 times.

● A-2. How kanji are made up of parts

Kanji are often composed of two or more *parts*. Complicated kanji, or in other words, kanji with many strokes, are just kanji with more parts. These *parts* are normally just other kanji stacked or standing next to each other.

For example, the kanji for "rain" is 雨. When 雨 (rain) is stacked on top of the kanji for "field" 田, it becomes 雷 which means "lightning". Cool right? Rain on a field makes lightning! This is a great example of simple kanji parts making up a bigger kanji.

Sometimes, one or more parts are not a kanji, but just a seemingly random line OR a random modification of an existing kanji.

For example, by adding a hooked line under 雷, we make 電, which means, "electric". But the "hooked line" itself isn't actually a kanji, it's just modification of 田. Imagine the hooked line is lightning coming from the *rain* over the *field* to make electricity.

rain	thunder and lightning	electric
雨	雷	電
"rain"	"rain" + "field	"rain" + "field" (with hook)

Conflicting origin stories

When I was in Japan, I learned the origin story of 電 (electricity) as taught in the prior section. It was THAT origin story that excited me at age 15 to go full on into learning kanji. And until writing this book, the origin story of 電 remained unchanged for me.

If you ever deep dive into the origin of any particular kanji, you might come across conflicting information. This is what happened to me with 電.

While doing research for this book, I learned that the 十 part of 田 in 雷 (lightning / thunder) actually represents "lightning". Alternatively, some sources say that 田 isn't a field, but is instead four 口 representing a "cluster of air" making the sound of lighting.

十 = lightning?

田 = 口+口+口+口?

Furthermore, the "hooked line" added to 田 (field) in 電 (electric) is said to be the character 电 (いなずま) which means "lightning bolt".

The problem with deep diving kanji origins

While it's interesting to learn of "possible" origin stories, these stories can be burdensome to a kanji learner. The problem is that 十 means, "10", and 口 means, "mouth, opening". Also, 电 isn't used in any other kanji in the 常用漢字 (じょうようかんじ) (Common Use Kanji).

So, assigning a new meaning to 十 or 口 just for one kanji to make a "cooler" story is counterproductive when there are thousands of kanji to be learned.

It also might not be effective use of your time to learn a unique meaning for a part used only once or twice in the over 2,000 Common Use Kanji. Instead, learning smaller, more often used parts, regardless of the actual or cooler origin story, is more effective.

HOWEVER, despite our goal of making "remembering the kanji" easier by using the most logical origin story, we will also sometimes include the deeper origin story to give the full picture of the kanji being taught.

● A-3. Looking up kanji you can't read

You can search for kanji that you can and can't read in one of three common ways:

1. **STROKE COUNT**

   Count the strokes then go to the back of the kanji dictionary / book and look at all kanji with that number of strokes until you find the kanji you are looking for. If the kanji you are looking for isn't listing ADD one stroke or REMOVE one stroke from your count just in case you might have miscounted.

Stroke order index example: **Kanji From Zero!** book 1

7 strokes

体	256
何	403
作	219
図	384
声	239
売	191
弟	248
形	395
村	107
来	182

雨	88
青	108

9 strokes

前	374
南	298
室	403
後	374
思	190
星	308
春	360
昼	373

週	288
野	331
雪	307
魚	269
鳥	269
黄	349
黒	350

12 strokes

場	322
晴	237
朝	373

2. **くんよみ (JAPANESE READING) AND おんよみ (CHINESE READING)**

   If you know ANY of the readings of a kanji you can look for the kanji based on that reading.

Readings index example: **Kanji From Zero!** book 1

は

は	羽	288
は(える)	生	79
は(やす)	生	79
は(らす)	晴	237
は(れる)	晴	237
はい(る)	入	120
はか(る)	図	384
はか(る)	計	200
ハク	白	109
はし(る)	走	181
はず(す)	外	341
ハチ	八	25

ひろ(がる)	広	170
ひろ(げる)	広	170
ひろ(まる)	広	170
ひろ(める)	広	170

び

ビャク	白	109

ふ

フ	歩	182
フ	父	247
フ	風	307

3. **RADICAL**

A "radical", called 部首 (ぶしゅ) in Japanese, is just the main part of a kanji in which it's indexed. It's most often the first part of the kanji written or the most prominent part. Kanji books often have a radical index with the kanji ordered by strokes that have a particular radical.

Radical / Parts index example: **Kanji From Zero!** book 2

3 strokes	
艹	苦 (#247) 落 (#310) 薬 (#376) 漢 (#380) 葉 (#389) 荷 (#404)
丂	号 (#358)
与	写 (#275)
凵	歯 (#429)
宀	安 (#242) 寒 (#246) 守 (#276) 定 (#296) 客 (#317) 宿 (#330) 宮 (#331) 実 (#395)

● A-4. The brutal truth about kanji

Kanji are often called, "pictographs". For example, consider this logical series of kanji.

Adding a tree next to a tree to make "woods" and three trees to make "forest" is purely genius and anyone can understand this logic.

There are other examples where kanji truly makes logical sense. Sometimes, it's so obvious that even a person who has never seen kanji can guess the meanings.

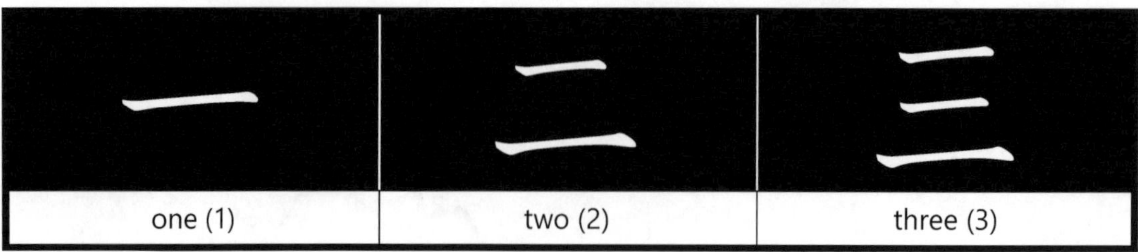

Some kanji, while not as easy to figure out as 一二三, are easy enough to imagine.

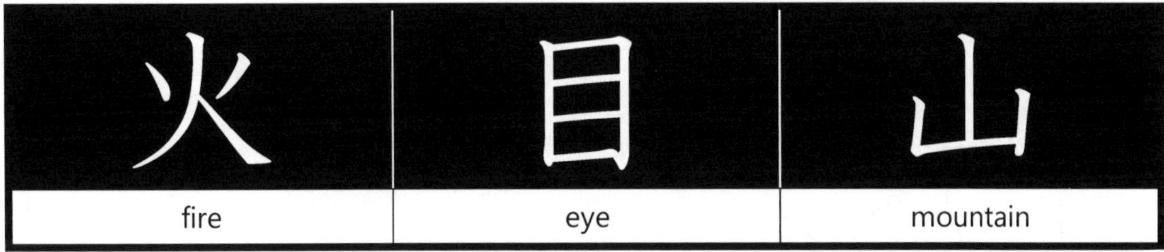

火	目	山
fire	eye	mountain

Unfortunately, the kanji pictograph often doesn't make sense unless you study the origins and sometimes make giant leaps in logic. Consider the following three kanji.

怒	悲	忠
anger	sorrow	loyalty

At first sight, I don't imagine anyone would have been able to guess the meanings. However, by breaking up kanji into its individual parts, you gain valuable hints that, while not outright telling you the meaning, will help you remember the meaning.

怒 is composed with 女 (woman) + 又 (again) + 心 (heart) to mean "anger"
悲 is composed with 非 (negative) + 心 (heart) to mean "sorrow"
忠 is composed with 中 (inside) + 心 (heart) to mean "loyalty"

These parts are also re-used in other kanji to have completely different meanings.

努	罪	沖
diligent	sin	open sea

努 is composed with 女 (woman) + 又 (again) + 力 (power) to mean "diligent"
罪 is composed with 罒 (net) + 非 (negative) to mean "sin"
沖 is composed with 氵 (water) + 中 (inside) to mean "open sea"

While it's true that some kanji absolutely make sense as a pictograph, the truth is the meaning of most kanji isn't easily figured out just by looking at them.

In book one of the "Kanji From Zero!" series, most of the kanji were simple and not made up of parts, so it required you to use raw memory to learn each character.

In this book, most of the kanji can be split into parts. This allows us to take advantage of the mind's incredible ability to remember patterns and more easily remember the kanji.

While initially there will be more time required to learn the parts AND the kanji, over time your ability to recognize and retain new kanji should improve dramatically, when compared to straight memorization techniques. More on this in the next section!

● A-5. Effectively "remembering the kanji" through mnemonics

There is a technique called a "mnemonic", (pronounced, "nuh·maa·nik"), which is a "device such as a pattern of letters, ideas, or associations that assists in remembering something".

I once made a video titled, "The case against mnemonics". **http://learnfz.com/against**

The case AGAINST mnemonics (from the video)

- Some mnemonics are "forced" into books and don't actually help.
- Not all characters are easily made into a mnemonic.
- Often kanji are created with parts based on sound NOT meaning.
- Mnemonics are often better when created by the learner.
- Sometimes it's easier to just learn the character.

Since that video my views have shifted. Now even this book has mnemonics. Here's why:

The case FOR mnemonics

- MANY viewers let me know how powerful mnemonics have been for them.
- I realized how powerful mnemonics had been for me (and still are)

While my opinion has evolved, I still believe mnemonics are more powerful when you invent your own. However, many students seem to like having mnemonics provided.

So, we have included several mnemonic devices for each kanji taught in this book based on its individual parts. Each part also has an associated meaning, to help make creating your own mnemonic easier if you wish. When new kanji is initially introduced, we provide the RAW parts that make up the kanji without providing any mnemonic.

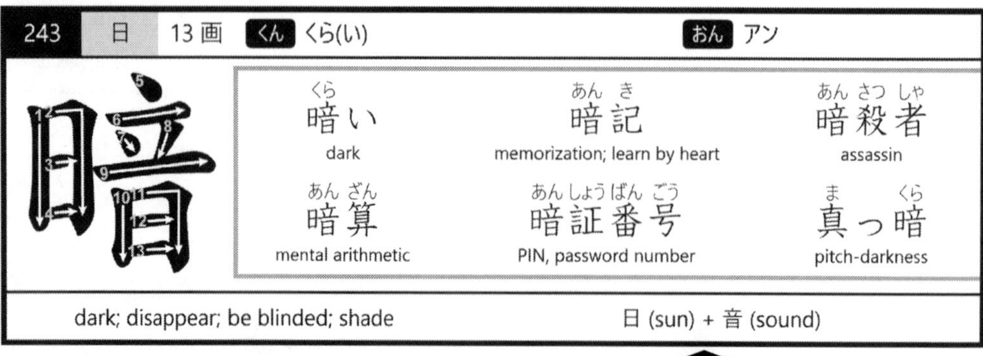

The "RAW" parts are provided, but we suggest you initially imagine your own mnemonic.

● A-6. How we created our mnemonic devices for each kanji

Mnemonic devices based on the kanji parts are provided to help you remember:
1. writing order, 2. the base kanji meaning, and 3. the individual readings of each kanji.
We have assigned meaning to each kanji part type based on these standards:

Our Part Type Preference Order

1. **Common** – parts with a proper Japanese name and meaning
   For these parts we always use with the original Japanese meaning.
2. **Uncommon** – parts with an ambiguous or "unhelpful" meaning
   For these parts we use the Japanese or Chinese meaning based on best fit.
3. **Unnamed** – parts that have no associated meaning, or are just additional lines
   For these parts we have imagined our own meaning based on look and fit.

Also, for simplicity, we use just ONE meaning per part even when multiple meanings exist. For example, 日 is "day" or "sun", but we chose "sun" as its single part meaning.

● A-7. The fine print about our mnemonics

Coming up with effective mnemonics for a wide array of students and learning styles is a difficult task, to say the least. Therefore, we suggest you only use our mnemonics if they are helpful. Furthermore, we encourage you to cross out "bad" mnemonics and write your own.

To make the most effective mnemonics, we have the following self-imposed limitations:

Our Mnemonic Rules

1. **Order** – The kanji parts MUST appear the same order as written.
2. **Kanji Meaning** – The meaning MUST be the last word in the mnemonic sentence.
3. **Avoid Words** – We MUST avoid words that could be confused as another part.

For example, the kanji 温 (warm) is written with these parts:

氵 (water) + 日 (sun) + 皿 (plate)

With our rules we made this mnemonic: (same order as written, ending with meaning)

氵 日 皿
Water in the sun on a plate is "warm".

Without our order and word limitations, perhaps we could have used:

"The water on the plate is '**warmed**' by the sun". While this sounds better, it doesn't help you remember the order of writing, and it isn't clear which of the words is the meaning.

● A-8. The problem with kanji parts

Learning the parts of the kanji can be VERY effective in learning how a kanji is written and even its underlying meaning. This is especially true when a part is commonly used amongst many kanji with a similar grouping. A great example of this are kanji that use 魚 (fish).

whale	carp	trout
鯨	鯉	鱒
fish + capital	fish + village	fish + nobility

There is a problem though. Kanji used as parts can be distorted from the familiar kanji you learned that make up the part. And those distorted versions can even look exactly like another kanji with a completely different meaning.

For example, moon is 月. So if you saw this kanji, 育 (to raise, grow up) you might think the bottom part is "moon," but it's actually a distorted / alternative version of 肉 which in this case means, "flesh" or "meat". Look at the following kanji that have a part that is 月.

月 as "flesh"		
stomach	**skin**	**back**
胃	肌	背
field + flesh	flesh + desk	north + flesh

月 as "moon"		
morning	**period; time**	**full moon**
朝	期	望
sun peeking thru grass + moon	that + moon	loss + moon + king

As you can see there is no way to easily distinguish "flesh" from "moon". To help see the difference we will use 月 for "flesh" and 月 for "moon" however they are both written as 月.

● A-9. How Kanji is introduced in this book

The following key shows the sections of the new kanji information boxes in the "New Kanji" section at the beginning of each lesson.

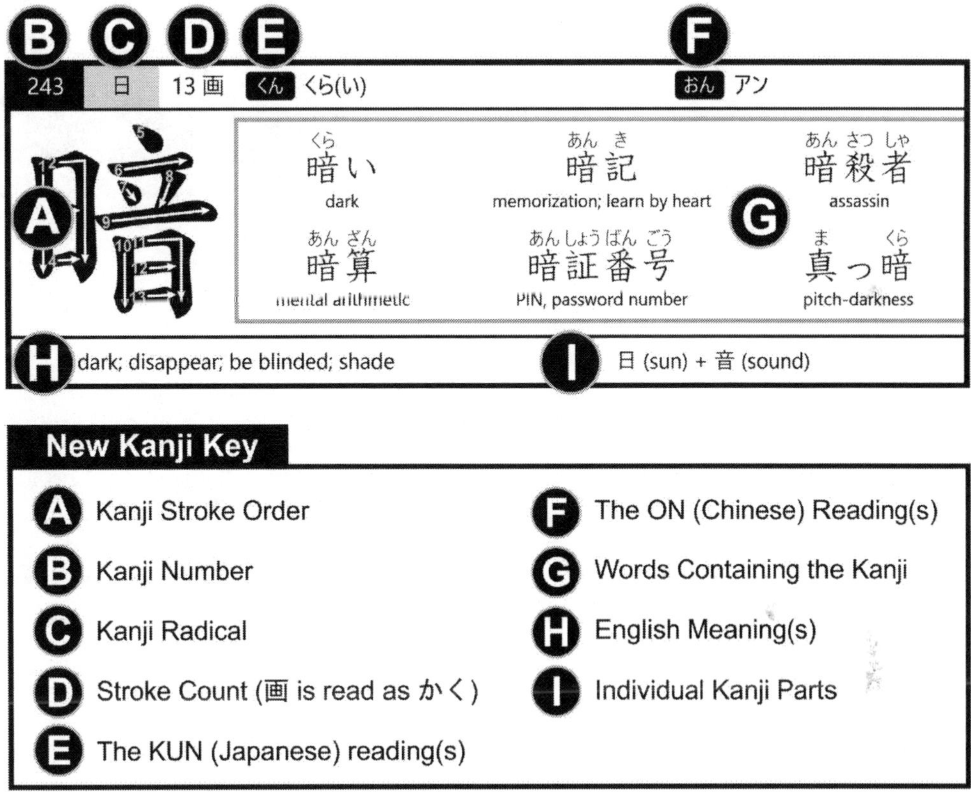

In the "Kanji Memory Tools" section, associated mnemonic devices for each kanji will be provided. PERHAPS this will help you remember the kanji. At least WE HOPE!

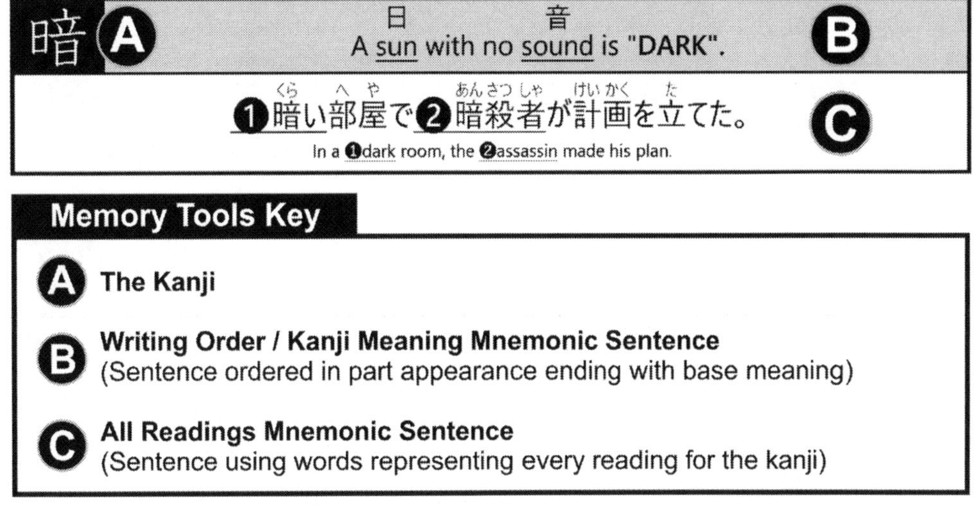

1 Kanji Lesson 1: 悪安暗温暑寒

241-246

Kanji that can be adjectives

1 New Kanji 新しい漢字

241	心	11 画	くん わる(い)	おん オ、アク

悪

わる 悪い bad	あく にん 悪人 bad person; villain	あく む 悪夢 nightmare; bad dream
あく じゅん かん 悪循環 vicious circle	さい あく 最悪 horrible; the worst	わる ぐち 悪口 slander; bad-mouthing

bad; vice; false; evil; wrong — 亜 (second-rate) + 心 (heart)

242	宀	6 画	くん やす(い)	おん アン

安

あん ぜん 安全 safety; safe	やす 安い cheap; inexpensive	あん しん 安心 ease; relief
ふ あん 不安 anxiety; uneasiness	やす う 安売り bargain; discount	やす 安っぽい cheap-looking; tawdry

inexpensive; peaceful; rested; relax — 宀 (roof) + 女 (woman)

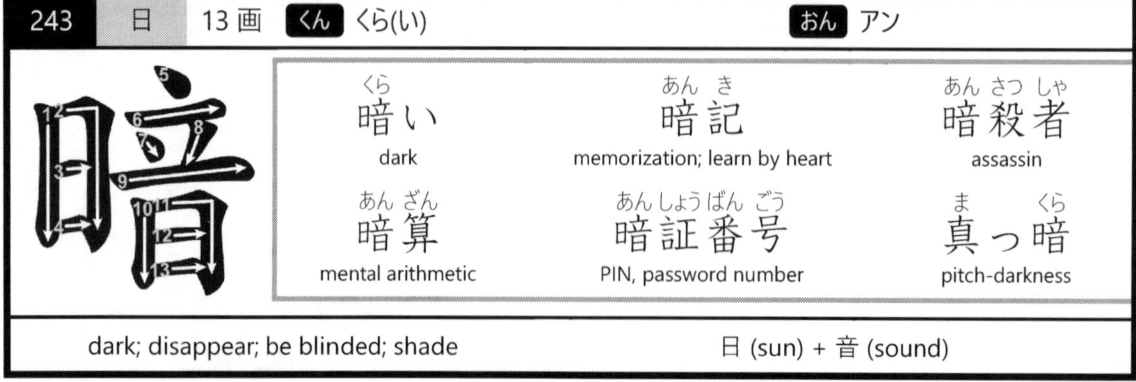

243	日	13 画	くん くら(い)	おん アン

暗

くら 暗い dark	あん き 暗記 memorization; learn by heart	あん さつ しゃ 暗殺者 assassin
あん ざん 暗算 mental arithmetic	あん しょう ばん ごう 暗証番号 PIN, password number	ま くら 真っ暗 pitch-darkness

dark; disappear; be blinded; shade — 日 (sun) + 音 (sound)

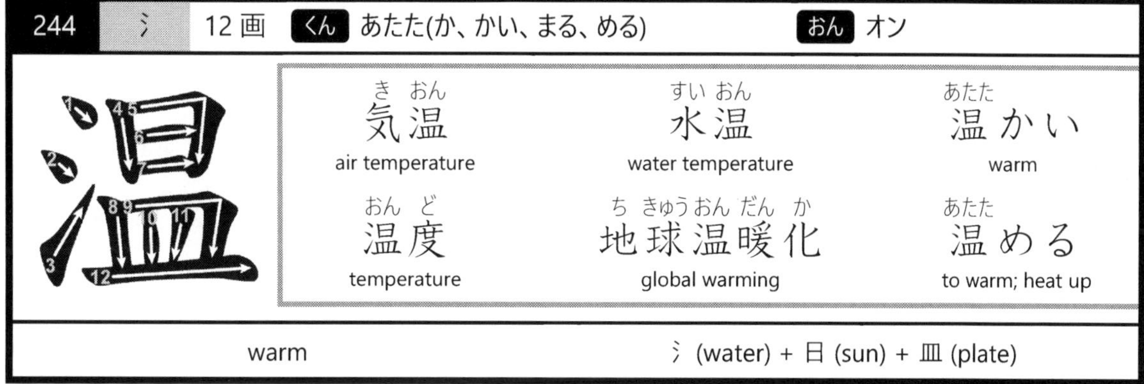

244 | 氵 | 12画 | くん あたた(か、かい、まる、める) | おん オン

温

き おん 気温 air temperature	すい おん 水温 water temperature	あたた 温かい warm
おん ど 温度 temperature	ち きゅう おん だん か 地球温暖化 global warming	あたた 温める to warm; heat up

warm | 氵 (water) + 日 (sun) + 皿 (plate)

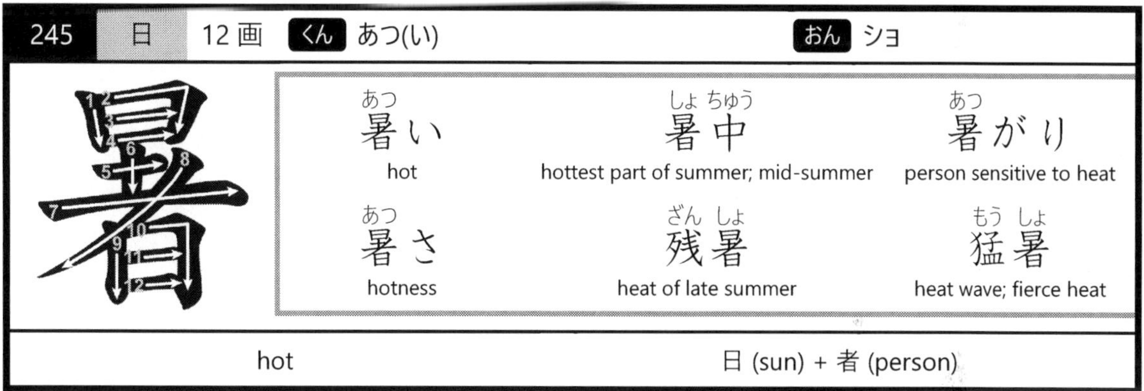

245 | 日 | 12画 | くん あつ(い) | おん ショ

暑

あつ 暑い hot	しょ ちゅう 暑中 hottest part of summer; mid-summer	あつ 暑がり person sensitive to heat
あつ 暑さ hotness	ざん しょ 残暑 heat of late summer	もう しょ 猛暑 heat wave; fierce heat

hot | 日 (sun) + 者 (person)

246 | 宀 | 12画 | くん さむ(い) | おん カン

寒

さむ 寒い cold	かん ちゅう 寒中 mid-winter; cold season	さむ 寒がり person sensitive to cold
さむ 寒さ coldness	お かん 悪寒 chill; the shakes	かん ぱ 寒波 cold wave

cold | 宀 (roof) + 其 (that, those) + ⺀ (slashes)

Kanji Parts used in the New Kanji

亜	second-rate	日	sun	者	person
心	heart	音	sound	其	that, those
宀	roof	氵	water	⺀	slashes
女	woman	皿	plate		

1 Kanji Memory Tools 漢字記憶術

This section helps you organically memorize kanji readings, meanings, and construction.

悪

亜 心

A second-rate heart is "**BAD**".

天気(てんき)の❶悪(わる)い日(ひ)は、寝(ね)る時(とき)に❷悪寒(おかん)がして、❸悪夢(あくむ)を見(み)ます。

On ❶bad weather days, when I sleep, I get the ❷chills and have ❸nightmares.

安

宀 女

A roof with a woman under it is "**PEACEFUL**".

給料(きゅうりょう)が❶安(やす)すぎるから、生活(せいかつ)が❷不安(ふあん)です。

Because my salary is ❶so cheap, I'm ❷anxious about my life.

暗

日 音

A sun with no sound is "**DARK**".

❶暗(くら)い部屋(へや)で❷暗殺者(あんさつしゃ)が計画(けいかく)を立(た)てた。

In a ❶dark room, the ❷assassin made his plan.

温

氵 日 皿

Water in the sun on a plate is "**WARM**".

❶気温(きおん)の低(ひく)い日(ひ)は❷室温(しつおん)を上げて風呂(ふろ)で❸温(あたた)まります。

On days when the ❶temperature is low, I raise the ❷room temperature and ❸warm up in the bath.

暑

日 者

Sun above a person makes them "**HOT**".

私(わたし)は❶暑(あつ)がりなので、❷猛暑(もうしょ)の日(ひ)は外(そと)に出(で)ません。

❶sensitive to heat, I don't go out on ❷an extremely hot day.

寒

宀 其 ⺀

A roof with those open slashes makes a house "**COLD**".

私(わたし)は❶寒(さむ)がりなので、❷寒中水泳(かんちゅうすいえい)はしません。

Since I'm ❶sensitive to cold, I don't ❷ swim in the cold.

1 Understanding Kanji Parts 漢字部分の理解

● 1-1. This, that, that over there in the olden days

In this lesson, the kanji part 其 (that, those) was introduced. In modern times, それ and その～ are written in hiragana, however, at one time they were written with kanji, 其(そ)れ and 其(そ)の. Here are others in the どれ and どの group that can be written in kanji:

これ	→	此(こ)れ	この	→	此(こ)の
それ	→	其(そ)れ	その	→	其(そ)の
あれ	→	彼(あ)れ	あの	→	彼(あ)の
どれ	→	何(ど)れ	どの	→	何(ど)の

It's recommended to only write them in hiragana since 彼(あ)の, without ふりがな would be read as 彼(かれ)の (his) and 何(ど)の would be read 何(なん)の and possibly create confusion.

● 1-2. Some kanji parts are "inferior" to others 亜

Not every kanji part plays a big role in kanji. A prime example is 亜 which only is used in a limited number of kanji. In modern Japan I have only been about to find three kanji that use 亜 (second-rate) as a part.

rank next; come after	bad; evil	muteness; speech impairment
亜	悪	唖
second-rate	second-rate + heart	mouth + second-rate

Even though country names are most often written using カタカナ, countries and places also have kanji names made up of 当(あ)て字(じ) (kanji chosen purely for their sound and not meaning). A common 当(あ)て字(じ) for place names for sound ア is 亜. Here are a few examples:

EXAMPLES

1. 亜米利加(アメリカ) (America)
2. 亜細亜(アジア) (Asia)
3. 亜剌比亜(アラビア) (Arabia)
4. 亜富汗斯坦(アフガニスタン) (Afghanistan)

* Full list of countries: LearnFZ.com/kanji-countries

亜 is used in countries purely for its sound, yet it does have a meaning. 亜 is an abbreviated (simplified) version (略字(りゃくじ)) of the original Chinese character 亞 which expresses the *platform* upon which a building sits. The *platform* is always pinned below the building, and unable to go to the top and therefore, "second-rate".

NOTE: 唖(おし) is considered a discriminative word, so use it cautiously or don't use it at all.

1 Kanji Usage 漢字の使い方

● 1-3. Talk is cheap (安)

安 can mean "inexpensive", but it's more commonly used in words relating with "peace of mind".

unease (not + peaceful)	public order (empty + room)
ふ　あん 不安	ち　あん 治安
If you are worried about a situation, then you can use 不安(ふあん) to say you are so.	治安(ちあん)が悪(わる)い or 治安(ちあん)がいい is a way to say a place is "dangerous" or "safe."

stable (peaceful + certain)	cheap yen (yen + cheap)
あん　てい 安定	えん　やす 円安
If something is "unstable", you can add 不(ふ) to make 不安定(ふあんてい) (unstable).	円安(えんやす) describes when the value of the yen drops in comparison to other currencies.

euthanasia (peaceful + comfort + death)	low priced; reasonable (status + cheap)
あん らく し 安楽死	かく やす 格安
Euthanasia means to end a life to end suffering when that is the only option.	格安 means "bargain priced" or "discounted." It isn't considered negative.

● 1-4. The bad part of kanji (悪)

悪 is part of some interesting words and Japanese idioms.

devil; demon (bad + evil spirit)	ill will; malice (bad + mind)
あく ま 悪魔	わる ぎ 悪気

nightmare (bad + dream)	bad person (bad + person)
あく む 悪夢	わる もの 悪者

bad smell; bad odor (bad + odor)	feelings of guilt (guilt + bad + feeling)
あく しゅう 悪臭	ざい あく かん 罪悪感

Here are some Japanese proverbs using 悪.

悪銭身に付かず
Easy come, easy go
Literally, "Ill-gotten gains (money) will not stick to you."

悪事千里を行く
Bad news travels a 1000 miles
One 里 is actually 3.927km or 2.44 miles, so bad news travels 2,440 miles.

● 1-5. Mid-winter (寒中)

寒中 (mid-winter; cold season) is written with 寒 (cold) + 中 (middle). Rather than using 寒中 to say "it's the cold season", it's commonly used in these two words.

checking up on someone in the cold season	swimming in the middle of the winter season
寒中見舞い	寒中水泳

寒中見舞い also describes a greeting card sent in the winter season when the weather is the coldest, from around January 7th until 節分, the last day of winter in the Japanese traditional calendar, around February 3rd or 4th. When a 年賀状 (New Year's Card) hasn't been sent, this will be the first greeting of the year. Luckily, with smartphones etc. there are now easier-to-send digital 年賀状 and 寒中見舞い.

When participating in 寒中水泳 (winter swimming) events, men will wear a traditional ふんどし (Japanese loincloth), or be completely naked during the swim. Woman and children will wear appropriate swimming attire.

● 1-6. い adjectives from the kanji

The kanji introduced in this lesson are all used to make い adjectives.
い adjectives can be conjugated into various tenses by dropping the final い, then adding to the word.

is~	was~	is not~	was not~
悪(わる)い (bad)	悪(わる)かった	悪(わる)くない	悪(わる)くなかった
安(やす)い (inexpensive)	安(やす)かった	安(やす)くない	安(やす)くなかった
暗(くら)い (dark)	暗(くら)かった	暗(くら)くない	暗(くら)くなかった
温(あたた)かい (warm)	温(あたた)かかった	温(あたた)かくない	温(あたた)かくなかった
暑(あつ)い (hot)	暑(あつ)かった	暑(あつ)くない	暑(あつ)くなかった
寒(さむ)い (cold)	寒(さむ)かった	寒(さむ)くない	寒(さむ)くなかった

1 Words You Can Write 書ける言葉

In this section, we introduce words you can write using the new kanji in the lesson.

悪い (わるい) bad

悪い

悪友 (あくゆう) undesirable friend; bad company; bad companion

悪友

安い (やすい) inexpensive

安い

安心 (あんしん) relief

安心

暗い(くらい) dark

暗	い										

明暗（めいあん）contrasting; lighting

明	暗										

気温（きおん）air temperature

気	温										

温室（おんしつ）glasshouse; greenhouse

温	室										

暑い（あつい）hot

暑	い										

暑中（しょちゅう）during summer heat

暑	中										

寒い（さむい）cold

寒	い										

室温（しつおん）room temperature

室	温										

悪口（わるぐち）bad mouth; insult; evil speaking

悪	口										

高温（こうおん）high temperature

高	温										

悪寒（おかん）chill; shakes; ague

悪	寒										

1 Kanji Workbook Activities

● 1. Stroke Order Check 書き順確認

Each kanji has a stroke with an arrow on it. Write its order number below the kanji.

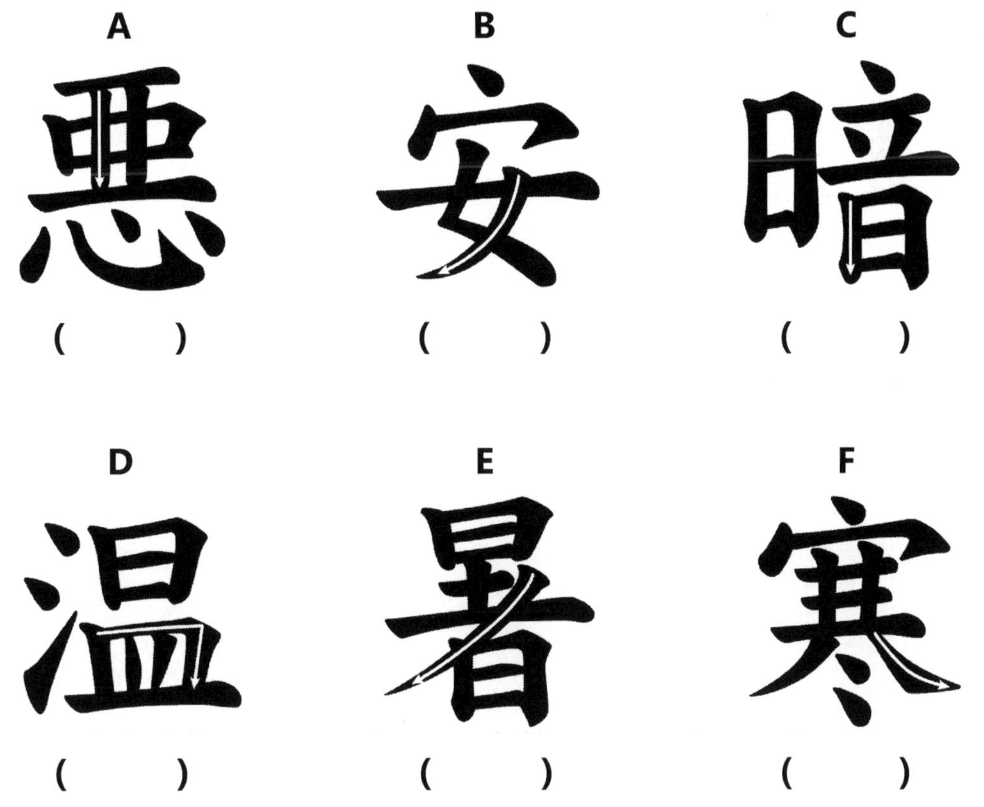

● 2. Kanji Meaning Match

Write the following kanji next to its meaning: 悪 寒 安 暑 暗 温 万 室 同

1. ____ cheap
2. ____ dark
3. ____ cold
4. ____ warm
5. ____ bad
6. ____ hot
7. ____ same
8. ____ room
9. ____ ten thousand

● 3. Kanji Readings

Write FURIGANA above the underlined kanji words.

1. アニメには、いつも悪人が 出ます。
2. お母さんといる時、安心します。
3. 今日の気温は、いつもより高いです。
4. わたしは スピーチを ぜんぶ 暗記しました。
5. わたしは暑いより、寒い方がいいです。

● 4. Fill in the Kanji

Fill in the appropriate kanji in the blanks for each sentence.

こ とし なつ あつ

1. ____ ____の____は ____いです。

Summer this year is hot.

に ほん い やす か

2. ____ ____ ____きの____いチケットを____いました。

I bought a cheap ticket to Japan.

さむ ひ あたた ちゃ の

3. ____い____は、____かい お____を____みましょう。

Let’s drink warm tea on cold days.

が　　　　　　　　　あく　にん　　で

4. あのえい ___には たくさんの___ ___が___てきます。

A lot of bad people appear in that movie.

よ　じ　　　　くら

5. さいきんは ___ ___ごろ、___ くなります。

Recently it's getting dark around 4pm.

お　かん　　　　　　　　の

6. ___ ___がするので、くすりを___みます。

Since I have the chills, I am going to take some medicine.

め　　まえ　　　くら

7. ___ の___がまっ___になりました。

It got pitch dark in front of my eyes.

● 5. Kanji Matching

Connect each kanji with an おん or くん reading. Use each reading only ONCE.

暑 •	• しょ
遠 •	• しん
安 •	• おん
楽 •	• おお
悪 •	• くら
寒 •	• やす
暗 •	• かん
多 •	• らく
温 •	• あく
新 •	• とお

1 Answer Key 答え合わせ

1. Stroke order check (answers)

A) 5 B) 5 C) 10

D) 9 E) 8 F) 10

2. Kanji meaning match (answers)

1. 安 cheap 2. 暗 dark 3. 寒 cold
4. 温 warm 5. 悪 bad 6. 暑 hot
7. 同 same 8. 室 room 9. 万 ten thousand

3. Kanji Readings (answers)

1. アニメには、いつも悪人(あくにん)が 出(で)ます。 Bad guys always appear in anime.
2. お母(かあ)さんといる時(とき)、安心(あんしん)します。 I'm at ease when my mother is here.
3. 今日(きょう)の気温(きおん)は、いつもより高(たか)いです。 Today's temperature is higher than normal.
4. わたしは スピーチを ぜんぶ 暗記(あんき)しました。 I memorized the entire speech.
5. わたしは暑(あつ)いより、寒(さむ)い方(ほう)がいいです。 I like cold more than hot.

4. Fill in the kanji (answers)

1. 今年の夏は、暑いです。
2. 日本行きの安いチケットを買いました。
3. 寒い日は、温かいお茶を飲みましょう。
4. あのえい画には、たくさんの悪人が出てきます。
5. さいきんは四時ごろ、暗くなります。
6. 悪寒がするので、くすりを飲みます。
7. 目の前がまっ暗になりました。

5. Kanji matching (answers)

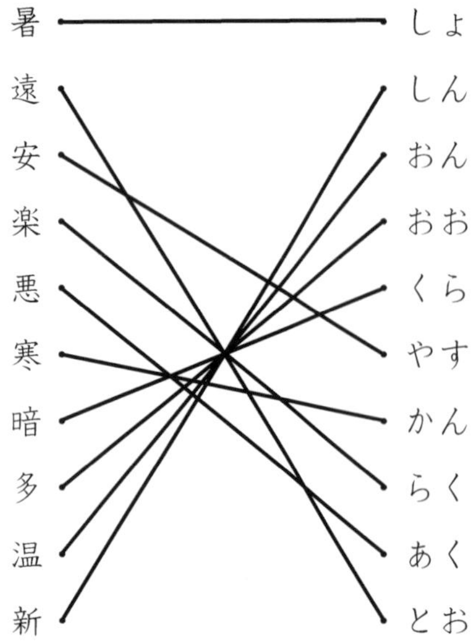

2 Kanji Lesson 2: 苦速重軽深短

247-252

More kanji that can be adjectives

2 New Kanji 新しい漢字

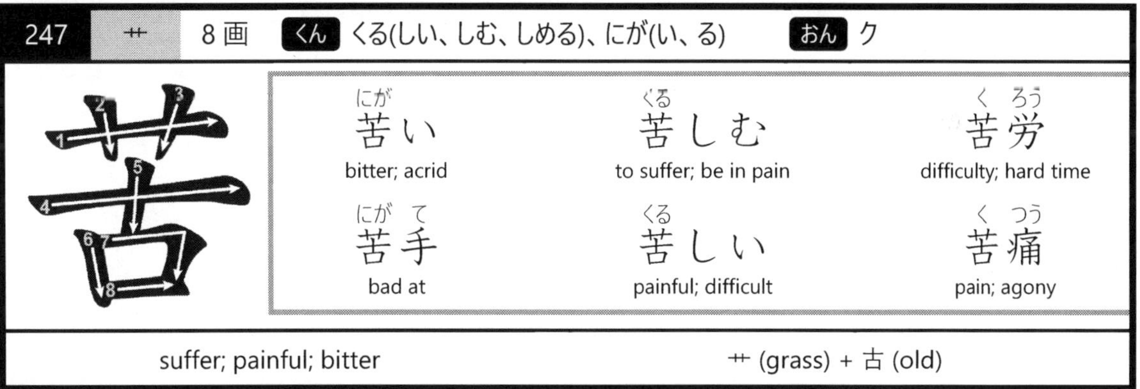

247
艹
8画
くん くる(しい、しむ、しめる)、にが(い、る)
おん ク
にが 苦い
bitter; acrid
くる 苦しむ
to suffer; be in pain
くろう 苦労
difficulty; hard time
にがて 苦手
bad at
くる 苦しい
painful; difficult
くつう 苦痛
pain; agony
suffer; painful; bitter
艹 (grass) + 古 (old)

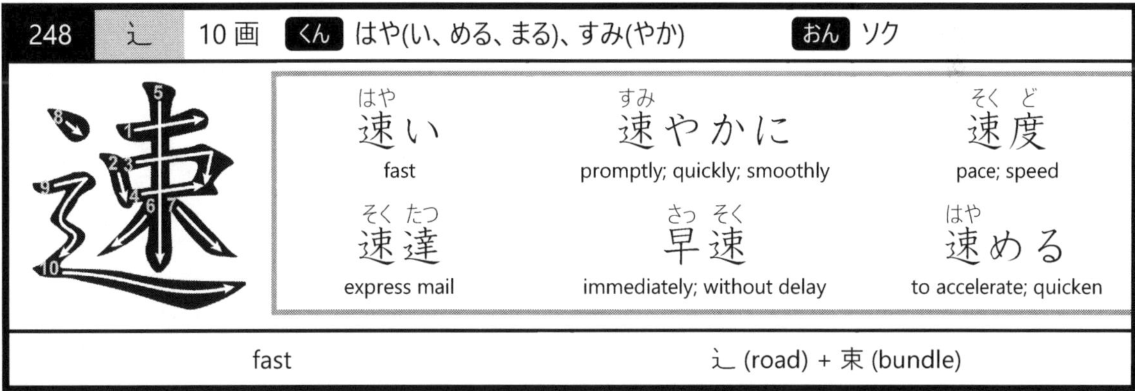

248
辶
10画
くん はや(い、める、まる)、すみ(やか)
おん ソク
はや 速い
fast
すみ 速やかに
promptly; quickly; smoothly
そくど 速度
pace; speed
そくたつ 速達
express mail
さっそく 早速
immediately; without delay
はや 速める
to accelerate; quicken
fast
辶 (road) + 束 (bundle)

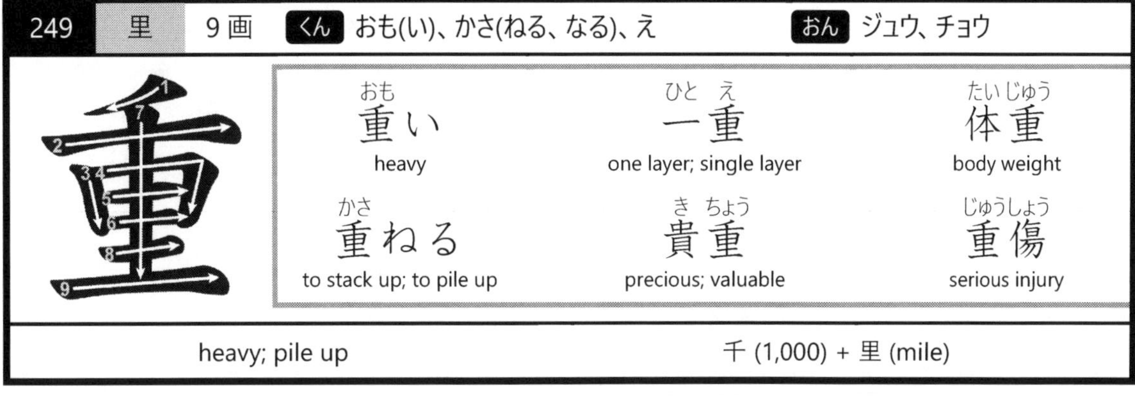

249
里
9画
くん おも(い)、かさ(ねる、なる)、え
おん ジュウ、チョウ
おも 重い
heavy
ひとえ 一重
one layer; single layer
たいじゅう 体重
body weight
かさ 重ねる
to stack up; to pile up
きちょう 貴重
precious; valuable
じゅうしょう 重傷
serious injury
heavy; pile up
千 (1,000) + 里 (mile)

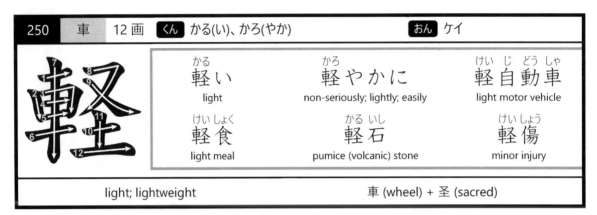

250	車	12 画	くん かる(い)、かろ(やか)	おん ケイ

軽

かる 軽い light	かろ 軽やかに non-seriously; lightly; easily	けい じ どう しゃ 軽自動車 light motor vehicle
けい しょく 軽食 light meal	かる いし 軽石 pumice (volcanic) stone	けい しょう 軽傷 minor injury

light; lightweight — 車 (wheel) + 圣 (sacred)

251	氵	11 画	くん ふか(い、まる、める)	おん シン

深

ふか 深い deep	ふか 深める to deepen / intensify	しん や 深夜 late night
しん かい 深海 deep ocean	すい しん 水深 depth of water	しん こ きゅう 深呼吸 deep breath

deep — 氵 (water) + 穴 (hole) + 木 (tree)

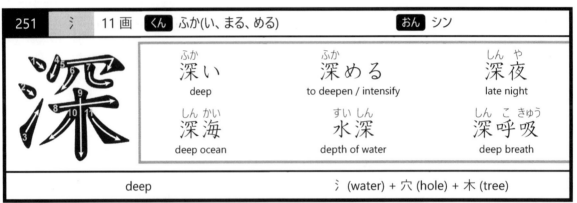

252	矢	12 画	くん みじか(い)	おん タン

短

みじか 短い short	たん ぶん 短文 short sentence	たん しょ 短所 bad point
たん じ かん 短時間 a short time	たん き だい がく 短期大学 junior college (2 or 3 year)	たん き 短気 short tempered

short — 矢 (arrow) + 豆 (bean)

Kanji Parts used in the New Kanji

艹	grass	里	mile	木	tree
古	old	車	wheel	矢	arrow
辶	road	圣	sacred	豆	bean
束	bundle	氵	water		
千	1,000	穴	hole		

2 Kanji Memory Tools 漢字記憶術

This section helps you organically memorize kanji readings, meanings, and construction.

苦

艹 古

Getting grass cuts when you're old is "**PAINFUL**".

❶苦(くる)しんでいる犬(いぬ)に❷苦(にが)い薬(くすり)を飲(の)ませるのは❸苦労(くろう)します。

You'll ❸have a hard time making a ❶suffering dog drink ❷bitter medicine.

速

⻌ 束

When crossing a road with a bundle you must be "**FAST**".

❶速達(そくたつ)は❷速(はや)い電車(でんしゃ)で、❸速(すみ)やかに運(はこ)びます。

❶Express mail is sent ❸promptly via a ❷fast train.

重

千 里

Walking 1,000 miles is hard when you are "**HEAVY**".

❶重(かさ)なった❷重(おも)い本(ほん)の❸重量(じゅうりょう)は 5 キロです。

The ❸weight of the ❷heavy ❶stacked books is 5 kilograms.

軽

車 圣

These wheels aren't sacred but they are "**LIGHT**".

❶軽自動車(けいじどうしゃ)は❷軽(かる)いし、❸軽(かろ)やかに走(はし)ります。

❶light motor vehicles are ❷light and drive ❸easily.

深

氵 穴 木

The water in the hole of the tree is "**DEEP**".

❶深夜(しんや)に❷深呼吸(しんこきゅう)をして❸深(ふか)いプールに飛(と)び込(こ)んだ。

❶Late night I took a ❷deep breath and dove into a ❸deep pool.

短

矢 豆

An arrow shot into a bean would have to be "**SHORT**".

❶短(みじか)い髪(かみ)の人(ひと)は、❷短気(たんき)が多(おお)いです。

Many people with ❶short hair are ❷short-tempered.

2 Understanding Kanji Parts 漢字部分の理解

● 2-1. How long is, and what is 里 (Chinese mile)

If you live in or have travelled the United States, you are likely aware of the distance called a "mile". A mile is approximately 1.6 kilometers. In this lesson, we introduce the kanji part 里 (り) as a "mile", also often called a "Chinese mile". One 里 is 3.927km or 2.44 miles. While the 里 was used in the past, in modern times you will probably only encounter it on period TV shows or in history books. A modern Japanese person most likely doesn't know how long a 里 is.

2 Kanji Usage 漢字の使い方

● 2-2. Don't be too fast when choosing kanji (速)

速 (fast), as in speed, and 早 (early) as in time, are commonly mistaken since they can both be read as はや.

to be fast	to be early
速(はや)い	早(はや)い

EXAMPLE SENTENCES

1. この車(くるま)は超(ちょう)速(はや)いです。
This car is super-fast.

2. 雅(まさ)さんはいつも起(お)きるのが早(はや)いです。
Masa is always early to wake up.

● 2-3. A short note about "short" (短)

短 (short) doesn't mean "short" as in height. Instead you say a person's height is "low" using 低い (ひくい).

short (length)	short (height)
短(みじか)い	背(せ)が低(ひく)い

EXAMPLE SENTENCES

1. 私(わたし)は短(みじか)い髪(かみ)が好(す)きです。
I like short hair.

2. うちのクラスには背(せ)が低(ひく)い人(ひと)が多(おお)いです。
There are a lot of short people in our class.

● 2-4. More い adjectives from the kanji

Similar to the last lesson, the kanji introduced in this lesson are all used to make い adjectives. い adjectives can be conjugated into various tenses.

is~	was~	is not~	was not~
苦(くる)しい (painful)	苦(くる)しかった	苦(くる)しくない	苦(くる)しくなかった
苦(にが)い (bitter)	苦(にが)かった	苦(にが)くない	苦(にが)くなかった
速(はや)い (fast)	速(はや)かった	速(はや)くない	速(はや)くなかった
重(おも)い (heavy)	重(おも)かった	重(おも)くない	重(おも)くなかった
軽(かる)い (lightweight)	軽(かる)かった	軽(かる)くない	軽(かる)くなかった
深(ふか)い (deep)	深(ふか)かった	深(ふか)くない	深(ふか)くなかった
短(みじか)い (short)	短(みじか)かった	短(みじか)くない	短(みじか)くなかった

EXAMPLE SENTENCES

1. 昼(ひる)に食(た)べ過(す)ぎてお腹(なか)が苦(くる)しいです。
   I ate so much at lunch my stomach is painful. (suffering)

2. テスラの車(くるま)は速(はや)いけど、充電時間(じゅうでんじかん)が長(なが)いです。
   Tesla cars are fast, but the charging time is long.

3. 飛行機(ひこうき)は離陸(りりく)する時(とき)は重(おも)いけど、着陸(ちゃくりく)の時(とき)は、燃料(ねんりょう)が減(へ)っているから軽(かる)いです。
   When airplanes take off, they are heavy, but when landing, due to less fuel, they are light.

4. 今朝(けさ)、飲(の)んだコーヒーは苦(にが)かったです。
   The coffee that I drank this morning was bitter.

5. このストローは、この深(ふか)いコップには短(みじか)すぎます。
   This straw is too short for this deep cup.

● 2-5. Compound kanji words vs phrases

The 熟語(じゅくご) (compound kanji word), 短気(たんき) means, "short temper" and 口軽(くちがる) means "unable to keep a secret". You can sometimes unwind a compound word into its parts to say the same thing. Be careful using 口軽(くちがる) as it is a fairly negative word.

Tanaka is short-tempered.	
田中(たなか)さんは短気(たんき)です。	田中(たなか)さんは気(き)が短(みじか)いです。

If you can't keep secrets, you can't make friends.	
口軽(くちがる)だと、友達(ともだち)ができません。	口(くち)が軽(かる)いと、友達(ともだち)ができません。

It takes longer to recover from a heavy wound than a light wound.	
軽傷(けいしょう)より重傷(じゅうしょう)は、治(なお)るのに時間(じかん)がかかる。	軽(かる)い傷(きず)より重(おも)い傷(きず)は、治(なお)るのに時間(じかん)がかかる。

It's a depressing Monday, but let's do our best.	
気重(きおも)な月曜日(げつようび)だけど、頑張(がんば)りましょう。	気(き)が重(おも)い月曜日(げつようび)だけど、頑張(がんば)りましょう。

2 Words You Can Write 書ける言葉

苦い(にがい) bitter

苦 い

苦心(くしん) painstaking

苦 心

苦手(にがて) bad at

苦 手

速い(はやい) fast

速	い										

時速(じそく) a speed per hour

時	速										

重い(おもい) heavy

重	い										

重大(じゅうだい) important

重	大										

軽い(かるい) light

軽	い										

軽食(けいしょく) light meal

軽	食										

深い(ふかい) deep

深	い										

短い(みじかい) short

短	い										

短気(たんき) short temper; quick temper

短	気										

高速(こうそく) high-speed; rapid; express

高	速										

重体 (じゅうたい) seriously ill; serious condition; critical state

重	体										

手軽 (てがる) easy; simple; informal; offhand; cheap

手	軽										

深夜 (しんや) late at night

深	夜										

2 Kanji Workbook Activities

● 1. Stroke Order Check 書き順確認

Each kanji has a stroke with an arrow on it. Write its order number below the kanji.

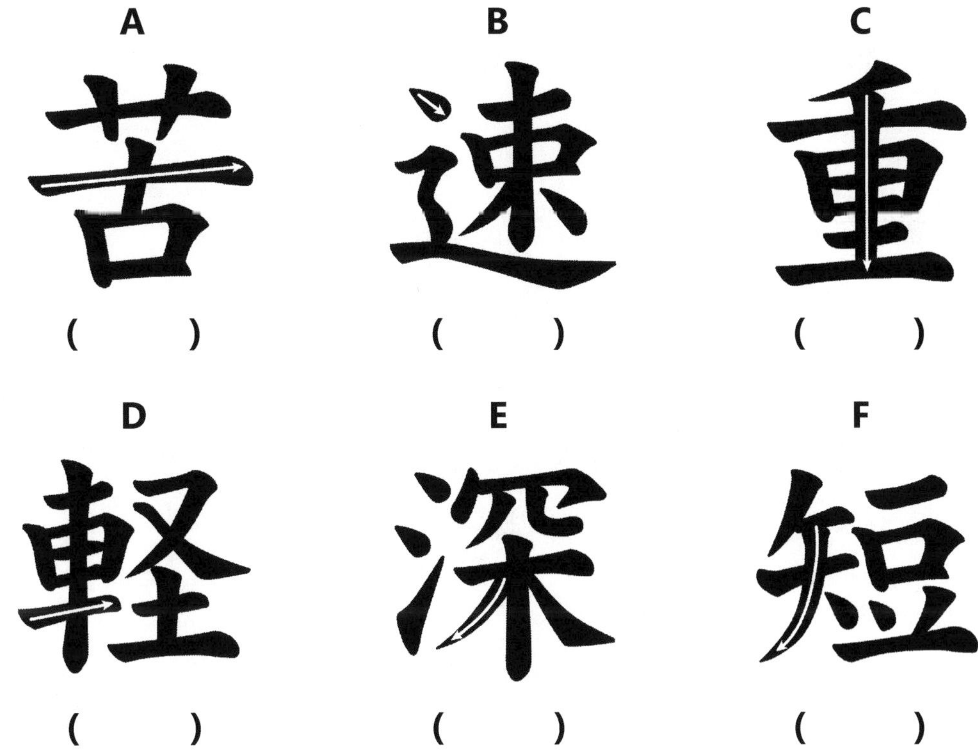

● 2. Kanji Readings

Write FURIGANA above the underlined kanji words.

1. 兄は そうじが 苦手です。
2. この道は、時速 40 キロで走りましょう。
3. 今日は、重大なニュースがあります。
4. あのレストランで 軽食を とりましょうか。
5. この海は、水深 何メートルですか。

3. Kanji Meaning Match

Write the following kanji next to its meaning: 苦 悪 速 寒 重 軽 深 温 短

1. ____ fast
2. ____ suffer; painful
3. ____ warm
4. ____ light
5. ____ cold
6. ____ heavy
7. ____ short
8. ____ deep
9. ____ bad

4. Fill in the Kanji

Fill in the appropriate kanji in the blanks for each sentence.

1. ____(にが)い____(くすり)は あまり____(の)みたくないです。
   I don't really want to drink bitter medicine.

2. わたしは____(ちい)さい____(とき)、____(はし)るのが____(はや)かったです。
   When I was small, I was fast at running.

3. さいきん、____(たい) ____(じゅう)がふえてしまいました。
   Recently my body weight has increased.

4. おばあちゃんは よく____(かる) ____(いし) をつかいます。
   My grandmother often uses a pumice stone.

5. このプールは____(ふか)いです。
   This pool sure is deep.

6. わたしの ____(いもうと) は____(たん) ____(き)なので、こまります。
   I'm troubled since my younger sister is short tempered.

7. ____(なつ) は____(ひる)が____(なが)くて、____(よる)が____(みじか) いです。
   Summer has long days and short nights.

● 5. Kanji Matching

Connect each kanji with an おん or くん reading. Use each reading only ONCE.

速 •	• けい
軽 •	• たん
暑 •	• しん
短 •	• やす
安 •	• はや
暗 •	• あつ
寒 •	• かん
重 •	• く
深 •	• くら
苦 •	• じゅう

2 Answer Key 答え合わせ

1. Stroke order check (answers)

A) 4　　B) 8　　C) 7

D) 6　　E) 10　　F) 4

3. Kanji meaning match (answers)

1. 速 fast	2. 苦 suffer; painful	3. 温 warm
4. 軽 light	5. 寒 cold	6. 重 heavy
7. 短 short	8. 深 deep	9. 悪 bad

2. Kanji Readings (answers)

1. 兄(あに)は そうじが 苦手(にがて)です。　My older brother isn't good at cleaning.
2. この道(みち)は、時速(じそく)40 キロで走(はし)りましょう。　Let's drive at a speed of 40 kilo on this street.
3. 今日(きょう)は、重大(じゅうだい)なニュースがあります。　I have important news today.
4. あのレストランで 軽食(けいしょく)を とりましょうか。　Shall we grab a light meal at that restaurant?
5. この海(うみ)は、水深(すいしん) 何(なん)メートルですか。　How many meters is the depth of this ocean?

4. Fill in the kanji (answers)

1. 苦い薬は あまり飲みたくないです。
2. わたしは小さい時、走るのが速かったです。
3. さいきん、体重がふえてしまいました。
4. おばあちゃんは よく軽石をつかいます。
5. このプールは深いです。
6. わたしの妹は短気なので、こまります。
7. 夏は昼が長くて、夜が短いです。

5. Kanji matching (answers)

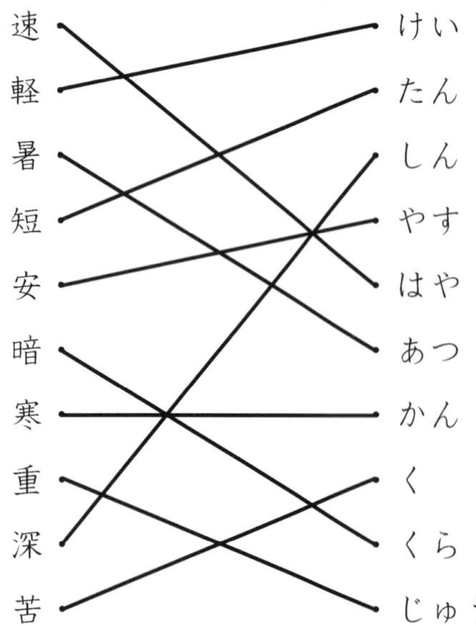

3 Kanji Lesson 3: 悲美幸曲助消

253-258

Kanji that can be adjectives or verbs

3 New Kanji 新しい漢字

253 心 12 画 くん かな(しい、しむ) おん ヒ

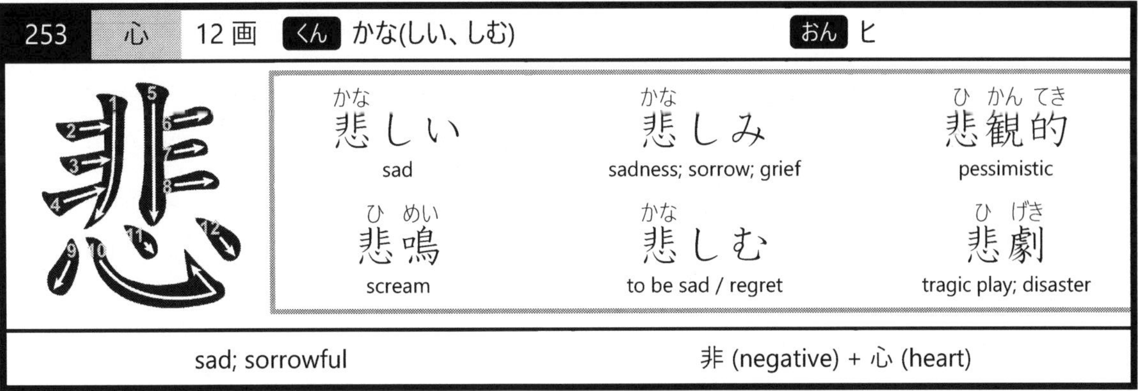

悲しい (かな) sad	悲しみ (かな) sadness; sorrow; grief	悲観的 (ひかんてき) pessimistic
悲鳴 (ひめい) scream	悲しむ (かな) to be sad / regret	悲劇 (ひげき) tragic play; disaster

sad; sorrowful — 非 (negative) + 心 (heart)

254 羊 9 画 くん うつく(しい) おん ビ

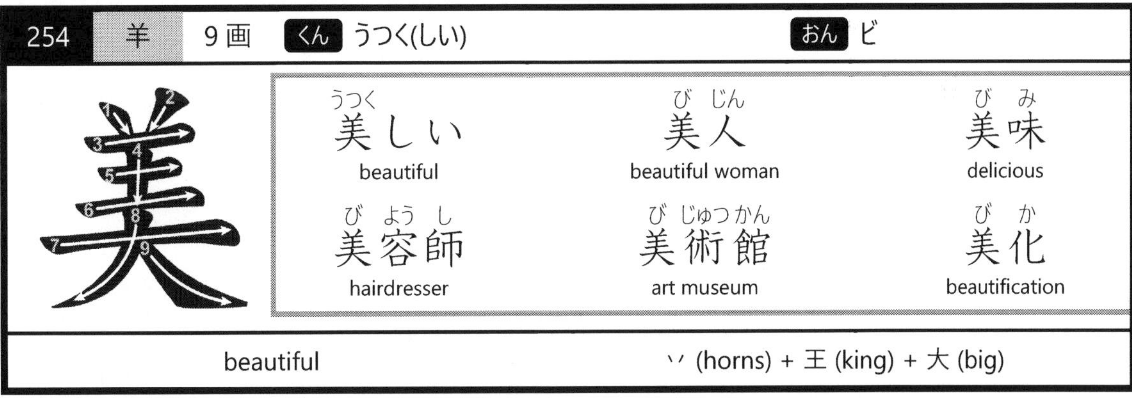

美しい (うつく) beautiful	美人 (びじん) beautiful woman	美味 (びみ) delicious
美容師 (びようし) hairdresser	美術館 (びじゅつかん) art museum	美化 (びか) beautification

beautiful — 丷 (horns) + 王 (king) + 大 (big)

255 干 8 画 くん さいわ(い)、しあわ(せ)、さち おん コウ

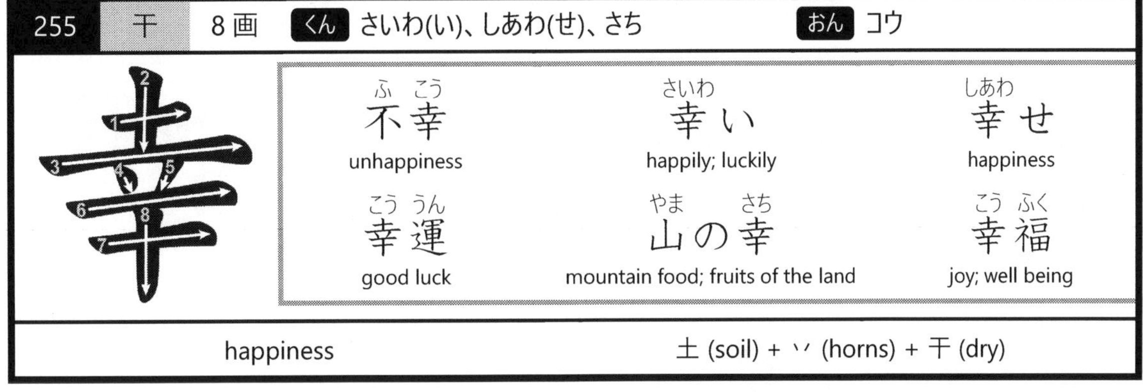

不幸 (ふこう) unhappiness	幸い (さいわ) happily; luckily	幸せ (しあわ) happiness
幸運 (こううん) good luck	山の幸 (やまさち) mountain food; fruits of the land	幸福 (こうふく) joy; well being

happiness — 土 (soil) + 丷 (horns) + 干 (dry)

256	日	6 画	くん ま(がる、げる)	おん キョク

曲

ま 曲げる to bend	きょくせん 曲線 curved line	さんきょく 三曲 three songs
ま 曲がる to make a turn	さっきょく 作曲 composition	しんきょく 新曲 new song

bend; curve; turn; song — 日 (reason) + || (towers)

257	力	7 画	くん たす(ける、かる)、すけ	おん ジョ

助

たす 助ける to help	すけ と 助っ人 supporter; backer; helper	じょしゅ 助手 assistant; helper
たす 助かる to be saved	じょし 助詞 particle (in Japanese grammar)	えんじょ 援助 support; assistance

help; assist; rescue — 且 (also) + 力 (power)

258	氵	10 画	くん き(える)、け(す)	おん ショウ

消

き 消える to disappear; to go off	け 消しゴム rubber eraser	しょうか 消化 digestion
しょうぼうし 消防士 firefighter	け 消す to erase; to snuff out; to turn off	しょうひぜい 消費税 consumption tax

erase; turn off; extinguish — 氵 (water) + | (sword) + 丷 (horns) + 月 (moon)

Kanji Parts used in the New Kanji

非	negative	土	soil	力	power
心	heart	干	dry	氵	water
丷	horns	日	reason	丨	sword
王	king	川	towers	月	moon
大	big	且	also		

3 Kanji Memory Tools 漢字記憶術

This section helps you organically memorize kanji readings, meanings, and construction.

悲

非 心
People with a negative heart are "**SAD**".

映画(えいが)の❶悲(かな)しいシーンで❷悲鳴(ひめい)を上(あ)げてしまった。

I ❷couldn't help screaming at the movie's ❶sad scene.

美

丷 王 大
The horns of the king's big goat are "**BEAUTIFUL**".

❶美人(びじん)の❷美容師(びようし)さんは❸美(うつく)しく髪(かみ)を切(き)ります。

The ❶beautiful woman ❷hairdresser cuts hair ❸beautifully.

幸

土 丷 干
Soil washed from horns then dried makes me "**HAPPY**".

私(わたし)は❶幸(さいわ)い、❷不幸(ふこう)がなくて❸幸(しあわ)せです。

❶Luckily, not having ❷unhappiness, I'm ❸happy.

曲

日 ||
For some reason these towers are built with a "**CURVE**".

有名(ゆうめい)な❶作曲家(さっきょくか)が左(ひだり)に❷曲(ま)がりました。

The famous ❶composer ❷ turned left.

助

且 力
Also, power is needed to "**HELP**".

親(おや)の❶援助(えんじょ)で❷助(たす)かっています。

I'm ❷being helped with ❶support from my parents.

消

氵 | 丷 月
With the water sword cut the horns to make the moon "**EXTINGUISH**".

❶消防士(しょうぼうし)は火(ひ)を❷消(け)すと、その場(ば)から❸消(き)えました。

❷Upon extinguishing the fire ❶the firefighters ❸disappeared from the area.

3 Understanding Kanji Parts 漢字部分の理解

● 3-1. 曰 (reason) and 日 (day, sun) look similar

曰 (say, reason) and 日 (day, sun) kanji parts look similar. 日 (day, sun) is used far more than 曰 (say, reason) as a kanji part. However, there is a common grammar pattern using 曰 (say, reason) that is powerful.

○○曰く (いわく)
according to ○○

EXAMPLE SENTENCES

1. 山田先生曰く、今日は学校がないそうです。
   According to Mr./Mrs. Yamada, it seems there isn't school today.

2. 家内曰く、私はいびきをかくそうです。
   According to my wife, it seems I snore.

3 Kanji Usage 漢字の使い方

● 3-2. Same sound, different words

Some English words have the same sound, but different spellings like PAIL / PALE and RED / READ. Japanese also has words with the same sound, but different kanji.

to criticize (not + difficult)	to escape; take refuge (avoid + trouble)
ひ なん 非難する	ひ なん 避難する
It's not difficult to criticize, but often very difficult to take criticism.	The context of the situation will help distinguish these similar words.

hair salon (beauty + form + institution)	hospital (illness + institution)
び よう いん 美容院	びょう いん 病院
These aren't the same sound, but are easy to confuse since they DO sound the same to the untrained ear. Imagine your friend says she is going to the "beauty shop", but you hear "hospital."	

● 3-3. The beauty of Japan (美)

In America, looking pale isn't considered healthy, so a tan look is popular. Japan and other parts of Asia are obsessed with keeping white skin that is undamaged from the sun. It's not uncommon to see women with a 日傘 (ひがさ) "parasol" on a sunny day to protect their skin from the sun's harmful rays.

The act of applying creams to whiten skin or other actions to protect the whiteness is called 美白 (びはく), which is written with "beauty" and "white".

Here are that and some other words containing 美.

whiteness care (beauty + white)	beautiful skin (beauty + skin)
び はく 美白	び はだ 美肌
美白 describes the actions to whiten skin or prevent it from getting damaged from the sun.	Many Japanese women and even men want 美肌 and cosmetics companies want to help!

art; fine arts (beautiful + technique)	Beauty cream (beauty + form + liquid)
び じゅつ 美術	び よう えき 美容液
In the anime NARUTO battle technique names end with 術 (じゅつ) to mean, "art" or "technique".	A good 美容液 (beauty lotion; essence) also has UV protection for 美白 purposes.

● 3-4. The luck of the Japanese

幸運 (こううん) means "good luck or fortune" in Japanese. "Luck" by itself is 運 (うん).

うん 運がいい	to have good luck
わたし とう うん 私のお父さんは、いつも運がいいです。 My father always has good luck.	

うん わる 運が悪い	to have bad luck
うん わる とき なに ほう 運が悪い時は、何もしない方がいいです。 You shouldn't do anything when your luck is bad.	

Japanese don't normally say "good luck" like we do in English. Instead they will say 頑張って (がんばって) (do your best) or make a direct "wish" for success in the specific action you are trying to accomplish.

勝ちますように。(か)	合格しますように。(ごうかく)
so that you may win~ (a game or sport match)	**so that you pass~** (a test, or get through an interview etc.)

NOTE: These are incomplete sentences and the "assumed" verb could be "I pray" or "I hope", or with negative conjugations "be careful to not~" when using しませんように～

● 3-5. More than one way to help (助)

In English, we can scream "HELP!" in a life and death situation, or we can say "help" when requesting someone to help carry a heavy object or other trivial task. Japanese has two separate verbs for "help".

HELP!	help / lend a hand (relay a hand)
助けて (たすけて)	手伝って (てつだって)
If you need to be saved, use this version of "HELP". (たすける)	If you need help doing homework or chores, use this version of "HELP". (てつだう)

3 Words You Can Write 書ける言葉

悲鳴（ひめい）scream

悲	鳴										

美人（びじん）beautiful woman

美	人										

幸せ（しあわせ）happiness

幸	せ										

幸い（さいわい）happily

幸	い										

曲線（きょくせん）curve line

曲	線										

消火（しょうか）fire extinction

消	火										

作曲 (さっきょく) musical composition

作	曲										

美白 (びはく) skin whitening

美	白										

助言 (じょげん) advice; suggestion

助	言										

手助け (てだすけ) helping hand

手	助	け									

助ける (たすける) to help

助	け	る									

消える (きえる) to disappear; to go out (light, fire, etc.); to vanish

消	え	る									

消しゴム (けしゴム) eraser

消	し	ゴ	ム								

助け合う (たすけあう) to help each other

助	け	合	う								

3 Kanji Workbook Activities

● 1. Stroke Order Check 書き順確認

Each kanji has a stroke with an arrow on it. Write its order number below the kanji.

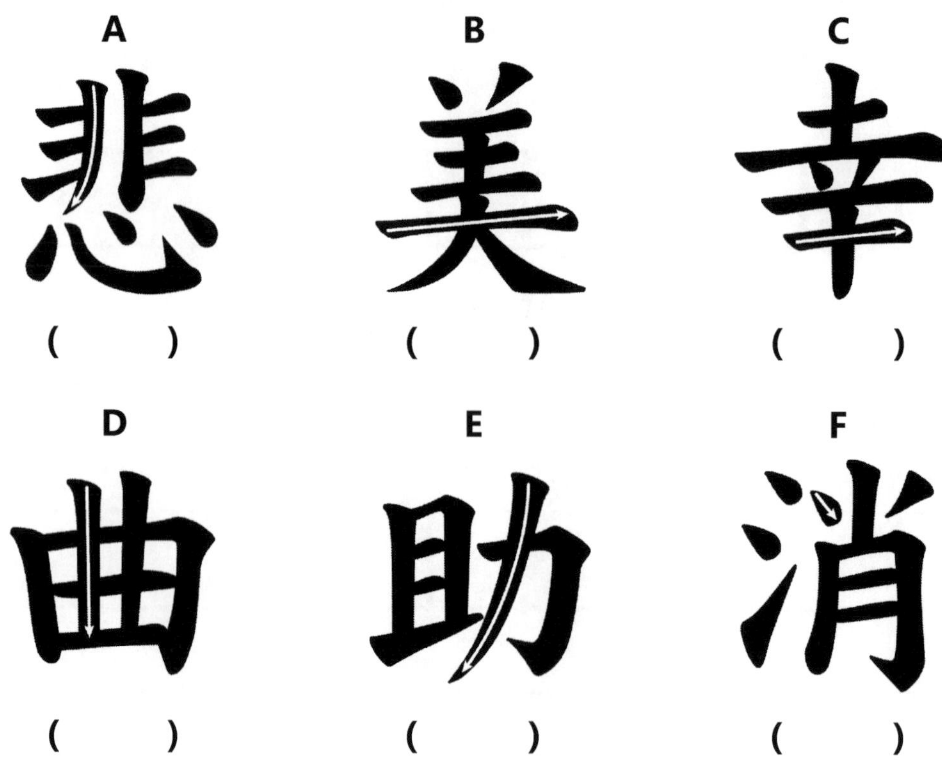

● 2. Kanji Meaning Match

Write the following kanji next to its meaning: 悲 短 消 美 軽 助 暑 曲 幸

1. ____ happiness
2. ____ sad
3. ____ help
4. ____ hot
5. ____ erase
6. ____ turn
7. ____ light
8. ____ short
9. ____ beautiful

● 3. Kanji Readings

Write FURIGANA above the underlined kanji words.

1. 悲しい曲より、楽しい曲をききましょう。
2. フランスで美しい絵画を見ました。
3. かの女と出会って、幸せになりました。
4. 消しゴムがどこかに消えてしまいました。
5. 友だちに引っこしを手つだってもらって、助かりました。

● 4. Fill in the Kanji

Fill in the appropriate kanji in the blanks for each sentence.

そと ひ めい き

1. ____で ____ ____が ____ こえました。

I heard a scream outside.

びじん

2. おばあちゃんは むかし、____ ____でした。

A long time ago, my grandmother was a beautiful woman.

かど ま くだ

3. その____で ____がって____さい。

Please turn at that corner.

さいわ　　　　てん　き

4. ___いにも、___ ___に めぐまれました。

Happily, we were blessed by the weather.

て　　　　　　　たす

5. いつも___つだってくれて、___かります。

I am helped by you always helping. / It helps that you always help.

ひ　　け　　くだ

6. ろうそくの___を ___ して___さい。

Please extinguish the candle's flame.

きょく　　　　しあわ　　き

7. この___を きくと、___せな___もちになります。

When I listen to this song, I get a happy feeling.

● 5. Kanji Matching

Connect each kanji with an おん or くん reading. Use each reading only ONCE.

曲 •	• じょ
寒 •	• しょう
幸 •	• ひ
助 •	• くる
速 •	• ま
消 •	• かん
悪 •	• こう
悲 •	• あく
美 •	• び
苦 •	• そく

3 Answer Key 答え合わせ

1. Stroke order check (answers)

A) 1　　B) 7　　C) 7

D) 3　　E) 7　　F) 5

2. Kanji meaning match (answers)

1. 幸 happiness　2. 悲 sad　3. 助 help

4. 暑 hot　5. 消 erase　6. 曲 turn

7. 軽 light　8. 短 short　9. 美 beautiful

3. Kanji Readings (answers)

1. 悲(かな)しい曲(きょく)より、楽(たの)しい曲(きょく)をききましょう。　Instead of sad songs let's listen to fun songs.
2. フランスで美(うつく)しい絵画(かいが)を見(み)ました。　I saw beautiful paintings in France.
3. かの女(じょ)と出(で)会(あ)って、幸(しあわ)せになりました。　I'm happy now that I've met her / my girlfriend.
4. 消(け)しゴムがどこかに消(き)えてしまいました。　My eraser disappeared somewhere.
5. 友(とも)だちに引(ひ)っこしを手(て)つだってもらって、助(たす)かりました。　I had a friend help me move and I was helped.

4. Fill in the kanji (answers)

1. 外で悲鳴が聞こえました。
2. おばあちゃんはむかし 美人でした。
3. その角で 曲がって下さい。
4. 幸いにも、天気にめぐまれました。
5. いつも手つだってくれて、助かります。
6. ろうそくの火を消して下さい。
7. この曲をきくと、幸せな気もちになります。

5. Kanji matching (answers)

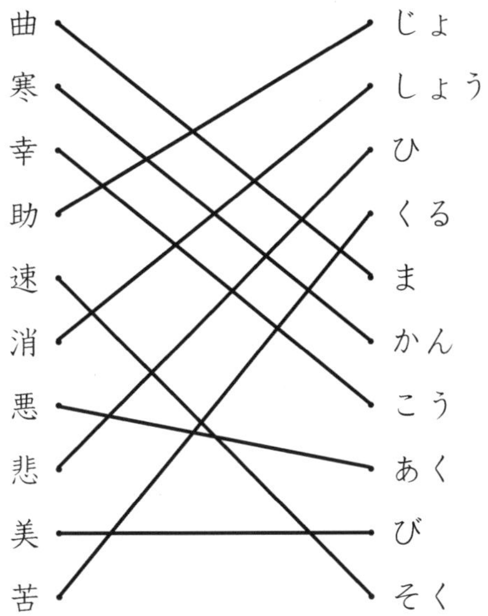

4 Kanji Lesson 4: 申乗植育飲泳

259-264

Kanji that can be verbs (part 2)

4 New Kanji 新しい漢字

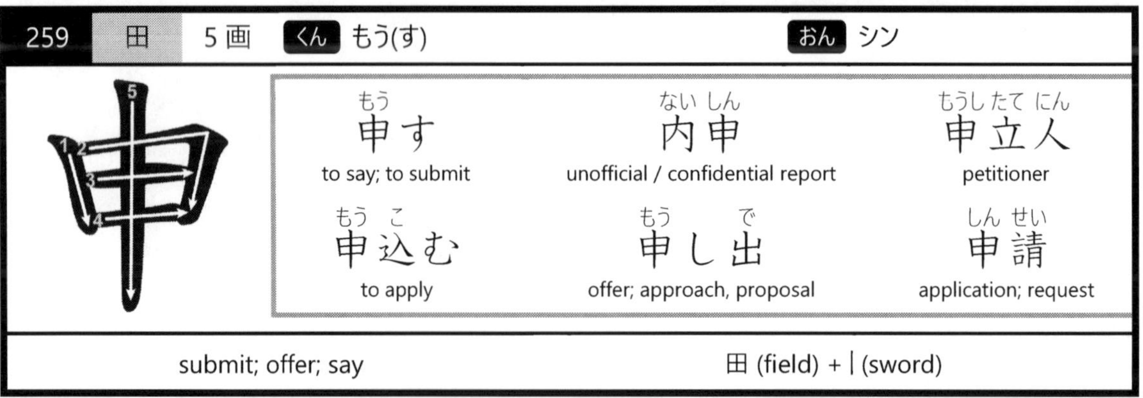

259 | 田 | 5 画 | くん もう(す) | おん シン

もう 申す to say; to submit	ない しん 内申 unofficial / confidential report	もうしたて にん 申立人 petitioner
もう こ 申込む to apply	もう で 申し出 offer; approach, proposal	しん せい 申請 application; request

submit; offer; say — 田 (field) + | (sword)

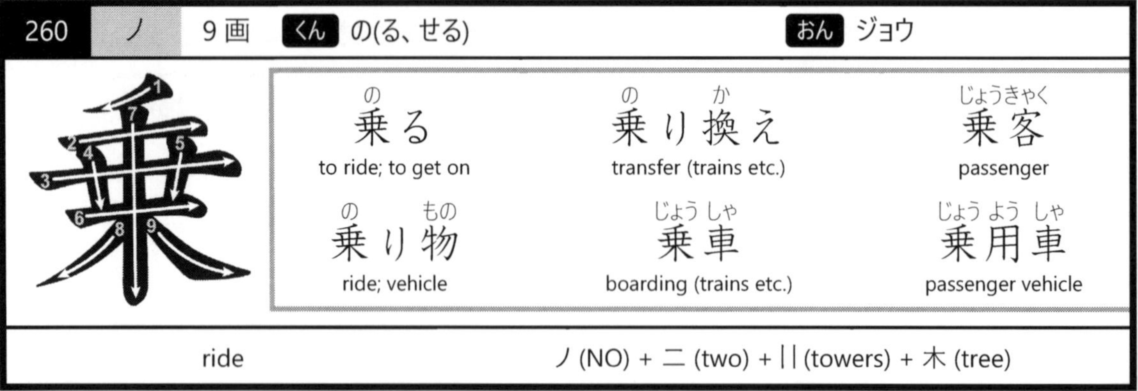

260 | ノ | 9 画 | くん の(る、せる) | おん ジョウ

の 乗る to ride; to get on	の か 乗り換え transfer (trains etc.)	じょうきゃく 乗客 passenger
の もの 乗り物 ride; vehicle	じょう しゃ 乗車 boarding (trains etc.)	じょう よう しゃ 乗用車 passenger vehicle

ride — ノ (NO) + 二 (two) + | | (towers) + 木 (tree)

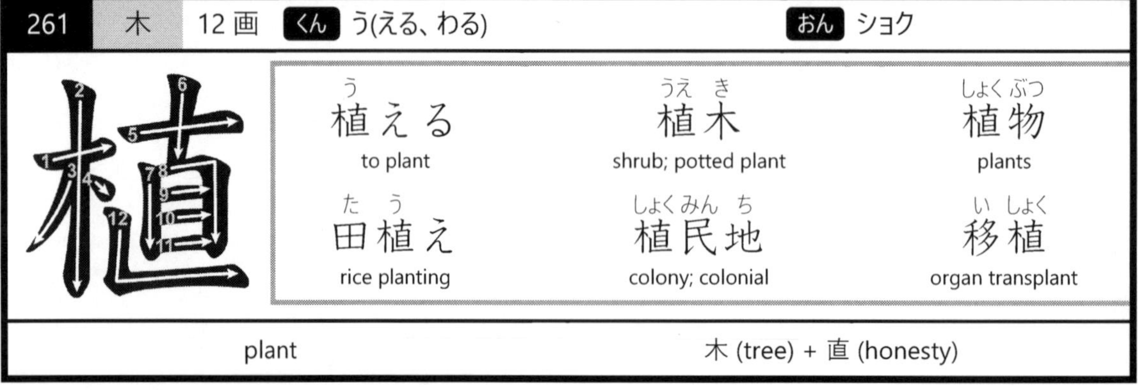

261 | 木 | 12 画 | くん う(える、わる) | おん ショク

う 植える to plant	うえ き 植木 shrub; potted plant	しょく ぶつ 植物 plants
た う 田植え rice planting	しょく みん ち 植民地 colony; colonial	い しょく 移植 organ transplant

plant — 木 (tree) + 直 (honesty)

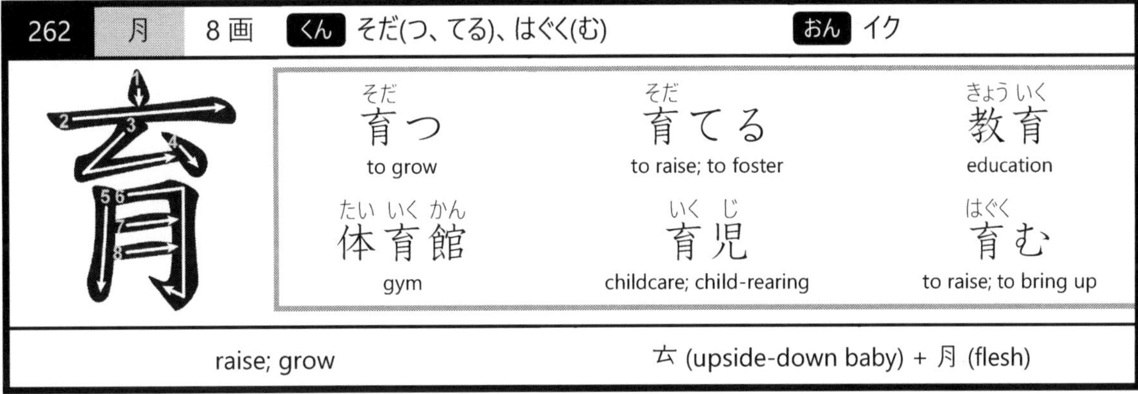

262	月	8 画	くん そだ(つ、てる)、はぐく(む)	おん イク

育

そだ 育つ	そだ 育てる	きょういく 教育
to grow	to raise; to foster	education
たいいくかん 体育館	いくじ 育児	はぐく 育む
gym	childcare; child-rearing	to raise; to bring up

raise; grow — 𠫓 (upside-down baby) + 月 (flesh)

263	食	12 画	くん の(む)	おん イン

飲

の 飲む	いんしゅうんてん 飲酒運転	いんりょう 飲料
to drink	drunk driving	beverage; drink
いんしょくてん 飲食店	いっきの 一気飲み	の みず 飲み水
restaurant	chugging; drink all at once	drinking water

drink — 食 (food) + 欠 (lack)

264	氵	8 画	くん およ(ぐ)	おん エイ

泳

およ 泳ぐ	およ かた 泳ぎ方	すいえい 水泳
to swim	way of swimming	swimming
ひらおよ 平泳ぎ	うちゅうゆうえい 宇宙遊泳	きょうえい 競泳
breaststroke	space walk	swimming race

swim — 氵 (water) + 永 (eternity)

Kanji Parts used in the New Kanji

田	field	木	tree	欠	lack
丨	sword	直	honesty	氵	water
ノ	NO	𠫓	upside-down baby	永	eternity
二	two	月	flesh		
〢	towers	食	food		

4 Kanji Memory Tools 漢字記憶術

This section helps you organically memorize kanji readings, meanings, and construction.

申

田 |
A field with a sword is what I "**OFFER**".

もう わけ しんせい ことわ
❶申し訳ないけど、フレンド❶申請をお断りします。

❶Sorry, but I refuse your friend ❷request.

乗

ノ 二 || 木
NO, the two towers won't give your tree a "**RIDE**".

じょうきゃく とうきょうえき の か
❶乗客は、東京駅で❷乗り換えました。

The ❶passenger ❷transferred at Tokyo station.

植

木 直
A tree filled with honesty is a great "**PLANT**".

しょくぶつ うえきばち う
❶植物を❷植木鉢に❸植えました。

I ❸planted ❶plants in a ❷flower pot.

育

𠫓 月
This upside-down baby is my flesh which I choose to "**RAISE**".

こども そだ がっこうきょういく たいせつ
子供を❶育てるには、❷学校教育が大切です。

❷School education is important in ❶raising of a child.

飲

食 欠
Food doesn't taste good if you lack a "**DRINK**".

こんや いんしゅうんてん さけ の
今夜❶飲酒運転しないように、お酒を❷飲みません。

So that I don't ❶drink and drive tonight, I ❷won't drink alcohol.

泳

氵 永
If there is water for eternity you must "**SWIM**".

すいえいきょうしつ ひらおよ なら
❶水泳教室で❷平泳ぎを習いました。

In ❶swimming school I learned ❷the breaststroke.

4 Understanding Kanji Parts 漢字部分の理解

● 4-1. The upside-down baby radical

If you use your imagination a bit, you can see how the "upside down baby" radical is ACTUALLY, the "child" radical rotated to show the head pointed down like in a breech birth.

● 4-2. The "flesh" radical にくづき (肉、月、月)

Radicals are sometimes "radically" different looking from the kanji they are based on. For example, 肉 (flesh; meat), in most cases, looks like the 月 (moon) radical. To distinguish "moon" and "flesh", we use 月 for "flesh". However, when written, 月 should be used. Kanji with 月 radical are often related to body words. When 月 (月) is on the left it's called にくづき.

arm

うで
腕

- 腕立て伏せ (うでたふ) — push-ups
- 腕を組む (うでく) — to fold one's arms

lower back

こし
腰

- 腰が低い (こしひく) — humble; modest
- 腰を掛ける (こしか) — to sit down

groin; thigh

また
股

- 内股 (うちまた) — pigeon-toed
- 二股 (ふたまた) — two-timing (cheating)

leg

あし
脚

- 三脚 (さんきゃく) — tripod
- 左脚 (ひだりあし) — left leg

elbow

ひじ
肘

- 肘掛 (ひじかけ) — armrest (of chair)
- テニス肘 (ひじ) — tennis elbow

knee

ひざ
膝

- 膝のお皿 (ひざさら) — kneecap
- 膝掛 (ひざかけ) — lap blanket

When 月 (⺼) is below, it's called just にく.

stomach		shoulder	
い 胃	い **胃がん** stomach cancer い つう **胃痛** stomach pain	かた 肩	かた に お **肩の荷が下りる** wait lifted from shoulders かた がき **肩書** title; position

height; back		grow up; raise	
せ 背	せ なか **背中** back (of body) はい けい **背景** background; scenery	育	そだ **育てる** to raise; to bring up きょう いく **教育** education; training

4 Kanji Usage 漢字の使い方

● 4-3. "Raising" things in Japan requires more than just 育

いく
育 meaning "raise" or "grow" is created using the parts 𠫓 (upside down baby) and 月 (flesh). Compound words using 育 tend to be related to human development.

education	nursing; rearing	breeding (animals)	physical ed
きょう いく 教育	ほ いく 保育	し いく 飼育	たい いく 体育
(teach + grow)	(keep + grow)	(raise + grow)	(body + grow)

Be aware that there are other kanji used for different types of growing and raising.

raising / planting plants	growing a beard / hair	raising / breeding animals
う 植える	は 生える	か 飼う

● 4-4. 十二支 (12 signs of the Chinese zodiac)

In the west, especially America, we base personalities on birth month with horoscopes. In Asia, including Japan, personalities are often based on birth year using the 干支 (えと) (Chinese Zodiac). You will eventually be asked, "What year are you?" so you should figure out what year you are to keep the conversation going.

Chinese Zodiac 干支					
rat/mouse	ox	tiger	rabbit/hare	dragon	snake
ねずみ年	うし年	とら年	うさぎ年	たつ年	へび年
子 (ね)	丑 (うし)	寅 (とら)	卯 (う)	辰 (たつ)	巳 (み)
horse	sheep	monkey	rooster	dog	pig/boar
うま年	ひつじ年	さる年	とり年	いぬ年	いのしし年
午 (うま)	未 (ひつじ)	申 (さる)	酉 (とり)	戌 (いぬ)	亥 (い)

The kanji used for the years might not be familiar to you since they are from the Chinese simplified kanji which Japan didn't adopt. The Chinese Zodiac is a 12-year cycle, so someone born in 1960, 1972, 1984, 1996, 2008 are all "year of the rat".

Conversation between friends

A: 何年生まれですか。
B: 申年生まれです。あなたは？
A: 辰年です。来年は何年ですか。
B: 今年はねずみ年だから、来年は丑年ですね。

何年 can be read as なんねん or なにどし. When read as なんねん, it means "what year." But as なにどし it's "what year of the zodiac?"

A: What year (of the zodiac) were you born?
B: I'm was born of the monkey. You?
A: I'm year of the dragon. What year (of the zodiac) is it next year?
B: Since this year is the year of the rat, next year is the year of the ox.

● 4-5. The difference between 言(い)う and 申(もう)す

申(もう)す is the humble form of 言(い)う and both mean "to say" or "to be called".

It's used to lower yourself and show respect to the listener.

EXAMPLE SENTENCES (申す)

1. 田中(たなか)と申(もう)します。よろしくお願(ねが)いします。
   I'm (called)Tanaka. I request to be in your favor.

   It's very common to say 申します when introducing yourself.

2. 安田(やすだ)と申(もう)しますが、西田社長(にしだしゃちょう)は いらっしゃいますか。
   I'm (called) Yasuda, is president Nishida here?

EXAMPLE SENTENCES (言う)

3. これは日本語(にほんご)で「教科書(きょうかしょ)」と言(い)います。
   This is called きょうかしょ (textbook) in Japanese.

4. これはフランス語(ご)で何(なん)と言(い)うの？
   What's this called in French?

4 Words You Can Write 書ける言葉

申す（もうす） to say; to submit

申	す										

乗る（のる） to ride

乗	る										

植木（うえき） garden tree

植	木										

育つ（そだつ） to grow

育	つ										

教育（きょういく） education

教育

飲む（のむ） to drink

飲む

泳ぐ（およぐ） to swim

泳ぐ

水泳（すいえい） swimming

水泳

体育(たいいく) physical education

体育

遠泳(えんえい) long-distance swimming

遠泳

申し出（もうしで） offer; approach

申し出

植える（うえる） to plant

植える

飲み水（のみみず） drinking water

飲み水

乗せる（のせる） to give (someone) a ride; to load; to carry

乗	せ	る									

乗り心地(のりごこち) comfort (of a vehicle); ride quality

乗	り	心	地								

4 Kanji Workbook Activities

● 1. Stroke Order Check 書き順確認

Each kanji has a stroke with an arrow on it. Write its order number below the kanji.

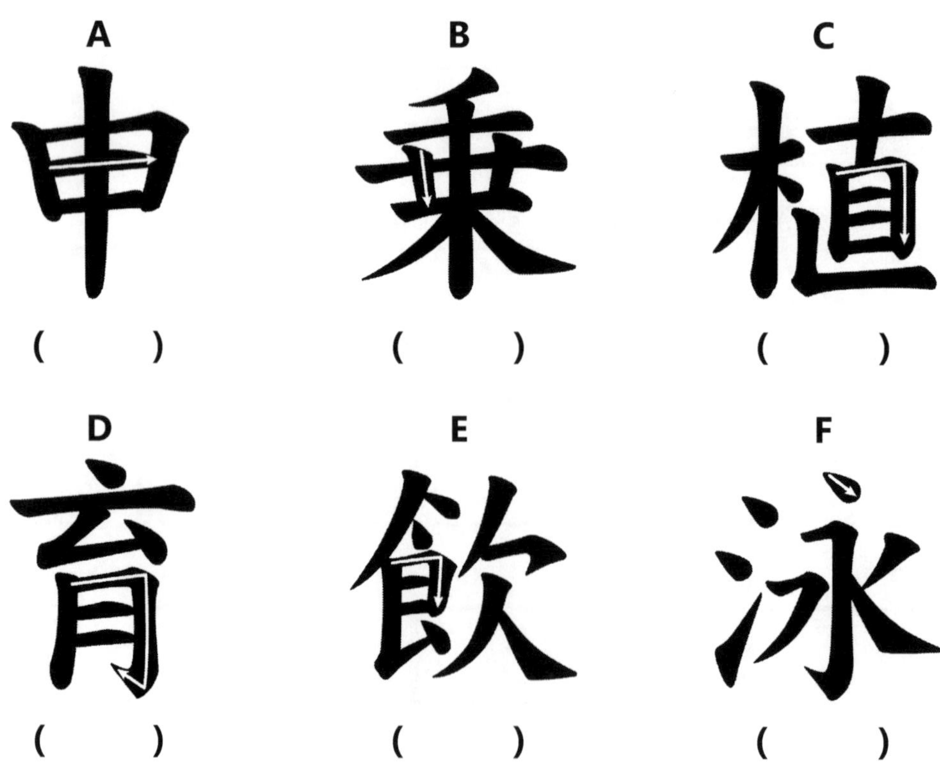

● 2. Kanji Meaning Match

Write the following kanji next to its meaning: 乗 育 泳 申 植 飲 曲 重 深

1. ____ deep
2. ____ swim
3. ____ say; submit
4. ____ turn
5. ____ ride
6. ____ drink
7. ____ plant
8. ____ grow
9. ____ heavy

● 3. Kanji Readings

Write FURIGANA above the underlined kanji words.

1. 先日、ある人から仕事の申し出がありました。
2. うちの会社は、乗用車を五台もっています。
3. よく行く公園に、さくらの木が植えられました。
4. 体育では、リレーが一番とくいです。
5. 泳いでいる時、プールの水を飲んでしまいました。

● 4. Fill in the Kanji

Fill in the appropriate kanji in the blanks for each sentence.

1. この____(あいだ)、____(すい) ____(えい)のクラスに____(もう)しこみました。

The other day I signed up for a swimming class.

2. ____(こ)どもが りっぱに____(そだ)って____(しあわ)せです。

I'm happy that my children grew up so splendidly.

うえ き て い

3. よく___ ___の___ ___れをします。

I often tend to my plants.

あつ ひ みず の

4. ___ い___ は、___をいっぱい___ みましょう。

Take care to (let's) drink a lot of water on hot days.

わる もう

5. むすこが ___いことをして ___ しわけありませんでした。

I apologize for my son doing bad things.

しゅう まつ くるま の うみ い

6. ___ ___によく___に ___って、___へ___きます。

I often get in my car and go to the beach on weekends.

あたら の ごこ ち

7. ___ しいバイクの___り___ ___は、どうですか。

How is the ride (quality) of your new bike (motorcycle)?

● 5. Kanji Matching

Connect each kanji with an おん or くん reading. Use each reading only ONCE.

申 •	• しょく
温 •	• もう
安 •	• いく
乗 •	• おん
植 •	• はや
軽 •	• じょう
育 •	• いん
速 •	• やす
飲 •	• およ
泳 •	• けい

4 Answer Key 答え合わせ

1. Stroke order check (answers)

A) 3　　B) 4　　C) 8

D) 6　　E) 4　　F) 4

2. Kanji meaning match (answers)

1. 深 deep　　2. 泳 swim　　3. 申 say
4. 曲 turn　　5. 乗 ride　　6. 飲 drink
7. 植 plant　　8. 育 grow　　9. 重 heavy

3. Kanji Readings (answers)

1. 先日(せんじつ)、ある人(ひと)から仕事(しごと)の申(もう)し出(で)がありました。 — The other day someone offered me a job.
2. うちの会社(かいしゃ)は、乗用車(じょうようしゃ)を五台(ごだい)もっています。 — My company has 5 passenger cars.
3. よく行(い)く公園(こうえん)に、さくらの木(き)が植(う)えられました。 — Cherry trees were planted in a park I often go.
4. 体育(たいいく)では、リレーが一番(いちばん)とくいです。 — For physical education, my best is relay.
5. 泳(およ)いでいる時(とき)、プールの水(みず)を飲(の)んでしまいました。 — I ended up drinking pool water when I was swimming.

4. Fill in the kanji (answers)

1. この間、水泳のクラスに申しこみました。
2. 子どもがりっぱに育って幸せです。
3. よく植木の手入れをします。
4. 暑い日は、水をいっぱい飲みましょう。
5. むすこが悪いことをして申しわけありませんでした。
6. 週末によく車に乗って、海へ行きます。
7. 新しいバイクの乗り心地は、どうですか。

5. Kanji matching (answers)

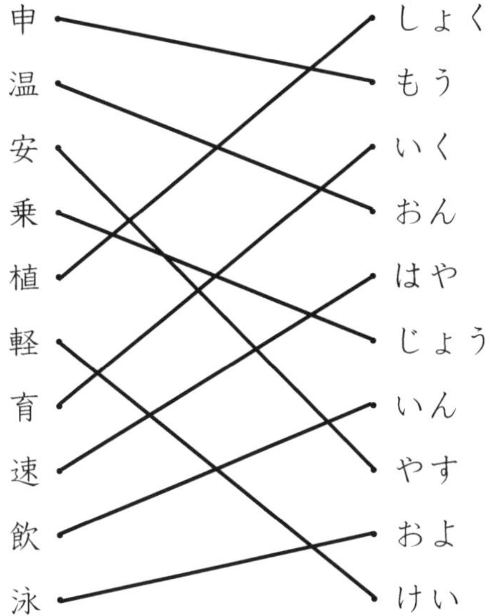

5 Kanji Lesson 5: 運開決想死感

265-270

Kanji that can be verbs (part 3)

5 New Kanji 新しい漢字

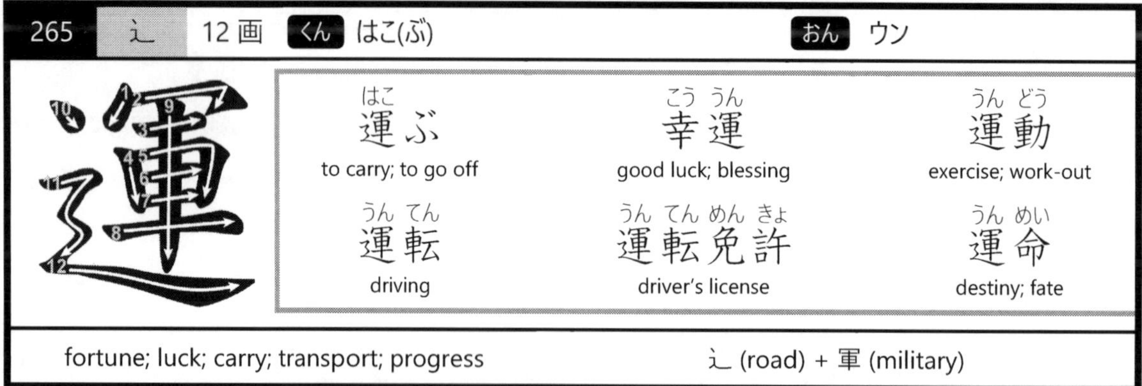

265 辶 12画 くん はこ(ぶ) おん ウン
運ぶ (はこ) to carry; to go off
幸運 (こううん) good luck; blessing
運動 (うんどう) exercise; work-out
運転 (うんてん) driving
運転免許 (うんてんめんきょ) driver's license
運命 (うんめい) destiny; fate
fortune; luck; carry; transport; progress
辶 (road) + 軍 (military)

266 門 12画 くん ひら(く、ける)、あ(く、ける) おん カイ
開く (ひら) to open; to hold
開く (あ) to be open; to be empty
開ける (あ) to open; to unlock
開店 (かいてん) open a store
開会式 (かいかいしき) opening ceremony
開発 (かいはつ) development
open; unfold; unseal
門 (gate) + 开 (start)

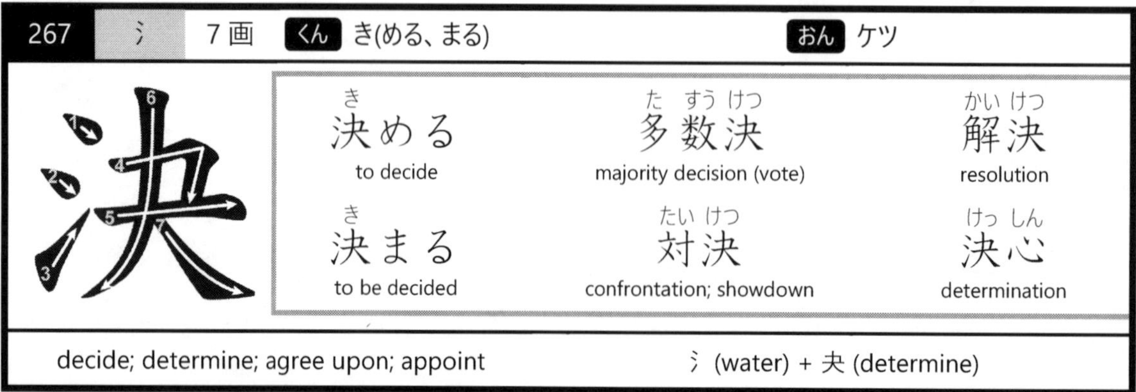

267 氵 7画 くん き(める、まる) おん ケツ
決める (き) to decide
多数決 (たすうけつ) majority decision (vote)
解決 (かいけつ) resolution
決まる (き) to be decided
対決 (たいけつ) confrontation; showdown
決心 (けっしん) determination
decide; determine; agree upon; appoint
氵 (water) + 夬 (determine)

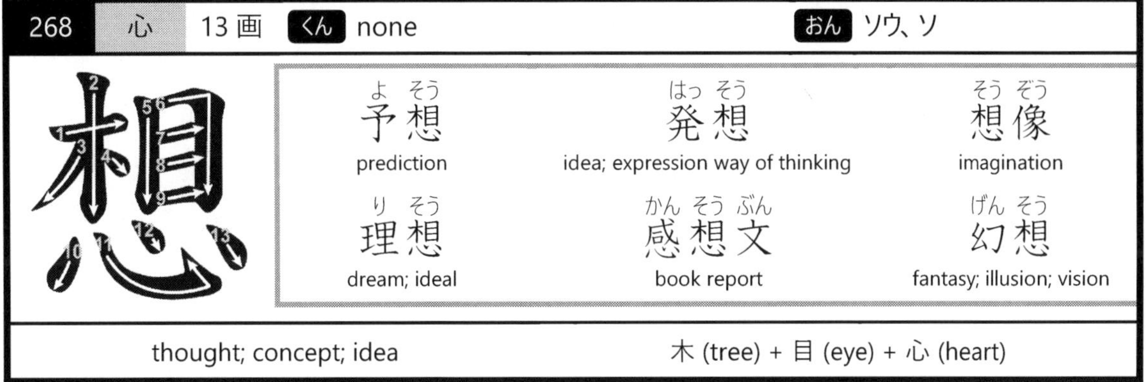

268 | 心 | 13 画 | くん none | おん ソウ、ソ

よ そう 予想 prediction	はっ そう 発想 idea; expression way of thinking	そう ぞう 想像 imagination
り そう 理想 dream; ideal	かん そう ぶん 感想文 book report	げん そう 幻想 fantasy; illusion; vision

thought; concept; idea — 木 (tree) + 目 (eye) + 心 (heart)

269 | 歹 | 6 画 | くん し(ぬ) | おん シ

し 死ぬ to die	し にん 死人 a dead person; corpse	し ぼう 死亡 death; mortality
そく し 即死 instant death	しょう し 焼死 burn to death	ひっ し 必死 desperate; frantic

death; die — 歹 (bare bones) + ヒ (spoon)

270 | 心 | 13 画 | くん none | おん カン

かん 感じる to feel	かんじょう 感情 emotion; feeling; sentiment	どう かん 同感 agree
かん しゃ 感謝 thankfulness	ざい あく かん 罪悪感 sense of guilt; guilty feelings	かん どう 感動 sensation, moving

feeling; emotion; sensation — 咸 (all) + 心 (heart)

Kanji Parts used in the New Kanji

辶	road	氵	water	心	heart
軍	military	夬	decide	歹	bare bones
門	gate	木	tree	ヒ	spoon
开	start	目	eye	咸	all

5 Kanji Memory Tools 漢字記憶術

This section helps you organically memorize kanji readings, meanings, and construction.

運

辶 軍
Many roads were designed for military "**TRANSPORT**".

ソファーを❶運ぶのは、いい❷運動になる。

❶Moving a sofa is a good ❷workout.

開

門 开
The gate will start to "**OPEN**".

お店を❶開いてから、❷開店時間にドアを❸開けたことがない。

❶Since opening the store, I've ❸never opened the doors at ❷opening time.

決

氵 夬
Water will determine what I "**DECIDE**".

映画を観る時は❶多数決で❷決める。

When we watch movies we ❷decide by ❶majority vote.

想

木 目 心
A tree with an eye and heart certainly has "**THOUGHTS**".

❶感想文を書くのに、❷想像力が必要です。

Writing an ❶book report requires ❷imagination.

死

歹 匕
Demons dug into his bare bones with a spoon until "**DEATH**".

❶死にたくないので、❷必死にクマから逃げました。

Because I ❶don't want to die, I ❷frantically ran from the bear.

感

咸 心
Use all your heart to express "**EMOTION**".

殺人鬼は❷罪悪感を❸感じません。

Bloodthirsty killers don't ❶feel ❷a sense of guilt.

5 Understanding Kanji Parts 漢字部分の理解

● 5-1. The road to 辶

辶 (しんにょう、しんにゅう) (road) is in a variety of words, many which have relation to a road, or path.

close; nearby		send	
近 road + fold	きんじょ 近所 neighborhood ちか 近い near	送 road + pass	そうしん 送信 transmission おく 送る to send; to transmit

road		week	
道 road + neck	ちかみち 近道 short cut どうぐ 道具 tool	週 road + perimeter	せんしゅう 先週 last week いっしゅうかん 一週間 one week

5 Kanji Usage 漢字の使い方

● 5-2. Kanji is killing you「死」

No one wants to think of death, but kanji forces us to.

びょうし 病死 death from illness	とうし 凍死 freezing to death	がし 餓死 starving to death
しょうし 焼死 death by fire	あんらくし 安楽死 euthanasia; painless death	かろうし 過労死 death from overwork
すいし 水死／できし 溺死 death by drowning	のうし 脳死 brain-dead	せんし 戦死 death in battle; killed in action

5-3. Same sound, different kanji あける

Imagine if English had three spellings for "open" depending on what you were opening. Well Japanese does this for あける.

to open; to unlock; to unwrap	to empty; to make space; to be away from	to end (of a period, season); to begin (of the New Year)
開(あ)ける	空(あ)ける	明(あ)ける
base kanji: to open	**base kanji: empty**	**base kanji: bright**
ドアを開(あ)ける open a door	**席(せき)を空(あ)ける** make a seat available	**夜(よ)が明(あ)ける** night recedes (to dawn)
口(くち)を開(あ)ける open one's mouth	**スケジュールを空(あ)ける** open one's schedule	**年(とし)が明(あ)ける** the year ends
プレゼントを開(あ)ける open a present	**家(いえ)を空(あ)ける** leave the house (make empty)	**梅雨(つゆ)が明(あ)ける** the rainy season ends

5-4. Various feelings using 感

Emotions are important in life and important with kanji.

Word	First Kanji	English
好感(こうかん)	好 = fond; like something	good feeling; favorable impression
共感(きょうかん)	共 = together; both; with	sympathy; empathy
痛感(つうかん)	痛 = pain; hurt; damage	acutely aware; fully realizing
同感(どうかん)	同 = same; equal; alike	same opinion; same feeling; sympathize
反感(はんかん)	反 = anti-	antipathy; antagonism
敏感(びんかん)	敏 = cleverness; agile; alert	sensitive; alert; aware
鈍感(どんかん)	鈍 = insensitive; dull; thick-skinned	thickheaded; insensitive
予感(よかん)	予 = beforehand; previous	premonition; hunch
音感(おんかん)	音 = sound; noise	sense of sound; sense of pitch

EXAMPLE SENTENCES

1. 友達(ともだち)の考(かんが)えに同感(どうかん)です。
   I'm of the same opinion as my friend's thought.

2. 上田(うえだ)さんは明(あか)るくて、かわいくて、好感(こうかん)が持(も)てます。
   Ueda-san being cheerful and cute has a favorable impression.

3. なんか、悪(わる)い予感(よかん)がしています。
   Man... I've got a bad feeling (about this).

4. 私(わたし)は寒(さむ)さに敏感(びんかん)です。
   I'm sensitive to the cold.

5. 私(わたし)が鈍感(どんかん)なせいで、相手(あいて)の気持(きも)ちに気付(きづ)かなかったと痛感(つうかん)しています。
   I'm keenly aware that due to my being thickheaded, I hadn't realized the other person's feelings.

5 Words You Can Write 書ける言葉

運ぶ（はこぶ） to carry

運 ぶ

幸運（こううん） good luck

幸 運

公開（こうかい） release; open for public

公 開

開く（ひらく） to open

開 く

理想（りそう） dream; ideal

理 想

空想（くうそう） dreamy thought

空	想										

死ぬ（しぬ） to die

死	ぬ										

直感（ちょっかん） instinct; hunch

直	感										

悪運（あくうん） bad luck

悪	運										

開花（かいか） blooming; flowering; showing results

開	花										

決行（けっこう） doing (with resolve); carrying out (e.g. a plan)

決	行										

死角（しかく） blind spot; dead space

死	角										

感心（かんしん） admiration; being impressed; admirable

感	心										

決める(きめる) to decide

決	め	る									

決まる（きまる） to be decided

決	ま	る									

感じる（かんじる） to feel

感	じ	る									

5 Kanji Workbook Activities

● 1. Stroke Order Check 書き順確認

Each kanji has a stroke with an arrow on it. Write its order number below the kanji.

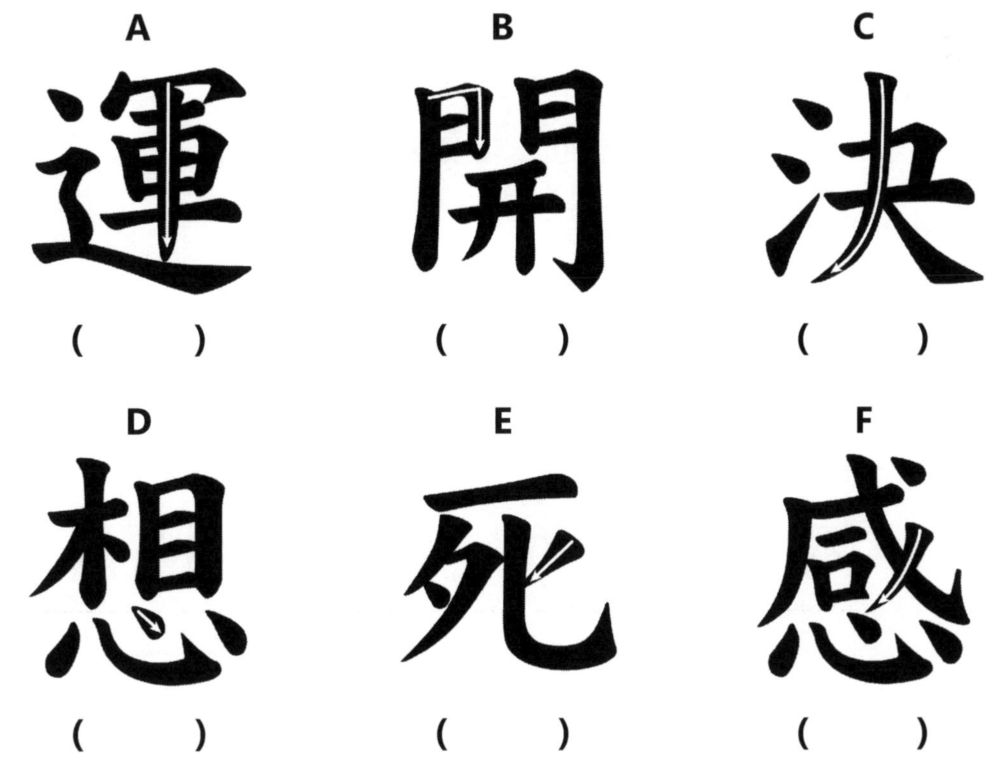

● 2. Kanji Meaning Match

Write the following kanji next to its meaning: 死 決 悲 感 運 寒 開 想 暗

1. ____ decide
2. ____ open
3. ____ die
4. ____ luck
5. ____ dark
6. ____ sad
7. ____ feel
8. ____ cold
9. ____ thought

● 3. Kanji Readings

Write FURIGANA above the underlined kanji words.

1. わたしは自分を幸運だと思っています。
2. あのえい画が公開する日は、何日でしたか。
3. 明日の遠足は、雨天決行です。
4. 先生は、わたしの読書感想文を読んで感心したそうです。
5. 車のサイドミラーには死角があるから、よく見て。

● 4. Fill in the Kanji

Fill in the appropriate kanji in the blanks for each sentence.

うん　とき　き　くだ

1. ____ てんする____ は ____をつけて____さい。

Please be careful when you drive.

あつ　あ

2. ____ いから、まどを ____けておきましょう。

Let's open up the windows since it's hot.

だい　がく　けっ　しん

3. ____ ____をやめることを____ ____ しました。

I have decided to quit college.

こ　　さん　にん　　　　　り　そう
4. ___ ども___ ___が わたしの ___ ___です。
Three children is my ideal.

きん　ぎょ　し　　　　　かな
5. ___ ___が___んでしまって ___しいです。
I'm sad since my goldfish ended up dying.

ちょっ　かん
6. わたしは___ ___ がよく あたります。
My intuition often hits. (I have good intuition.)

とお　か　　　　かん　そう　ぶん　か
7. ___ ___までに ___ ___ ___を___かなければなりません。
I have to write a book report by the 10th.

● 5. Kanji Matching

Connect each kanji with an おん or くん reading. Use each reading only ONCE.

感 •	• かい
想 •	• し
助 •	• うん
開 •	• ふか
苦 •	• かん
決 •	• じょ
死 •	• そう
深 •	• く
運 •	• き
消 •	• け

5 Answer Key 答え合わせ

1. Stroke order check (answers)

A) 9　　B) 2　　C) 6

D) 12　　E) 5　　F) 8

2. Kanji meaning match (answers)

1. 決 decide　2. 開 open　3. 死 die
4. 運 luck　5. 暗 dark　6. 悲 sad
7. 感 feel　8. 寒 cold　9. 想 thought

3. Kanji Readings (answers)

1. わたしは自分(じぶん)を幸運(こううん)だと思(おも)っています。　I think of myself as lucky.
2. あのえい画(が)が公開(こうかい)する日(ひ)は、何日(なんにち)でしたか。　What date was that movie is to be released?
3. 明日(あした)の遠足(えんそく)は、雨天決行(うてんけっこう)です。　Tomorrow's excursion will be held rain or shine.
4. 先生(せんせい)は、わたしの読書感想文(どくしょかんそうぶん)を読(よ)んで感心(かんしん)したそうです。　The teacher read my book report and was impressed.
5. 車(くるま)のサイドミラーには死角(しかく)があるから、よく見(み)て。　Look carefully since there are blind spots in the car's side mirrors.

4. Fill in the kanji (answers)

1. 運てんする時は気をつけて下さい。
2. 暑いから、まどを開けておきましょう。
3. 大学をやめることを決心しました。
4. 子ども三人がわたしの理想です。
5. 金魚が死んでしまって悲しいです。
6. わたしは直感がよくあたります。
7. 十日までに感想文を書かなければなりません。

5. Kanji matching (answers)

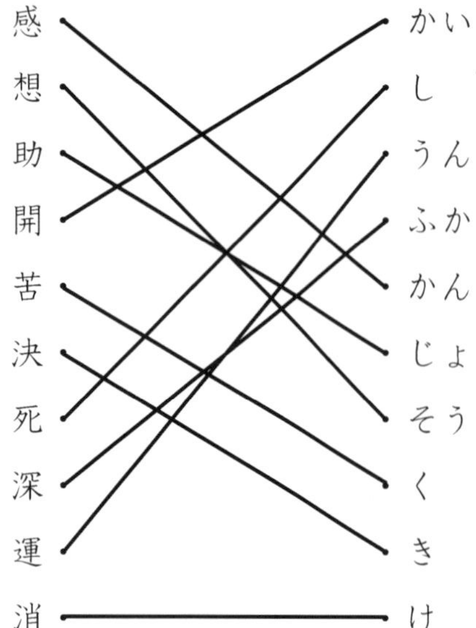

Kanji Lessons 1-5: Super Review 1

From the teacher...

Test your knowledge of the kanji learned in the last 5 lessons.

● 1. Build-a-Kanji 漢字の組み合わせ

Combine the left and right parts to make seven of the kanji learned in lessons 1-5.

RULES
1. You can use the radical and kanji parts as many times as you want.
2. Some kanji can use two kanji parts.

部首 (Radical)		
氵	日	广
辶	十	亻
木	矢	力
宀	心	艹

Other Kanji Parts		
直	日	相
豆	一	音
田	皿	古
女	力	軍

SAMPLE	1	2	3	4	5	6	7
安							

● 2. Okurigana drill 送り仮名ドリル

Circle the correct 漢字(かんじ) + 送り仮名(おくがな) combination.

1. あたたかい	・温かい	・温たかい
2. くるしい	・苦い	・苦しい
3. かさねる	・重ねる	・重さねる
4. みじかい	・短い	・短かい
5. うつくしい	・美くしい	・美しい
6. さいわい	・幸い	・幸わい
7. まがる	・曲がる	・曲る
8. そだてる	・育る	・育てる

● 3. Kanji selection 漢字の選択

Select the best kanji to replace the underlined section of the sentence.

1. わたしは つめたいスープより、____かいスープのほうがすきです。
   A. 暑　　B. 軽　　C. 温　　D. 寒

2. かえりの にもつが 2 キロ____くなっていました。
   A. 速　　B. 重　　C. 短　　D. 悪

3. 赤ちゃんは____しそうな顔をしていますね。おなかがいたいんでしょうか。
   A. 幸　　B. 悲　　C. 美　　D. 苦

4. 人を____けるしごとは すばらしいですね。
   A. 開　　B. 助　　C. 消　　D. 感

● 4. Kanji reading selection 読みの選択

Select the best reading for the underlined kanji.

1. わたしが苦手なのは、歌うことです。
   A. く　　B. くる　　C. にが　　D. にく

2. つぎの角で右に曲がって下さい。
   A. お　　B. み　　C. ひ　　D. ま

3. 新しい えい画が 公開されるのは、七月二十日です。
   A. かい　　B. ひら　　C. あ　　D. もん

4. 幸い、天気にめぐまれました。
   A. さち　　B. しあわ　　C. さいわ　　D. こう

● 5. Compound kanji word puzzle 熟語パズル

Fill in the correct kanji based on the list below the puzzle.

1)		2)
	3)	
	4)	
5)		6)

Down ↓	
English meaning	**Hiragana**
2) book report	かんそうぶん
Left to Right →	
1) decision	けっしん
4) short sentence	たんぶん
5) drinking and eating	いんしょく
← Right to Left	
2) admiration	かんしん
3) good luck	こううん
4) short temper	たんき
6) light meal	けいしょく

SR1 Answer Key 答え合わせ

1. Build-a-Kanji (answers) (order can vary)

SAMPLE 安 1) 暗 2) 温 3) 苦 4) 短 5) 運 6) 想 7) 植

2. Okurigana drill (answers)

1. あたたかい	**・温かい**	・温たかい	5. うつくしい	・美くしい	**・美しい**
2. くるしい	・苦い	**・苦しい**	6. さいわい	**・幸い**	・幸わい
3. かさねる	**・重ねる**	・重さねる	7. まがる	**・曲がる**	・曲る
4. みじかい	**・短い**	・短かい	8. そだてる	・育る	**・育てる**

3. Kanji selection (answers)

1. C – 温(あたた)かい — I like warm soup more than cold soup.
2. B – 重(おも)く — My return luggage had gotten 2 kilos heavier.
3. D – 苦(くる)しそう — The baby is making a seemingly suffering face. Perhaps their stomach hurts.
4. B – 助(たす)ける — Work that helps people is amazing.

4. Kanji reading selection (answers)

1. C – 苦手(にがて) — What I'm not good at is singing.
2. D – 曲(ま)がって — Please turn right at the next corner.
3. A – 公開(こうかい) — The new movie will be released on July 20th.
4. C – 幸(さいわ)い — Luckily, we were blessed with good weather.

5. Compound kanji word puzzle (answers)

決	心	感
運	幸	想
気	短	文
飲	食	軽

6 Kanji Lesson 6: 起使始終写守

271-276

Kanji that can be verbs (part 4)

6 New Kanji 新しい漢字

271	走	10 画	くん お(きる、こす、こる)	おん キ

起

起こる (お) to happen; to occur	起こす (お) to cause; to wake someone up	早起き (はや お) early rising
起床 (き しょう) getting out of bed; rising	起きる (お) to wake up; to get up; to occur	縁起 (えん ぎ) omen; sign of luck

wake up; take place; happen — 走 (run) + 己 (self)

272	イ	8 画	くん つか(う)	おん シ

使

使う (つか) to use	使命 (し めい) mission; duty; obligation	使用中 (し よう ちゅう) in use
天使 (てん し) angel	使い方 (つか かた) how to use	使い捨て (つか す) disposable

use; messenger; envoy — イ (person) + 吏 (official)

273	女	8 画	くん はじ(める、まる)	おん シ

始

始める (はじ) to start; to initiate	年始 (ねん し) beginning of the year	始発 (し はつ) initial; first train etc.
始まる (はじ) to begin; to start	原始人 (げん し じん) primitive man; caveman	始業式 (し ぎょう しき) opening ceremony

begin; start — 女 (woman) + 台 (platform)

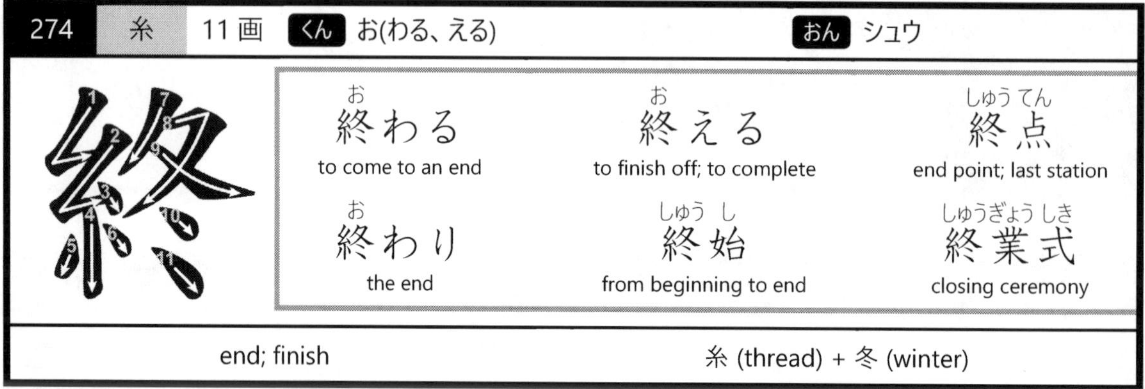

274 | 糸 | 11 画 | くん お(わる、える) | おん シュウ

終

終わる (お) to come to an end	終える (お) to finish off; to complete	終点 (しゅう てん) end point; last station
終わり (お) the end	終始 (しゅう し) from beginning to end	終業式 (しゅうぎょう しき) closing ceremony

end; finish — 糸 (thread) + 冬 (winter)

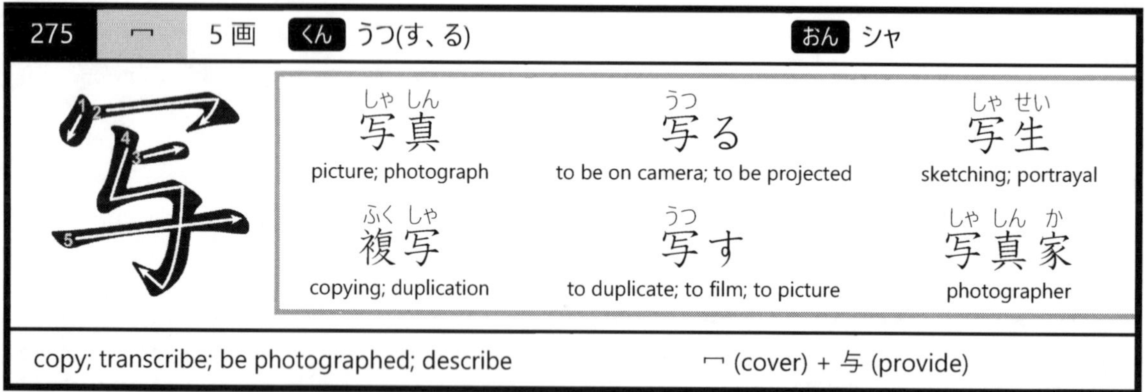

275 | 冖 | 5 画 | くん うつ(す、る) | おん シャ

写

写真 (しゃ しん) picture; photograph	写る (うつ) to be on camera; to be projected	写生 (しゃ せい) sketching; portrayal
複写 (ふく しゃ) copying; duplication	写す (うつ) to duplicate; to film; to picture	写真家 (しゃ しん か) photographer

copy; transcribe; be photographed; describe — 冖 (cover) + 与 (provide)

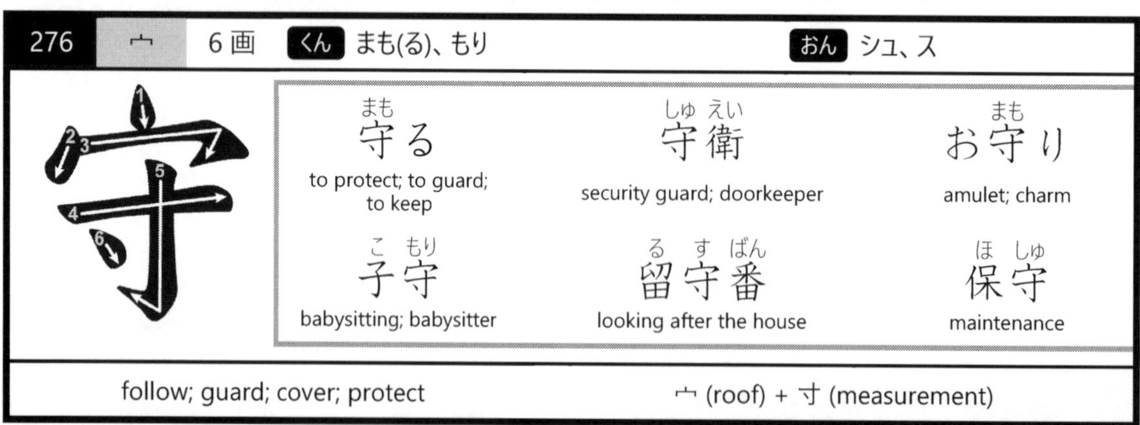

276 | 宀 | 6 画 | くん まも(る)、もり | おん シュ、ス

守

守る (まも) to protect; to guard; to keep	守衛 (しゅ えい) security guard; doorkeeper	お守り (まも) amulet; charm
子守 (こ もり) babysitting; babysitter	留守番 (る す ばん) looking after the house	保守 (ほ しゅ) maintenance

follow; guard; cover; protect — 宀 (roof) + 寸 (measurement)

Kanji Parts used in the New Kanji

走	run	女	woman	冖	cover
己	self	台	platform	与	provide
イ	person	糸	thread	宀	roof
吏	official	冬	winter	寸	measurement

6 Kanji Memory Tools 漢字記憶術

This section helps you organically memorize kanji readings, meanings, and construction.

起

走 己
Run by yourself to "**WAKE UP**".

にほんご お じかん きしょうじかん い
日本語で❶「起きる時間」は❷「起床時間」と言います。

In Japanese the ❶"time you wake up" is called ❷"wake up time".

使

亻 吏
This is something only a person that's an official can "**USE**".

つか ぜんぶ しようちゅう
トイレが❶使いたいのに、全部❷使用中でした。

Even though I ❶want to use the toilet, they were all ❷in use.

始

女 台
The woman next to the platform said "**START**".

しぎょうしき はじ まえ じこしょうかい はじ
❶始業式が❷始まる前に、自己紹介を❸始めましょう。

❸Let's start self-introductions before the ❶opening ceremony ❷starts.

終

糸 冬
This thread means that winter will "**END**".

しゅうぎょうしき お しゃしんさつえい お
❶終業式が❷終わるまでに、写真撮影を❸終えました。

We ❸finished taking photos ❷by the end of the ❶closing ceremony.

写

冖 与
The cover you provide can be a "**COPY**".

しゃしん だれ うつ
この❶写真に、誰が❷写っていますか。

Who is ❷in this ❶picture?

守

宀 寸
The roof has a measurement that is easy to "**GUARD**".

しゅえい だんな るす とき わたし まも
❶守衛さんは旦那が❷留守の時、私を❸守ります。

❶The security guard ❸protects me when my husband is ❷away from home.

6 Understanding Kanji Parts 漢字部分の理解

● 6-1. How long is, and what is 寸 (measurement)

The kanji part 寸 (すん) meaning is listed as "measurement". One 寸 is 30.3 millimeters, or 1.193 inches. In modern times, it's not used except when talking about traditional structures build during the time when 寸 was still used. Not that it matters, but it's 1/10 of a 尺 (しゃく). Here are some words that use 寸.

measurement; dimension; size	just before; on the verge of	cutting; tearing into pieces
すん ぽう 寸法	すん ぜん 寸前	すん だん 寸断
(measurement + law)	(measurement + before)	(measurement + decision)

EXAMPLE SENTENCES

1. 携帯電話(けいたいでんわ)のケースと電話(でんわ)の寸法(すんぽう)に合(あ)わないです。
   The cell phone case and the phone dimensions don't match.

2. 寝落(ねお)ち寸前(すんぜん)に、電話(でんわ)が鳴(な)って目(め)が覚(さ)めた。
   On the verge of falling asleep, my phone rang, and I woke up.

3. 台風(たいふう)のせいで、道路(どうろ)が寸断(すんだん)されました。
   Due to the typhoon, the road got torn up.

● 6-2. The "person" radical にんべん (亻)

The "person" radical is called にんべん and the kanji containing にんべん tend to be people related. However, this isn't always the case.

close; nearby		body	
作	つく 作る to make; to create	体	からだ 体 body; torso
person + concurrently	さっ か 作家 author; writer; novelist	person + main	たい けい 体型 figure; body shape

rest; day off		what	
休 person + tree	やす **休み** rest; recess; vacation きゅうじつ **休日** holiday; day off	何 person + possibility	なん じ **何時** what time? なん にん **何人** how many people?

use; order; messenger		reside; live; inhabit	
使 person + history	つか **使う** to use し よう にん **使用人** servant; employee	住 person + master	す **住む** to live; to reside じゅう にん **住人** resident; dweller

person in charge; duty		other; another; the others	
係 person + thread	かかり **係** person in charge; clerk かん けい **関係** relation; connection	他 person + to be	ほか **他** other (place, person, thing) た にん **他人** another person; outsider

6 Kanji Usage 漢字の使い方

● 6-3. The beginning and the end 始、終

It's important to know the difference between these similar sounding verbs.

to start (I / he / she started it)	to start (it started)
はじ 始める	はじ 始まる

to end (I / he / she ended it)	to end (it ended)
お 終える	お 終わる

EXAMPLE SENTENCES

1. 先生(せんせい)が授業(じゅぎょう)を始(はじ)めました。
   The teacher started the class.
   A person did an action to make the class start.
2. 10時(じ)に授業(じゅぎょう)が始(はじ)まりました。
   Class began at 10 o'clock.
   This sentence just states that class began. No person required.
3. 先生(せんせい)が授業(じゅぎょう)を終(お)えました。
   The teacher ended the class.
   A person did an action to make the class end.
4. 12時(じ)に授業(じゅぎょう)が終(お)わりました。
   Class ended at 12 o'clock.
   This sentence just states that class ended regardless of if a person was involved or not.

Notice the different particles used before each verb depending on if the action was actively done by a person, or whether the state just occurred.

6 Words You Can Write 書ける言葉

起立（きりつ） to stand up

起	立										

天使（てんし） angel

天	使										

使う（つかう） to use

使	う										

終点（しゅうてん） end point; last stop (e.g. train)

終	点										

写す（うつす） to copy; to duplicate; to film

写	す										

写生（しゃせい） sketching; portrayal

写	生										

守る（まもる） to guard; to follow

守	る										

起用（きよう） being used for a role; promotion

起	用										

使用（しよう） use; application; utilization

使	用										

年始（ねんし） beginning of the year

年	始										

終日（しゅうじつ） all day; for a whole day

終	日										

起きる（おきる） to get up

起	き	る									

始める（はじめる） to begin

始	め	る									

終わる（おわる） to come to an end

終	わ	る									

使い方（つかいかた） how to use

使	い	方									

写メール（しゃメール） email from cell phones; containing pictures

写	メ	ー	ル								

6 Kanji Workbook Activities

● 1. Stroke Order Check 書き順確認

Each kanji has a stroke with an arrow on it. Write its order number below the kanji.

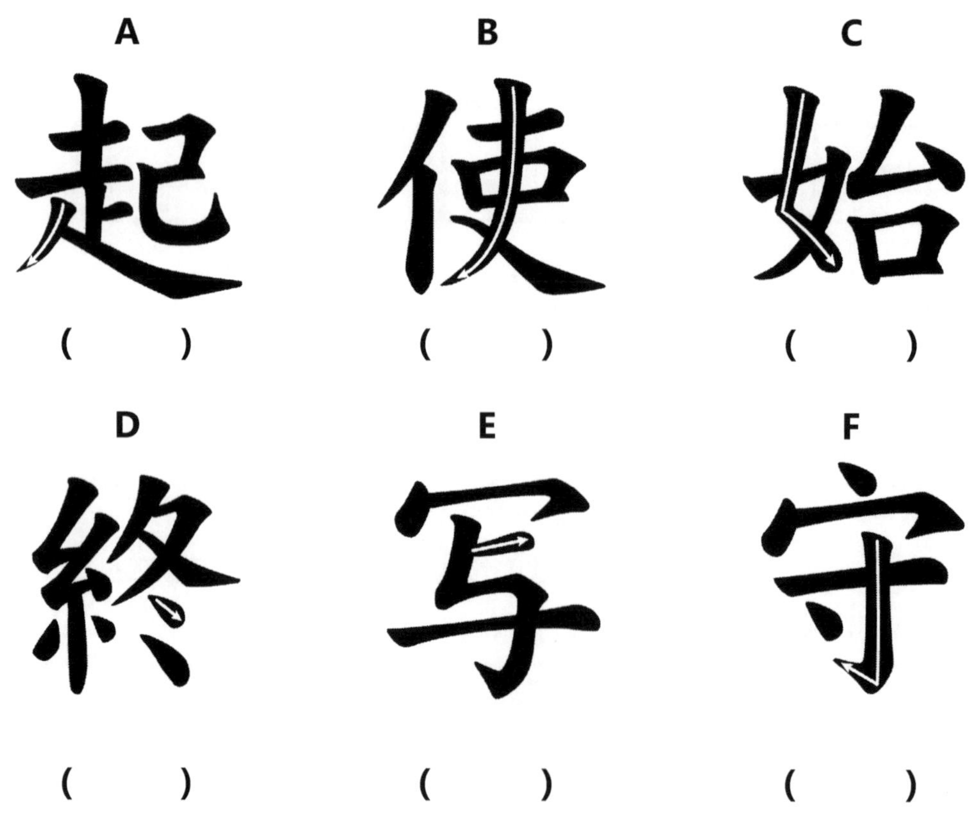

● 2. Kanji Meaning Match

Write the following kanji next to its meaning: 守 終 使 乗 写 助 始 短 起

1. ____ get up
2. ____ help
3. ____ end
4. ____ short
5. ____ ride
6. ____ copy
7. ____ begin
8. ____ follow
9. ____ use

● 3. Kanji Readings

Write FURIGANA above the underlined kanji words.

1. 日本の学校では、先生がクラスを始める時、起立します。
2. お父さん、明日 車を使ってもいい？
3. 年始は、何日からお店を開けますか。
4. 社長はパーティーで 終始 楽しそうでした。
5. 高校一年生の時は、よく六さいの弟の子守をしていました。

● 4. Fill in the Kanji

Fill in the appropriate kanji in the blanks for each sentence.

1. わたしは ___(まい) ___(あさ) ___(ろく) ___(じ)に ___(お)きます。
   I get up at 6 o'clock every morning.

2. おばあちゃんはパソコンの___(つか) い___(かた) が ___(わ) かりません。
   My grandmother doesn't know how to use a PC (personal computer)

3. ___(さき) に___(た) べ___(はじ)めて___(くだ)さい。
   Please begin to eat first.

しゅう てん い

4. このバスで___ ___まで___ きましょう。

Let's go to the last stop on this bus.

くら しゃ

5. そこは ___いから、___しんがとれません。

You can't take a photo there since it's dark.

に ほん か まも たい せつ

6. ___ ___で___ ったお___ りを ___ ___にしています。

I cherish the charms that I bought in Japan.

やま かわ しゃ せい

7. わたしは___ や___で ___ ___ するのがすきです。

I like sketching at the mountain or the river.

● 5. Kanji Matching

Connect each kanji with an おん or くん reading. Use each reading only ONCE.

使 •	• しゅ
終 •	• しゃ
消 •	• しゅう
守 •	• つか
安 •	• しょう
起 •	• もう
苦 •	• はじ
始 •	• く
写 •	• き
申 •	• あん

6 Answer Key 答え合わせ

1. Stroke order check (answers)

A) 6　B) 7　C) 1

D) 10　E) 3　F) 5

2. Kanji meaning match (answers)

1. 起 get up　2. 助 help　3. 終 end

4. 短 short　5. 乗 ride　6. 写 copy

7. 始 begin　8. 守 follow　9. 使 use

3. Kanji Readings (answers)

1. 日本の学校では、先生がクラスを始める時、起立します。
   In Japanese schools, when the teacher starts class, we stand up.
2. お父さん、明日 車を使ってもいい？
   Dad, can I use the car tomorrow?
3. 年始は、何日からお店を開けますか。
   What day does the story open at the beginning of the New Year?
4. 社長はパーティーで 終始 楽しそうでした。
   The president seemed to enjoy the part from start to finish.
5. 高校一年生の時は、よく六さいの 弟 の子守をしていました。
   When I was in 10th grade, I often babysat my 6-year-old brother.

4. Fill in the kanji (answers)

1. わたしは毎朝六時に起きます。
2. おばあちゃんはパソコンの使い方が分かりません。
3. 先に食べ始めて下さい。
4. このバスで終点まで行きましょう。
5. そこは暗いから、写しんがとれません。
6. 日本で買ったお守りを大切にしています。
7. わたしは山や川で写生するのがすきです。

5. Kanji matching (answers)

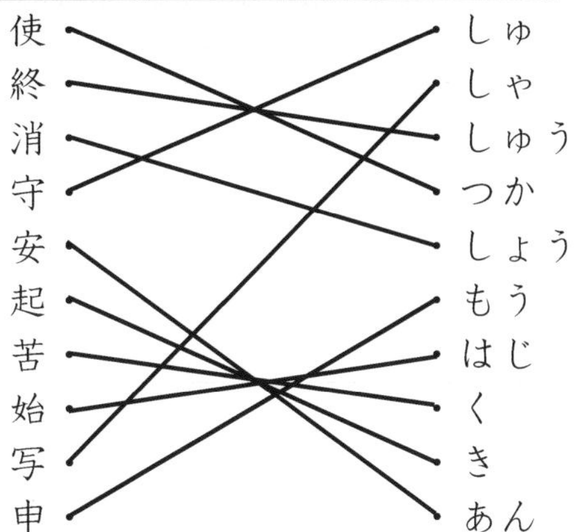

7 Kanji Lesson 7: 277-282

取受拾持習集

Kanji that can be verbs (part 5) (hand related)

7 New Kanji 新しい漢字

277 | 又 | 8 画 | くん と(る) | おん シュ

取る (と) to take; to pick up	取れる (と) to come off; to be removed	取得 (しゅ とく) acquisition; obtaining
草取り (くさ と) pulling weeds	取材 (しゅ ざい) news gathering; interview	取っ手 (と て) handle; grip; knob

take; fetch; take up — 耳 (ear) + 又 (again)

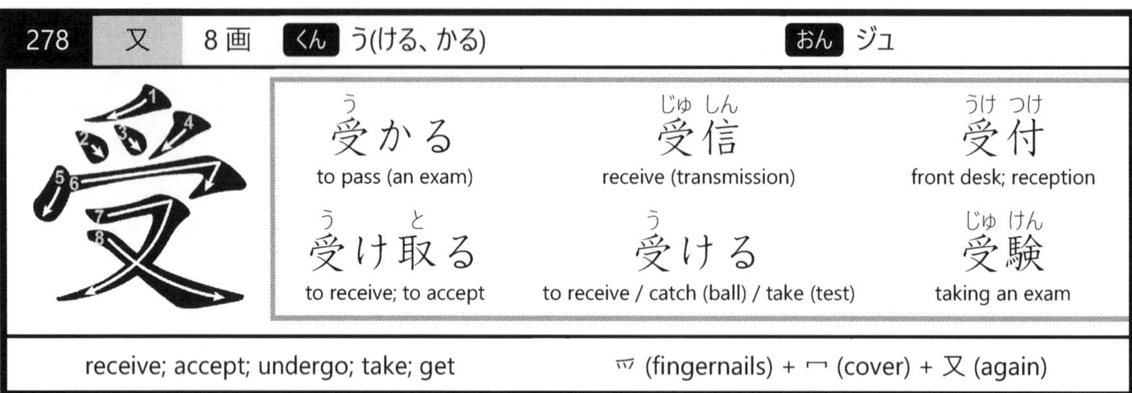

278 | 又 | 8 画 | くん う(ける、かる) | おん ジュ

受かる (う) to pass (an exam)	受信 (じゅ しん) receive (transmission)	受付 (うけ つけ) front desk; reception
受け取る (う と) to receive; to accept	受ける (う) to receive / catch (ball) / take (test)	受験 (じゅ けん) taking an exam

receive; accept; undergo; take; get — 爫 (fingernails) + 冖 (cover) + 又 (again)

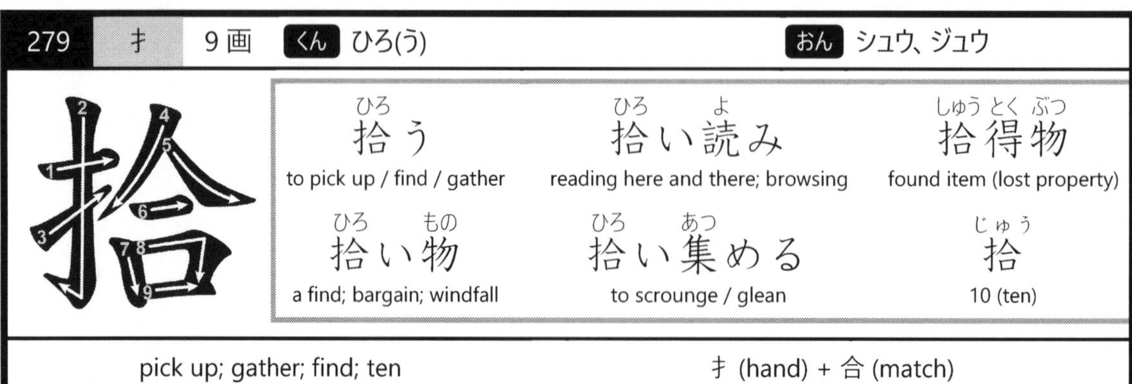

279 | 扌 | 9 画 | くん ひろ(う) | おん シュウ、ジュウ

拾う (ひろ) to pick up / find / gather	拾い読み (ひろ よ) reading here and there; browsing	拾得物 (しゅう とく ぶつ) found item (lost property)
拾い物 (ひろ もの) a find; bargain; windfall	拾い集める (ひろ あつ) to scrounge / glean	拾 (じゅう) 10 (ten)

pick up; gather; find; ten — 扌 (hand) + 合 (match)

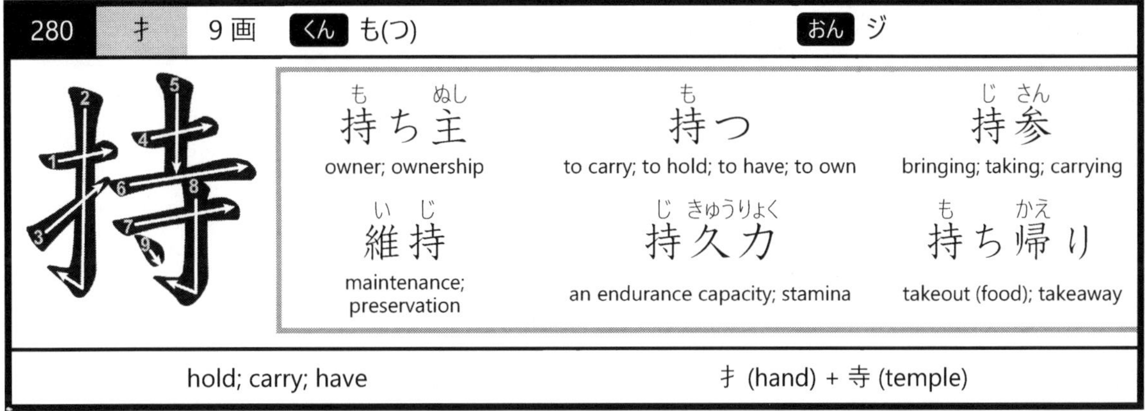

280	扌	9 画	くん も(つ)	おん ジ

持ち主 (も ぬし) owner; ownership	持つ (も) to carry; to hold; to have; to own	持参 (じ さん) bringing; taking; carrying
維持 (い じ) maintenance; preservation	持久力 (じ きゅうりょく) an endurance capacity; stamina	持ち帰り (も かえ) takeout (food); takeaway

hold; carry; have — 扌 (hand) + 寺 (temple)

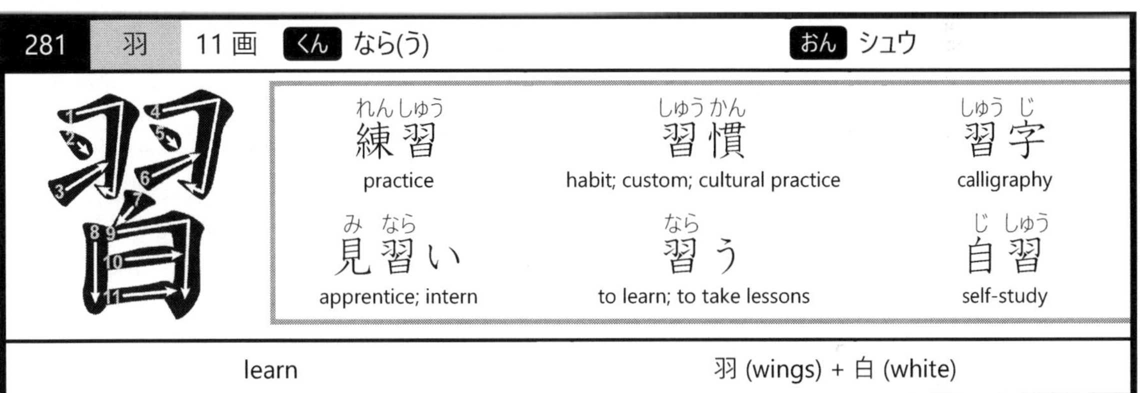

281	羽	11 画	くん なら(う)	おん シュウ

練習 (れんしゅう) practice	習慣 (しゅうかん) habit; custom; cultural practice	習字 (しゅう じ) calligraphy
見習い (み なら) apprentice; intern	習う (なら) to learn; to take lessons	自習 (じ しゅう) self-study

learn — 羽 (wings) + 白 (white)

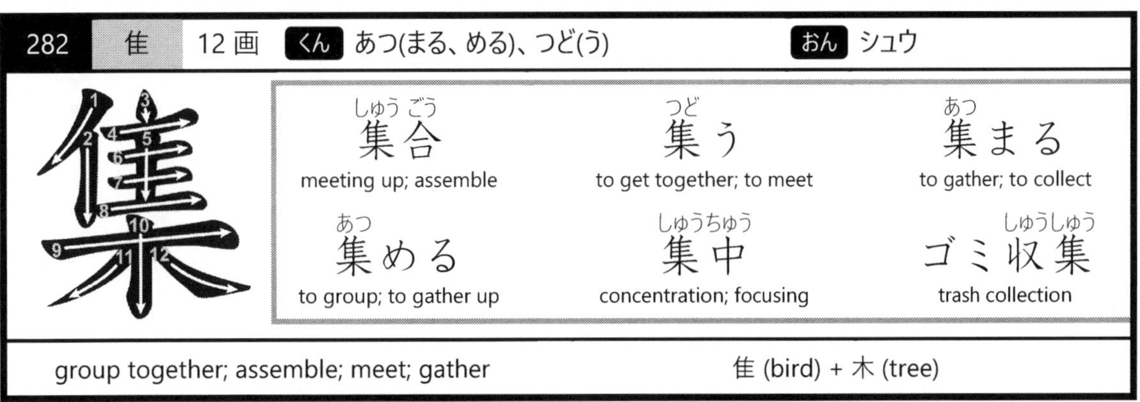

282	隹	12 画	くん あつ(まる、める)、つど(う)	おん シュウ

集合 (しゅう ごう) meeting up; assemble	集う (つど) to get together; to meet	集まる (あつ) to gather; to collect
集める (あつ) to group; to gather up	集中 (しゅうちゅう) concentration; focusing	ゴミ収集 (しゅうしゅう) trash collection

group together; assemble; meet; gather — 隹 (bird) + 木 (tree)

Kanji Parts used in the New Kanji

耳	ear	扌	hand	白	white
又	again	合	match	隹	bird
爫	fingernails	寺	temple	木	tree
冖	cover	羽	wings		

7 Kanji Memory Tools 漢字記憶術

This section helps you organically memorize kanji readings, meanings, and construction.

取

耳 又
It's your ear that again I will "**TAKE**".

テレビの❶取材（しゅざい）の途中（とちゅう）に、入（い）れ歯（ば）が❷取（と）れた。

In the middle of a TV ❶interview, my dentures ❷came off.

受

⺤ 又
Just tap your fingernails again and ye shall "**RECEIVE**".

大学（だいがく）❶受験（じゅけん）に❷受（う）かったかどうかは、明日（あした）分（わ）かります。

I will know tomorrow if I ❷passed (or not) the college entrance ❶exam.

拾

扌 合
If your hand is a match you can "**PICK (IT) UP**".

落（お）とし物（もの）を❶拾（ひろ）ったら、その拾（ひろ）った物（もの）は❷「拾得物（しゅうとくぶつ）」と言（い）います。

When lost property is ❶picked up, that picked-up item is called a ❷ "found article".

持

扌 寺
Yoda: Your hand on the temple, much power it will "**HOLD**".

高級車（こうきゅうしゃ）を❶持（も）っていると❷維持費（いじひ）が高（たか）いです。

If you ❶have a luxury car the ❷cost of maintenance is expensive.

習

羽 白
Wings of white yearn to "**LEARN**".

日本人（にほんじん）は❶習字（しゅうじ）を❷習（なら）う ❸習慣（しゅうかん）がある。

Japanese people have a ❸custom of ❷learning ❶calligraphy.

集

隹 木
Birds in trees tend to "**GATHER**".

人（ひと）が❶集（あつ）まる時間（じかん）は❷「集合時間（しゅうごうじかん）」と言（い）います。

The time when people ❶gather is called, ❷"meet time".

7 Understanding Kanji Parts 漢字部分の理解

● 7-1. Kanji Part: "again" 又

The 又 part is officially called 又部 (ゆうぶ), but it's almost always referred to as また (again). The meaning of 又 can be "right hand" or "hand movement". In this book we use "again" for its meaning to avoid conflict with other parts that more closely represent "hand".

friend		anti-	
友 one + no + again	ともだち 友達 friend しんゆう 親友 best friend	反 cliff + again	はんたい 反対 opposition; objection はんこうき 反抗期 rebellious phase or age
receive		**take; obtain**	
受 fingernails + cover + again	う 受ける to receive うけつけ 受付 reception (desk)	取 ear + again	しゅとく 取得する to acquire; to obtain とっとりけん 鳥取県 Tottori Prefecture

7 Kanji Usage 漢字の使い方

● 7-2. Obtaining and Acquisition (取)

Here are some other interesting words you might hear using 取.

the first goal	intake; absorption
せんしゅてん 先取点	せっしゅ 摂取
(prior + acquire + point)	(take + acquire)
transactions; business	**to cancel; to withdraw; to revoke**
とりひき 取引	と け 取り消す
(acquire + pull)	(take + erase)

● 7-3. Subtle Difference, Big Changes

You can avoid similar looking kanji by looking at which parts they are formed from.

Buddhist temple		hold; carry; have	
寺	てら **寺** temple (Buddhist) やま でら **山寺** mountain temple	持	も **持つ** to hold / carry し じ **支持** support; backing
soil + measurement		hand + temple	

wait; depend on		waiter; samurai; serve	
待	ま **待つ** to wait / anticipate き たい **期待** expectation; hope	侍	さむらい **侍** warrior; samurai じ じょ **侍女** lady attendant; maid
move forward + temple		person + temple	

poem; poetry		time; hour	
詩	し **詩** poem; verse of poetry し じん **詩人** poet	時	いち じ **一時** one o'clock じ かん **時間** time
speak + temple		sun + temple	

etc., and so forth; class; equal		special	
等	いっ とう **一等** first-class; first-rank びょう どう **平等** equality; evenness	特	とく **特に** particularly; especially とく べつ **特別** special; particular
bamboo + temple		cow + temple	

● 7-4. The difference between 習(なら)う、勉強(べんきょう)する and 学(まな)ぶ

習(なら)う、勉強(べんきょう)する、and 学(まな)ぶ all relate to learning, but each have slight variations.

❶ 習(なら)う (to learn)
to learn something specific (arts; handicrafts, etc.) from someone

- The learning is specific and not abstract.
- There is always a teacher directly teaching.
- Learning through repetition.

❷ 学(まな)ぶ (to learn)
to acquire knowledge or obtain skill in a craft

- The learning is abstract.
- This can be used for self-teaching or with a teacher.

❸ 勉強(べんきょう)する (to study, to learn)
to learn through time, effort, or experience

- The learning can be a result of effort OR through passive experiences.
- The learning is of school subjects, technique, and specific arts and crafts.

to take lessons in; to be taught; to learn (from a teacher)	to study (in depth); to learn	to study; to work
習(なら)う	学(まな)ぶ	勉強(べんきょう)する
ピアノを習(なら)う learn piano	失敗(しっぱい)から学(まな)ぶ learn from mistakes	毎日(まいにち)、勉強(べんきょう)する study everyday
テニスを習(なら)う learn tennis	人生(じんせい)について学(まな)ぶ learn about life	日本語(にほんご)を勉強(べんきょう)する study Japanese
日本語(にほんご)を習(なら)う learn Japanese	新(あたら)しい事(こと)を学(まな)ぶ learn a new thing	この仕事(しごと)はいい勉強(べんきょう)になった the job taught me good (a lot).

● 7-5. Different types of learning 習

習 is used in many 熟語 (じゅくご) compound kanji words.

Japanese	Meaning of the first kanji	English
予習 (よしゅう)	予 = beforehand; previous	preparation for a lesson
復習 (ふくしゅう)	復 = restore; revert; resume	review; revision
実習 (じっしゅう)	実 = reality; truth	practice (in the field); training; drill
練習 (れんしゅう)	練 = practice; train; drill; polish	practice; practicing
自習 (じしゅう)	自 = oneself	self-study; teaching oneself
補習 (ほしゅう)	補 = supplement; assistant; offset	supplementary lessons
風習 (ふうしゅう)	風 = wind; style; manner	custom

7 Words You Can Write 書ける言葉

取る（とる） to take; to pick up

取る

拾う（ひろう） to pick up; to find

拾う

持つ（もつ） to hold; to carry

持つ

習う（ならう） to learn

習う

集合（しゅうごう） aggregate; ingathering

集合

学習（がくしゅう） study; learning

学習

草取り（くさとり） pulling weeds by hand

草取り

受ける（うける） to receive

受ける

力持ち（ちからもち） powerful person

力持ち

見習い（みならい） apprentice; intern

見習い

集まる（あつまる） to gather; to meet

集まる

集める（あつめる） to group; to gather up

集める

取っ手（とって） handle; grip; knob

取っ手

気持ち（きもち） feeling; sensation; mood

気	持	ち									

受け取る（うけとる） to receive; to get; to accept

受	け	取	る								

拾い読み（ひろいよみ） reading (just the parts one is interested in)

拾	い	読	み								

7 Kanji Workbook Activities

● 1. Stroke Order Check 書き順確認

Each kanji has a stroke with an arrow on it. Write its order number below the kanji.

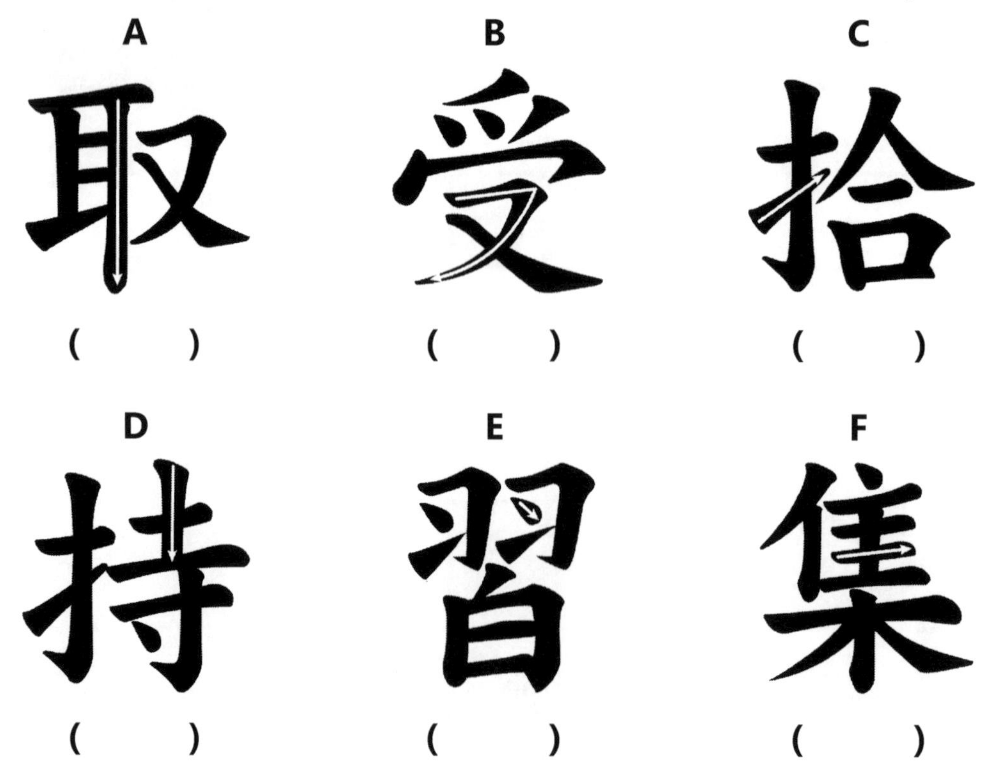

● 2. Kanji Meaning Match

Write the following kanji next to its meaning: 取 開 受 温 拾 持 消 習 集

1. ____ gather	2. ____ receive	3. ____ warm
4. ____ erase	5. ____ take	6. ____ hold; carry
7. ____ pick up	8. ____ open	9. ____ learn

● 3. Kanji Readings

Write FURIGANA above the underlined kanji words.

1. ドアの取っ手を持ったら、取れてしまいました。
2. すみませんが、ここに受取のサインをして下さい。
3. わたしはよく、書店で拾い読みをします。
4. 先生に助言をいただいて、気持ちが楽になりました。
5. 大工の見習いになって、今はしごとに集中しています。

● 4. Fill in the Kanji

Fill in the appropriate kanji in the blanks for each sentence.

1. ___(あか)チームが ___(せん) ___(しゅ) ___(てん)を___(と)りました。
The red team got the first goal.

2. ___(はやし)さんは ___(うけ) ___(つけ)のしごとをしています。
Hayashi-san does receptionist work. a

3. ___(がっ) ___(こう)の___(えん) ___(そく)で、くりを たくさん ___(ひろ) いました。
On our school excursion (trip), we gathered (picked up) a lot of chestnuts.

も　し
4. このかばんの___ ちぬしを___っていますか。

Do you know the owner of this bag?

ちい　とき　しゅう　じ　なら
5. わたしは___ さい___、___ ___を___っていました。

When I was small (young), I was learning calligraphy.

あした　こう　えん　しゅう　ごう
6. ___ ___ は この ___ ___で___ ___ しましょう。

Let's meet up at the park tomorrow.

せん　せい　う　と
7. きのう、___ ___からメールを ___け___りました。

I received an email from the teacher yesterday.

● 5. Kanji Matching

Connect each kanji with an おん or くん reading. Use each reading only ONCE.

持 •	• ひ
取 •	• ひろ
悲 •	• し
受 •	• じ
速 •	• と
拾 •	• じゅ
軽 •	• そく
習 •	• けい
死 •	• あつ
集 •	• なら

7 Answer Key 答え合わせ

1. Stroke order check (answers)

A) 6　B) 7　C) 3

D) 5　E) 5　F) 7

2. Kanji meaning match (answers)

1. 集 gather　2. 受 receive　3. 温 warm

4. 消 erase　5. 取 take　6. 持 hold; carry

7. 拾 pick up　8. 開 open　9. 習 learn

3. Kanji Readings (answers)

1. ドアの取(と)っ手(て)を持(も)ったら、取(と)れてしまいました。
   When I grabbed the door handle it came off.
2. すみませんが、ここに受取(うけとり)のサインをして下(くだ)さい。
   Excuse me but please sign the receipt here.
3. わたしはよく、書店(しょてん)で拾(ひろ)い読(よ)みをします。
   I often browse read at the bookstore.
4. 先生(せんせい)に助言(じょげん)をいただいて、気持(きも)ちが楽(らく)になりました。
   I feel better after getting advice from the teacher (or doctor).
5. 大工(だいく)の見習(みなら)いになって、今(いま)はしごとに集中(しゅうちゅう)しています。
   I become a carpenter's apprentice and now I'm concentrating on my work.

4. Fill in the kanji (answers)

1. 赤チームが先取点を取りました。
2. 林さんは受付のしごとをしています。
3. 学校の遠足で、くりを たくさん拾いました。
4. このかばんの持ちぬしを知っていますか。
5. わたしは小さい時、習字を習っていました。
6. 明日は この公園で集合しましょう。
7. きのう、先生からメールを受け取りました。

5. Kanji matching (answers)

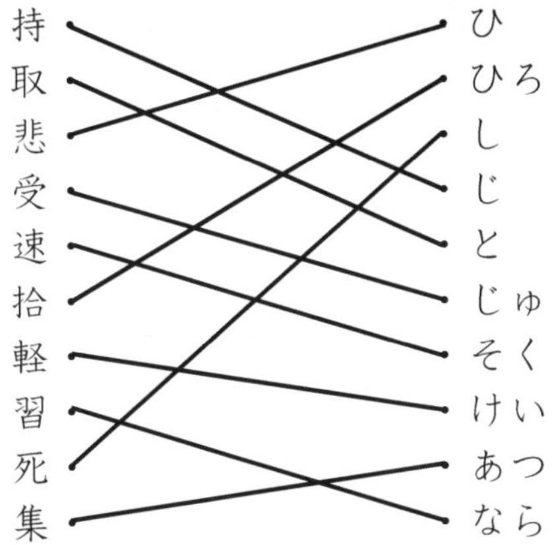

8 Kanji Lesson 8: 住向急去進整

283-288

Kanji that can be verbs (part 6)

8 New Kanji 新しい漢字

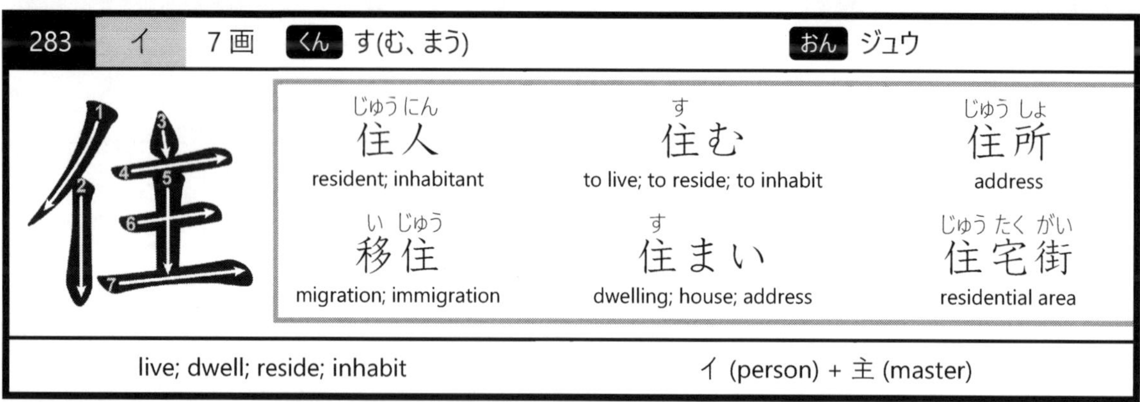

283
亻
7 画
くん す(む、まう)
おん ジュウ
じゅうにん 住人 resident; inhabitant
す 住む to live; to reside; to inhabit
じゅうしょ 住所 address
いじゅう 移住 migration; immigration
す 住まい dwelling; house; address
じゅうたくがい 住宅街 residential area
live; dwell; reside; inhabit
亻 (person) + 主 (master)

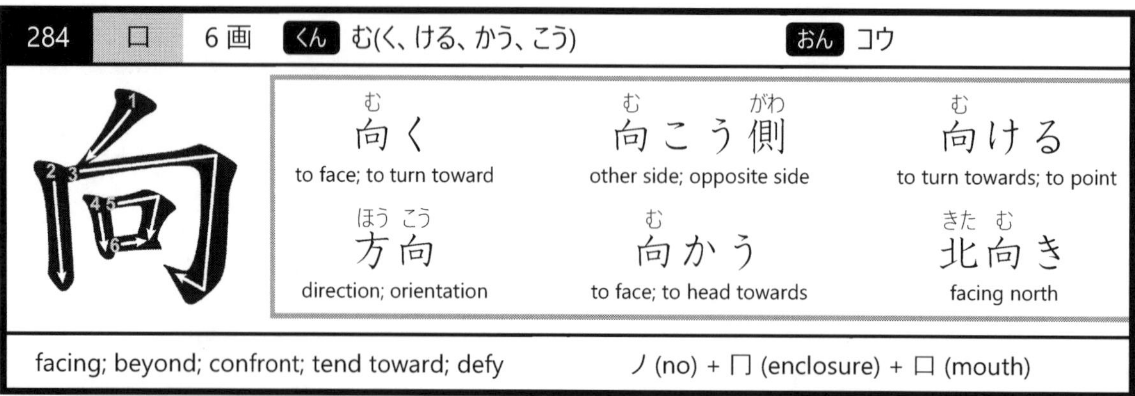

284
口
6 画
くん む(く、ける、かう、こう)
おん コウ
む 向く to face; to turn toward
む がわ 向こう側 other side; opposite side
む 向ける to turn towards; to point
ほうこう 方向 direction; orientation
む 向かう to face; to head towards
きた む 北向き facing north
facing; beyond; confront; tend toward; defy
丿 (no) + 冂 (enclosure) + 口 (mouth)

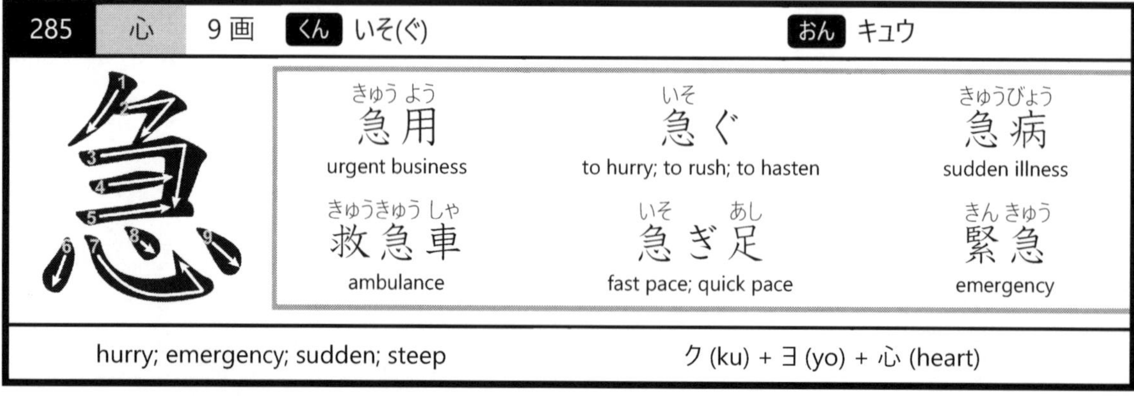

285
心
9 画
くん いそ(ぐ)
おん キュウ
きゅうよう 急用 urgent business
いそ 急ぐ to hurry; to rush; to hasten
きゅうびょう 急病 sudden illness
きゅうきゅうしゃ 救急車 ambulance
いそ あし 急ぎ足 fast pace; quick pace
きんきゅう 緊急 emergency
hurry; emergency; sudden; steep
ク (ku) + ヨ (yo) + 心 (heart)

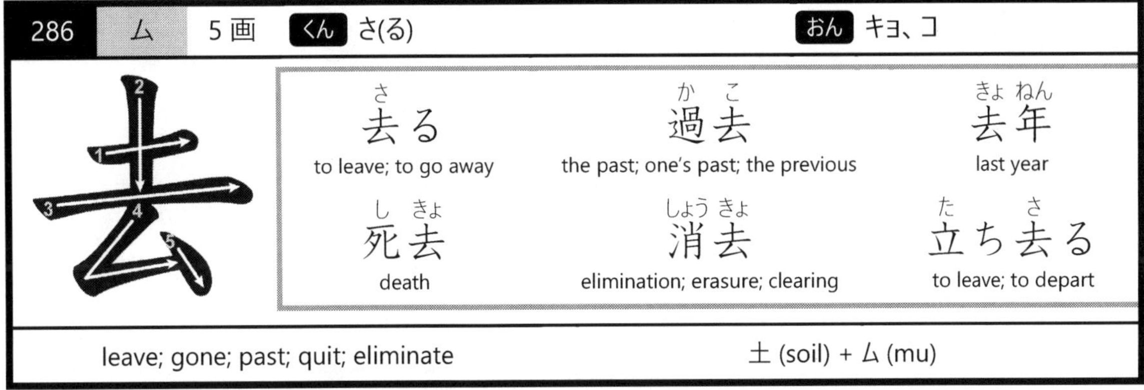

286 ム 5画 くん さ(る) おん キョ、コ
さ 去る to leave; to go away
かこ 過去 the past; one's past; the previous
きょねん 去年 last year
しきょ 死去 death
しょうきょ 消去 elimination; erasure; clearing
たちさる 立ち去る to leave; to depart
leave; gone; past; quit; eliminate
土 (soil) + ム (mu)

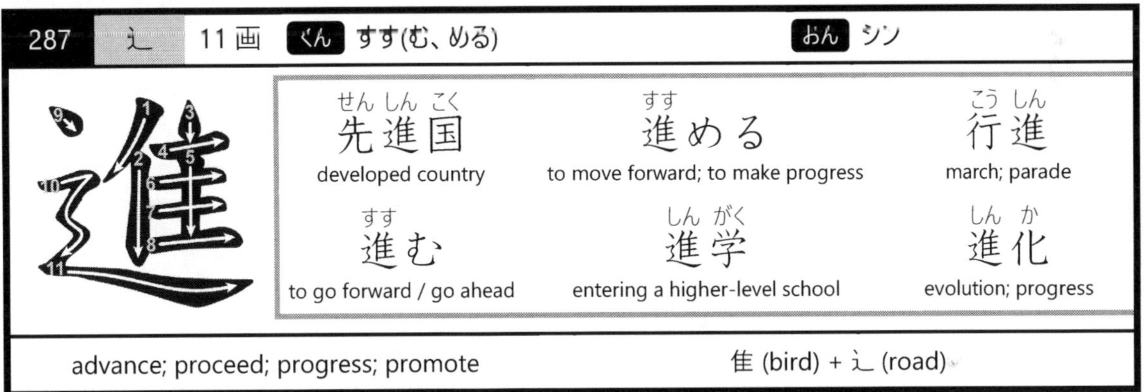

287 辶 11画 くん すす(む、める) おん シン
せんしんこく 先進国 developed country
すす 進める to move forward; to make progress
こうしん 行進 march; parade
すす 進む to go forward / go ahead
しんがく 進学 entering a higher-level school
しんか 進化 evolution; progress
advance; proceed; progress; promote
隹 (bird) + 辶 (road)

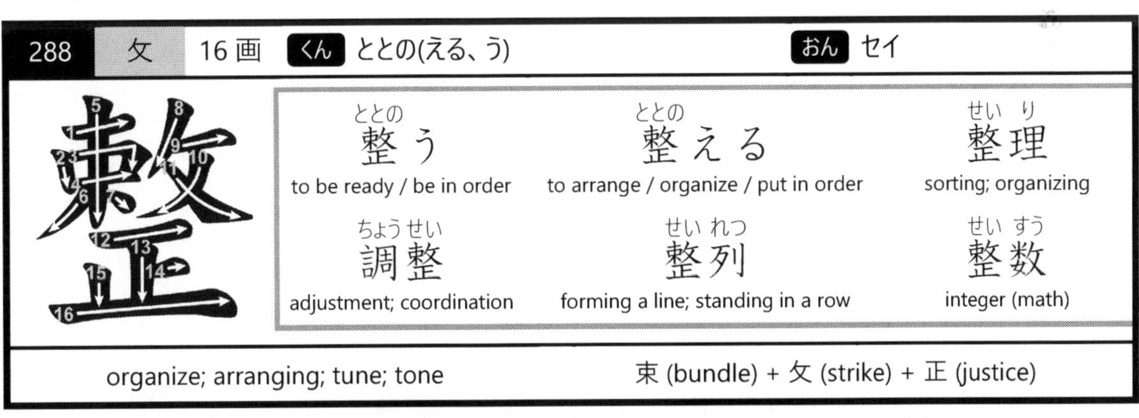

288 攵 16画 くん ととの(える、う) おん セイ
ととの 整う to be ready / be in order
ととの 整える to arrange / organize / put in order
せいり 整理 sorting; organizing
ちょうせい 調整 adjustment; coordination
せいれつ 整列 forming a line; standing in a row
せいすう 整数 integer (math)
organize; arranging; tune; tone
束 (bundle) + 攵 (strike) + 正 (justice)

Kanji Parts used in the New Kanji

イ	person	ク	ku	隹	bird
主	master	ヨ	yo	辶	road
ノ	no	心	heart	束	bundle
冂	enclosure	土	soil	攵	strike
口	mouth	ム	mu	正	justice

8 Kanji Memory Tools 漢字記憶術

This section helps you organically memorize kanji readings, meanings, and construction.

住

亻 主
The person with the chief is with whom I "**LIVE**".

私(わたし)はこの❶住所(じゅうしょ)に❷住(す)んでいます。
I ❷live at this ❶address.

向

ノ 冂 口
NO enclosure can keep my mouth from what it's "**FACING**".

友達(ともだち)は❶向上心(こうじょうしん)があって、夢(ゆめ)に❷向(む)かって頑張(がんば)っています。
My friend has a ❶desire to improve herself and works hard ❷heading towards her dreams.

急

ク ヨ 心
Katakana ku and yo are weighing on my heart so "**HURRY**".

❶急用(きゅうよう)があるから、❷急(いそ)いでいます。
I'm ❷rushing, because I have ❶urgent business.

去

土 ム
In this soil draw a katakana mu then "**LEAVE**".

元恋人(もとこいびと)の写真(しゃしん)を❶消去(しょうきょ)しても、❷過去(かこ)は❸葬(ほうむ)り去(さ)れない。
Even if you ❶erase your prior girlfriend's pictures, you ❸can't bury ❷the past.

進

隹 辶
The bird used the road to "**PROCEED**".

❶先進国(せんしんこく)の技術(ぎじゅつ)は、途上国(とじょうこく)より❷進(すす)んでいます。
The technology of ❶developed countries is more ❷advanced than that of developing countries.

整

束 攵 正
Use this bundle to strike for justice and "**ORGANIZE**".

書類(しょるい)を❶整(ととの)えてから、スケジュールを❷調整(ちょうせい)します。
I will ❷adjust my schedule after I ❶organize the documents.

8 Understanding Kanji Parts 漢字部分の理解

● 8-1. The "movement" radical しんにょう (⻌)

The English name for しんにょう has alternatives. It may be translated to "move ahead", "road" or "walk".

distant; far	
遠	遠い (とお) far; distant; far away
road + long robe	遠足 (えんそく) excursion; outing; trip

near; early	
近	近い (ちか) near; close
road + axe	近所 (きんじょ) neighborhood

traffic; pass through; commute	
通	通る (とお) to go by; to go past
walk + walled road	通学 (つうがく) commuting to school

road-way; street; district; course	
道	道 (みち) road; path; street
road + neck	鉄道 (てつどう) railroad; railway

carry; luck; destiny; fate; transport	
運	運ぶ (はこ) to carry; to transport
road + army	運転 (うんてん) operate; driving

advance; proceed; progress	
速	高速 (こうそく) high speed
road + bundle	速度 (そくど) speed; velocity

8 Kanji Usage 漢字の使い方

● 8-2. Japanese Proverbs using 住・急・去

Let's look at some proverbs that include some of the new kanji taught in this lesson. Proverbs can give your Japanese some extra pizzazz.

住(す)めば都(みやこ)	**Literally** If you live there, it's the capital. **Equivalents** Home is where you make it. Wherever you live, you come to love it.

急(いそ)がば回(まわ)れ	**Literally** When you are in a hurry, go around. **Equivalents** More haste, less speed. Slow and steady wins the race.

去(さ)る者(もの)は日々(ひび)にうとし	**Literally** People that go away, day after day become distant. **Equivalents** Out of sight, out of mind. Long absent, soon forgotten.

EXAMPLE CONVERSATIONS

1. Polite conversation between friends

A: 東京(とうきょう)の生活(せいかつ)は大変(たいへん)でしょう？
B: 確(たし)かに、物価(ぶっか)も高(たか)いし、人(ひと)も多(おお)いけど、
しばらく住(す)んでからは、本当(ほんとう)に好(す)きになりました。
A: 「住(す)めば都(みやこ)」ですね。

A: It's hard living in Tokyo, right?
B: It's true that the cost of living is high, and there are many people,
but after living there for a while, I've really come to like it.
A: So, it's "if you live there, it's the capital."

2. Casual conversation between friends

A: 急(いそ)がないと間(ま)に合(あ)わないよ。

B: 落(お)ち着(つ)いて。事故(じこ)をしたら、もっと遅(おく)れちゃう。

A: そうだね。だから「急(いそ)がば回(まわ)れ」というのかな。

A: We won't make it in time if you don't hurry.

B: Calm down. If we have an accident, we'll end up being more late.

A: You're right. I wonder if that's why they say, "when in a hurry, go around."

8 Words You Can Write 書ける言葉

住む（すむ） to live

住	む										

住人（じゅうにん） resident; inhabitant

住	人										

向く（むく） to face; to turn toward

向	く										

去る（さる） to get off

去	る										

去年（きょねん） last year

去	年										

進む（すすむ） to move forward

進	む										

急行（きゅうこう） express (train); rushing; hastening

急行

直進（ちょくしん） going right on; going straight ahead

直進

前進（ぜんしん） advance; moving forward; progress

前進

南向き（みなみむき） southern direction

南向き

急ぎ足 (いそぎあし） fast pace; quick pace

急ぎ足

進め方（すすめかた） format; procedure

進め方

整える (ととのえる） arrange

整える

前向き (まえむき） front-facing; forward-looking; positive

前向き

向上心 (こうじょうしん) ambition; desire to improve oneself

向	上	心									

写メール (しゃメール) email with attached photos from a mobile phone

写	メ	ー	ル								

8 Kanji Workbook Activities

● 1. Stroke Order Check 書き順確認

Each kanji has a stroke with an arrow on it. Write its order number below the kanji.

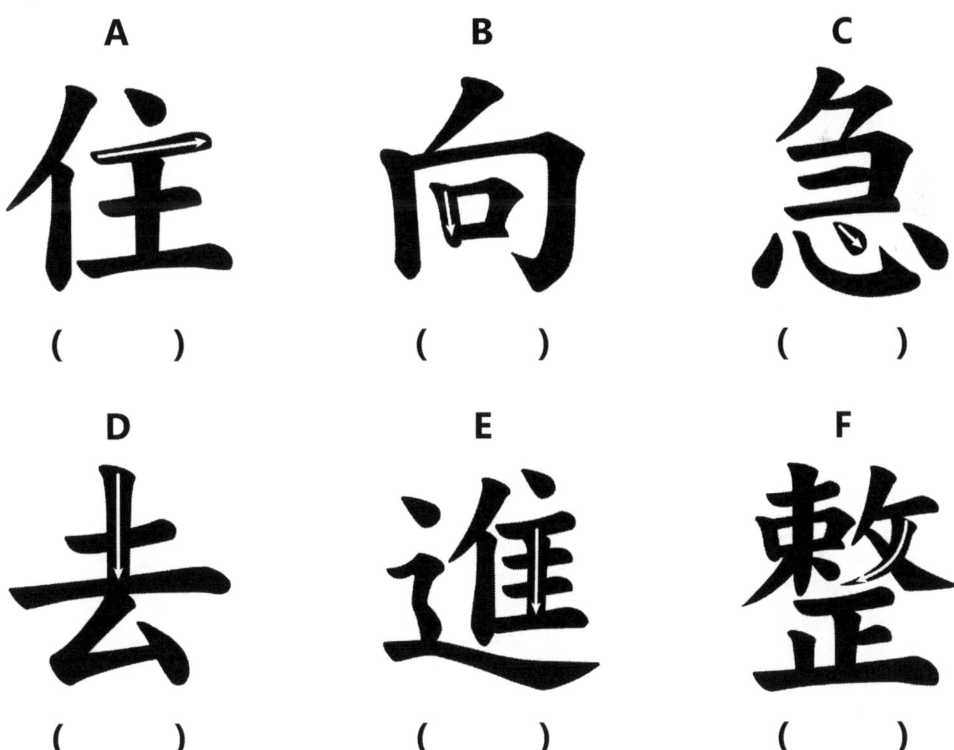

● 2. Kanji Meaning Match

Write the following kanji next to its meaning: 急 住 進 死 向 去 整 幸 感

1. ____ feel
2. ____ move ahead
3. ____ death
4. ____ arrange
5. ____ hurry
6. ____ leave
7. ____ face
8. ____ live
9. ____ happy

● 3. Kanji Readings

Write FURIGANA above the underlined kanji words.

1. 明日、東京に住んでいる友だちと集まります。
2. どっちの方向に進んだらいいか分かりません。
3. 急用を思い出したので、帰ります。
4. 去年、習字を習い始めました。
5. じゅんびが整ったので、行きましょう。

● 4. Fill in the Kanji

Fill in the appropriate kanji in the blanks for each sentence.

1. このアパートの___(じゅう) ___(にん)は、みんな___(しん) ___(せつ)です。
   All (everyone) the residents of this apartment are kind.

2. ___(なに)が あっても、わたしは ___(まえ) ___(む)きに ___(かんが)えます。
   No matter what happens, I always think positively.

3. ___(ろく) ___(がつ)になって ___(きゅう)に ___(あつ)くなりました。
   It turned to June and suddenly got hot.

しょう　きょ　くだ

4. きのう、おくったデータを ___ ___して___さい。

Please erase the data that I sent you yesterday.

だい　がく　しん　がく　ゆう　じん

5. わたしは___ ___に___ ___しますが、___ ___はしません。

I'm going to proceed to college, but my friend will not.

おとうと　せい　り　にが　て

6. ___ は___ ___するのが___ ___です。

My younger brother isn't good at organizing.

あめ　いそ　あし　かえ

7. ___ がふってきたので、___ぎ ___で___りました。

Since it started to rain, I returned home with a quick pace.

● 5. Kanji Matching

Connect each kanji with an おん or くん reading. Use each reading only ONCE.

整 •	• すす
助 •	• き
進 •	• そう
曲 •	• せい
去 •	• じゅう
決 •	• じょ
急 •	• む
想 •	• いそ
向 •	• さ
住 •	• ま

8 Answer Key 答え合わせ

1. Stroke order check (answers)

A) 4 B) 4 C) 8

D) 2 E) 5 F) 10

2. Kanji meaning match (answers)

1. 感 feel 2. 進 move ahead 3. 死 death
4. 整 arrange 5. 急 hurry 6. 去 leave
7. 向 face 8. 住 live 9. 幸 happy

3. Kanji Readings (answers)

1. 明日(あした)、東京(とうきょう)に住(す)んでいる友(とも)だちと集(あつ)まります。 Tomorrow I'm gathering with friends living in Tokyo.
2. どっちの方向(ほうこう)に進(すす)んだらいいか分(わ)かりません。 I don't know which direction to progress in.
3. 急用(きゅうよう)を思(おも)い出(だ)したので、帰(かえ)ります。 I remembered something urgent, so I'm going home.
4. 去年(きょねん)、習字(しゅうじ)を習(なら)い始(はじ)めました。 I started learning calligraphy last year.
5. じゅんびが整(ととの)ったので、行(い)きましょう。 My preparations are in order, so let's go.

4. Fill in the kanji (answers)

1. このアパートの住人は みんな親切です。
2. 何があっても、わたしは前向きに考えます。
3. 六月になって 急に暑くなりました。
4. きのう、おくったデータを消去して下さい。
5. わたしは大学に進学しますが、友人はしません。
6. 弟は整理するのが苦手です。
7. 雨がふってきたので、急ぎ足で帰りました。

5. Kanji matching (answers)

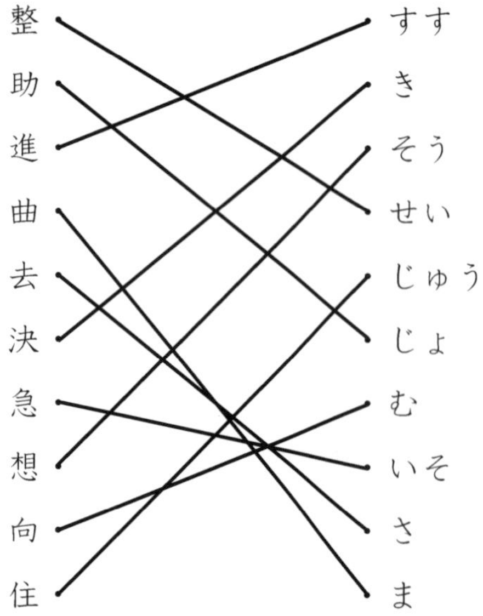

9 Kanji Lesson 9: 送打待代着調

289-294

Kanji that can be verbs (part 7)

9 New Kanji 新しい漢字

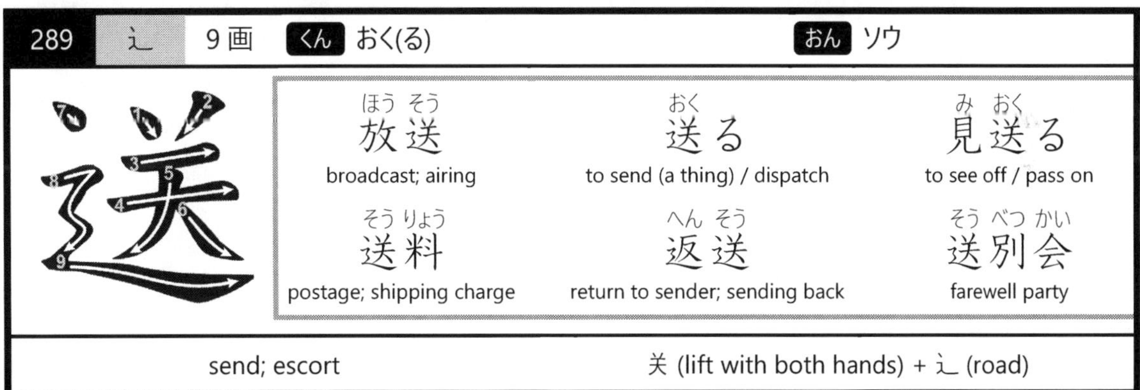

289 ⻌ 9画 くん おく(る) おん ソウ

ほうそう 放送 broadcast; airing	おく 送る to send (a thing) / dispatch	みおく 見送る to see off / pass on
そうりょう 送料 postage; shipping charge	へんそう 返送 return to sender; sending back	そうべつかい 送別会 farewell party

send; escort — 关 (lift with both hands) + ⻌ (road)

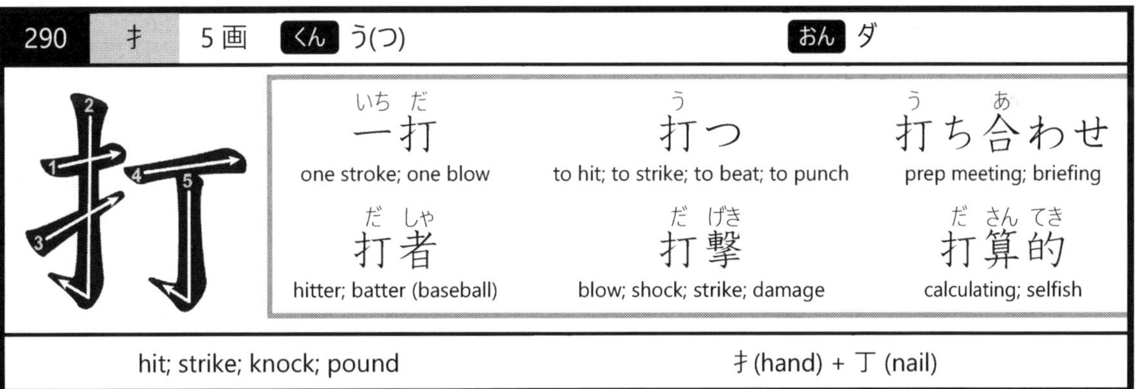

290 扌 5画 くん う(つ) おん ダ

いちだ 一打 one stroke; one blow	う 打つ to hit; to strike; to beat; to punch	うあ 打ち合わせ prep meeting; briefing
だしゃ 打者 hitter; batter (baseball)	だげき 打撃 blow; shock; strike; damage	ださんてき 打算的 calculating; selfish

hit; strike; knock; pound — 扌(hand) + 丁 (nail)

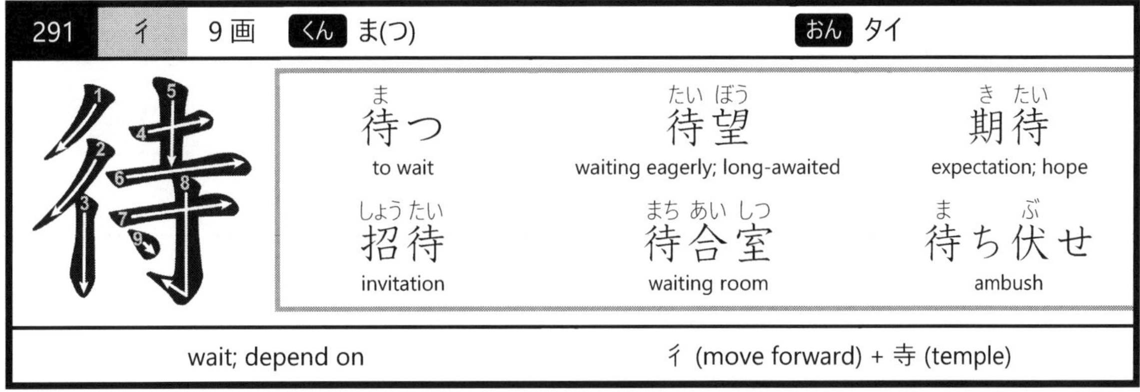

291 彳 9画 くん ま(つ) おん タイ

ま 待つ to wait	たいぼう 待望 waiting eagerly; long-awaited	きたい 期待 expectation; hope
しょうたい 招待 invitation	まちあいしつ 待合室 waiting room	まぶ 待ち伏せ ambush

wait; depend on — 彳 (move forward) + 寺 (temple)

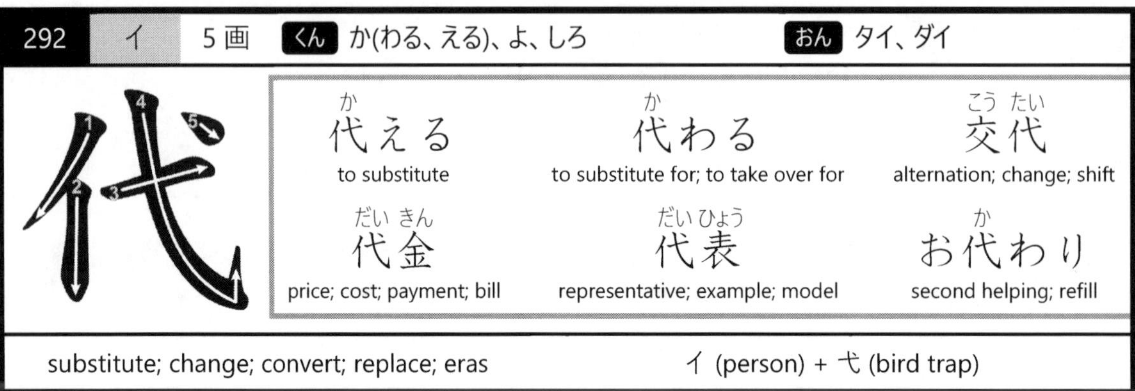

292 | イ | 5 画 | くん か(わる、える)、よ、しろ | おん タイ、ダイ

代

か 代える to substitute	か 代わる to substitute for; to take over for	こう たい 交代 alternation; change; shift
だい きん 代金 price; cost; payment; bill	だい ひょう 代表 representative; example; model	か お代わり second helping; refill

substitute; change; convert; replace; eras — イ (person) + 弋 (bird trap)

293 | 羊 | 12 画 | くん き(る、せる)、つ(く、ける) | おん チャク、ジャク

着

き 着る to wear; to put on	せん ちゃく じゅん 先着順 first-come-first-served basis	し ちゃく 試着 trying on clothing
つ 着く to arrive at; to reach	みず ぎ 水着 swimsuit; bathing suit	とう ちゃく 到着 arrival

arrive; wear; counter for suits of clothing — ⺍ (horns) + 王 (king) + ノ (no) + 目 (eye)

294 | 言 | 15 画 | くん しら(べる)、ととの(う、える) | おん チョウ

調

しら 調べる to do a search; to find out	ちょう ちょう 長調 major key (music)	たん ちょう 短調 minor key (music)
ととの 調える to prepare; to arrange	たい ちょう 体調 physical condition	ちょう し 調子 condition; form; health

investigate; prepare; harmonize; tune; tone — 言 (speak) + 周 (perimeter)

Kanji Parts used in the New Kanji

关	lift with both hands	寺	temple	ノ	no
辶	road	イ	person	目	eye
扌	hand	弋	bird trap	言	speak
丁	nail	⺍	horns	周	perimeter
彳	move forward	王	king		

9 Kanji Memory Tools 漢字記憶術

This section helps you organically memorize kanji readings, meanings, and construction.

送

关 辶

First lift with both hands on this road then you can "**SEND**".

そうりょう たか おく

❶送料が高いので、❷送れません。

Because the ❶shipping charges are expensive, I ❷can't send it.

打

扌 丁

Please hand me a nail to "**HIT**".

だい だ う おどろ

❶代打がホームランを❷打って、驚いた。

I was surprised that the ❶pinch-hitter ❷hit a homerun.

待

彳 寺

Move forward to temple and "**WAIT**".

おい た もの き たい ま

美味しい食べ物を❶期待して❷待ちました。

I ❷waited in ❶anticipation of delicious food.

代

亻 弋

The person next to the bird trap is a "**SUBSTITUTE**".

こう たい うん てん か なが きゅうけい と

❶交代で運転をする❷代わりに長い休憩を取りました。

We took long breaks ❶instead of ❷taking turns driving.

着

丷 王 ノ 目

Horns honoring the king with no left eye will soon "**ARRIVE**".

つ とき みず ぎ し ちゃくしつ

デパートに❶着いた時、❷水着の❸試着室がいっぱいだった。

When I ❶arrived at the department store, the ❷bathing suit ❸dressing room was full.

調

言 周

Dare to speak of the perimeter and I will "**INVESTIGATE**"!

りょ こう じゅん び ととの とき たいちょう わる

旅行の❶準備を調えている時、❷体調が悪くなった。

While I was ❶getting ready for my trip, my ❷physical condition worsened.

9 Kanji Usage 漢字の使い方

● 9-1. Kinds of Clothing 着

Most people have heard of 着物(きもの), but there are other types of clothing that use 着.

dressing warmly; wearing thick clothes	being lightly dressed
厚着(あつぎ)	薄着(うすぎ)

coat; jacket; outer garment	underwear; under garment
上着(うわぎ)	下着(したぎ)

vintage clothes; secondhand clothing	bathing suit; swimsuit
古着(ふるぎ)	水着(みずぎ)

EXAMPLE SENTENCES

1. 今日は寒いから、厚着をした方がいいかも知れません。
   It might be better to dress warmly since today is cold.

2. 冬に薄着で出かけるのは、健康にいいと思う人がいます。
   There are people that think going out in winter lightly dressed is good for your health.

3. 荷物に水着と上着を入れたけど、下着を忘れてしまいました。
   I put a bathing suit and a coat in my luggage, but I ended up forgetting underwear.

4. 日本では古着が大人気です。
   Vintage clothing is really popular in Japan.

● 9-2. Same sound, different words「ととのえる」

Sometimes Japanese words have the same sound but use a different kanji. Sometimes the meaning can be similar but used in different circumstances. Let's look at ととのえる, which is 整える in lesson 8, and 調える in this lesson.

「調える」－To prepare in advance / To gather required items
「整える」－To put in order / To put properly into shape

※ Notice that even though the sentences have the same sound, using one kanji over another changes the meaning.

to get ready; to prepare; to arrange; to supply; to assemble		to put in order; to tidy up; to adjust; to fix; to straighten	
調える		整える	
資金を調える	to gather up funding	服装を整える	to dress to the occasion
夕食を調える	to prepare dinner	髪を整える	to fix one's hair
味を調える	to adjust the flavor	体調を整える	to get body in shape
※道具を調える	to prepare tools	※道具を整える	to tidy up tools

When prepping in advance, use「調える」

When tidying up, use「整える」

● 9-3. How many can you hit? 打

打 is used in many phrases.

Japanese	English	Japanese	English
花火を打ち上げる	to set off fireworks	ホームランを打つ	to hit a homerun
頭を打つ	to hit your head	先手を打つ	to take the initiative
注射を打つ	to inject a shot	釘を打つ	to hammer a nail
手を打つ	to strike a deal	心を打つ	to touch a person's heart

There are also a lot of commonly used words that have 打ち in it.

value; worth; merit	whisper
値打(ねう)ち	耳打(みみう)ち

to input (data)	prep meeting; briefing session
打(う)ち込(こ)む	打(う)ち合(あ)わせ

EXAMPLE SENTENCES

1. 古(ふる)いコインは、値打(ねう)ちがあります。
   There is value in old coins.

2. 友達(ともだち)が耳打(みみう)ちして、テストの答(こた)えを教(おし)えてくれた。
   A friend whispered and told me the test answer(s).

3. 朝(あさ)までデータを打(う)ち込(こ)んだけど、まだまだ終(お)わりそうにないです。
   I entered data until the morning, but it's nowhere near the end.

4. 真面目(まじめ)に打(う)ち合(あ)わせしてるようで、実(じつ)は昼(ひる)ご飯(はん)のことを考(かんが)えています。
   It appears that I'm seriously having a meeting, but actually I'm thinking about lunch.

9 Words You Can Write 書ける言葉

送る（おくる） to send (a thing); to take (a person somewhere)

送る

打つ（うつ） to hit; to strike; to beat; to punch

打つ

強打（きょうだ） hard blow; bashing

強打

待つ（まつ） to wait

待つ

時代（じたい） period; era; age; the times

時代

着く（つく） to arrive; to reach

着く

上着（うわぎ） coat; outer wear

上着

体調（たいちょう） physical condition

体調

安打（あんだ） safe hit

安	打										

送金（そうきん） money transfer

送	金										

代打（だいだ） pinch-hitting

代	打										

口調（くちょう） tone of voice; way of speaking

口	調										

調べる（しらべる） to do a search; to find out

調	べ	る									

下調べ(したしらべ) preparatory study; prep

下	調	べ									

代わり(かわり) substitute; replacement; exchange; return

代	わ	り									

先送り(さきおくり) postpone

先	送	り									

待たせる(またせる) to keep (a person) waiting

待	た	せ	る								

9 Kanji Workbook Activities

● 1. Stroke Order Check 書き順確認

Each kanji has a stroke with an arrow on it. Write its order number below the kanji.

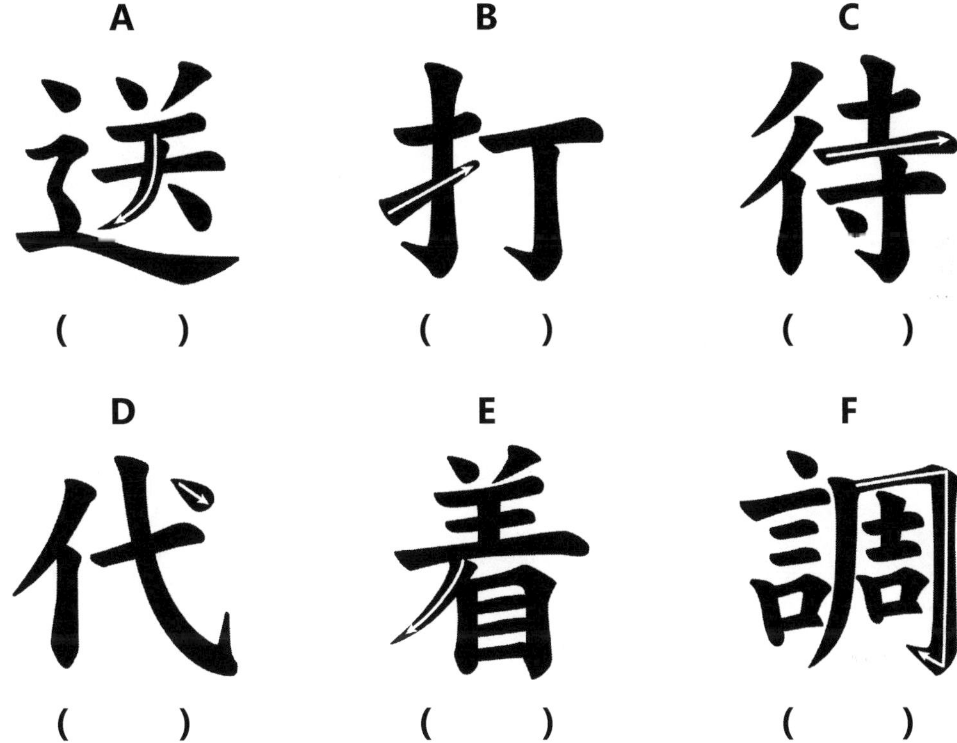

● 2. Kanji Readings

Write FURIGANA above the underlined kanji words.

1. この手紙に切手をはって、送って下さい。
2. 先手を打って早めにびょういんに行きました。
3. 友だちを待たせなくないから、走って行きましょう。
4. 代金は、しょうひんを受け取った時に はらって下さい。
5. 今日は寒いから、コートを着た方がいいです。

● 3. Kanji Meaning Match

Write the following kanji next to its meaning: 調 送 着 急 代 決 待 運 打

1. ____ hit
2. ____ search
3. ____ decide
4. ____ carry
5. ____ send
6. ____ hurry
7. ____ wait
8. ____ arrive
9. ____ switch

● 4. Fill in the Kanji

Fill in the appropriate kanji in the blanks for each sentence.

くう　ゆう　じん　み　おく　い

1. ____ こうまで____ ____を____ ____りに____きます。

I'm going to the airport to send off my friend.

だ　しゃ　まえ　う

2. あの ____ ____は この____ 、ホームランを____ちました。

う　いそ　あたま　う

2. ____ちあわせに ____いでいたら、____を ____った

When I was rushing to the meeting, I hit my head.

まち　あい　しつ　む　い

3. この____ ____ ____ は いっぱいだから、____こうへ ____こう。

Let's go over there since this waiting room is full.

さむ　うわ　ぎ　も　い　くだ

4. ____ いから、____ ____を ____って____って____さい。

Take a jacket since it's cold.

きょう　はは　か　つく

5. ____ ____は ____ の____わりに ばんごはんを____ります。

I will make dinner tonight instead of my mother.

いま　たい　ちょう　わる　なに　たべ

6. ____ は____ ____が ____ くて、____ も____られません。

My condition is so bad right now, I can't eat anything.

でん　しゃ　　なん　じ　　く　　　しら

7. つぎの____ ____ が____ ____に____ るか____ べましょう。

Let's look up what time the next train comes.

● 5. Kanji Matching

Connect each kanji with an おん or くん reading. Use each reading only ONCE.

悲 •	• ひ
送 •	• つ
調 •	• ちょう
打 •	• しょう
消 •	• し
待 •	• だ
写 •	• ま
代 •	• か
始 •	• そう
着 •	• しゃ

9 Answer Key 答え合わせ

1. Stroke order check (answers)

A) 5　B) 3　C) 6

D) 5　E) 7　F) 9

3. Kanji meaning match (answers)

1. 打 hit　2. 調 search　3. 決 decide
4. 運 carry　5. 送 send　6. 急 hurry
7. 待 wait　8. 着 arrive　9. 代 switch

2. Kanji Readings (answers)

1. この手紙(てがみ)に切手(きって)をはって、送(おく)って下(くだ)さい。 Please stick a stamp on this letter and send it.
2. 先手(せんて)を打(う)って早(はや)めにびょういんに行(い)きました。 I took the initiative and went to the hospital early.
3. 友(とも)だちを待(ま)たせなくないから、走(はし)って行(い)きましょう。 Let's run since I don't want to make my friends wait.
4. 代金(だいきん)は、しょうひんを受(う)け取(と)った時(とき)に はらって下(くだ)さい。 Please pay the fee when you receive the goods.
5. 今日(きょう)は寒(さむ)いから、コートを着(き)た方(ほう)がいいです。 You should wear a coat since it's cold today.

4. Fill in the kanji (answers)

1. 空こうまで友人を見送りに行きます。
2. 打ちあわせに急いでいたら、頭を打った。
3. この待合室はいっぱいだから、向こうへ行こう。
4. 寒いから、上着を持って行って下さい。
5. 今日は母の代わりに ばんごはんを作ります。
6. 今は体調が悪くて、何も食べられません。
7. つぎの電車が何時に来るか調べましょう。

5. Kanji matching (answers)

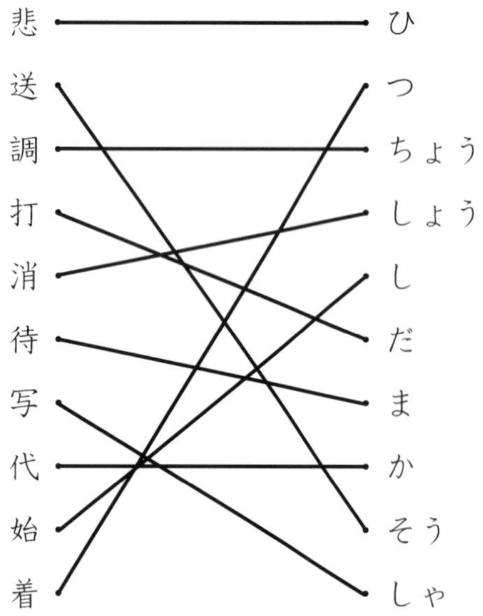

10 Kanji Lesson 10: 追定転投登動

295-300

Kanji that can be verbs (part 8)

10 New Kanji 新しい漢字

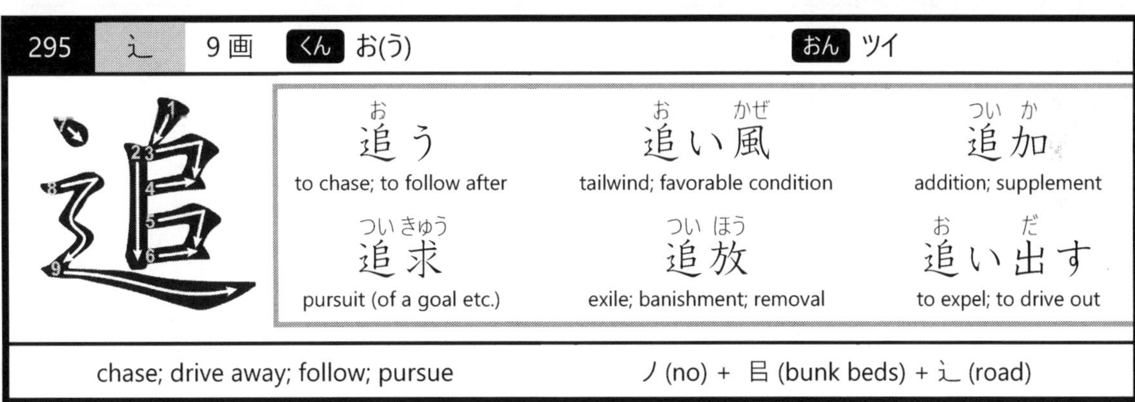

295 | ⻌ | 9画 | くん お(う) | おん ツイ

追

追う (お) to chase; to follow after	追い風 (お・かぜ) tailwind; favorable condition	追加 (つい・か) addition; supplement
追求 (つい・きゅう) pursuit (of a goal etc.)	追放 (つい・ほう) exile; banishment; removal	追い出す (お・だ) to expel; to drive out

chase; drive away; follow; pursue — ノ (no) + 𠂤 (bunk beds) + ⻌ (road)

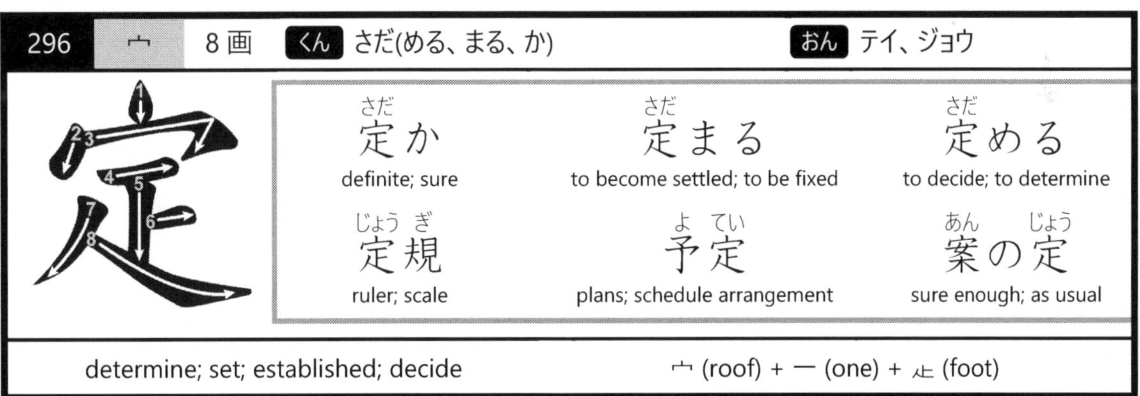

296 | 宀 | 8画 | くん さだ(める、まる、か) | おん テイ、ジョウ

定

定か (さだ) definite; sure	定まる (さだ) to become settled; to be fixed	定める (さだ) to decide; to determine
定規 (じょう・ぎ) ruler; scale	予定 (よ・てい) plans; schedule arrangement	案の定 (あん・じょう) sure enough; as usual

determine; set; established; decide — 宀 (roof) + 一 (one) + 𤴓 (foot)

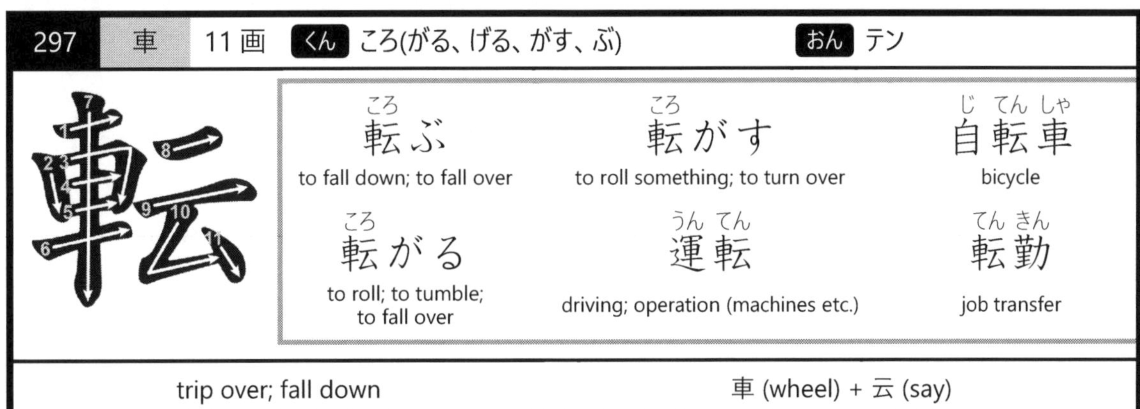

297 | 車 | 11画 | くん ころ(がる、げる、がす、ぶ) | おん テン

転

転ぶ (ころ) to fall down; to fall over	転がす (ころ) to roll something; to turn over	自転車 (じ・てん・しゃ) bicycle
転がる (ころ) to roll; to tumble; to fall over	運転 (うん・てん) driving; operation (machines etc.)	転勤 (てん・きん) job transfer

trip over; fall down — 車 (wheel) + 云 (say)

298	扌	7画	くん な(げる)	おん トウ

投

投(な)げる to throw; to cast away	投(とう)じる to throw; to cast; to invest; to put in	投資(とうし) investment
投手(とうしゅ) pitcher (baseball)	投稿(とうこう) submission; post (websites etc.)	投票(とうひょう) voting; poll

throw; discard; abandon; invest in — 扌 (hand) + 几 (table) + 又 (again)

299	癶	12画	くん のぼ(る)	おん ト、トウ

登

登(のぼ)る to climb; to ascend	登場人物(とうじょうじんぶつ) character (in a play or novel)	登山(とざん) mountain climbing
登校(とうこう) attending school	木登(きのぼ)り tree climbing	登録(とうろく) registration; register

climb up; ascend — 癶 (footsteps) + 豆 (beans)

300	力	11画	くん うご(く、かす)	おん ドウ

動

動(うご)く to move; to operate	動(うご)かす to set in motion; to move; to shift	動物(どうぶつ) animal(s)
動画(どうが) video; movie; animation	感動(かんどう) deep emotion; excitement	動詞(どうし) verb

move; motion; change; confusion; shift — 重 (heavy) + 力 (power)

Kanji Parts used in the New Kanji

ノ	no	疋	foot	又	again
目	stacked boxes	車	wheel	癶	footsteps
辶	road	云	say	豆	beans
宀	roof	扌	hand	重	heavy
一	one	几	table	力	power

10 Kanji Memory Tools 漢字記憶術

This section helps you organically memorize kanji readings, meanings, and construction.

追

ノ 𠂤 辶

There are no bunk beds on this road to "**PURSUE**".

このレストランでは❶追加注文(ついかちゅうもん)しないと、❷追(お)い出(だ)される。

At this restaurant if don't make an ❶additional order, you will ❷be kicked out.

定

宀 一 龰

Under my roof don't step even one foot until I "**DETERMINE**".

❶定(さだ)かじゃないけど、この店(みせ)の❷定休日(ていきゅうび)は日曜日(にちようび)です。

I'm ❶not sure, but store's ❷fixed closed day is Sunday.

転

車 云

♪ The wheels on the bus say, don't "**FALL DOWN**". ♪

子供(こども)が❶自転車(じてんしゃ)で❷転(ころ)んだ。

The child ❷fell over on their ❶bicycle.

投

扌 几 又

Put your hand on the table again and it's you I will "**THROW**".

❶投手(とうしゅ)が時速(じそく)160 キロでボールを❷投(な)げました。

The ❶pitcher ❷threw the ball at a speed of 160 kilometers per hour.

登

癶 豆

The giant's footsteps reverberate on the bean stalk as we "**ASCEND**".

この小説(しょうせつ)の❶登場人物(とうじょうじんぶつ)は、山(やま)に❷登(のぼ)るのが好(す)きです。

The ❶characters in this novel like to ❷climb mountains.

動

重 力

This is heavy but with power it will "**MOVE**".

❶動物(どうぶつ)は❷動(うご)く物(もの)です。

❶Animals are ❷moving things.

10 Kanji Usage 漢字の使い方

● 10-1. Compound words using 定

定 is used in many common compound words.

regularly closed day	retail price (list price)
ていきゅうび 定休日	ていか 定価
(fixed + day off)	(fixed + price)

capacity (bus, elevator etc.)	timetable; schedule
ていいん 定員	ていこく 定刻
(fixed + number/member)	(fixed+ time)

assumption	undecided; pending
かてい 仮定	みてい 未定
(temporary + decided)	(not yet + decided)

affirmation	denial; negation
こうてい 肯定	ひてい 否定
(consent + established)	(deny + established)

● 10-2. 定食(ていしょく) (set meals)

Often Japanese restaurants offer 定食(ていしょく) (set meals), which are pre-defined meals having a main dish and pre-determined sides, and typically rice and 味噌汁(みそしる) (miso soup).

定食 (ていしょく) set meal

Unlike America, Japan doesn't often allow substitutions which honestly has frustrated me (George) beyond belief as an entitled American.

コーンスープ下さい!

One time in a restaurant, I saw some corn soup in a rather large bowl go by on a tray to another table. My stomach churned for one of my favorites, so I asked our waitress if I could get some in a smaller bowl. I was told "we can't put corn soup in a smaller bowl, since it's part of a set meal".

Already having too much food in front of me I insisted, "how about half the amount in the large bowl?". I was again met with resistance, "we can't put less soup in the bowl". I assured her I would pay full price for the soup, but still the answer was "no".

You might be thinking, "why not just leave half of the soup in the bigger bowl", but at this point I wasn't fighting for soup, but against years of injustice. I just had to win the battle of perceived illogic that I often face when trying to do anything customized in a Japanese restaurant.

Well... I lost my battle and left with no corn soup in my belly. And I'm ashamed to say that I didn't lose graciously... as each time the waitress passed by with corn soup on the tray I said audibly in Japanese, コーンスープいいなぁ (Oh man, the corn soup looks good.) I'm 100% sure I was an ugly American that day.

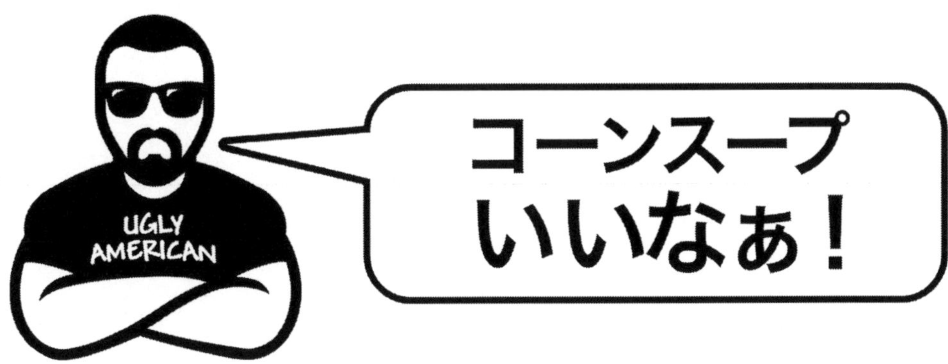

● 10-3. Japanese proverbs with 投

Just knowing kanji for the sake of kanji is boring, and not unique. Learning some idiomatic phrases with the kanji you just learned will cause quite a stir.

一石を投じる

Literally, this means "throwing one stone", but its true meaning is, "to cause or make a stir". In English we might say, "cause ripples" which would be the result of throwing a stone in a placid lake or pond.

EXAMPLE SENTENCES

1. 彼が作った曲は、音楽業界に一石を投じました。
   The song that he created caused a stir in the music world.

2. 僕は新人議員として、今の政治に一石を投じたいです。
   As a new congressman, I want to shake things up in current politics.

身を投じる

Literally, this means "throwing one's body". It means, "to devote or throw oneself into something".

EXAMPLE SENTENCES

1. 会社を辞めて、演劇の世界に身を投じます。
   I'm going to quit the company (my job) and throw myself into the world of theatre.

2. 漢字との闘いに身を投じてから、2年経ちました。
   Two years have passed since throwing myself into the battle with kanji.

Using 投じる, you can also say 一票を投じる (to cast a vote).

10 Words You Can Write 書ける言葉

追う (おう) to chase; to pursue; to run after

追	う										

安定（あんてい） stability; steadiness

安	定										

一定（いってい） constant; steady

一	定										

転ぶ（ころぶ） to fall down; to trip over

転	ぶ										

運転（うんてん） driving; operation

運	転										

投書（とうしょ） letter (e.g. of complaint); letter from a reader

投	書										

登る（のぼる） to climb; to ascend

登	る										

登山（とざん） mountain climbing

登	山										

運動（うんどう） exercise; physical training; work-out

運	動										

行動（こうどう） action; conduct; behavior

行	動										

決定（けってい） decision; determination

決	定										

定食（ていしょく） set meal; special (of the day)

定	食										

追い風（おいかぜ） tailwind; fair wind; favorable condition

追	い	風									

定休日（ていきゅうび） regular holiday; fixed day off

定	休	日									

自転車（じてんしゃ） bicycle

自	転	車									

投げる（なげる) to throw

投	げ	る									

10 Kanji Workbook Activities

● 1. Stroke Order Check 書き順確認

Each kanji has a stroke with an arrow on it. Write its order number below the kanji.

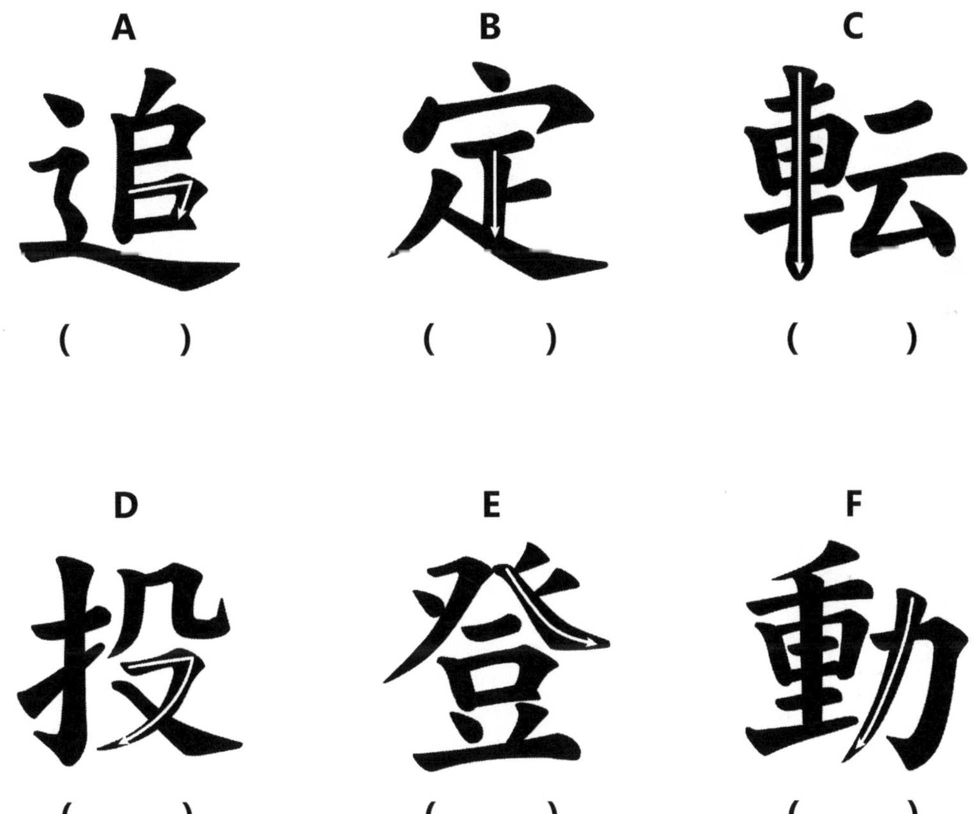

● 2. Kanji Meaning Match

Write the following kanji next to its meaning: 追 転 登 調 動 投 打 定 待

1. ____set
2. ____ find out
3. ____ move
4. ____ chase
5. ____ wait
6. ____ hit
7. ____ fall down
8. ____ throw
9. ____ climb

● 3. Kanji Readings

Write FURIGANA above the underlined kanji words.

1. マラソンをしていた時、追い風に助けられました。
2. ピアノ・リサイタルの会場が決定しました。
3. うちの子は、ボールを投げたり転がしたりするのがすきです。
4. 毎週日曜日に友人と登山をしています。
5. わたしはよく、スマホでかわいい動物の動画を見ます。

● 4. Fill in the Kanji

Fill in the appropriate kanji in the blanks for each sentence.

いぬ　お

1. うちの___ は、ボールを___ いかけるのがすきです。

Our dog likes chasing after balls.

さだ　たい　せつ

2. もくひょうを ___ めるのは、___ ___です。

Establishing goals is important.

じゅう　はっ　さい　くるま　うん　てん　はじ

3. わたしは___ ___ ___で___の___ ___ を___めました。

I started driving at 18 years old.

に　ほん　いち　ばん　とう　しゅ

4. ___ ___ の___ ___すきな ___ ___は、だれですか。

Who is your favorite Japanese baseball pitcher?

はち　じ　はん　とう　こう

5. いつも ___ ___ ___に___ ___ します。

I always arrive at school at 8:30.

ちち　じ　どう　しゃ　に　だい　も

6. ___ は___ ___ ___ を___ ___、___っています。

My father has 2 automobiles.

きょく　かん　どう

7. ラジオできいた___に ___ ___しました。

I was moved by a song I heard on the radio.

● 5. Kanji Matching

Connect each kanji with an おん or くん reading. Use each reading only ONCE.

動 •	• お
投 •	• な
定 •	• そう
送 •	• すす
追 •	• どう
進 •	• ととの
運 •	• てい
登 •	• と
転 •	• てん
整 •	• うん

10 Answer Key 答え合わせ

1. Stroke order check (answers)

A) 5 B) 5 C) 7

D) 6 E) 4 F) 11

2. Kanji meaning match (answers)

1. 定 set 2. 調 find out 3. 動 move
4. 追 chase 5. 待 wait 6. 打 hit
7. 転 fall down 8. 投 throw 9. 登 climb

3. Kanji Readings (answers)

1. マラソンをしていた時(とき)、追(お)い風(かぜ)に助(たす)けられました。 When I was running a marathon, a tailwind helped me.
2. ピアノ・リサイタルの会場(かいじょう)が決定(けってい)しました。 The venue for the piano recital has been decided.
3. うちの子(こ)は、ボールを投(な)げたり転(ころ)がしたりするのがすきです。 My child likes to throw and roll balls.
4. 毎週日曜日(まいしゅうにちようび)に友人(ゆうじん)と登山(とざん)をしています。 I mountain climb with my friend every Sunday.
5. わたしはよく、スマホでかわいい動物(どうぶつ)の動画(どうが)を見(み)ます。 I often watch cute animal videos on my phone.

4. Fill in the kanji (answers)

1. うちの[犬]は、ボールを[追]いかけるのがすきです。
2. もくひょうを[定]めるのは、[大切]です。
3. わたしは[十八才]で[車]の[運転]を[始]めました。
4. [日本]の[一番]すきな[投手]は、だれですか。
5. いつも[八時半]に[登校]します。
6. [父]は[自動車]を[二台]、[持]っています。
7. ラジオできいた[曲]に[感動]しました。

5. Kanji matching (answers)

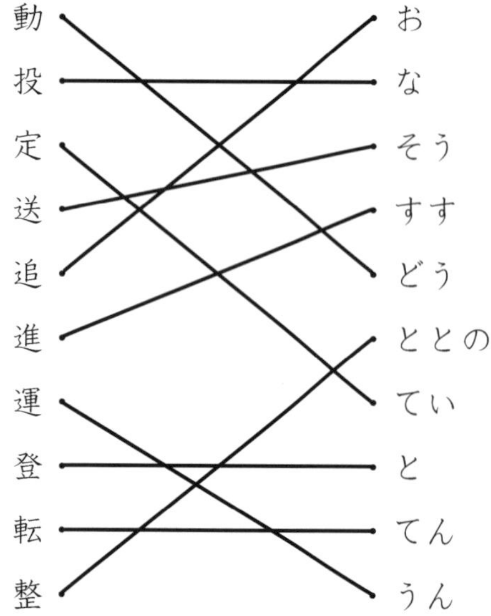

Kanji Lessons 6-10:

Super Review 2

From the teacher...

Test your knowledge of the kanji learned in the last 5 lessons.

● 1. Build a Kanji 漢字の組み合わせ

Combine the left and right parts to make seven of the kanji learned in lessons 6-10.

RULES
1. You can use the radical and kanji parts as many times as you want.
2. Some kanji can use two kanji parts.

部首 (Radical)		
氵	扌	糸
辶	羽	亻
木	女	力
宀	又	艹

Other Kanji Parts		
ム	日	寸
冬	白	合
田	口	古
寺	丁	耳

SAMPLE	1	2	3	4	5	6	7
始							

● 2. Kanji selection 漢字の選択

Select the best kanji to replace the underlined section of the sentence.

1. あそこでタクシーを____っているのは、だれですか。
   A. 持　　B. 使　　C. 待　　D. 送

2. えい画が____わってから、ごはんを食べに行きましょう。
   A. 代　　B. 動　　C. 写　　D. 終

3. 石を____げたら、あぶないですよ。
   A. 投　　B. 拾　　C. 取　　D. 集

4. 朝、会社へ行く前に、かみを____えます。
   A. 着　　B. 整　　C. 調　　D. 定

● 3. Kanji reading selection 読みの選択

Select the best reading for the underlined kanji.

1. 少しつかれたので、交代しませんか。
   A. か　　B. よ　　C. だい　　D. たい

2. 今年、新しい水着を買いました。
   A. き　　B. ぎ　　C. じゃく　　D. ちゃく

3. すずしくなったら 登山に行きましょう。
   A. と　　B. とう　　C. のぼ　　D. の

4. この待合室はこんでいるから、外で待ちましょう。
   A. ま　　B. まつ　　C. まち　　D. たい

● 4. Okurigana drill 送り仮名ドリル

Circle the correct 漢字 + 送り仮名 combination.

1. おきる　・起きる　・起る
2. はじまる　・始じまる　・始まる
3. うける　・受ける　・受る

4. ならう	・習う	・習らう
5. むかう	・向かう	・向う
6. すすめる	・進める	・進る
7. ととのえる	・整のえる	・整える
8. かわる	・代わる	・代る

● 5. Compound kanji word puzzle 熟語パズル

Fill in the correct kanji based on the list below the puzzle.

1)	2)		3)
4)		5)	
6)	7)		
	8)	9)	10)

Down ↓

English meaning	Hiragana
2) driving	うんてん
3) book report; an essay	かんそうぶん
6) last year	きょねん

Left to Right →

English meaning	Hiragana
1) good luck	こううん
2) exercise	うんどう
4) swirl; spin around	かいてん
5) ideal; dream	りそう
7) fire extinction	しょうか
9) procedure; progression	しんこう

← Right to Left

English meaning	Hiragana
3) sensation; throb	かんどう
7) erasing; elimination	しょうきょ
8) year in school	がくねん
9) education continuance	しんがく
10) march; procession	こうしん

SR2 Answer Key 答え合わせ

1. Build-a-Kanji (answers) (order can vary)

SAMPLE 始　1) 終 2) 守 3) 取 4) 拾 5) 持 6) 習 7) 打

2. Kanji selection (answers)

1. C – 待(ま)っている　Who is that waiting for a taxi over there?
2. D – 終(お)わってから　Let's go to eat after this movie ends.
3. A – 投(な)げたら　It's dangerous if you throw rocks.
4. B – 整(ととの)えます。　Before I go to work in the morning, I set my hair.

3. Kanji reading selection (answers)

1. D – 交代(こうたい)　Won't you change out (driving etc.) since I'm a bit tired.
2. B – 水着(みずぎ)　I bought a new bathing suit this year
3. A – 登山(とざん)　Once it gets cooler, let's go mountain climbing.
4. C – 待合室(まちあいしつ)　Let's wait outside since this waiting room is crowded.

4. Okurigana drill (answers)

1. おきる	**・起きる**	・起る	5. むかう	**・向かう**	・向う
2. はじまる	・始じまる	**・始まる**	6. すすめる	**・進める**	・進る
3. うける	**・受ける**	・受る	7. ととのえる	・整のえる	**・整える**
4. ならう	**・習う**	・習らう	8. かわる	**・代わる**	・代る

5. Compound kanji word puzzle (answers)

幸	運	動	感
回	転	理	想
去	消	火	文
年	学	進	行

11 Kanji Lesson 11: 配表勝負返放

301-306

Kanji that can be verbs (part 9)

11 New Kanji 新しい漢字

301 配

301	酉	10 画	くん くば(る)	おん ハイ

くば 配る to hand out; to distribute	て はい 手配 arrangement; preparations	たく はい びん 宅配便 express home delivery
はい ぐう しゃ 配偶者 spouse; partner	き くば 気配り care; attention; consideration	はい しん 配信 stream (internet)

hand out; deal; circularize — 酉 (liquor pot) + 己 (self)

302 表

302	衣	8 画	くん おもて、あらわ(す、れる)	おん ヒョウ

あらわ 表す to express; to show	あらわ 表れる to express itself; to find voice	ひょうじょう 表情 expression (face, voice)
おもてどお 表通り main street	ひょう し 表紙 front cover; cover; board	ひょう げん 表現 expression; presentation

exterior; surface; table; chart; diagram — 十 (ten) + 一 (one) + 衣 (clothes)

303 勝

303	力	12 画	くん か(つ)、まさ(る)	おん ショウ

か 勝つ to win; to gain victory	しょう はい 勝敗 outcome (of game, battle)	まさ 勝る to excel; to exceed
けっ しょう 決勝 finals (in sports)	ゆう しょう 優勝 victory; championship	あっ しょう 圧勝 overwhelming victory

win; victory; excel — 月 (moon) + 关 (lift with both hands) + 力 (power)

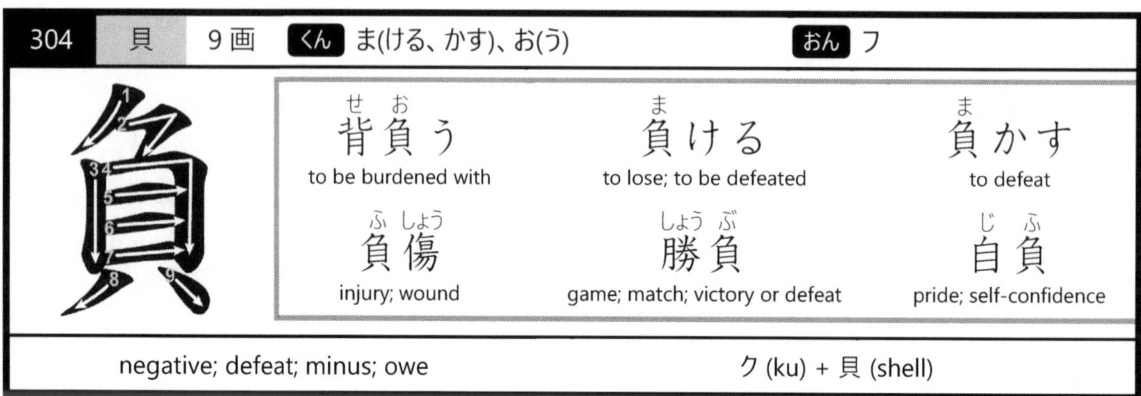

304	貝	9画	くん ま(ける、かす)、お(う)	おん フ

負

背負う（せおう） to be burdened with	負ける（まける） to lose; to be defeated	負かす（まかす） to defeat
負傷（ふしょう） injury; wound	勝負（しょうぶ） game; match; victory or defeat	自負（じふ） pride; self-confidence

negative; defeat; minus; owe — ク (ku) + 貝 (shell)

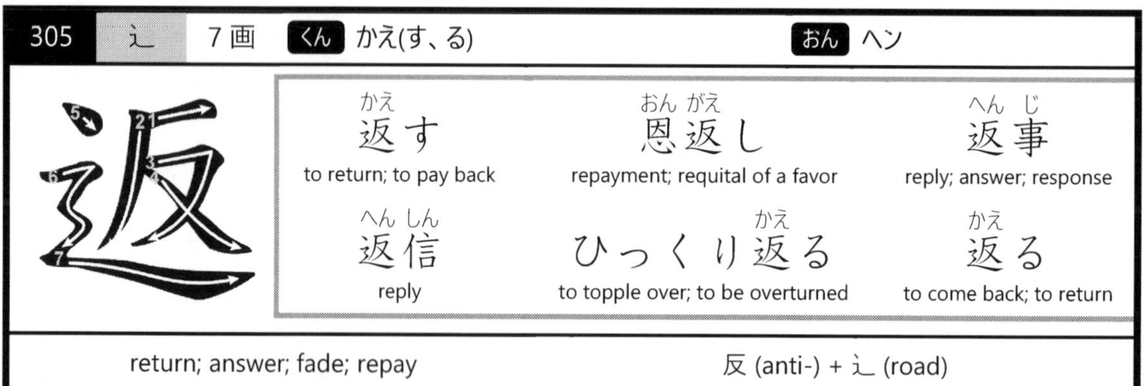

305	辶	7画	くん かえ(す、る)	おん ヘン

返

返す（かえす） to return; to pay back	恩返し（おんがえし） repayment; requital of a favor	返事（へんじ） reply; answer; response
返信（へんしん） reply	ひっくり返る（ひっくりかえる） to topple over; to be overturned	返る（かえる） to come back; to return

return; answer; fade; repay — 反 (anti-) + 辶 (road)

306	攵	8画	くん はな(す、つ、れる)、ほう(る)	おん ホウ

放

放す（はなす） to let go; to let loose	放れる（はなれる） to get free (from); to be released	放つ（はなつ） to set free; to release; to emit (to fire)
放送（ほうそう） airing; broadcast	開放（かいほう） leaving open; opening up	手放す（てばなす） to part with; to relinquish

let go; release — 方 (direction) + 攵 (strike)

Kanji Parts used in the New Kanji

酉	liquor pot	月	moon	貝	shell
己	self	券	ticket	反	anti-
十	ten	关	lift with both hands	辶	road
一	one	力	power	方	direction
衣	clothes	ク	katakana KU	攵	strike

11 Kanji Memory Tools 漢字記憶術

This section helps you organically memorize kanji readings, meanings, and construction.

配

酉 己

The liquor pot has a self help pamphlet to "**HAND OUT**".

ピザ屋(や)さんは❶宅配(たくはい)ピザの割引券(わりびきけん)を❷配(くば)っています。

The pizza shop is ❷handing out ❶delivery pizza discount coupons.

表

十 一 衣

Odds are ten to one that your clothes match your "**EXTERIOR**".

❶表(おもて)に見(み)せない感情(かんじょう)は、時(とき)に❷表情(ひょうじょう)に❸表(あらわ)れる。

From time to time, ❷emotions that you don't show on the ❶surface appear in ❸facial expressions.

勝

月 关 力

I reached the moon via a mountain pass using my power so, I "**WIN**"!

今日(きょう)、❶勝(か)ったら、❷三連勝(さんれんしょう)になります。

❶If I win today, it will be my ❷third win in a row.

負

ク 貝

The katakana ku on this shell signals "**DEFEAT**".

この❶勝負(しょうぶ)に❷負(ま)けたら、借金(しゃっきん)を❸背負(せお)うことになる。

❷If I lose this ❶match, I will ❸be burdened with debt.

返

反 辶

This anti- road isn't the way to "**RETURN**".

商品(しょうひん)を❶返(かえ)したら、❷返金(へんきん)された。

When I ❶returned the product it ❷was refunded.

放

方 攵

In this direction we strike until they "**RELEASE**".

❶放送中(ほうそうちゅう)はカメラから❷目(め)を放(はな)さないほうがいいです。

You should ❷not take your eyes off the camera ❶during the broadcast (on air).

11 Kanji Usage 漢字の使い方

● 11-1. Same sound, different kanji「はなす」

放す, from this lesson, and 離す are close in meaning, but used in different situations.

「放す」– to let something go free that had been captured

「離す」– to split or divide items that were connected

to release; to let go; to set free		to separate; to part; to divide; to keep apart	
放す		離す	
庭に犬を放す	let the dog into the yard	目を離す	take your eye off of~
かごから鳥を放す	release bird from cage	犬を離す	separate the dogs
子供の手を放す	let go of a child's hand	つないだ手を離す	separate held hands

When releasing something captured, use「放す」

When separating connected items, use「離す」

● 11-2. The visible and hidden parts of kanji 表と裏

表 (front) and 裏 (back) can be used for two-sided items like paper, buildings, etc.

EXAMPLE SENTENCES

1. アメリカの一ドル札の表には、ワシントン大統領の肖像画があります。
   裏には、鷲とピラミッドの絵があります。
   There is a portrait of President Washington on the front of the American 1-dollar bill.
   On the back, there is a picture of an eagle and a pyramid.

2. この店の表の看板には、裏に駐車場があると書いてあります。
   The sign in front of this store says there is a parking lot in the back.

表 and 裏 can also be used to describe things that are visible and hidden. For people, 表 is the side a person outwardly shows while 裏 is what is hidden inside.

EXAMPLE SENTENCES

3. 彼女は表裏のない性格です。
   She is of a personality that doesn't hide anything.

4. 私は同僚の表の顔しか知りません。
   I only know the face that my co-workers show me.

5. これは個人情報なので、表に出せません。
   We can't disclose this since it's personal information.

6. 俺の裏の顔は誰にも見せられない。
   I can't show anyone my hidden face.

裏 can also refer to an unseen location, such as the stockroom in a store.

EXAMPLE SENTENCE

The store staff would never say あなた. They instead say お客様 (customer).

7. お客様の靴のサイズは、裏の倉庫にあるかも知れません。少々お待ち下さい。
   We might have your shoe size in the storage room in the back. Please wait a moment.

● 11-3. Winning and losing in kanji 勝・負

In competitive activities, a competitor's consecutive wins are counted with 連勝. However, consecutive losses is 連敗 and uses 敗 (loss, defeat, reversal) instead of 負 (loss).

EXAMPLE SENTENCES

The Hiroshima Carp is a famous Japanese baseball team.

1. おとといの試合で、広島カープが８連勝した。
   At the match the day before yesterday, the Hiroshima Carp had their 8th consecutive victory.

勝 and 敗 are counters for wins and losses.

2. 囲碁の大会で一勝二敗して、決勝に進めませんでした。
   I couldn't move forward to the finals after one victory and two losses in the Go tournament.

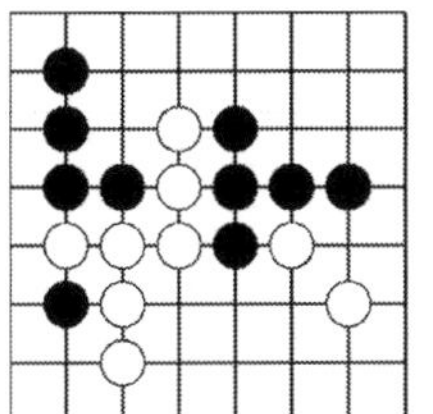

"Go" is an abstract strategy board game for two players in which the aim is to surround more territory than the opponent.

The game was invented in China more than 2,500 years ago and is believed to be the oldest board game continuously played to the present day. - Wikipedia

● 11-4. The origin of the term 負け犬 (loser)

負け犬 is a derogatory term meaning "loser" or "unsuccessful person", literally meaning "a dog that loses a fight and runs away." The origin of 負け犬 is from the 2003 best-selling novel written by Junko Sakai about an unmarried woman in her 30s without children, titled 負け犬の遠吠え (Howling of a Losing Dog).

11 Words You Can Write 書ける言葉

集配（しゅうはい） pickup and delivery; collection and delivery

集 配

心配（しんぱい） worry; anxiety; concern

心 配

表す（あらわす） to express; to show

表 す

公表（こうひょう） airing; exposure; publication

公 表

代表（だいひょう） representative; model; main number

代 表

勝ち（かち） win; victory

勝 ち

勝負（しょうぶ） game; match

勝 負

自負（じふ） pride; being proud of one's abilities or achievements

自	負										

返金（へんきん） repayment

返	金										

返送（へんそう） sending back; return to sender

返	送										

追放（ついほう） cast out; ban; throw out

追	放										

放送（ほうそう） airing; broadcast

放	送										

配送（はいそう） delivery

配	送										

楽勝（らくしょう） easy victory

楽	勝										

負ける（まける） to be defeated

負	け	る									

勝ち目(かちめ) chance (of success); odds

勝	ち	目									

11 Kanji Workbook Activities

● 1. Stroke Order Check 書き順確認

Each kanji has a stroke with an arrow on it. Write its order number below the kanji.

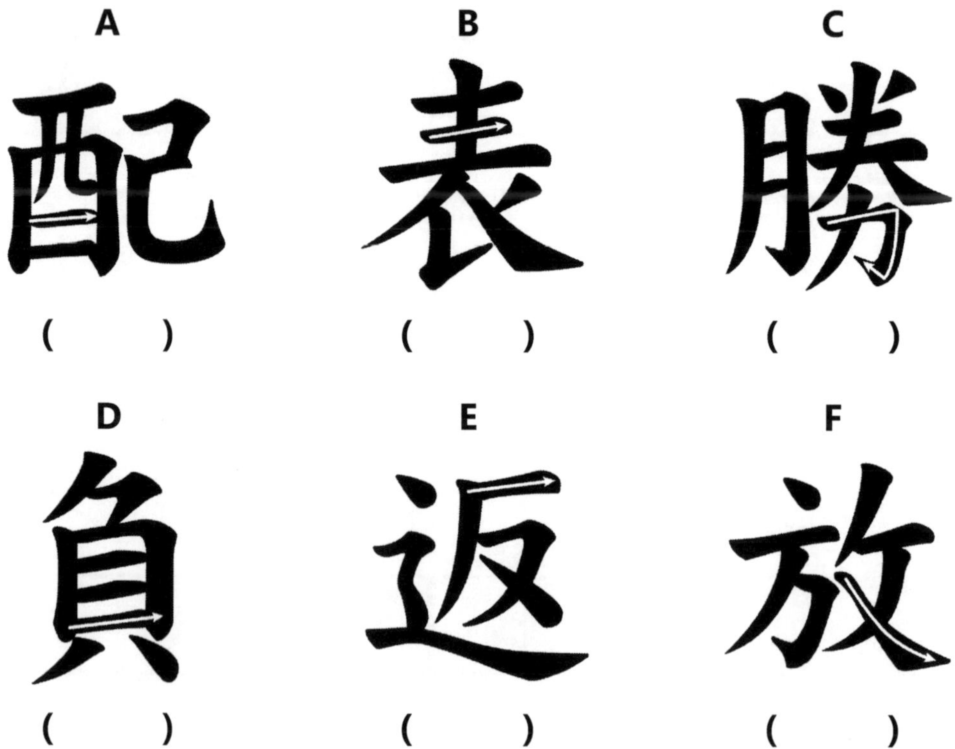

● 2. Kanji Readings

Write FURIGANA above the underlined kanji words.

1. <u>今</u>、タクシーを<u>手配</u>したので、お<u>待</u>ち<u>下</u>さい。
2. <u>表通り</u>に、よくティッシュを<u>配</u>っている<u>人</u>がいます。
3. うちのサッカーチームは<u>決勝</u>まで<u>進</u>みました。
4. <u>前回</u>はライバルに<u>負</u>けたけど、<u>今回</u>は<u>負</u>かします。
5. <u>四月</u>から、<u>新</u>しい<u>歌番組</u>が<u>放送</u>されるそうです。

● 3. Kanji Meaning Match

Write the following kanji next to its meaning: 放 負 転 表 登 配 勝 返 待

1. ____ hand out
2. ____lose
3. ____ let go; shoot
4. ____ express
5. ____ give back
6. ____ climb
7. ____ win
8. ____ wait
9. ____ fall down

● 4. Fill in the Kanji

Fill in the appropriate kanji in the blanks for each sentence.

1. ____ ____のことが ____ ____で、ねられませんでした。(あした / しん ぱい)

Being worried about tomorrow, I couldn't sleep.

2. クラスの ____ ____で スピーチをすることになりました。(だい ひょう)

It was decided that I do a speech as the class representative.

3. もう____ ____ は____まりました。(しょう ぶ / き)

The match was already decided.

4. ____ の____ りょうりに____るものは、ないです。(はは / て / まさ)

Nothing beats mother's home cooking.

5. ____ い バックパックをせ____ うのは、すきじゃないです。(おも / お)

I don't like carrying a heavy backpack on my back.

6. 「つるの おん ____ し」という____を____ っていますか。(がえ / はなし / し)

Do you know the story, "The Crane's Gratitude"?

7. ____を____ に____してあげました。(さかな / かわ / はな)

I released the fish into the river.

● 5. Kanji Matching

Connect each kanji with an おん or くん reading. Use each reading only ONCE.

代 •	• ほう
放 •	• ちょう
終 •	• おもて
配 •	• だい
調 •	• しゅう
負 •	• へん
勝 •	• な
表 •	• ま
返 •	• くば
投 •	• しょう

11 Answer Key 答え合わせ

1. Stroke order check (answers)

A) 6　B) 3　C) 11

D) 7　E) 1　F) 8

3. Kanji meaning match (answers)

1. 配 hand out　2. 負 lose　3. 放 let go; shoot
4. 表 express　5. 返 give back　6. 登 climb
7. 勝 win　8. 待 wait　9. 転 fall down

2. Kanji Readings (answers)

1. 今(いま)、タクシーを手配(てはい)したので、お待(ま)ち下(くだ)さい。 — I just arranged for a taxi, so please wait.
2. 表通(おもてどお)りに、よくティッシュを配(くば)っている人(ひと)がいます。 — There are often people handing out tissues on the main street.
3. うちのサッカーチームは決勝(けっしょう)まで進(すす)みました。 — My soccer team proceeded to the finals.
4. 前回(ぜんかい)はライバルに負(ま)けたけど、今回(こんかい)は負(ま)かします。 — Last time I lost to my rival, but this time I will defeat them.
5. 四月(しがつ)から、新(あたら)しい歌番組(うたばんぐみ)が放送(ほうそう)されるそうです。 — It seems there'll be a new song show broadcasting from April.

4. Fill in the kanji (answers)

1. 明日のことが心配で、ねられませんでした。
2. クラスの代表でスピーチをすることになりました。
3. もう勝負は決まりました。
4. 母の手りょうりに勝るものは、ないです。
5. 重いバックパックをせ負うのは、すきじゃないです。
6. 「つるのおん返し」という話を知っていますか。
7. 魚を川に放してあげました。

5. Kanji matching (answers)

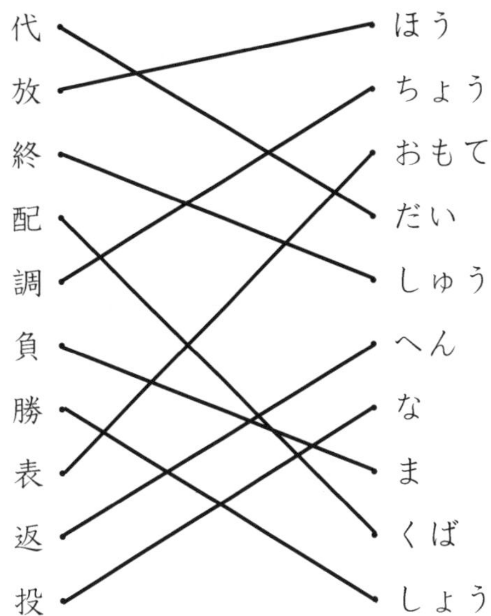

12 Kanji Lesson 12: 問有遊落流練

307-312

Kanji that can be verbs (part 10)

12 New Kanji 新しい漢字

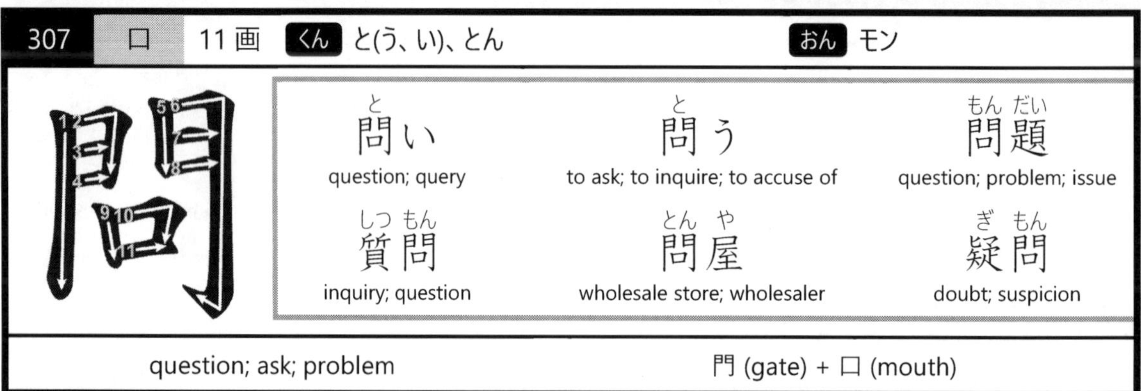

307	口	11 画	くん と(う、い)、とん	おん モン

問

問い (とい) question; query	問う (とう) to ask; to inquire; to accuse of	問題 (もんだい) question; problem; issue
質問 (しつもん) inquiry; question	問屋 (とんや) wholesale store; wholesaler	疑問 (ぎもん) doubt; suspicion

question; ask; problem — 門 (gate) + 口 (mouth)

308	月	6 画	くん あ(る)	おん ユウ、ウ

有

有る (ある) to be; to exist; to have	有頂天 (うちょうてん) to go to one's head	有名 (ゆうめい) famous
所有 (しょゆう) ownership, possession	有無 (うむ) existence or non-existence; yes or no	有料 (ゆうりょう) paid; not free

possess; have; exist; happen; occur — ナ (right hand) + 月 (flesh)

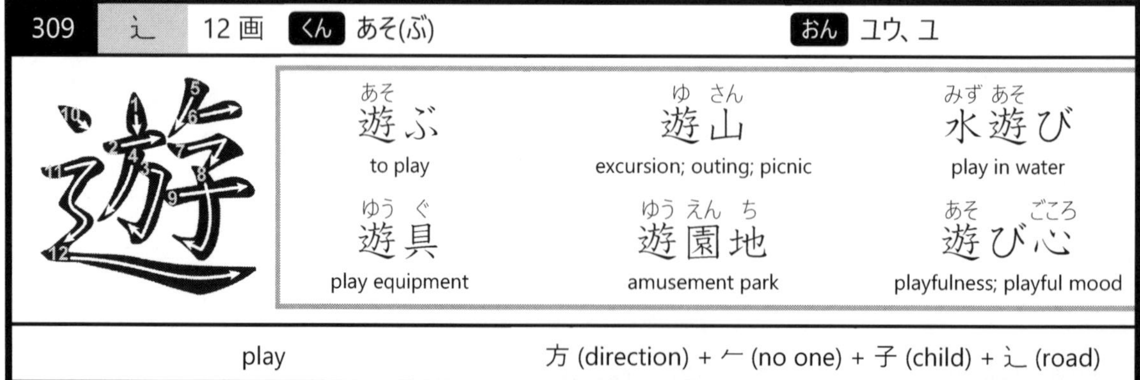

309	辶	12 画	くん あそ(ぶ)	おん ユウ、ユ

遊

遊ぶ (あそぶ) to play	遊山 (ゆさん) excursion; outing; picnic	水遊び (みずあそび) play in water
遊具 (ゆうぐ) play equipment	遊園地 (ゆうえんち) amusement park	遊び心 (あそびごころ) playfulness; playful mood

play — 方 (direction) + 𠂉 (no one) + 子 (child) + 辶 (road)

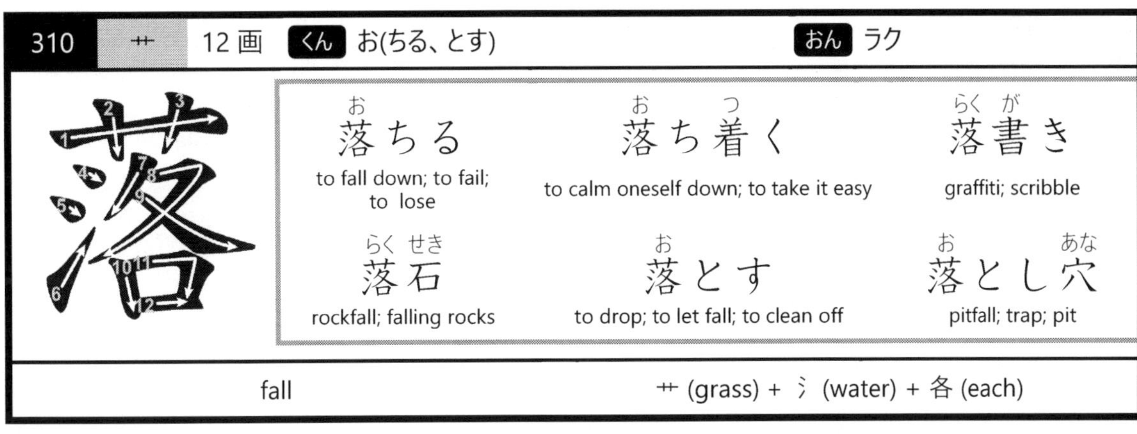

310 | 艹 | 12画 | くん お(ちる、とす) | おん ラク

落

落ちる (お) to fall down; to fail; to lose	落ち着く (お つ) to calm oneself down; to take it easy	落書き (らく が) graffiti; scribble
落石 (らく せき) rockfall; falling rocks	落とす (お) to drop; to let fall; to clean off	落とし穴 (お あな) pitfall; trap; pit

fall — 艹 (grass) + 氵 (water) + 各 (each)

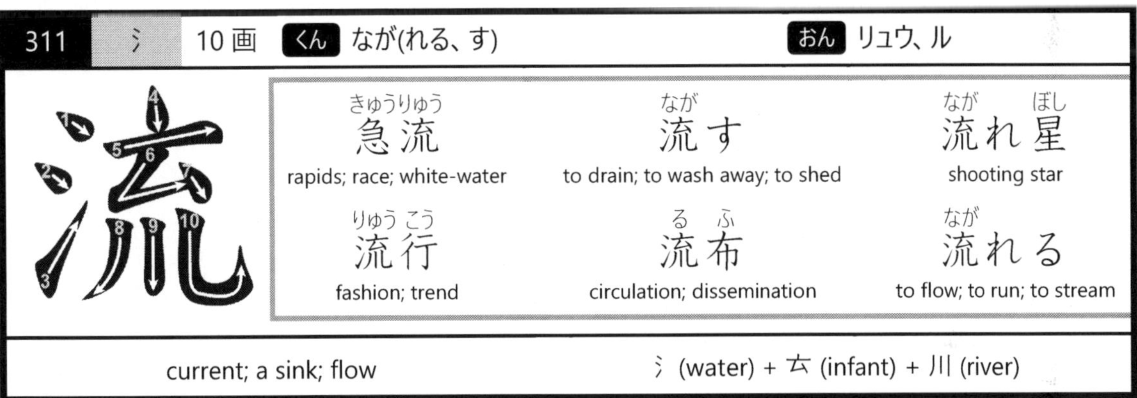

311 | 氵 | 10画 | くん なが(れる、す) | おん リュウ、ル

流

急流 (きゅうりゅう) rapids; race; white-water	流す (なが) to drain; to wash away; to shed	流れ星 (なが ぼし) shooting star
流行 (りゅう こう) fashion; trend	流布 (る ふ) circulation; dissemination	流れる (なが) to flow; to run; to stream

current; a sink; flow — 氵 (water) + 𠫓 (infant) + 川 (river)

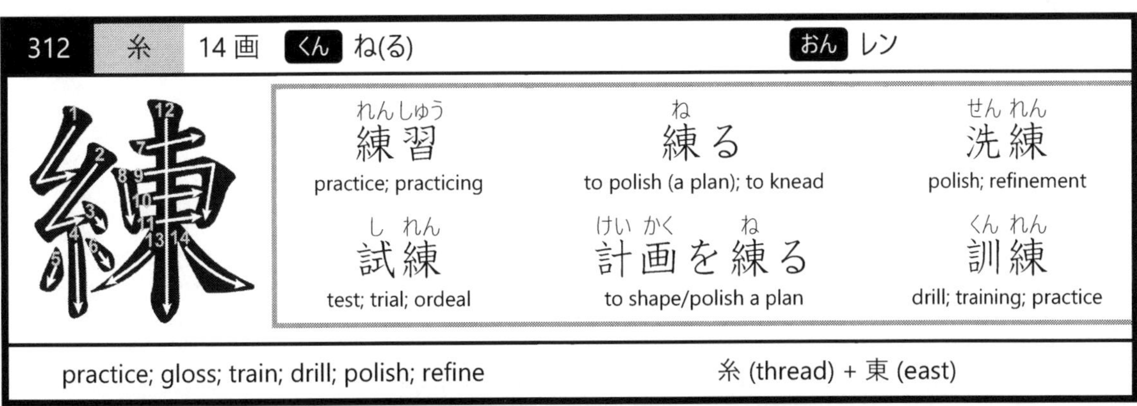

312 | 糸 | 14画 | くん ね(る) | おん レン

練

練習 (れんしゅう) practice; practicing	練る (ね) to polish (a plan); to knead	洗練 (せん れん) polish; refinement
試練 (し れん) test; trial; ordeal	計画を練る (けい かく ね) to shape/polish a plan	訓練 (くん れん) drill; training; practice

practice; gloss; train; drill; polish; refine — 糸 (thread) + 東 (east)

Kanji Parts used in the New Kanji

門	gate	子	child	川	river
口	mouth	艹	grass	糸	thread
ナ	right hand	氵	water	東	east
月	flesh	各	each		
方	direction	𠫓	infant		

12 Kanji Memory Tools 漢字記憶術

This section helps you organically memorize kanji readings, meanings, and construction.

問

門 口
You must open the gate of your mouth to ask a "**QUESTION**".

とんや か もの もんだい
❶問屋で買った物には❷問題があった。
The things I bought at the ❶wholesaler, had a ❷problem.

有

ナ 月
My right hand holds the flesh I "**POSSESS**".

うちゅうじん うむ ぎろん ゆうめい あ
宇宙人の❶有無を議論する❷有名なポッドキャストが❸有る。
❸There is a ❷famous podcast that debates the ❶existence or non-existence of aliens.

遊

方 𠂉 子 辶
No matter the direction, no one's child on the road should "**PLAY**".

ゆうえんち あそ みずあそ
❶遊園地で❷遊んでから、プールで❸水遊びしたいです。
After ❷playing at ❶the amusement park I want to ❸play in water at the pool.

落

艹 氵 各
Grass needs water for each to soften a "**FALL**".

いし お らくせき い
石が❶落ちることを❷「落石」と言います。
The ❶falling of rocks is called, ❷"falling rocks".

流

氵 㐬 川
Unafraid of the water, the infant lept into the river "**FLOW**".

なが ぼし み い りゅうこう
❶流れ星を観に行くツアーが❷流行している。
Tours to go see ❷shooting stars are ❶popular.

練

糸 東
Darning thread from the east is how I "**PRACTICE**".

しゅうまつ かんじ れんしゅうけいかく ね
週末の漢字の❶練習計画を❷練っています。
I'm ❷devising a kanji ❶practice plan on the weekends.

12 Understanding Kanji Parts 漢字部分の理解

● 12-1. The "gate" radical もんがまえ (門)

The "gate" radical, もんがまえ is used in many kanji.

Meaning	Kanji	Parts	Word	Reading	Word meaning
gate	門	gate	門	もん	gate; division
			専門	せんもん	specialty; expert
question; ask; problem	問	gate + mouth	問題	もんだい	question; problem
			問い合わせ	と あ	inquiry; query
interval; space	間	gate + sun	時間	じかん	time; hour
			人間	にんげん	human being; person
connection; gateway; involve	関	gate + lift with both hands	関係	かんけい	relation; connection
			関心	かんしん	concern; interest
open; unfold; unseal	開	gate + start	開ける	あ	to open; to unwrap
			開始	かいし	start; beginning
closed; shut	閉	gate + genius	閉める	し	to close; to shut
			閉鎖	へいさ	closing; shutdown

There are no perfect humans!

Before marrying my Japanese wife, I sent letters to her from America to Japan almost daily (pre-internet). In one of my letters, after explaining a mistake I had made, I wrote in large letters what I had learned as a result. My intention was to write, "There are no perfect humans", 「完璧(かんぺき)な人間(にんげん)がいない！」 but unfortunately, I missed ONE part of the kanji and wrote, 「完璧(かんぺき)な人門(にんもん)がいない！」 which nonsensically means, "There are no perfect people gates". 25 years later my wife and I still say the mistaken phrase to each other when a mistake is made.

12 Kanji Usage 漢字の使い方

● 12-2. Go with the "kanji" flow 流

For the purposes of remembering the kanji 流, the final part in the kanji memory tools for 流 is listed as "river". While appearing similar, it's actually meant to be hair. Imagine the hair of an infant flowing down the river.

If you are a camper or like to fish, the following words using 流 might come in handy.

downstream	upstream
下流 (か りゅう)	上流 (じょう りゅう)
(down + current)	(up + current)

Here are some other words that you might come across using 流.

Compound	Meaning of the paired kanji	English
水流 (すい りゅう)	水 = water	water current
合流 (ごう りゅう)	合 = fit; suit; join	merge (traffic); linking up; coming together
逆流 (ぎゃく りゅう)	逆 = inverted; reverse; opposite	counter-current; adverse tide; reverse flow
電流 (でん りゅう)	電 = electricity	electric current
流行 (りゅう こう)	行 = going; journey; act; line	fashion; vogue; craze
流星 (りゅう せい)	星 = star; spot; dot; mark	meteor; falling star
流血 (りゅう けつ)	血 = blood	bloodshed
血流 (けつ りゅう)	血 = blood	blood flow

HANDY PHRASES USING 流す

1. トイレを流す。 to flush the toilet
2. 血を流す。 to shed blood; to bleed
3. 涙を流す。 to flow tears; to cry

● 12-3. Flowing sounds with 流

When a sound is playing in the background the verb 流れる (to be flowing) or 流す (to make flow) can be used to show that it's continuing.

EXAMPLE SENTENCES

1. 私はいつも、音楽を流しながら、宿題をします。
   I always play (let flow) music when I do my homework.

2. エレベーターの中では、いつもクラシック音楽が流れています。
   There's always classical music playing (flowing) on the elevator.

12 Words You Can Write 書ける言葉

問い（とい） question; query

問い

学問（がくもん） learning; study; scholarship

学問

有名（ゆうめい） famous

有名

遊ぶ（あそぶ） to play

遊ぶ

転落（てんらく） fall; tumble; dive; slump

転 落

流行（りゅうこう） fashion; trend

流 行

練習（れんしゅう） practice

練 習

練る（ねる） to draw up; to knead

練 る

有力（ゆうりょく） influential; strong; prominent; likely

有 力

集落（しゅうらく） settlement; village; community; town

集 落

上流（じょうりゅう） upper stream; upstream; upper classes

上 流

遊園地（ゆうえんち） amusement park

遊 園 地

落書き（らくがき） graffiti; scribble

落 書 き

流れる（ながれる） to flow; to run; to stream

流	れ	る									

流れ星（ながれぼし） shooting star

流	れ	星									

遊歩道（ゆうほどう） promenade; esplanade; walking trail

遊	歩	道									

12 Kanji Workbook Activities

● 1. Stroke Order Check 書き順確認

Each kanji has a stroke with an arrow on it. Write its order number below the kanji.

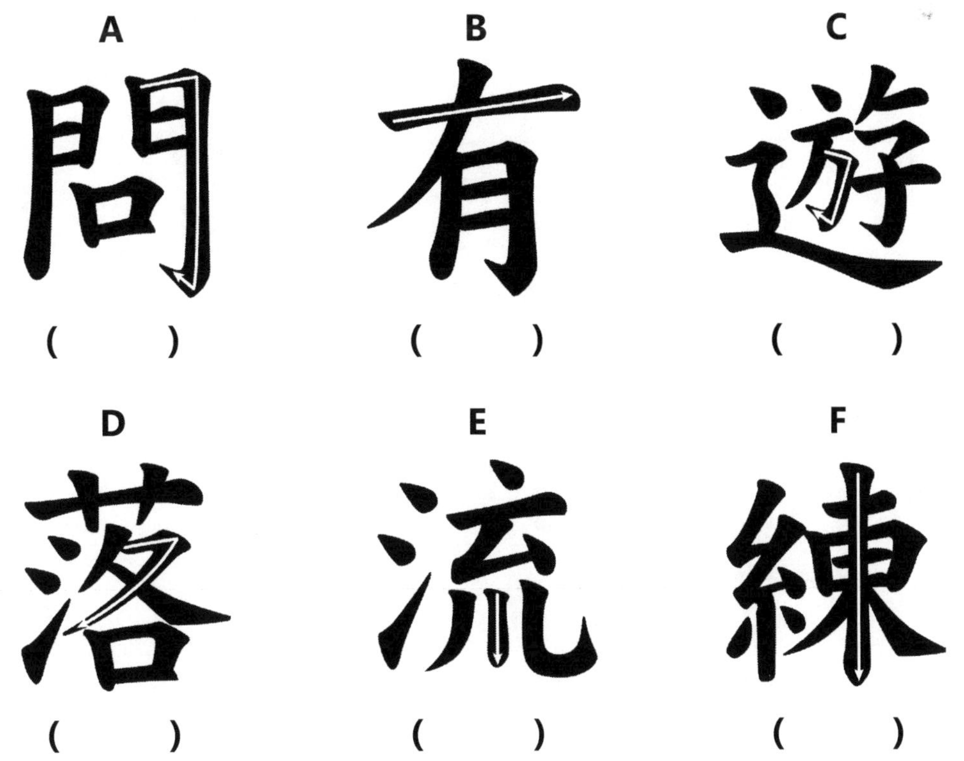

● 2. Kanji Readings

Write FURIGANA above the underlined kanji words.

1. この問いに答えて下さい。
2. かれは、一番有力なバスケットボールせん手です。
3. 遊園地で急流すべりに乗りました。
4. 落ち着いて、ゆっくり話しましょう。
5. もっと計画を練らなければなりません。

● 3. Kanji Meaning Match

Write the following kanji next to its meaning: 練 落 負 問 流 動 遊 有 配

1. ____ question	2. ____ play	3. ____ flow
4. ____ to be	5. ____ fall	6. ____ polish
7. ____ hand out	8. ____ lose	9. ____ move

● 4. Fill in the Kanji

Fill in the appropriate kanji in the blanks for each sentence.

がっ こう せん せい もん

1. ____ ____ で____ ____ にしつ____ しました。

I asked a question to the teacher at school.

せん じつ ゆう めい か しゅ あ

2. ____ ____ 、____ ____な____ ____に____ いました。

Last week, I met a famous singer.

こう えん みず あそ たの

3. ____ ____で ____ ____ びをするのは、____しいです。

It's fun to play in the water at the park.

あいだ　みち　お　ひろ

4. この ＿＿、＿＿ で＿＿としものを＿＿いました。

The other day I picked up an item that had been dropped on the street.

まち　ちゅう　しん　おお　かわ　なが

5. ＿＿ の ＿＿ ＿＿に＿＿きい ＿＿ が＿＿れています。

There is a large river (flowing) in the center of the town.

ご　ご　れん　しゅう

6. ＿＿ ＿＿からテニスの ＿＿ ＿＿があります。

I have tennis practice from the afternoon.

らく　せき　き　くだ

7. ＿＿ ＿＿に＿＿をつけて＿＿さい。

Please be careful of falling rocks.

● 5. Kanji Matching

Connect each kanji with an おん or くん reading. Use each reading only ONCE.

練 •	• れん
落 •	• あ
有 •	• もん
流 •	• しゅう
登 •	• のぼ
打 •	• りゅう
問 •	• ちゃく
遊 •	• あそ
集 •	• らく
着 •	• だ

12 Answer Key 答え合わせ

1. Stroke order check (answers)

A) 6 B) 2 C) 3

D) 8 E) 9 F) 12

3. Kanji meaning match (answers)

1. 問 question 2. 遊 play 3. 流 flow
4. 有 to be 5. 落 fall 6. 練 polish
7. 配 hand out 8. 負 lose 9. 動 move

2. Kanji Readings (answers)

1. この問(と)いに答(こた)えて下(くだ)さい。 Please answer this question.
2. かれは、一番(いちばん)有力(ゆうりょく)なバスケットボールせん手(しゅ)です。 He's the most influential basketball player.
3. 遊園地(ゆうえんち)で急流(きゅうりゅう)すべりに乗(の)りました。 I rode the whitewater slide at the amusement park.
4. 落(お)ち着(つ)いて、ゆっくり話(はな)しましょう。 Calm down and let's take our time and talk.
5. もっと計画(けいかく)を練(ね)らなければなりません。 We need to formulate our plan more.

4. Fill in the kanji (answers)

1. 学校で先生にしつ問しました。
2. 先日、有名な歌手に会いました。
3. 公園で水遊びをするのは、楽しいです。
4. この間、道で落としものを拾いました。
5. 町の中心に大きい川が流れています。
6. 午後からテニスの練習があります。
7. 落石に気をつけて下さい。

5. Kanji matching (answers)

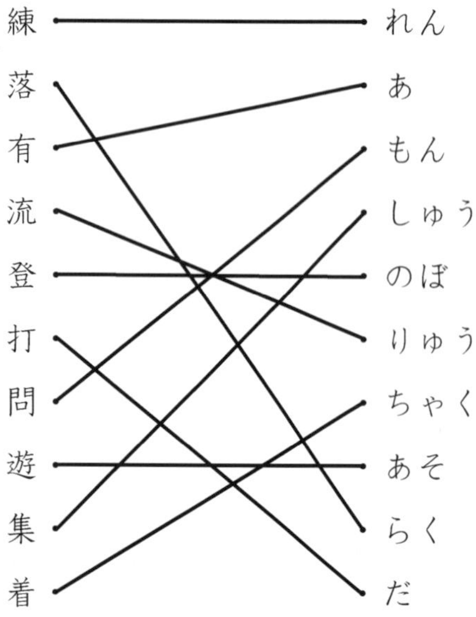

13 Kanji Lesson 13: 君者主相客係

313-318

Kanji related to people

13 New Kanji 新しい漢字

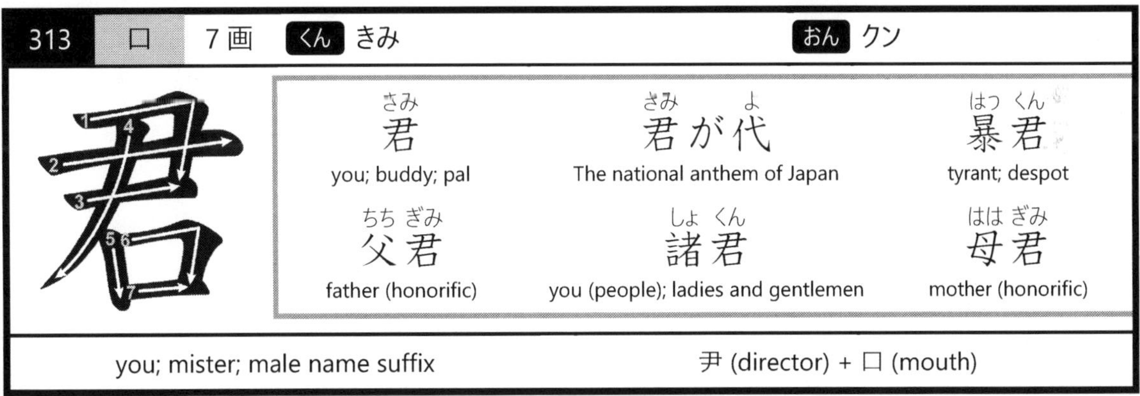

313 | 口 | 7 画 | くん きみ | おん クン

君

君 (さみ) you; buddy; pal	君が代 (さみ よ) The national anthem of Japan	暴君 (はつ くん) tyrant; despot
父君 (ちち ぎみ) father (honorific)	諸君 (しょ くん) you (people); ladies and gentlemen	母君 (はは ぎみ) mother (honorific)

you; mister; male name suffix — 尹 (director) + 口 (mouth)

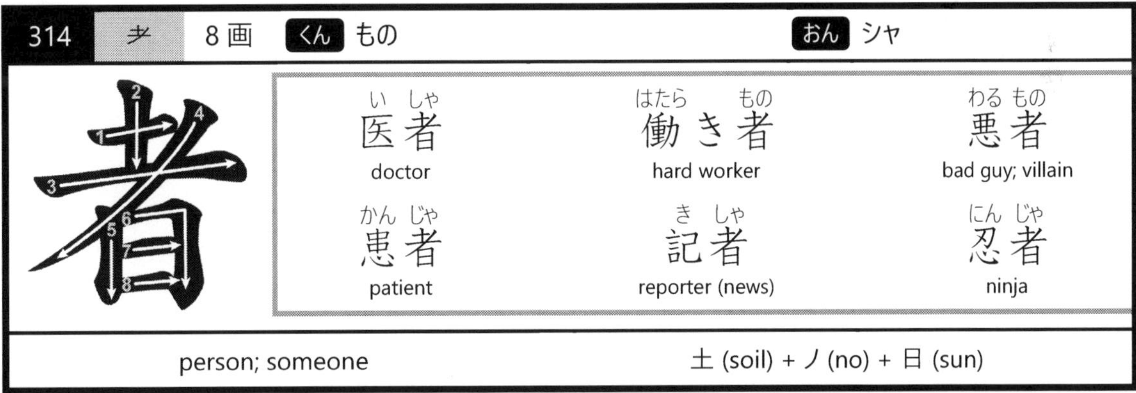

314 | 耂 | 8 画 | くん もの | おん シャ

者

医者 (い しゃ) doctor	働き者 (はたら もの) hard worker	悪者 (わる もの) bad guy; villain
患者 (かん じゃ) patient	記者 (き しゃ) reporter (news)	忍者 (にん じゃ) ninja

person; someone — 土 (soil) + ノ (no) + 日 (sun)

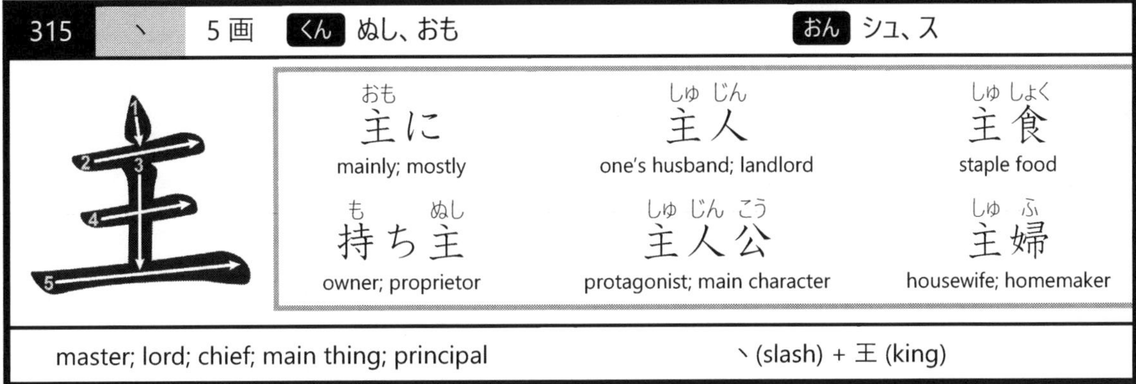

315 | 丶 | 5 画 | くん ぬし、おも | おん シュ、ス

主

主に (おも) mainly; mostly	主人 (しゅ じん) one's husband; landlord	主食 (しゅ しょく) staple food
持ち主 (も ぬし) owner; proprietor	主人公 (しゅ じん こう) protagonist; main character	主婦 (しゅ ふ) housewife; homemaker

master; lord; chief; main thing; principal — 丶 (slash) + 王 (king)

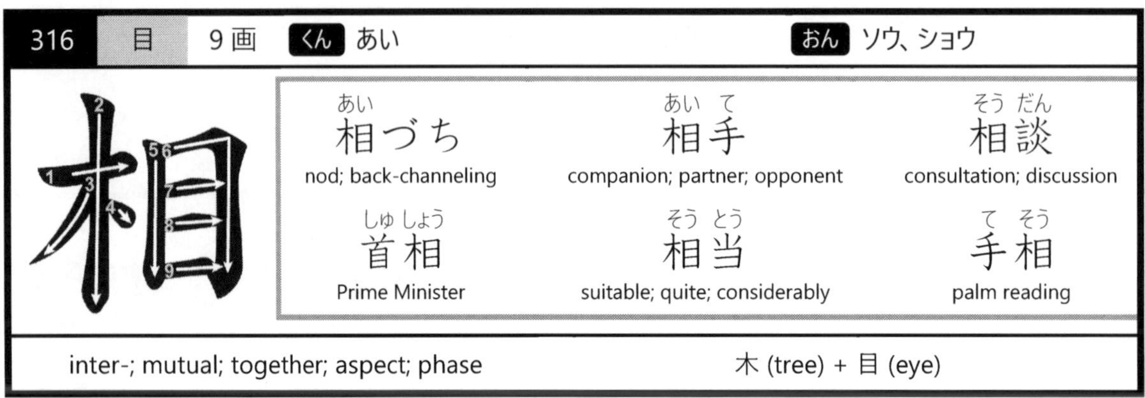

316 | 目 | 9画 | くん あい | おん ソウ、ショウ

相

相づち (あい)	相手 (あい て)	相談 (そう だん)
nod; back-channeling	companion; partner; opponent	consultation; discussion
首相 (しゅ しょう)	相当 (そう とう)	手相 (て そう)
Prime Minister	suitable; quite; considerably	palm reading

inter-; mutual; together; aspect; phase — 木 (tree) + 目 (eye)

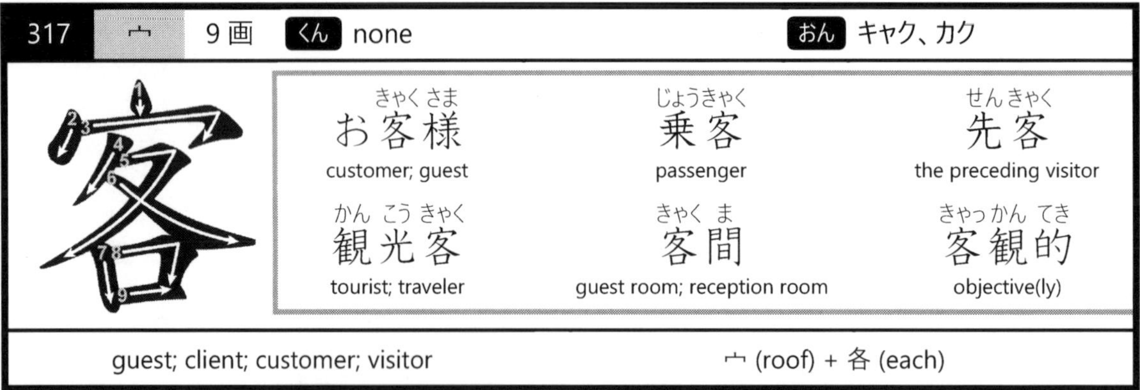

317 | 宀 | 9画 | くん none | おん キャク、カク

客

お客様 (きゃく さま)	乗客 (じょうきゃく)	先客 (せん きゃく)
customer; guest	passenger	the preceding visitor
観光客 (かん こう きゃく)	客間 (きゃく ま)	客観的 (きゃっ かん てき)
tourist; traveler	guest room; reception room	objective(ly)

guest; client; customer; visitor — 宀 (roof) + 各 (each)

318 | イ | 9画 | くん かか(る)、かかり | おん ケイ

係

係 (かかり)	係る (かか)	係員 (かかり いん)
charge; duty; clerk; official	to concern; to affect; to involve	attendant; staff
関係 (かん けい)	上下関係 (じょう げ かん けい)	受付係 (うけ つけ がかり)
relationship; connection	hierarchical relations; pecking order	receptionist; clerk

person in charge; duty; connection — イ (person) + ノ (no) + 糸 (thread)

Kanji Parts used in the New Kanji

尹	director	丶	slash	各	each
口	mouth	王	king	イ	person
土	soil	木	tree	糸	thread
ノ	no	目	eye		
日	sun	宀	roof		

13 Kanji Memory Tools 漢字記憶術

This section helps you organically memorize kanji readings, meanings, and construction.

君

尹 口
The director of your mouth is "**YOU**".

❶森君は先生に「❷君は甘いよ」と言われた。

❶Mori was told by his teacher, "❷You are naïve".

者

土 ノ 口
Soil with no sun feeds no "**PERSON**".

弟は❶忍者になって、❷悪者を倒したいって。

My younger brother said he wants to become a ❶ninja and bring down ❷bad guys.

主

丶 王
I shall slash the king for my "**MASTER**".

❶主人は❷主に日本株の❸株主です。

❶My husband is ❷primarily a ❸stockholder of Japanese stocks.

相

木 目
I looked my tree in the eye and the respect was "**MUTUAL**".

❶首相は、❷相談する❸相手を選びました。

The ❶Prime Minister chose a ❸partner to ❷consult with.

客

宀 各
Under my roof, each of you is a "**GUEST** ".

❶お客さんの中に❷刺客がいた。

Amongst the ❶visitors, there was an ❷assassin.

係

亻 ノ 糸
A person with no thread will never be a "**PERSON IN CHARGE**".

❶イベント係と❷会計係は❸関係ないです。

The ❶person in charge of the event and then ❷person in charge of accounting are ❸not related.

13 Kanji Usage 漢字の使い方

● 13-1. The relationships of kanji 関係

There are some powerful ways to use 関係. For example, it can be used to say "It doesn't matter" with 関係がないです or the more informal 関係ない. Let's look at some interesting ways 関係 is used with relationships.

love triangle	pecking order; hierarchical relationship
さん かく かん けい 三角関係	じょう げ かん けい 上下関係
(triangle + relation)	(up down + relation)

human relations; personal relationships	parent-child relations
にん げん かん けい 人間関係	おや こ かん けい 親子関係
(human + relation)	(parent + child + relation)

EXAMPLE SENTENCES

1. 僕は親友と親友の彼女との三角関係で、苦しんでいます。
   I'm suffering due to a love triangle with my best friend and my best friend's girlfriend.
2. 日本の社会では、上下関係が厳しいです。
   Pecking order is strict in Japanese society.
3. 私は人間関係が何よりも難しいと思います。
   I think that human relationships are more difficult than anything.
4. 子供が大人になると、親子関係がよくなることが多いです。
   Often when a child becomes an adult, the parent-child relation improves.

● 13-2. Describing many kinds of people using 者 (person)

We know that 人(ひと) is used when talking about people, such as 日本人(にほんじん) (Japanese people), 主人(しゅじん) (husband) etc. 者(もの) is also used when defining people.

Compound	Meaning of the other kanji	English
記者(きしゃ)	記 = scribe; account; narrative	reporter
作者(さくしゃ) 著者(ちょしゃ) 筆者(ひっしゃ)	作 = make; production; prepare 著 = renowned; publish; write 筆 = writing brush; writing	author; writer
読者(どくしゃ)	読 = read	reader
走者(そうしゃ)	走 = run	runner
信者(しんじゃ)	信 = faith; truth; trust	believer; adherent; devotee
役者(やくしゃ)	役 = duty; labor; service; role	actor; actress; man of wits
忍者(にんじゃ)	忍 = endure; conceal; sneak	ninja
実力者(じつりょくしゃ)	実 = reality; truth 力 = power; strength	powerful person; big wheel
当事者(とうじしゃ)	当 = hit; right; appropriate 事 = matter; thing; fact; reason	person concerned; related party
第三者(だいさんしゃ)	第 = No.; residence 三 = three	third party; outsider; disinterested person
死者(ししゃ)	死 = death; die	casualty; deceased
悪者(わるもの)	悪 = bad; evil; wrong	bad fellow; rascal
若者(わかもの)	若 = young; immature	young people; youngsters

● 13-3. Affectionate name additions 君 and ちゃん

You might see 君 (くん) or ちゃん added to the end of last or first names. They are both used to show affection but are not limited to just that. ちゃん is mostly used after girls' names and 君 after boys' names. ちゃん is used quite often after children's names, regardless of the sex of the child. It's also not unusual for a higher-up in a company to refer to the female staff members with a 君 following their names.

When NOT to use

ちゃん and 君 should never be used when addressing people above you in social status. If you ever hear someone addressing another person with 君 or ちゃん, you can assume that the speaker is equal or higher in status.

The UBER cute version of ちゃん

When speaking to animals, babies, or speaking to someone who is particularly adorable, you might hear ちゃん be converted to the much cuter form たん. It's very "cutesy" to use this version, so make sure you use it appropriately and with the right person.

13 Words You Can Write 書ける言葉

主君（しゅくん） master; lord

主	君										

学者（がくしゃ） scholar

学	者										

店主（てんしゅ） shopkeeper

店	主										

相手（あいて） companion; partner; opponent

相	手										

手相（てそう） palm reading

手	相										

来客（らいきゃく） visitor; caller; customer

来	客										

客足（きゃくあし） customer traffic

客	足										

作者（さくしゃ）author; writer; composer; artist

作	者										

家主（やぬし）landlord; house owner; home owner

家	主										

打者（だしゃ）batter; hitter

打	者										

係長（かかりちょう） subsection head; assistant manager

係	長										

君が代（きみがよ） The national anthem of Japan

君	が	代									

人気者（にんきもの） popular person

人	気	者									

主人公（しゅじんこう） main character

主	人	公									

図書係（としょがかり） a person who is in charge at a library

図	書	係									

田中君(たなかくん) Tanaka (last name)

田	中	君									

13 Kanji Workbook Activities

● 1. Stroke Order Check 書き順確認

Each kanji has a stroke with an arrow on it. Write its order number below the kanji.

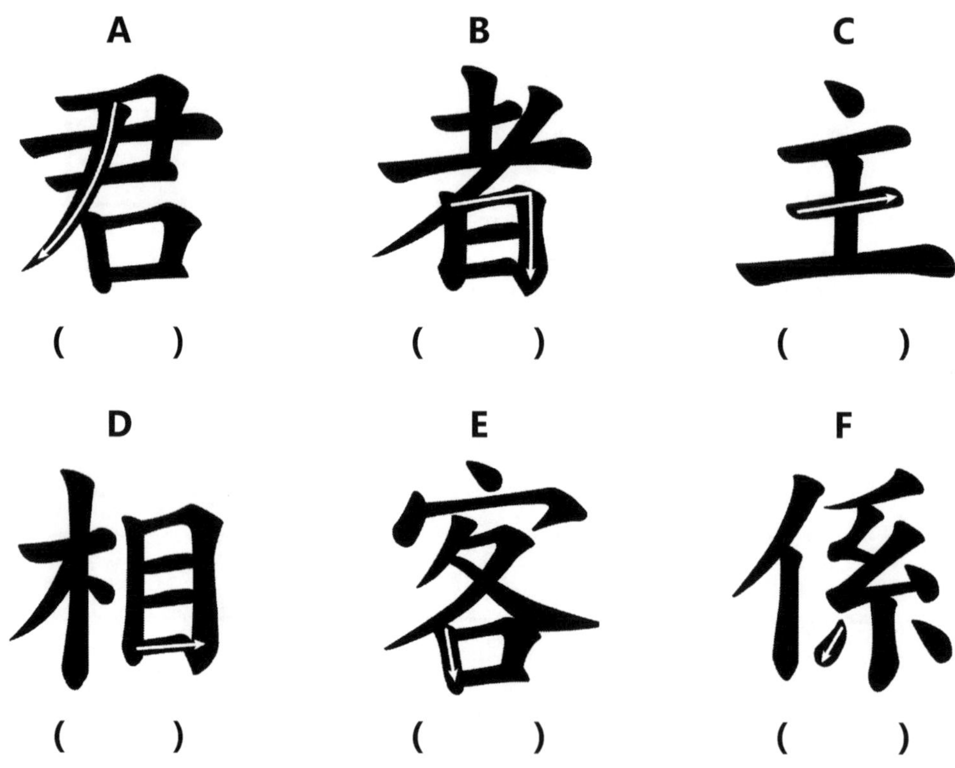

● 2. Kanji Meaning Match

Write the following kanji next to its meaning: 君 者 遊 主 相 返 客 係 進

1. ____ person 2. ____ play 3. ____ return

4. ____ progress 5. ____ main, major 6. ____ mutual

7. ____ you 8. ____ customer 9. ____ duty

● 3. Kanji Readings

Write FURIGANA above the underlined kanji words.

1. 君が新しく会社に入った人かな。

2. わたしは、この絵本の作者に会ったことがあります。

3. 店主は今、お客さんの相手をしています。

4. 台風のせいで、どこも客足がへってしまいました。

5. お客さんにサービスに係るアンケートを配った。

● 4. Fill in the Kanji

Fill in the appropriate kanji in the blanks for each sentence.

やま だ くん うち

1. ___ ___ ___の___はどこですか。

Where is Yamada's house?

なか むら こう こう とき にん き もの

2. ___ ___さんは ___ ___の___、___ ___ ___でした。

Nakamura was popular when he was in high-school.

に ほん じん しゅ しょく こめ

3. ___ ___ ___の___ ___は、お___です。

Japanese people's staple food is rice.

きょう　て　そう　み

4. ___ ___、___ ___を___ てもらいました。

Today I got my palm read.

きゃく　らい　てん　ま

5. お___ さま、またのご___ ___ をお___ちしています。

Customer, I await the next time you visit the store.

がっ　こう　がかり

6. わたしは___ ___で、そうじ___をしています。

I'm in charge of cleaning at school.

おも　せい　り

7. わたしの ___ なしごとは、しょるいの___ ___です。

My main work is document organization.

● 5. Kanji Matching

Connect each kanji with an おん or くん reading. Use each reading only ONCE.

係 •	• そう
客 •	• もの
流 •	• りゅう
相 •	• かかり
配 •	• はい
主 •	• しゅ
整 •	• つい
者 •	• きゃく
君 •	• くん
追 •	• せい

13 Answer Key 答え合わせ

1. Stroke order check (answers)

A) 4 B) 6 C) 4
D) 9 E) 7 F) 8

2. Kanji meaning match (answers)

1. 者 person 2. 遊 play 3. 返 return
4. 進 progress 5. 主 master 6. 相 mutual
7. 君 you 8. 客 customer 9. 係 duty

3. Kanji Readings (answers)

1. 君(きみ)が新(あたら)しく会社(かいしゃ)に入(はい)った人(ひと)かな。
   I guess you're the new person in the company.
2. わたしは、この絵本(えほん)の作者(さくしゃ)に会(あ)ったことがあります。
   I've met the author of this picture book.
3. 店主(てんしゅ)は今(いま)、お客(きゃく)さんの相手(あいて)をしています。
   The owner is dealing with a customer now.
4. 台風(たいふう)のせいで、どこも客足(きゃくあし)がへってしまいました。
   Due to the typhoon, foot traffic has decreased everywhere.
5. お客(きゃく)さんにサービスに係(かか)るアンケートを配(くば)った。
   A questionnaire pertaining to the service was distributed to the customers.

4. Fill in the kanji (answers)

1. 山田君の家はどこですか。
2. 中村さんは高校の時、人気者でした。
3. 日本人の主食は、お米です。
4. 今日、手相を見てもらいました。
5. お客さま、またのご来店をお待ちしています。
6. わたしは学校で、そうじ係わるをしています。
7. わたしの主なしごとは、しょるいの整理です。

5. Kanji matching (answers)

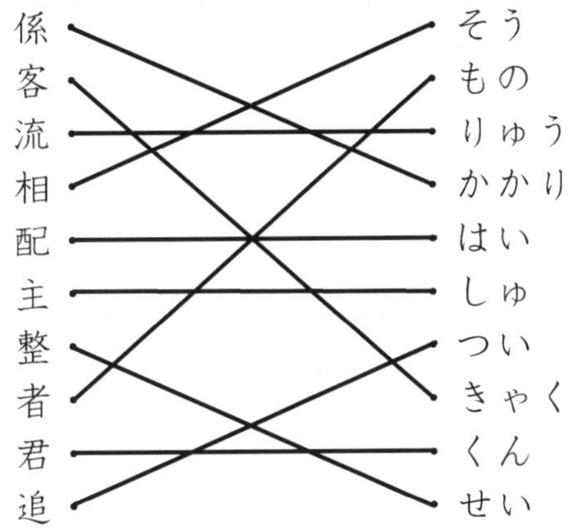

14 Kanji Lesson 14: 族他役童神様

319-324

Kanji related to people (part 2)

14 New Kanji 新しい漢字

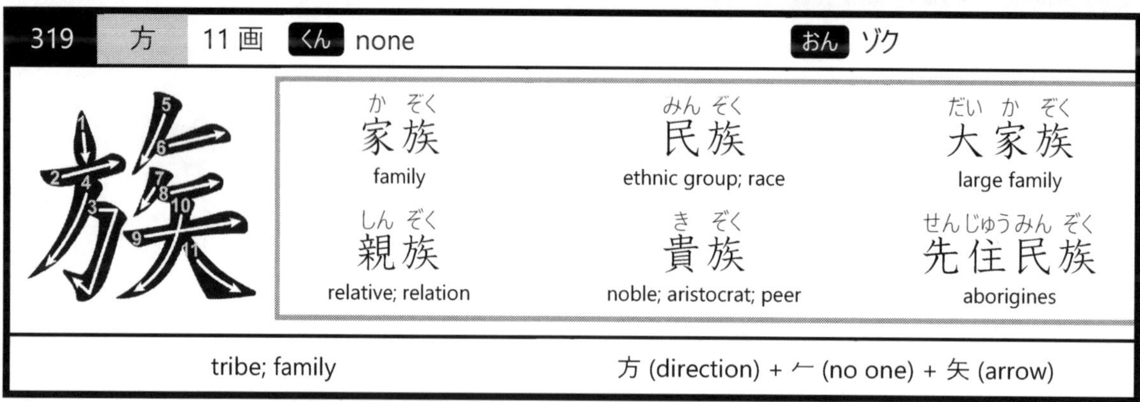

319 方 11画 くん none おん ゾク

族

家族 (かぞく) family	民族 (みんぞく) ethnic group; race	大家族 (だいかぞく) large family
親族 (しんぞく) relative; relation	貴族 (きぞく) noble; aristocrat; peer	先住民族 (せんじゅうみんぞく) aborigines

tribe; family — 方 (direction) + 𠂉 (no one) + 矢 (arrow)

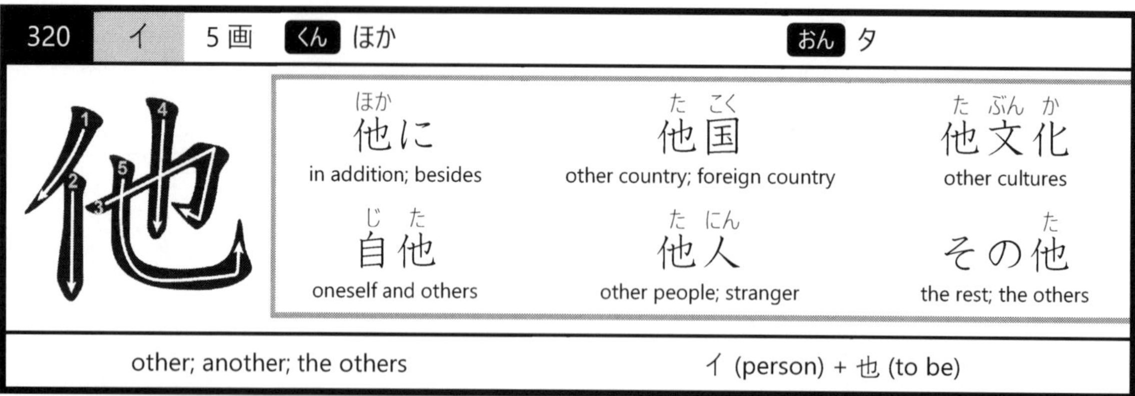

320 イ 5画 くん ほか おん タ

他

他に (ほかに) in addition; besides	他国 (たこく) other country; foreign country	他文化 (たぶんか) other cultures
自他 (じた) oneself and others	他人 (たにん) other people; stranger	その他 (そのた) the rest; the others

other; another; the others — イ (person) + 也 (to be)

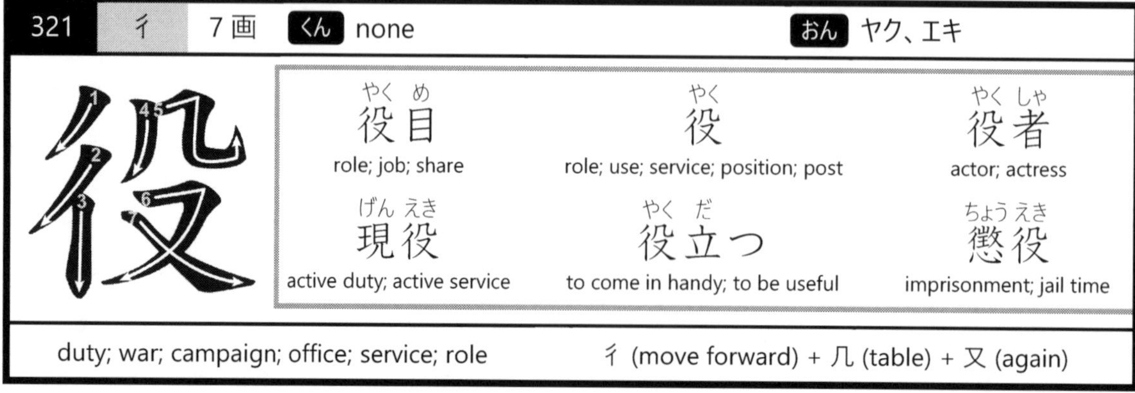

321 彳 7画 くん none おん ヤク、エキ

役

役目 (やくめ) role; job; share	役 (やく) role; use; service; position; post	役者 (やくしゃ) actor; actress
現役 (げんえき) active duty; active service	役立つ (やくだつ) to come in handy; to be useful	懲役 (ちょうえき) imprisonment; jail time

duty; war; campaign; office; service; role — 彳 (move forward) + 几 (table) + 又 (again)

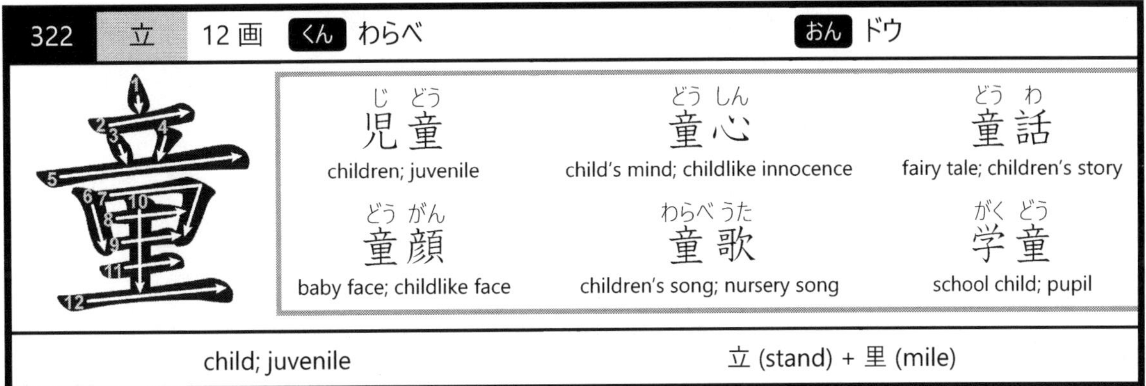

322	立	12 画	くん わらべ	おん ドウ

児童 (じ どう) children; juvenile	童心 (どう しん) child's mind; childlike innocence	童話 (どう わ) fairy tale; children's story
童顔 (どう がん) baby face; childlike face	童歌 (わらべ うた) children's song; nursery song	学童 (がく どう) school child; pupil

child; juvenile — 立 (stand) + 里 (mile)

323	ネ	9 画	くん かみ、かん、こう	おん シン、ジン

神様 (かみ さま) god	神主 (かん ぬし) chief Shinto priest (of a shrine)	神話 (しん わ) myth; legend
神社 (じん じゃ) Shinto shrine	死神 (しに がみ) grim reaper; god of death	神々しい (こう ごう) divine; sublime; solemn

gods; mind; soul — ネ (altar) + 申 (say)

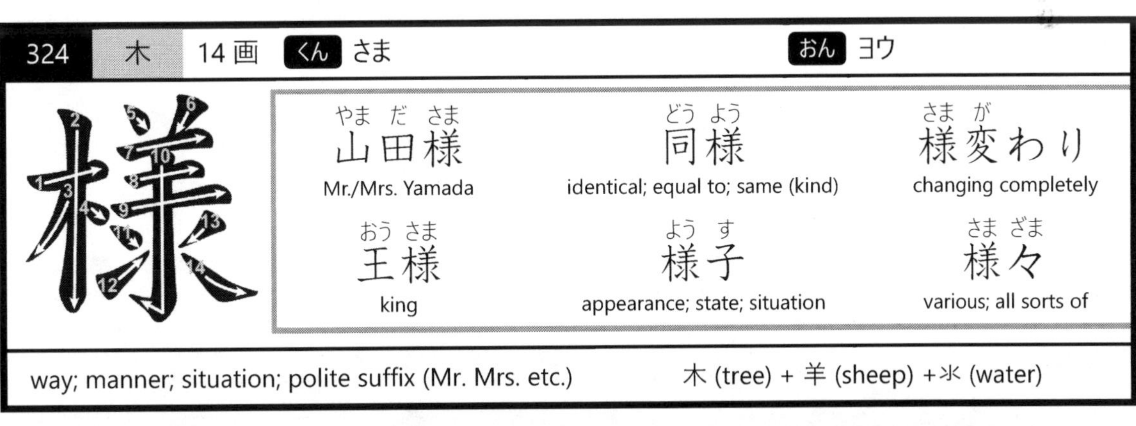

324	木	14 画	くん さま	おん ヨウ

山田様 (やま だ さま) Mr./Mrs. Yamada	同様 (どう よう) identical; equal to; same (kind)	様変わり (さま が) changing completely
王様 (おう さま) king	様子 (よう す) appearance; state; situation	様々 (さま ざま) various; all sorts of

way; manner; situation; polite suffix (Mr. Mrs. etc.) — 木 (tree) + 羊 (sheep) +氺 (water)

Kanji Parts used in the New Kanji

方	direction	彳	move forward	ネ	altar
𠂉	no one	几	table	申	say
矢	arrow	又	again	木	tree
イ	person	立	stand	羊	sheep
也	to be	里	mile	氺	water

14 Kanji Memory Tools 漢字記憶術

This section helps you organically memorize kanji readings, meanings, and construction.

族

方 𠂉 矢

The direction from which no one shoots an arrow is your "**TRIBE**".

じつ わたし か ぞく おう ぞく

実は、私の❶家族は❷王族です。

Actually, my ❶family is ❷royalty.

他

亻 也

A person can only want to be one or the "**OTHER**".

た こく ほか た にん きょう み

❶他国の❷他に、❸他人にも興味がありません。

❷In addition to ❶other countries, I also have no interest in ❸other people.

役

彳 几 又

Move forward to the table again and perform your "**DUTY**".

ねんかん げん えき やく しゃ いん たい

50年間❶現役だった❷役者が❸引退しました。

An ❷actor that was ❶active for 50 years ❸retired.

童

立 里

If you stand at mile marker 69, that is really "**JUVENILE**".

よう ち えん わらべうた うた どう わ よ

幼稚園では、❶童歌を歌ったり、❷童話を読んだりします。

In kindergarten they do things like, sing ❶children songs, and read ❷fairy tales.

神

ネ 申

The altar is where you say your prayers to the "**GODS**".

じん じゃ かん ぬし こう ごう め がみ え み

❶神社の❷神主さんは、❸神々しい❹女神の絵を見た。

This ❶Shinto shrine's ❷chief priest looked at the ❸solemn painting of a ❹Goddess.

様

木 羊 氺

The tree and sheep were immersed in water in a strange "**MANNER**".

た なか さま いえ よう す さま が

❶田中様の家の❶様子が❷様変わりしていました。

The ❷state of ❶Mr. Tanaka's home ❸had changed completely.

14 Kanji Usage 漢字の使い方

● 14-1. Gods, Lords, and people coming home late 様

様 is the honorific added to the end of Japanese names to mean "Mr., Mrs., Ms. etc.", but it's also used in some common words.

かみ さま 神様	ほとけ さま 仏様	との さま 殿様	ご ぜん さま 午前様
God	a Buddha	lord; master; your highness	one who gets home after midnight

午前様 – This is said not in a mean way, but more jokingly similar to sarcasm.

● 14-2. Phrases that use 様

There are also some common everyday Japanese phrases that use 様

ち そう さま ご馳走様でした。	Thank you for treating me to dinner.
This is said after someone has provided you a meal, whether it was cooked or purchased. It's also fun to say when getting the bill at a restaurant to signal that your friend will be paying for you. Try it out and you might get a laugh.	

く ろう さま ご苦労様でした。	Thank you for your efforts.
This is said at the end of work or task that someone has done. It's a nice phrase to hear to know that someone appreciates the effort you have made. **NOTE** This can be rude if saying it to someone higher in status than you.	

様(さま)になる	to become good-looking; to start looking appropriate
光君(ひかるくん)は、背(せ)が高(たか)くてかっこいいから、何(なに)を着(き)ても様(さま)になります。 Because Hikaru is tall and cool, he looks good no matter what he wears.	

様変(さまが)わりする	to alter; to undergo a radical transformation; to take on new dimensions
今(いま)の東京(とうきょう)は、二十年前(にじゅうねんまえ)と比(くら)べると、すっかり様変(さまが)わりしました。 If you compare Tokyo now to 20 years ago, it's undergone a complete transformation.	

● 14-3. The many roles kanji can play 役

役 is used in many everyday words, especially related to roles in movies.

Compound	Meaning of the other kanji / word	English
大役(たいやく)	大 = large; big	important role; major part (e.g. in a movie)
脇役(わきやく)	脇 = armpit; the other way; another place	supporting role; minor role
主役(しゅやく)	主 = lord; master; main thing	leading part; leading actor
悪役(あくやく)	悪 = bad; vice; evil; wrong	villain; baddie; the villain's part
適役(てきやく)	適 = suitable; rare; qualified	suitable post or role
子役(こやく)	子 = child	dramatic role for child; child actor
相手役(あいてやく)	相手 = companion; partner	opposing role; partner
当(あ)たり役(やく)	当たり = hit; success; prediction	successful role role where actor excels
ちょい役(やく)	ちょい = a little; a bit; slightly	bit part (e.g. in a film); extra

14 Words You Can Write 書ける言葉

家族（かぞく） family

家族

親族（しんぞく） relative

親族

他者（たしゃ） another person; others

他者

他社（たしゃ） another company; other company

他社

役者（やくしゃ） actor; performer

役者

主役（しゅやく） leading part; leading actor

主役

童顔（どうがん） baby fase; childlike face

童顔

童話（どうわ） fairy tale; children's story

童話

神様（かみさま） god

神	様										

神父（しんぷ） Catholic priest; abbe; reverend father; minister

神	父										

王様（おうさま） king

王	様										

様子（ようす） appearance; situation

様	子										

代役（だいやく） substitute (e.g. actor); stand-in; double

代	役										

童心（どうしん） child's mind; childlike innocence

童	心										

女神（めがみ） goddess; female deity

女	神										

多様（たよう） diverse; varied

多	様										

14 Kanji Workbook Activities

● 1. Stroke Order Check 書き順確認

Each kanji has a stroke with an arrow on it. Write its order number below the kanji.

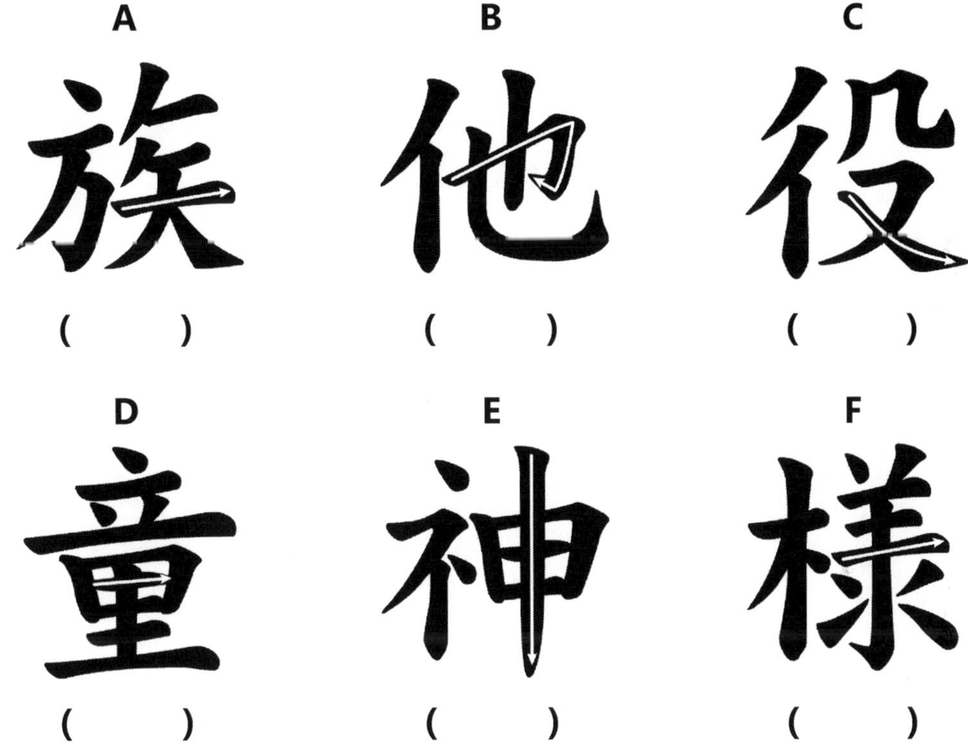

● 2. Kanji Readings

Write FURIGANA above the underlined kanji words.

1. 水族かんで、たくさんの魚を見ました。
2. 他に何か聞きたいことはありますか。
3. 友人の妹はホラー映画の死神役をしたことがある。
4. 童話の中では「ももたろう」が一番すきです。
5. うちの社長はよく「お客様は神様です」と言います。

● 3. Kanji Meaning Match

Write the following kanji next to its meaning: 族 様 他 遊 神 練 役 童 返

1. ____ return 2. ____ Mr. 3. ____ play

4. ____ group 5. ____ part; role 6. ____ god

7. ____ children 8. ____ knead 9. ____ other

● 4. Fill in the Kanji

Fill in the appropriate kanji in the blanks for each sentence.

しょう がつ しん ぞく あつ
1. お ___ ___ に___ ___が___まりました。
On New Year's, our relatives gathered.

はは じ ぶん た にん
2. ___は、___ ___ にきびしくて、___ ___にやさしいです。
My mother is tough on herself, but kind to others.

やく しゃ で
3. しょうらいは ___ ___ になって、ドラマに___たいです。
In the future I want to be an actor and appear in TV dramas.

わらべ うた うた
4. むかしは よく______を ___ いました。
A long time ago I often sang nursery rhymes.

じん じゃ い かみ さま
5. ___ ___に___ って、___ ___におねがいをしました。
I went to a temple and requested to God.

まち よう す
6. ___ の___ ___がかわって、おどろきました。
I was surprised how the appearance of the town had changed.

か ぞく なつ やす
7. ___ ___ で___ ___みに キャンプをしました。
We camped as a family on our summer vacation.

● 5. Kanji Matching

Connect each kanji with an おん or くん reading. Use each reading only ONCE.

様 •	• もの
童 •	• やく
他 •	• どう
者 •	• かみ
族 •	• さま
役 •	• た
係 •	• かかり
神 •	• くん
落 •	• らく
君 •	• ぞく

14 Answer Key 答え合わせ

1. Stroke order check (answers)

A) 9　B) 3　C) 7

D) 8　E) 9　F) 9

2. Kanji Readings (answers)

1. 水族(すいぞく)かんで、たくさんの魚(さかな)を見(み)ました。

   I saw a lot of fish at the aquarium.

2. 他(ほか)に何(なに)か聞(き)きたいことはありますか。

   Is there anything else you would like to ask?

3. 友人(ゆうじん)の 妹(いもうと) はホラー映画(えいが)の死神役(しにがみやく)をしたことがある。

   A friend's younger sister once played the grim reaper in a horror movie.

4. 童話(どうわ)の中(なか)では「ももたろう」が一番(いちばん)すきです。

   Of all the fairy tales, "Momotaro" is my favorite.

5. うちの社長(しゃちょう)はよく「お客様(きゃくさま)は神様(かみさま)です」と言(い)います。

   Our president says, "the customer is God".

3. Kanji meaning match (answers)

1. 返 return　2. 様 Mr.　3. 遊 play

4. 族 group　5. 役 part; role　6. 神 god

7. 童 children　8. 練 knead　9. 他 other

4. Fill in the kanji (answers)

1. お正月に親族が集まりました。
2. 母は、他人にやさしくて、自分にきびしいです。
3. しょうらいは役者になって、ドラマに出たいです。
4. むかしはよく童歌を歌いました。
5. 神社に行って、神様におねがいをしました。
6. 町の様子がかわって、おどろきました。
7. 家族で夏休みにキャンプをしました。

5. Kanji matching (answers)

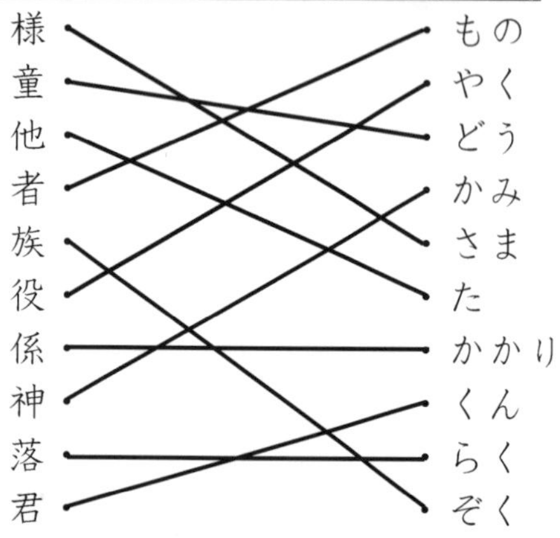

15 Kanji Lesson 15: 医院駅屋館宿

325-330

Kanji related to places and animals

15 New Kanji 新しい漢字

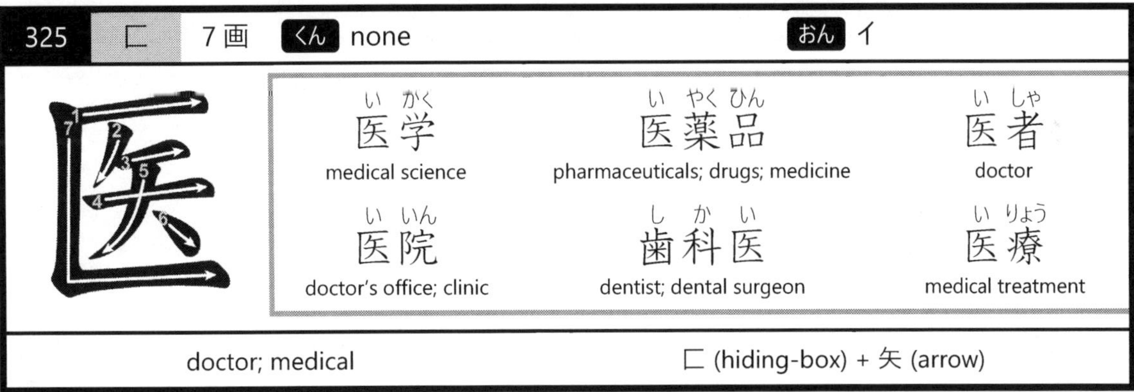

325 | 匚 | 7画 | くん none | おん イ

いがく 医学 medical science	いやくひん 医薬品 pharmaceuticals; drugs; medicine	いしゃ 医者 doctor
いいん 医院 doctor's office; clinic	しかい 歯科医 dentist; dental surgeon	いりょう 医療 medical treatment

doctor; medical — 匚 (hiding-box) + 矢 (arrow)

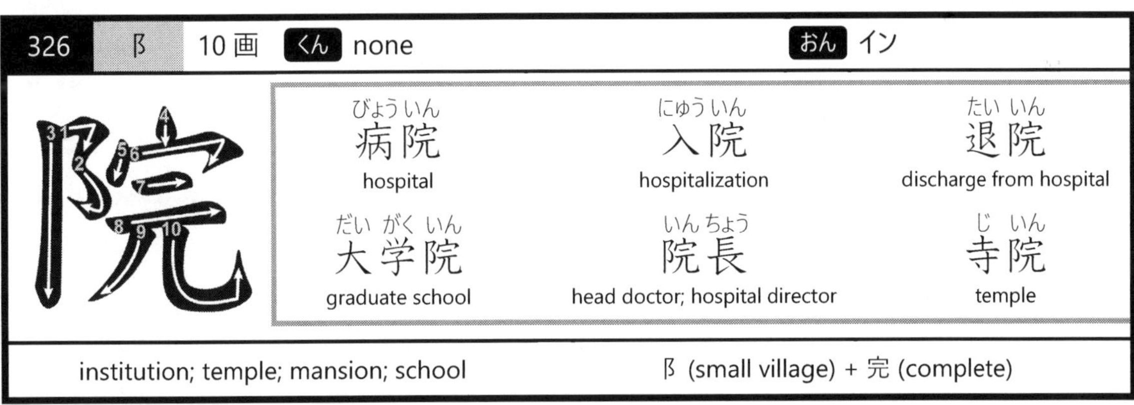

326 | 阝 | 10画 | くん none | おん イン

びょういん 病院 hospital	にゅういん 入院 hospitalization	たいいん 退院 discharge from hospital
だいがくいん 大学院 graduate school	いんちょう 院長 head doctor; hospital director	じいん 寺院 temple

institution; temple; mansion; school — 阝 (small village) + 完 (complete)

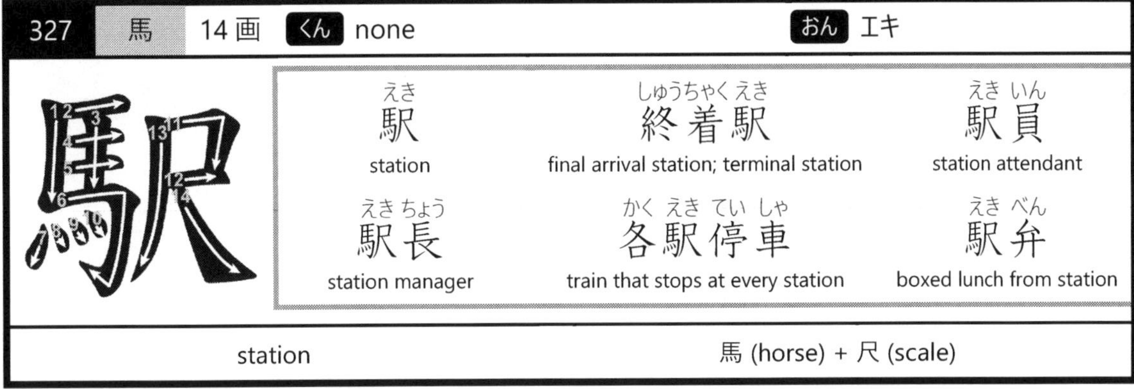

327 | 馬 | 14画 | くん none | おん エキ

えき 駅 station	しゅうちゃくえき 終着駅 final arrival station; terminal station	えきいん 駅員 station attendant
えきちょう 駅長 station manager	かくえきていしゃ 各駅停車 train that stops at every station	えきべん 駅弁 boxed lunch from station

station — 馬 (horse) + 尺 (scale)

328	尸	9画	くん や	おん オク

屋

おくじょう 屋上 rooftop	へ や 部屋 room; apartment; pad; stable	おく がい 屋外 outdoors
や ね 屋根 roof	はな や 花屋 flower shop	おく ない 屋内 indoor

roof; shop; dealer; seller; house — 尸 (flag) + 至 (arrive)

329	食	16画	くん やかた	おん カン

館

たい いく かん 体育館 gymnasium	やかた 館 mansion; palace; castle	たい し かん 大使館 embassy
りょ かん 旅館 Japanese inn	えい が かん 映画館 movie theater	すい ぞく かん 水族館 aquarium

building; mansion; large building; palace — 食 (food) + 官 (bureaucrat)

330	宀	11画	くん やど、やど(る、す)	おん シュク

宿

がっしゅく 合宿 lodging together; training camp	やど 宿る to dwell; to stay at; to be pregnant	やど 宿 lodging; inn; hotel
しゅくだい 宿題 homework; assignment	げ しゅく 下宿 boarding; lodging; boarding house	の じゅく 野宿 sleeping outdoors

lodging; inn; dwell; home — 宀 (roof) + イ (person) + 百 (100)

Kanji Parts used in the New Kanji

匚	hiding-box	尺	scale	宀	roof
矢	arrow	尸	flag	イ	person
阝	small village	至	arrive	百	100
完	complete	食	food		
馬	horse	官	bureaucrat		

15 Kanji Memory Tools 漢字記憶術

This section helps you organically memorize kanji readings, meanings, and construction.

医

匚 矢

In my hiding-box is an arrow with an inscription that says, "**MEDICAL**".

❶医者(いしゃ)になるか❷獣医(じゅうい)になるか迷(まよ)っています。

I'm not sure whether to become a ❶medical doctor or a ❷veterinarian.

院

阝 完

This small village is so complete it's an "**INSTITUTION**".

❶大学院生(だいがくいんせい)の時(とき)、❷総合病院(そうごうびょういん)に❸入院(にゅういん)した。

When I was a ❶graduate student I ❸was admitted to a ❷general hospital.

駅

馬 尺

You must weigh your horse on the scale at the "**STATION**".

❶駅長(えきちょう)も❷駅員(えきいん)も、よく❸駅弁(えきべん)を食(た)べます。

The ❶station manager and also the ❷station attendants often eat ❸boxed lunches from the station.

屋

尸 至

The flag will arrive soon at the "**SHOP**".

私(わたし)のホテルの❶部屋(へや)の近(ちか)くに❷屋外(おくがい)プールと❸ラーメン屋(や)があります。

There is an ❷outside pool and ❸ramen shop near my hotel ❶room.

館

食 官

The food for the bureaucrat is in that "**BUILDING**".

古(ふる)い❶館(やかた)が❷旅館(りょかん)に改装(かいそう)された。

The old ❶mansion house was remodeled into an ❷Japanese inn.

宿

宀 亻 百

The roof collapsed on a person 100 years ago at this "**LODGING**".

❶宿(やど)で❷宿題(しゅくだい)をした。

I did my ❷homework at ❶the inn.

15 Kanji Usage 漢字の使い方

● 15-1. Something about train stations 駅

Japanese society, especially in cities, is built around train stations. How far a business is from a train station can make or break it. Many advertisements for apartments and stores use the distance from the train station as a key selling point. Here are some great words you will see everywhere in Japan related to distance from the train station.

in front of the station	nearest station
えき まえ 駅前	も よ えき 最寄り駅

● 15-2. Shops and people 屋

In English we add "-er" to a word to denote that someone does a certain task. For example, someone who "buys" is a "buyer" and someone who "writes" is a "writer". Japanese has a similar method to denote a person's current position in life.

Shop / Person	Meaning
ほん や **本屋(さん)**	bookstore; book seller
にく や **肉屋(さん)**	butcher shop; butcher
や お や **八百屋(さん)**	vegetable shop; greengrocer
とこ や **床屋(さん)**	barbershop; barber
や **クリーニング屋(さん)**	dry cleaner; cleaner (as a job)
とん や **問屋(さん)**	wholesale store; wholesale dealer
ふ どう さん や **不動産屋(さん)**	real estate office; realtor
ころ や **殺し屋**	hit man; professional killer

NOTE: People who commit crimes, such as a "hit man", do not have さん added to their profession since they are generally not respected.

● 15-3. Building with kanji 院・館

Kanji can help us recognize that something is a building of some sort even if we don't know what type it is. Here are some common ones.

Buildings using 院

1. びょう いん
   病院
   hospital
2. い いん
   医院
   doctor's office; clinic
3. だい がく いん
   大学院
   graduate school
4. じ いん
   寺院
   temple
5. しゅう ぎ いん
   衆議院
   House of Representatives
6. しゅう どう いん
   修道院
   monastery; convent; abbey

Buildings using 館

1. び じゅつ かん
   美術館
   art gallery; art museum
2. はく ぶつ かん
   博物館
   museum
3. りょう じ かん
   領事館
   consulate
4. こう みん かん
   公民館
   community center; public hall
5. か がく かん
   科学館
   science museum
6. すい ぞく かん
   水族館
   aquarium

15 Words You Can Write 書ける言葉

医院（いいん） doctor's office; clinic

医 院

女医（じょい） woman doctor

女 医

院長（いんちょう） hospital director; head doctor

院 長

会館（かいかん） meeting hall; assembly hall

会 館

駅長（えきちょう） station manager

駅 長

駅前（えきまえ） in front of a station

駅 前

本屋（ほんや） book store

本 屋

屋台（やたい） food stall; stand

屋 台

宿屋（やどや） lodging; inn

宿屋

名医（めいい） noted doctor; excellent physician

名医

屋内（おくない） indoor (court, pool, etc.)

屋内

外科医（げかい） surgeon

外科医

終着駅（しゅうちゃくえき） arrival station; terminal station

終着駅

図書館（としょかん） library

図書館

雨宿り（あまやどり） taking shelter from rain

雨宿り

館内放送（かんないほうそう） announcement in a building

館内放送

15 Kanji Workbook Activities

● 1. Stroke Order Check 書き順確認

Each kanji has a stroke with an arrow on it. Write its order number below the kanji.

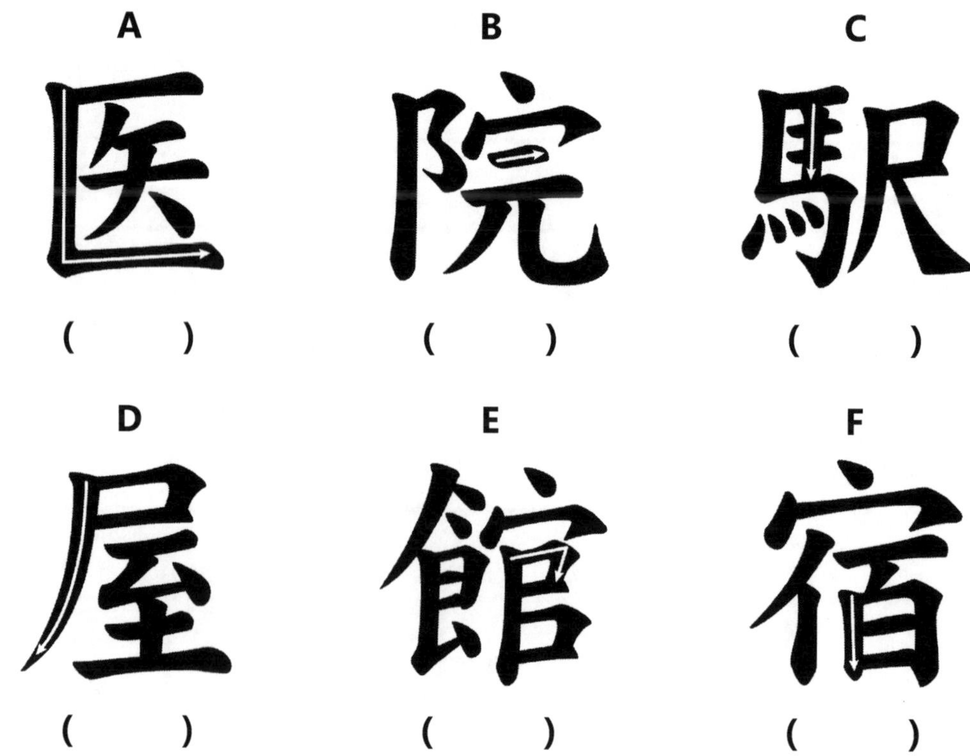

● 2. Kanji Readings

Write FURIGANA above the underlined kanji words.

1. 森医院では、いつも一時間ぐらい待たされます。
2. 図書館は、終着駅から五分のところにあります。
3. 北海道にいた時、屋外ライブに行きました。
4. 父は、アメリカ大使館ではたらいています。
5. 下宿するなら、駅の近くがいいです。

● 3. Kanji Meaning Match

Write the following kanji next to its meaning: 医 宿 係 院 館 登 駅 屋 負

1.____ lose　　2. ____ lodging　　3. ____ institution

4. ____ station　　5. ____ roof　　6. ____ climb

7. ____ mansion　　8. ____ medical　　9. ____ duty

● 4. Fill in the Kanji

Fill in the appropriate kanji in the blanks for each sentence.

い　しゃ　はなし　き　ほう

1. ___ ___の___を よく___いた___がいいです。

You should listen well to what the doctor says.

た　なか　くん　に　しゅう　かん　にゅう　いん

2. ___ ___ ___は___ ___ ___ 、___ ___しました。

Tanaka was in (the) hospital for two weeks.

きょ　う　えき　ちょう　やす

3. ___ ___ 、___ ___は お___みを いただいています。

Today the station master is taking a day off.

と　しょ　かん　ちか　や　た

4. ___ ___ ___ の ___くの ラーメン___で___べるのが すきです。

I like eating at the ramen shop near the library.

いま　かん　ない　ほう　そう　なが

5. ___、___ ___ ___ ___が___れています。

There is an in-building announcement going on right now.

はな　や　あま　やど

6. この___ ___で ___ ___りを しましょう。

Let's take shelter from the rain in this flower shop.

きん　よう　び　えき　まえ　あ

7. ___ ___ ___に___ ___で___いましょう。

Let's meet in front of the station on Friday.

5. Kanji Matching

Connect each kanji with an おん or くん reading. Use each reading only ONCE.

宿 •	• しゅく
屋 •	• とう
院 •	• や
表 •	• ひょう
医 •	• わらべ
投 •	• いん
駅 •	• えき
館 •	• かん
童 •	• い
放 •	• はな

15 Answer Key 答え合わせ

1. Stroke order check (answers)

A) 7　　B) 7　　C) 3

D) 3　　E) 13　　F) 8

3. Kanji meaning match (answers)

1. 負 lose	2. 宿 lodging	3. 院 institution
4. 駅 station	5. 屋 roof	6. 登 climb
7. 館 mansion	8. 医 medical	9. 係 duty

2. Kanji Readings (answers)

1. 森医院(もりいいん)では、いつも一時間(いちじかん)ぐらい待(ま)たされます。 At Mori Clinic, I'm always made to wait an hour.
2. 図書館(としょかん)は、終着駅(しゅうちゃくえき)から五分(ごふん)のところにあります。 The library is 5 minutes from the final station.
3. 北海道(ほっかいどう)にいた時(とき)、屋外(おくがい)ライブに行(い)きました。 When I was in Hokkaido, I went to an outdoor concert.
4. 父(ちち)は、アメリカ大使館(たいしかん)ではたらいています。 My father words at the American Embassy.
5. 下宿(げしゅく)するなら、駅(えき)の近(ちか)くがいいです。 If you're going to stay at a boarding house, it should be near a train station.

4. Fill in the kanji (answers)

1. 医者の話をよく聞いた方がいいです。
2. 田中君は二週間、入院しました。
3. 今日、駅長は お休みをいただいています。
4. 図書館の近くのラーメン屋で食べるのがすきです。
5. 今、館内放送が流れています。
6. この花屋で雨宿りをしましょう。
7. 金曜日に駅前で会いましょう。

5. Kanji matching (answers)

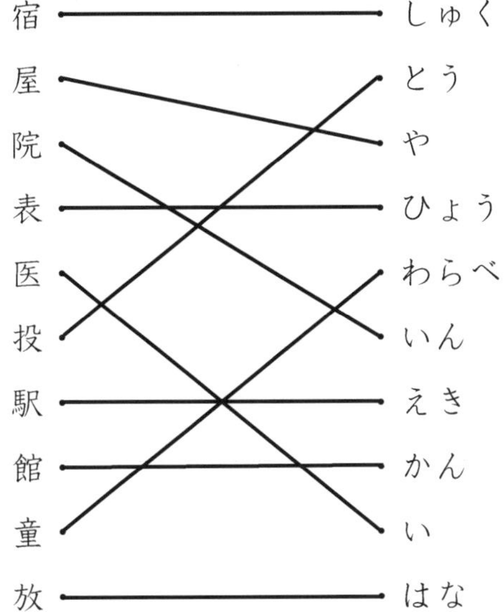

SR3 Kanji Lessons 10-15: Super Review 3

From the teacher...

Test your knowledge of the kanji learned in the last 5 lessons.

● 1. Build-a-Kanji 漢字の組み合わせ

Combine the left and right parts to make seven of the kanji learned in lessons 10-15.

RULES
1. You can use the radical and kanji parts as many times as you want.
2. Some kanji can use two kanji parts.

部首 (Radical)		
匚	日	广
辶	阝	亻
立	糸	力
宀	口	礻

Other Kanji Parts		
完	イ	反
門	一	東
田	矢	古
里	申	百

SAMPLE	1	2	3	4	5	6	7
返							

● 2. Okurigana drill 送り仮名ドリル

Circle the correct 漢字(かんじ) + 送り仮名(おくがな) combination.

1. あらわす	・表す	・表わす
2. まさる	・勝る	・勝さる
3. はなつ	・放つ	・放なつ
4. ながれる	・流る	・流れる
5. くばる	・配る	・配ばる
6. まける	・負る	・負ける

● 3. Kanji selection 漢字の選択

Select the best kanji to replace the underlined section of the sentence.

1. 弟は、学校でそうじの____をしています。
   A. 係　B. 者　C. 役　D. 配

2. 日本の古い____にとまりました。
   A. 院　B. 館　C. 屋　D. 宿

3. あの人は、____名な画家です。
   A. 有　B. 勝　C. 表　D. 遊

4. この公園では犬を____さないで下さい。
   A. 返　B. 放　C. 遊　D. 流

● 4. Kanji reading selection 読みの選択

Select the best reading for the underlined kanji.

1. この間、教会で神父様に会いました。
   A. かみ　B. かん　C. しん　D. じん

2. 運動会で勝負しましょう。
   A. か　B. まさ　C. しょう　D. ぶ

3. 表通りを歩くのがすきです。
   A. あらわ　B. おもて　C. ひょう　D. しょう

4. そこに落書きをしないで下さい。
   A. お　B. おと　C. らく　D. ら

● 5. Compound kanji word puzzle 熟語パズル

Fill in the correct kanji based on the list below the puzzle.

<table>
<tr><td>1)</td><td></td><td>2)</td><td></td></tr>
<tr><td></td><td>3)</td><td>4)</td><td></td></tr>
<tr><td>5)</td><td></td><td>6)</td><td>7)</td></tr>
<tr><td></td><td>8)</td><td>9)</td><td></td></tr>
</table>

Down ↓

English meaning	Hiragana
1) baby face	どうがん
2) God	かみさま
3) temple	じいん
5) doctor	いしゃ
7) relative	しんぞく

Left to Right →

English meaning	Hiragana
1) fairy story	どうわ
2) shrine	じんじゃ
4) appearance, condition	ようす
5) doctor's office	いいん
9) family	かぞく

← Right to Left

English meaning	Hiragana
2) myth	しんわ
6) hospitalization	にゅういん
8) actor, performer	やくしゃ

SR3 Answer Key 答え合わせ

1. Build-a-Kanji (answers) (order can vary)

SAMPLE 返 1) 問 2) 練 3) 院 4) 童 5) 神 6) 医 7)宿

2. Okurigana drill (answers)

1. あらわす	**・表す**	・表わす	4. ながれる	・流る	**・流れる**
2. まさる	**・勝る**	・勝さる	5. くばる	**・配る**	・配ばる
3. はなつ	**・放つ**	・放なつ	6. まける	・負る	**・負ける**

3. Kanji selection (answers)

1. A – そうじの係(かかり) My younger brother is in charge of cleaning at the school.
2. D – 宿(やど) I stayed in an old inn in Japan.
3. A – 有名(ゆうめい) That person is a famous artist.
4. B – 放(はな)さないで下(くだ)さい Don't let your dog loose in this park.

4. Kanji reading selection (answers)

1. C – 神父様(しんぷさま) The other day I met the priest at church.
2. C – 勝負(しょうぶ) Let's compete at the sports day event.
3. B – 表通り(おもてどお) I like walking the main street.
4. C – 落書き(らくが) Don't scribble there.

5. Compound kanji word puzzle (answers)

童	話	神	社
顔	寺	様	子
医	院	入	親
者	役	家	族

16 Kanji Lesson 16: 宮局所州県区

331-336

Kanji related to location

16 New Kanji 新しい漢字

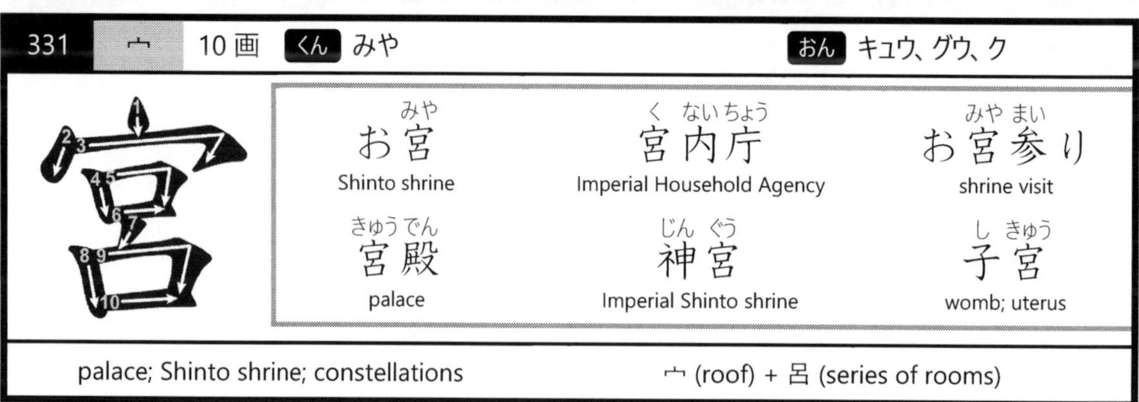

331	宀	10 画	くん みや	おん キュウ、グウ、ク

宮

みや お宮 Shinto shrine	く ないちょう 宮内庁 Imperial Household Agency	みや まい お宮参り shrine visit
きゅうでん 宮殿 palace	じん ぐう 神宮 Imperial Shinto shrine	し きゅう 子宮 womb; uterus

palace; Shinto shrine; constellations — 宀 (roof) + 呂 (series of rooms)

332	尸	7 画	くん none	おん キョク

局

すい どう きょく 水道局 water department	けっ きょく 結局 after all; in the end; eventually	やっ きょく 薬局 pharmacy; drugstore
ゆう びん きょく 郵便局 post office	し がい きょく ばん 市外局番 (telephone) area code	は きょく 破局 breakup; split; collapse

bureau; department; office; channel — 尸 (flag) + 句 (phrase)

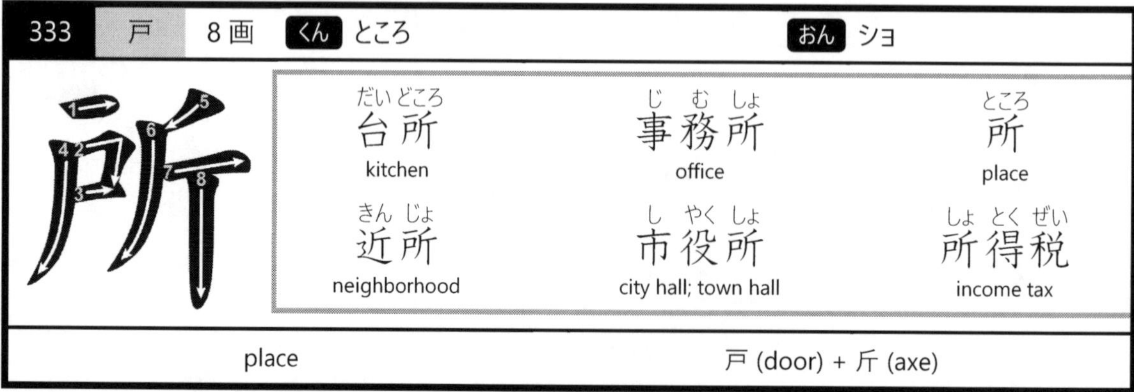

333	戸	8 画	くん ところ	おん ショ

所

だいどころ 台所 kitchen	じ む しょ 事務所 office	ところ 所 place
きん じょ 近所 neighborhood	し やく しょ 市役所 city hall; town hall	しょ とく ぜい 所得税 income tax

place — 戸 (door) + 斤 (axe)

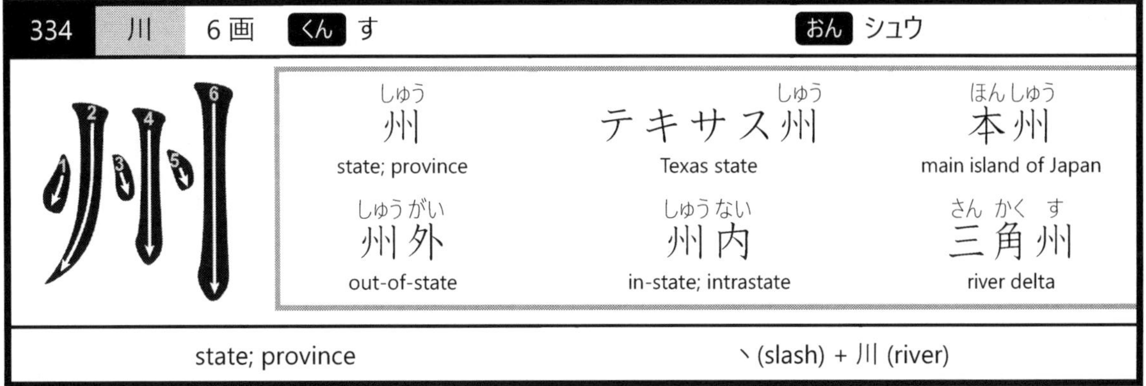

334	川	6 画	くん す	おん シュウ

しゅう 州 state; province	しゅう テキサス州 Texas state	ほんしゅう 本州 main island of Japan
しゅうがい 州外 out-of-state	しゅうない 州内 in-state; intrastate	さんかくす 三角州 river delta

state; province	丶 (slash) + 川 (river)

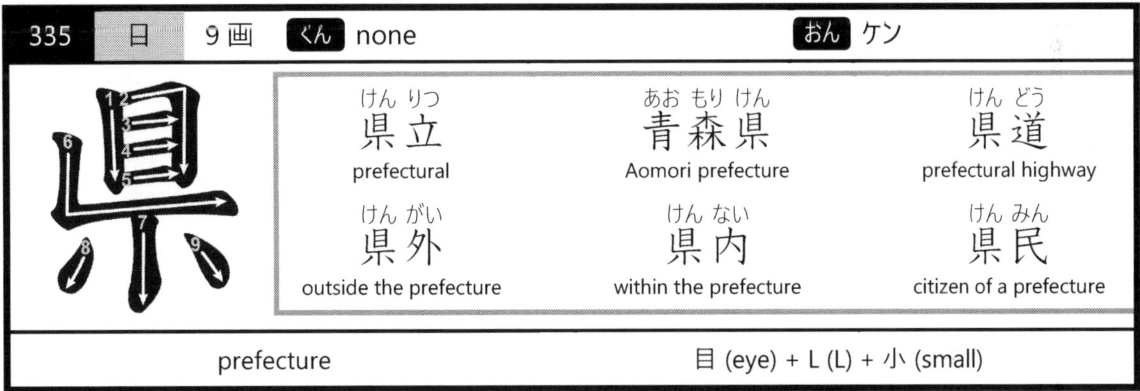

335	日	9 画	くん none	おん ケン

けんりつ 県立 prefectural	あおもりけん 青森県 Aomori prefecture	けんどう 県道 prefectural highway
けんがい 県外 outside the prefecture	けんない 県内 within the prefecture	けんみん 県民 citizen of a prefecture

prefecture	目 (eye) + L (L) + 小 (small)

336	匸	4 画	くん none	おん ク

くぎ 区切る to divide; to mark off	くかん 区間 section (of track); segment; interval	くべつ 区別 distinction; differentiation
ちく 地区 district; section; sector	くいき 区域 zone; territory; area; limits	くみん 区民 ward residents

district; region; county	匸 (hiding-box) + メ (X)

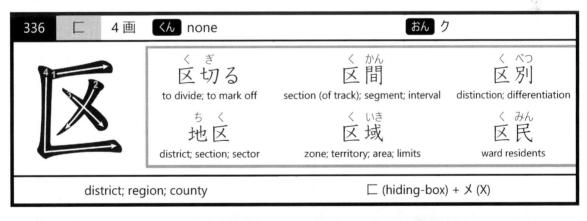

Kanji Parts used in the New Kanji

宀	roof	斤	axe	小	small
呂	spine	丶	slash	匸	hiding-box
尸	flag	川	river	メ	X
句	phrase	目	eye		
戸	door	L	L		

16 Kanji Memory Tools 漢字記憶術

This section helps you organically memorize kanji readings, meanings, and construction.

宮

宀 呂
A roof covering a series of rooms is a "**SHINTO SHRINE**".

今年(ことし)❶明治神宮(めいじじんぐう)を❷お宮参り(みやまい)したし、❸バッキンガム宮殿(きゅうでん)にも行(い)きました。

This year I made a ❷shrine visit to ❶Meiji Shrine and also went to ❸Buckingham Palace.

局

尸 句
The flag has the phrase "kanji is fun" at this "**BUREAU**".

❶結局(けっきょく)、❷薬局(やっきょく)と❸郵便局(ゆうびんきょく)の❹市外局番(しがいきょくばん)は同(おな)じだった。

The ❷pharmacy and ❸post office's ❹area code were the same ❶after all.

所

戸 斤
The door was destroyed with an axe at this "**PLACE**".

❶事務所(じむしょ)に❷台所(だいどころ)と寝(ね)る❸場所(ばしょ)が欲(ほ)しいです。

I want a kitchen and a place to sleep in the office. ❶neighborhood cat came close to the ❷kitchen window.

州

丶 川
We must slash the river budget in our "**STATE**".

❶九州(きゅうしゅう)に❷三角州(さんかくす)があります。

There is a ❷river delta in ❶Kyuushuu.

県

目 L 小
They keep an eye on the letter L in our small "**PREFECTURE**".

私(わたし)は❶兵庫県(ひょうごけん)の❷県立病院(けんりつびょういん)で生(う)まれました。

I was born at ❶Hyogo Prefecture's ❷prefectural hospital.

区

匚 メ
My hiding-box is buried at the X on this map of our "**DISTRICT**".

東京(とうきょう)は２３❶区(く)に❷区切(くぎ)られています。

Tokyo is ❶divided into 23 ❷districts.

16 Understanding Kanji Parts 漢字部分の理解

● 16-1. X marks the spot

The "X" inside of 区 is a variation of the 品 kanji which means "goods, article" or "elegance, grace". The original kanji used to be written as 區, but now is only written as 区. For the purposes of remembering how to write the kanji, we will be calling the メ part just, "X".

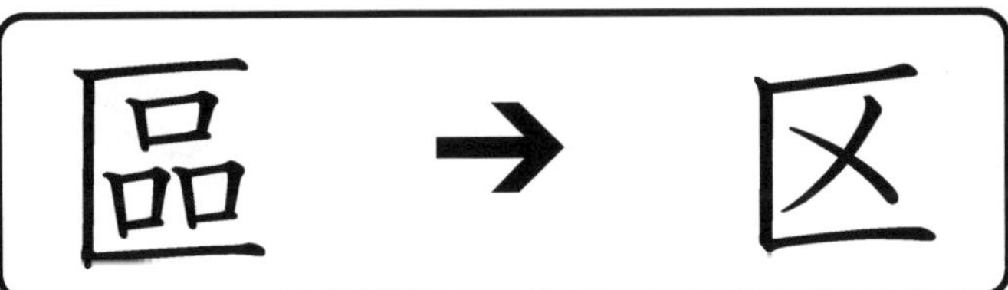

16 Kanji Usage 漢字の使い方

● 16-2. The states of kanji 州

When saying any of the 50 states from the United States, you will add 州 after them. Keep in mind that Japanese people tend to always properly say 州 after a state even though it sounds weird in English to always add it.

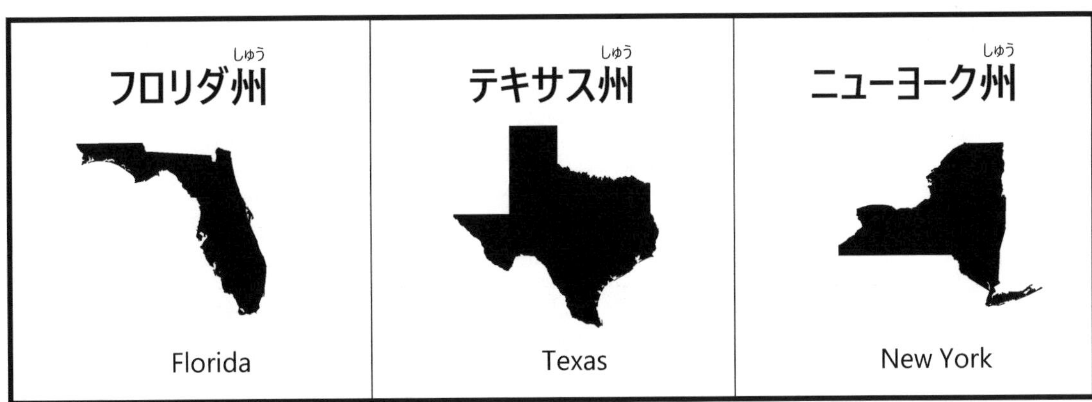

EXAMPLE SENTENCES

1. 私はネバダ州に住んでいます。
   I live in Nevada (state).
2. 私はカリフォルニア州で生まれました。
   I was born in California (state).

States in Japan??
Japan is made up of 4 main islands.

Two of the four main islands of Japan use 州 in their name.

However, they are not referred to as states.

The 州 is just part of their name.

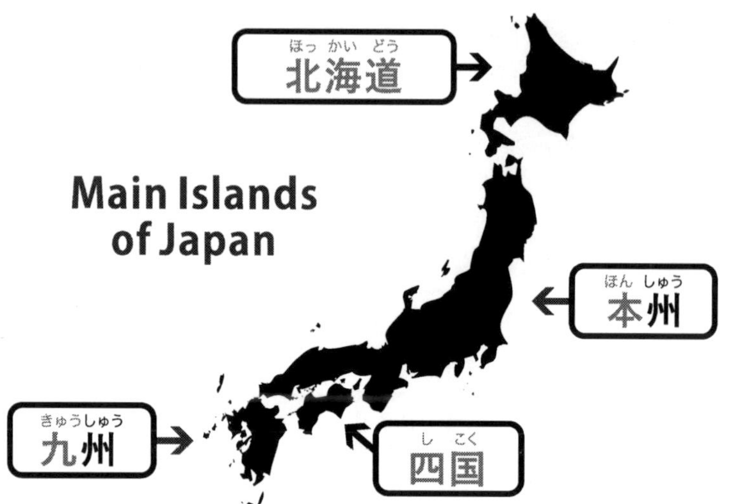

● 16-3. Tokyo divided by 区

Tokyo, one of the largest cities in the world by population and area, is split into 23 区(く) (districts). Here are Tokyo's 23 districts, referred to in Japanese simply as, 東京(とうきょう)２３区(く).

①千代田区(ちよだく)
②中央区(ちゅうおうく)
③港区(みなとく)
④新宿区(しんじゅくく)
⑤文京区(ぶんきょうく)
⑥台東区(たいとうく)
⑦墨田区(すみだく)
⑧江東区(こうとうく)
⑨品川区(しながわく)
⑩目黒区(めぐろく)
⑪大田区(おおたく)
⑫世田谷区(せたがやく)
⑬渋谷区(しぶやく)
⑭中野区(なかのく)
⑮杉並区(すぎなみく)
⑯豊島区(としまく)
⑰北区(きたく)
⑱荒川区(あらかわく)
⑲板橋区(いたばしく)
⑳練馬区(ねりまく)
㉑足立区(あだちく)
㉒葛飾区(かつしかく)
㉓江戸川区(えどがわく)

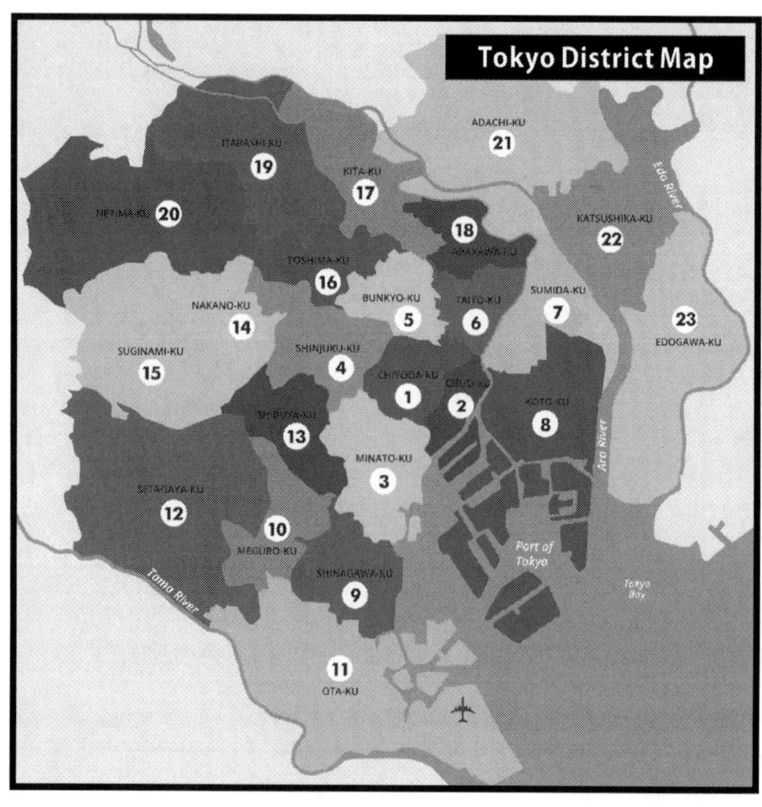

16-4. The royal kanji 宮

You might have noticed many words with 宮 seem to be related to royal things. Here are some interesting ones:

prince; princess (emperor's children)	Palace of the Dragon King
みや さま 宮様	りゅう ぐう じょう 竜宮城
The other words for "prince", 王子 (おうじ) and "princess", 王女 (おうじょ) only apply to children of a king. The emperor's children are called 宮様 (みやさま) which can mean "prince" or "princess" depending on gender. SIDE NOTE: While there have been many emperors throughout history, the only one left on earth is the on currently in Japan.	This is a fictional Palace, said to be located at the bottom of the sea, from the Japanese traditional story 浦島太郎 (うらしま・たろう). Read or listen to this story on ***From Zero!*** http://fromzero.com/japanese/stories/urashima-tarou

There two prefectures that have 宮 in their name.

Miyazaki Prefecture	Miyagi Prefecture
みや ざき けん 宮崎県	みや ぎ けん 宮城県
palace + cape (small peninsula)	palace + castle

16 Words You Can Write 書ける言葉

宮中（きゅうちゅう） imperial court

宮 中

王宮（おうきゅう） royal palace

王 宮

県道（けんどう） prefectural highway

県 道

長所（ちょうしょ） strong point; good point

長 所

所有（しょゆう） ownership; possession

所 有

州内（しゅうない） in-state

州 内

九州（きゅうしゅう） Kyushu (southernmost of the 4 main islands of Japan)

九 州

県立（けんりつ） prefectural

県 立

学区（がっく） school district; school area

学区

短所（たんしょ） demerit; weak point; disadvantage

短所

場所（ばしょ） place; location; spot; position; space

場所

州立（しゅうりつ） state-funded; state-supported

州立

水道局（すいどうきょく） waterworks department; water company

水道局

青森県（あおもりけん） Aomori prefecture

青森県

区切る（くぎる） to separate; to mark off

区切る

市外局番（しがいきょくばん） (telephone) area code

市外局番

16 Kanji Workbook Activities

● 1. Stroke Order Check 書き順確認

Each kanji has a stroke with an arrow on it. Write its order number below the kanji.

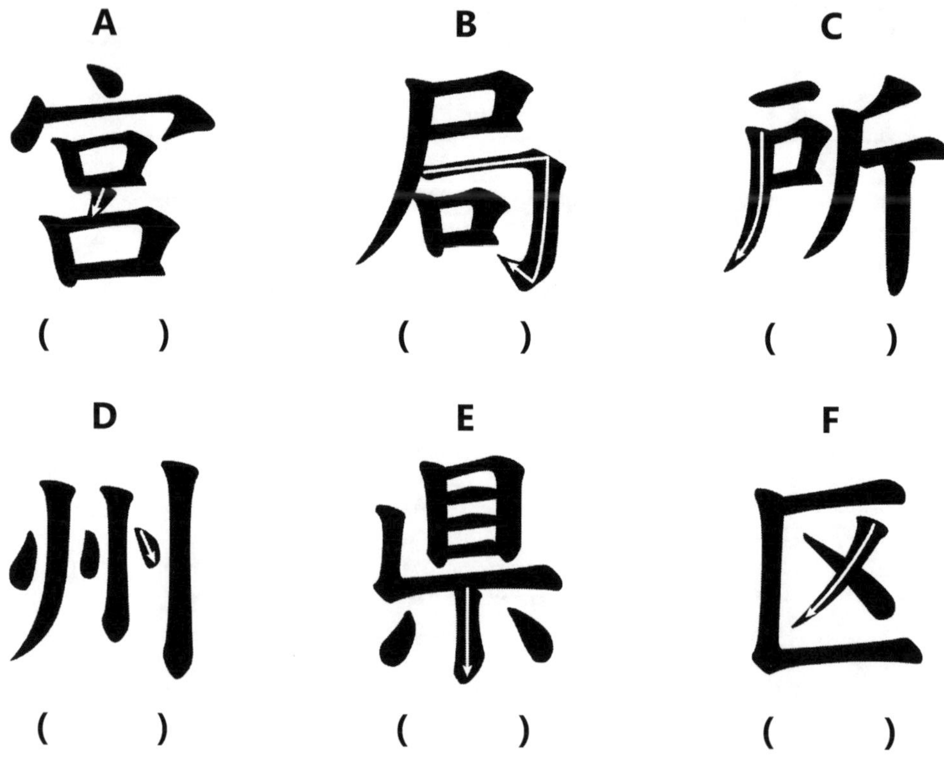

● 2. Kanji Readings

Write FURIGANA above the underlined kanji words.

1. 国王と王女は、王宮に住んでいます。
2. 住所がかわったので、市役所に行きました。
3. この州立図書館は大きいです。
4. 青森県つがる市の市外局番を教えて下さい。
5. 体育館を二つに区切って、バスケットボールをしました。

● 3. Kanji Meaning Match

Write the following kanji next to its meaning: 区 州 医 局 宮 駅 所 県 役

1.____ district 2. ____ place 3. ____ agency

4. ____ prefecture 5. ____ medical 6. ____ palace

7. ____ state 8. ____ station 9. ____ part; role

● 4. Fill in the Kanji

Fill in the appropriate kanji in the blanks for each sentence.

せん げつ みや い

1. ____ ____、お____ まいりに____きました。

I went to visit shrines last month.

ちち すい どう きょく

2. ____ は____ ____ ____で はたらいています。

My father works at the water company.

きん じょ こ あそ

3. むすめは よく____ ____ の____と____んでいます。

My daughter often plays with a neighborhood kid.

とも しゅう す

4. ____ だちは アメリカのネバダ____に____ んでいます。

My friend lives in Nevada, America.

あに けん りつ だい がく かよ

5. ____ は ____ ____ ____ ____に____っています。

My older brother is attending a prefectural college (university).

ち く がっ こう

6. あの ____ ____ には いい____ ____がたくさんあります。

There are a lot of good schools in that district.

きょく じゅう しょ しら

7. ゆうびん____の____ ____を____ べてほしいです。

I want you to find (look up) the address for the post office.

● 5. Kanji Matching

Connect each kanji with an おん or くん reading. Use each reading only ONCE.

宮 •	• く
客 •	• きゃく
定 •	• けん
区 •	• しゅう
県 •	• きゅう
局 •	• きょく
州 •	• しょ
所 •	• てい
相 •	• そう
童 •	• どう

16 Answer Key 答え合わせ

1. Stroke order check (answers)

A) 7 B) 4 C) 4
D) 5 E) 7 F) 2

3. Kanji meaning match (answers)

1. 区 district 2. 所 place 3. 局 agency
4. 県 prefecture 5. 医 medical 6. 宮 palace
7. 州 state 8. 駅 station 9. 役 part; role

2. Kanji Readings (answers)

1. 国王(こくおう)と王女(おうじょ)は、王宮(おうきゅう)に住(す)んでいます。 The king and the princess live in the royal palace.
2. 住所(じゅうしょ)がかわったので、市役所(しやくしょ)に行(い)きました。 I went to city hall because my address changed.
3. この州立(しゅうりつ)図書館(としょかん)は大(おお)きいです。 This state library is large.
4. 青森県(あおもりけん)つがる市(し)の市外局番(しがいきょくばん)を教(おし)えて下(くだ)さい。 Please tell me the area code of Aomori Prefecture, Tsugaru city.
5. 体育館(たいいくかん)を二(ふた)つに区切(くぎ)って、バスケットボールをしました。 We divided the gym into two and played basketball.

4. Fill in the kanji (answers)

1. 先月、お宮まいりに行きました。
2. 父は水道局で はたらいています。
3. むすめは よく近所の子と遊んでいます。
4. 友だちは アメリカのネバダ州に住んでいます。
5. 兄は 県立大学に通っています。
6. あの地区には いい学校がたくさんあります。
7. ゆうびん局の住所を調べてほしいです。

5. Kanji matching (answers)

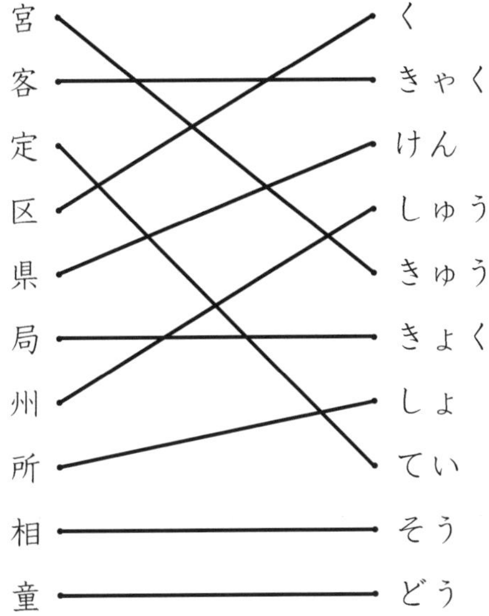

17 Kanji Lesson 17: 岸橋湖港庭畑

337-342

Kanji that is related to water and nature

17 New Kanji 新しい漢字

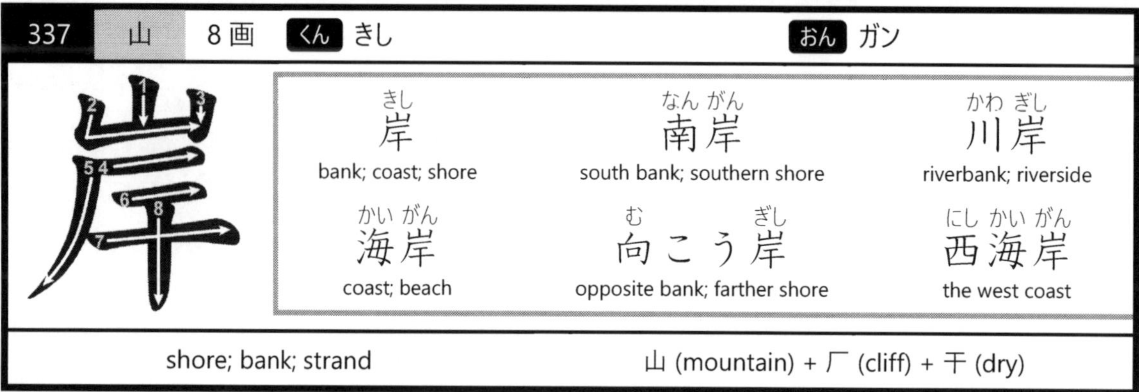

337 山 8画 くん きし おん ガン

きし 岸 bank; coast; shore	なんがん 南岸 south bank; southern shore	かわぎし 川岸 riverbank; riverside
かいがん 海岸 coast; beach	む ぎし 向こう岸 opposite bank; farther shore	にしかいがん 西海岸 the west coast

shore; bank; strand — 山 (mountain) + 厂 (cliff) + 干 (dry)

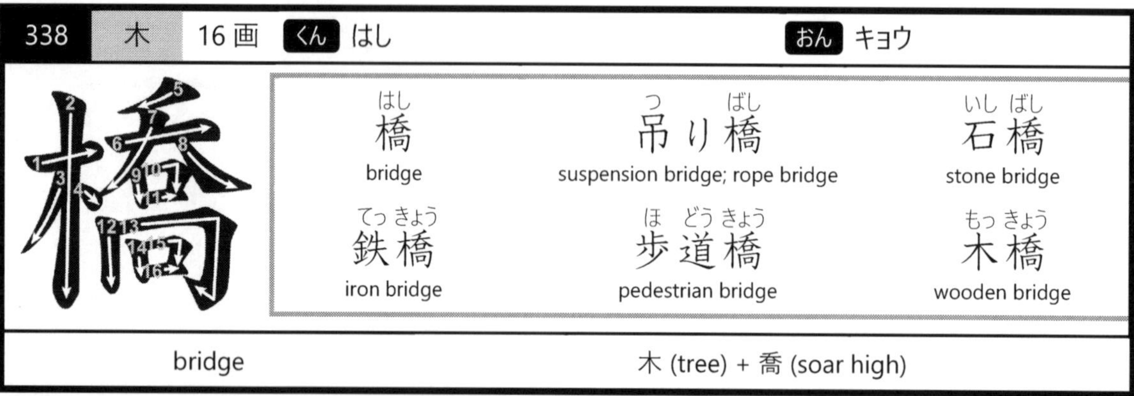

338 木 16画 くん はし おん キョウ

はし 橋 bridge	つ ばし 吊り橋 suspension bridge; rope bridge	いしばし 石橋 stone bridge
てっきょう 鉄橋 iron bridge	ほどうきょう 歩道橋 pedestrian bridge	もっきょう 木橋 wooden bridge

bridge — 木 (tree) + 喬 (soar high)

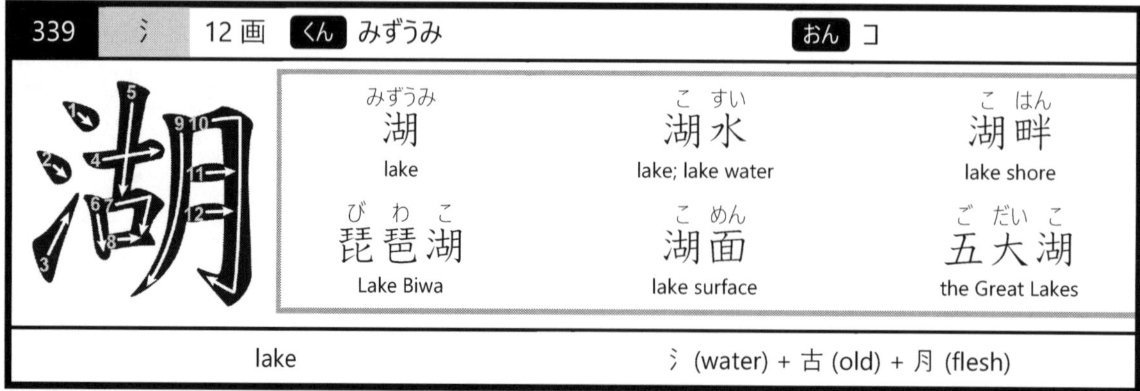

339 氵 12画 くん みずうみ おん コ

みずうみ 湖 lake	こすい 湖水 lake; lake water	こはん 湖畔 lake shore
びわこ 琵琶湖 Lake Biwa	こめん 湖面 lake surface	ごだいこ 五大湖 the Great Lakes

lake — 氵 (water) + 古 (old) + 月 (flesh)

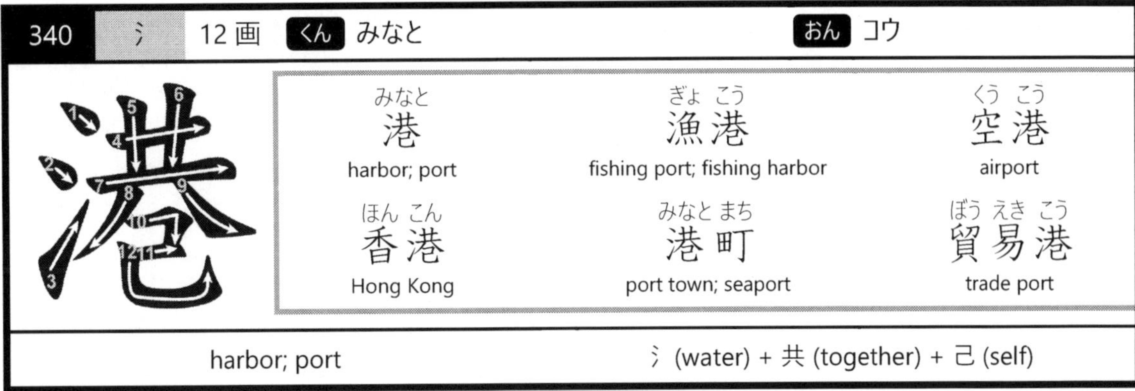

340	氵	12 画	くん みなと	おん コウ

港

みなと 港 harbor; port	ぎょ こう 漁港 fishing port; fishing harbor	くう こう 空港 airport
ほん こん 香港 Hong Kong	みなと まち 港町 port town; seaport	ぼう えき こう 貿易港 trade port

harbor; port	氵 (water) + 共 (together) + 己 (self)

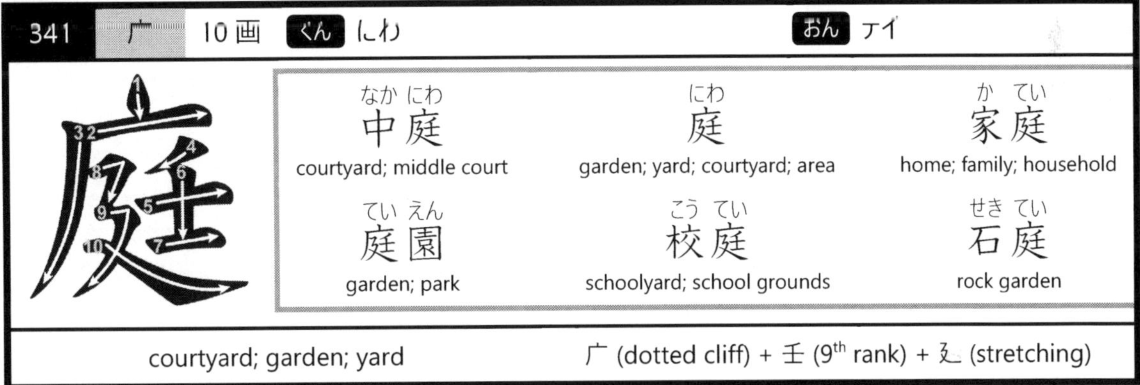

341	广	10 画	くん にわ	おん テイ

庭

なか にわ 中庭 courtyard; middle court	にわ 庭 garden; yard; courtyard; area	か てい 家庭 home; family; household
てい えん 庭園 garden; park	こう てい 校庭 schoolyard; school grounds	せき てい 石庭 rock garden

courtyard; garden; yard	广 (dotted cliff) + 壬 (9th rank) + 廴 (stretching)

342	田	9 画	くん はた、はたけ	おん none

畑

はたけ 畑 field; vegetable plot	た はた 田畑 fields (of rice and other crops)	はたけ ちが 畑違い out of one's field
はな ばたけ 花畑 field of flowers	はたけ し ごと 畑仕事 farming chores; field work	いちご ばたけ 苺畑 strawberry field (forever)

field; land	火 (fire) + 田 (rice field)

Kanji Parts used in the New Kanji

山	mountain	氵	water	广	dotted cliff
厂	cliff	古	old	廴	stretching
干	dry	月	flesh	壬	9th rank
木	tree	共	together	火	fire
喬	soar high	己	self	田	rice field

17 Kanji Memory Tools 漢字記憶術

This section helps you organically memorize kanji readings, meanings, and construction.

岸

山 厂 干
The mountain on the cliff is dry below until the "**SHORE**".

❶「海岸(かいがん)」は海(うみ)の❷岸辺(きしべ)で❸「川岸(かわぎし)」は川(かわ)の❹岸辺(きしべ)です。

❶"Kaigan" is the ❷shore of an ocean, and ❸"kawagishi" is the ❹shore of a river.

橋

木 喬
The tree that once soared high is now a "**BRIDGE**".

私(わたし)は❶吊(つ)り橋(ばし)や❷歩道橋(ほどうきょう)が高(たか)いから怖(こわ)いです。

I'm scared of ❶suspension bridges and ❷pedestrian bridges because they are high up.

湖

氵 古 月
The water is old and filled with flesh but it's still a "**LAKE**".

❶琵琶湖(びわこ)は❷湖(みずうみ)です。

❶Lake Biwa is a ❷lake.

港

氵 共 己
I think of water, us together, and myself at the "**PORT**".

❶空港(くうこう)には飛行機(ひこうき)、❷港(みなと)には船(ふね)があります。

At ❶the airport there are planes and at ❷the port there are boats.

庭

广 壬 廴
Below the dotted cliff is a 9th rank guard stretching in the "**GARDEN**".

日本(にほん)の❶家庭(かてい)の多(おお)くは❷庭(にわ)があります。

Many Japanese ❶households have a ❷ garden.

畑

火 田
Setting fire to a rice field improves the health of the "**FIELD**".

私(わたし)の苗字(みょうじ)は❶「畑中(はたなか)」なのに、❷畑(はたけ)の中(なか)には住(す)んでません。

Even though my is ❷"Hatanaka", I don't live in a ❶field.

17 Understanding Kanji Parts 漢字部分の理解

● 17-1. The "field" radical た (田)

Here are some common kanji that contain the 田 (た) radical.

Meaning	Kanji	Parts	Example 1	Meaning	Example 2	Meaning
rice field; rice paddy	田	field	田んぼ (た)	rice field	水田 (すいでん)	(water-filled) rice paddy
armor; high (voice); first class	甲	field + bottom sword	甲乙 (こうおつ)	first and second; A and B	生き甲斐 (い、がい)	something one lives for
have the honor to	申	field + middle sword	申す (もう)	to say; to be called	申し込み (もう、こ)	application; request
wherefore; a reason	由	field + upper sword	自由 (じゆう)	freedom; liberty	理由 (りゆう)	reason; motive
male	男	field + power	男の人 (おとこ、ひと)	man	長男 (ちょうなん)	eldest son; first-born son
brush-stroke; picture	画	one + field + upside down box	画面 (がめん)	screen; scene; picture	画家 (がか)	painter; artist
world; boundary	界	field + caregiving	世界 (せかい)	the world; society	限界 (げんかい)	limit; bound
farm; field; garden	畑	fire + field	麦畑 (むぎばたけ)	wheat field	畑仕事 (はたけしごと)	working in the fields; working on a farm

● 17-2. To split or not to split...

The 常用漢字 (じょうようかんじ) (Common Use Kanji) are the 2136 most commonly used kanji in Japan determined by the Japanese Ministry of Education. This list helps us determine the most efficient way to split up a kanji for the "Memorization Techniques" areas in this book.

There is often a debate as to split or not split a kanji. We often decide to split based on how we feel it will affect the student's ability to remember the kanji. In this lesson there are three kanji that we decided to split and one we decided to combine parts.

	Part of 橋 (bridge), 喬 means "soar high". We originally had split it into 夭 (drink) + 冋 (distant border) but realized that there are only two kanji in all of the *Common Use Kanji* that use either 夭 or 喬. So, there was no advantage in separating the parts.
	Part of 湖 (lake), 胡 means a variety of things including "barbarian" and "cover the ground". Since it's used in only ONE of the *Common Use Kanji*, we decided to split it into its smaller parts, 古 (old) and 月 (flesh), as they are commonly used with other kanji.
	Part of 港 (port), 巷 means, "road" amongst other things. However, it's only used in one *Common Use Kanji* so we chose to split into its more commonly used parts of 共 (together) and 己 (self)
	Part of 庭 (garden), 廷 means "imperial court", but its subparts, 廴 (stretching) and 壬 (9th rank) are FAR MORE common in the *Common Use Kanji*, so we decided splitting it had the most benefit for the learner.

● 17-3. The ten heavenly stems... 壬 is weird (a rant against kanji)

Kanji is often romanticized as a "story picture" and while there are many kanji that might have made logical sense when created over a thousand years ago, some stories certainly don't hold up in modern world.

With mnemonics (memory devices), it's often true that the more ridiculous the mnemonic, the easier the idea sticks. However, it was our goal to keep our mnemonic sentences relatively sane. We wrote our mnemonic sentences using the following rules:

1) The mnemonic sentence parts must appear in the same order as written.
2) The mnemonic sentence MUST end with the base meaning of the kanji.
3) "Power" words that distract from the kanji part meanings should be avoided.

When 壬 came up as part of 庭 in this lesson, the mnemonic sentence was truly a challenge. The meaning listed in dictionaries for 壬 is "9th rank". This led me to ask, "9th rank of what??" So, I started doing research.

It turns out there's a concept from ancient China, also adapted into Japan, called, 十干 (じっかん), which means, "the 10 heavenly stems". The 十干 is part of the *Chinese Five Elements* and *Yin-Yang* (darkness and light) which is part of 東洋学 (とうようがく) "Orientalism".

These "heavenly stems" are ranked from 1-10 with the 9th of these being 壬. If you are bored, you can read up on this as I did, but you might come away with more information clouding your head than required for remembering the kanji. Here is the list:

The 10 Heavenly Stems									
1	2	3	4	5	6	7	8	9	10
甲 (こう)	乙 (おつ)	丙 (へい)	丁 (てい)	戊 (ぼ)	己 (き)	庚 (こう)	辛 (しん)	壬 (じん)	辛 (しん)

Sometimes knowing the origin of the parts makes learning more complicated. Even an average Japanese person often hasn't heard of 十干 (じっかん). In fact, when I asked a few of my native Japanese friends, none of them were familiar with "the 10 heavenly stems".

An interesting common usage of the 十干 (じっかん) is that rank 1 and 2, 甲 (こう) and 乙 (おつ), are often used in contracts, with 甲 normally being "the company" and 乙 being "the contractor" or "other party" in the contract.

For me, the most interesting thing about the *10 heavenly stems* is that in Taiwan they use 甲乙丙丁戊 plus 優 (superior) in school report cards instead of A-B-C-D-F grades.

17 Kanji Usage 漢字の使い方

● 17-4. Famous landmarks in Japan 湖 橋 港 畑 庭

Here are some famous Japanese landmarks that have kanji from this lesson in their name.

Landmark	Why it's famous	Location
琵琶湖 (びわこ)	Largest lake in Japan	Shiga prefecture
サロマ湖 (こ)	Third largest lake in Japan	Hokkaido
明石海峡大橋 (あかしかいきょうおおはし)	Largest suspension bridge in the world	Links Kobe city and Awaji Island
瀬戸大橋 (せとおおはし)	Largest truss bridge in Japan World's longest two-tiered bridge system	Okayama prefecture
成田国際空港 (なりたこくさいくうこう)	Japan's busiest international airport	Chiba prefecture
関西国際空港 (かんさいこくさいくうこう)	The first offshore airport built on a completely man-made island	Osaka bay, Osaka
なよろひまわり畑 (ばたけ)	Sunflower field with approx. 5 million sunflowers that bloom in August	Nayoro City, Hokkaido
浜離宮恩賜庭園 (はまりっきゅうおんしていえん)	62-acre park located near Tokyo Bay surrounded by skyscrapers	Tokyo

17 Words You Can Write 書ける言葉

川岸（かわぎし） riverbank; riverside

川岸

海岸（かいがん） coast; seashore

海岸

石橋（いしばし） stone bridge

石橋

湖水（こすい） lake; lake water

湖水

港町（みなとまち） port town; seaport

港町

空港（くうこう） airport

空港

中庭（なかにわ） central courtyard

中庭

家庭（かてい） home; household

家庭

畑作（はたさく） dry field farming; dry field crop

畑 作

湖岸（こがん） lakeshore; lakeside

湖 岸

開港（かいこう） opening a port; starting operations at a port

開 港

帰港（きこう） returning to port

帰 港

庭木（にわき） garden tree

庭 木

火口湖（かこうこ） crater lake

火 口 湖

歩道橋（ほどうきょう） crossover bridge

歩 道 橋

ぶどう畑（ぶどうばたけ） vineyard

ぶ ど う 畑

17 Kanji Workbook Activities

● 1. Stroke Order Check 書き順確認

Each kanji has a stroke with an arrow on it. Write its order number below the kanji.

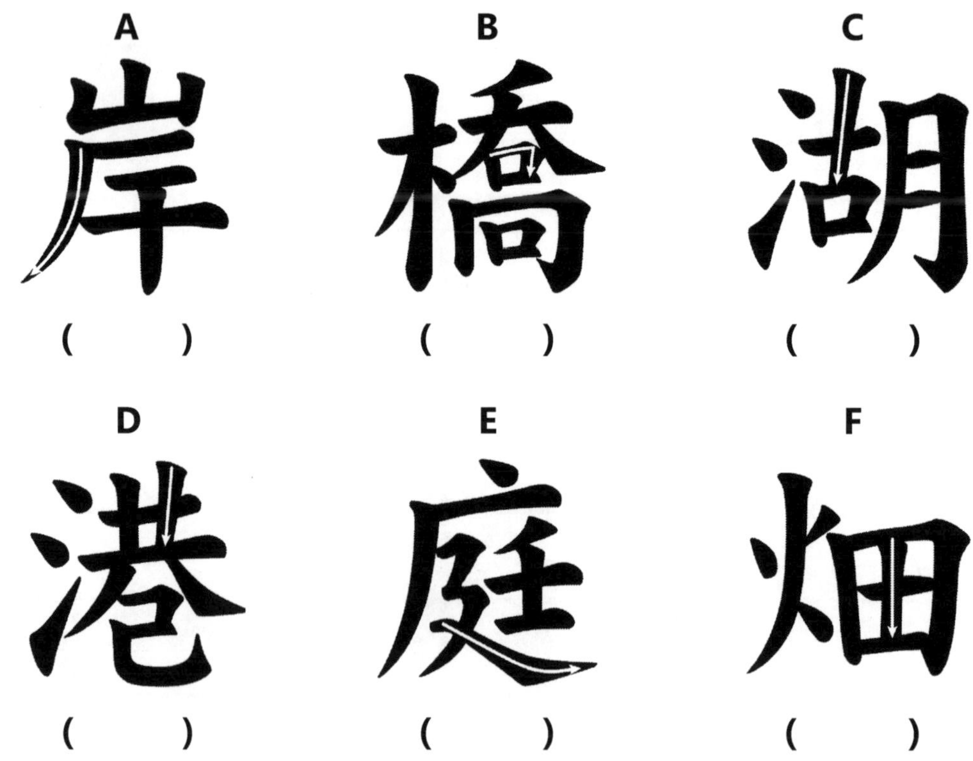

● 2. Kanji Readings

Write FURIGANA above the underlined kanji words.

1. あの橋で向こう岸に わたりましょう。
2. 今日の午後、湖岸を歩いてみませんか。
3. ロサンゼルスの空港で有名人に会いました。
4. 父は庭木の手入れをするのがすきです。
5. うちは、ぶどう畑を所有しています。

● 3. Kanji Meaning Match

Write the following kanji next to its meaning: 畑 港 橋 局 館 岸 湖 庭 県

1.____ shore 2. ____ prefecture 3. ____ harbor

4. ____ bridge 5. ____ agency; office 6. ____ garden

7. ____ lake 8. ____ mansion 9. ____ field

● 4. Fill in the Kanji

Fill in the appropriate kanji in the blanks for each sentence.

かい がん かい あつ
1. ___ ___ で___を ___めるのが すきです。
I like to collect shells at the beach.

ふる いし ばし いま つか
2. ローマは、___い___ ___が___も___われています。
In Rome, old stone bridges are being used even now.

はく ちょう みずうみ
3. バレエダンサーが「___ ___の ___ 」をおどりました。
The ballet dancer danced "Swan Lake".

みなと まち まい にち よ じ ふね で
4. あの___ ___ から___ ___ ___ ___ に ___ が ___ます。
A boat leaves from that port town every day at 4 o'clock.

うち なか にわ いぬ あそ
5. よく___の___ ___で___ と___びます。
I often play with our dog in our yard (courtyard).

はたけ ほう
6. ___ちがいな ことは、しない___がいいです。
It's better to not do something that's out of one's field.

くるま おお ほ どう きょう
7. ___が ___ いから、___ ___ ___をわたりましょう。
Since there's a lot of cars let's cross the pedestrian bridge.

● 5. Kanji Matching

Connect each kanji with an おん or くん reading. Use each reading only ONCE.

庭 •	• はたけ
湖 •	• しゅく
岸 •	• きし
畑 •	• しゅう
宿 •	• ぞく
族 •	• こ
港 •	• えき
橋 •	• はし
州 •	• てい
駅 •	• みなと

17 Answer Key 答え合わせ

1. Stroke order check (answers)

A) 5 B) 10 C) 5

D) 6 E) 10 F) 7

3. Kanji meaning match (answers)

1. 岸 shore 2. 県 prefecture 3. 港 harbor
4. 橋 bridge 5. 局 agency 6. 庭 garden
7. 湖 lake 8. 館 mansion 9. 畑 field

2. Kanji Readings (answers)

1. あの橋(はし)で向(む)こう岸(ぎし)に わたりましょう。 Let's cross to that opposite shore on that bridge.
2. 今日(きょう)の午後(ごご)、湖岸(こがん)を歩(ある)いてみませんか。 Why don't you walk the lakeshore this afternoon?
3. ロサンゼルスの空港(くうこう)で有名人(ゆうめいじん)に会(あ)いました。 I met a famous person at the Los Angeles airport.
4. 父(ちち)は庭木(にわき)の手入(てい)れをするのがすきです。 My father likes to take care of the garden trees.
5. うちは、ぶどう畑(ばたけ)を所有(しょゆう)しています。 We own a vineyard.

4. Fill in the kanji (answers)

1. 海岸で貝を集めるのがすきです。
2. ローマは、古い石橋が今も使われています。
3. バレエダンサーが「白鳥の湖」をおどりました。
4. あの港町から毎日四時に船が出ます。
5. よく家の中庭で犬と遊びます。
6. 畑ちがいなことは、しない方がいいです。
7. 車が多いから、歩道橋をわたりましょう。

5. Kanji matching (answers)

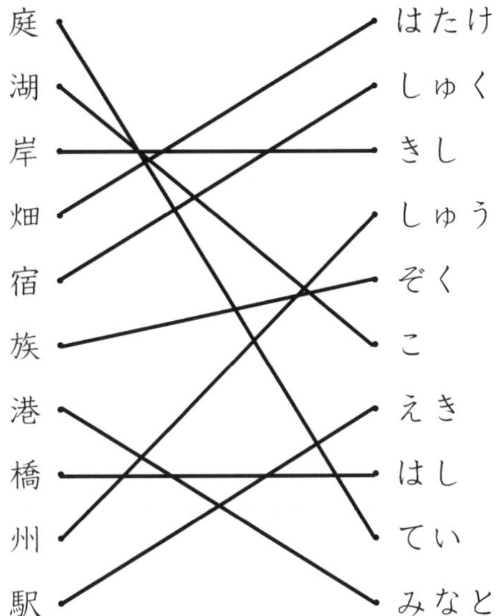

18 Kanji Lesson 18: 都島坂路庫式

343-348

Kanji related to places + plus one other

18 New Kanji 新しい漢字

343 阝 11 画 くん みやこ おん ト、ツ

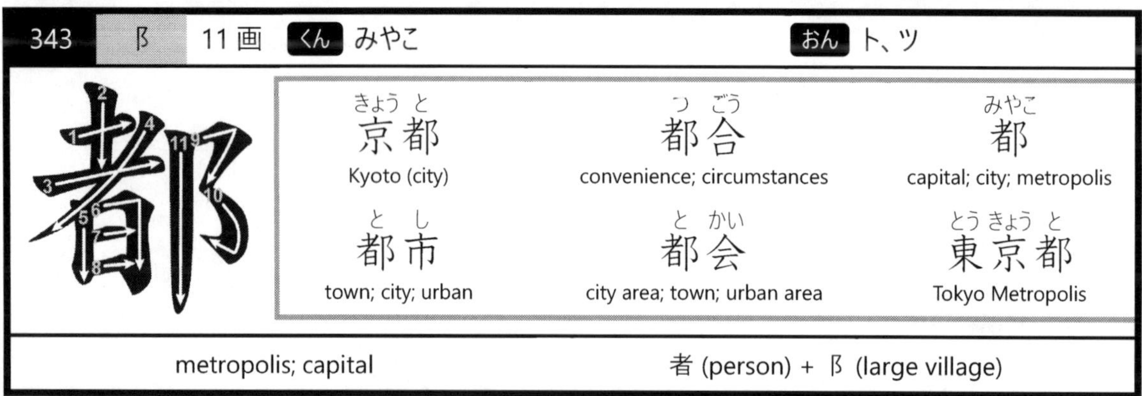

きょうと 京都 Kyoto (city)	つごう 都合 convenience; circumstances	みやこ 都 capital; city; metropolis
とし 都市 town; city; urban	とかい 都会 city area; town; urban area	とうきょうと 東京都 Tokyo Metropolis

metropolis; capital — 者 (person) + 阝 (large village)

344 山 10 画 くん しま おん トウ

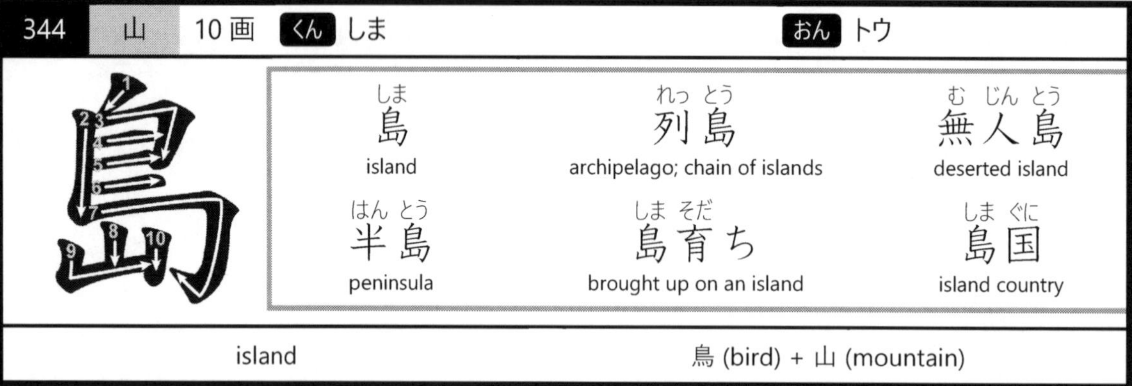

しま 島 island	れっとう 列島 archipelago; chain of islands	むじんとう 無人島 deserted island
はんとう 半島 peninsula	しまそだ 島育ち brought up on an island	しまぐに 島国 island country

island — 鳥 (bird) + 山 (mountain)

345 土 7 画 くん さか おん ハン

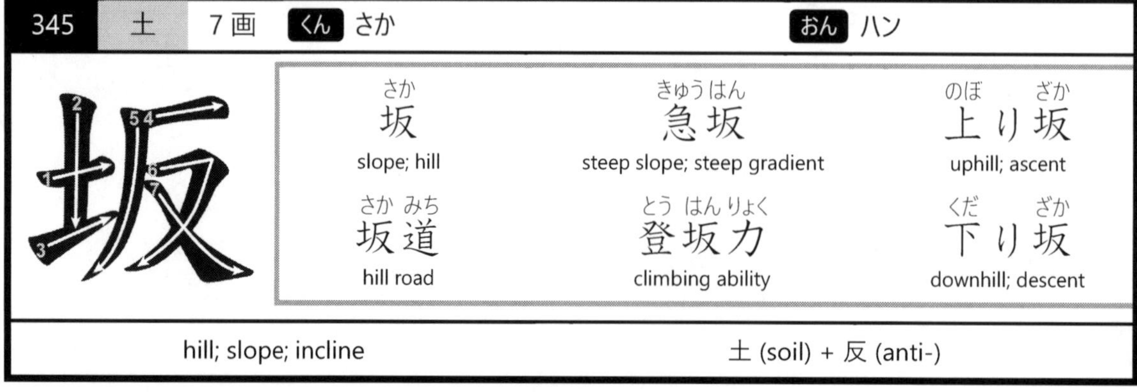

さか 坂 slope; hill	きゅうはん 急坂 steep slope; steep gradient	のぼ ざか 上り坂 uphill; ascent
さかみち 坂道 hill road	とうはんりょく 登坂力 climbing ability	くだ ざか 下り坂 downhill; descent

hill; slope; incline — 土 (soil) + 反 (anti-)

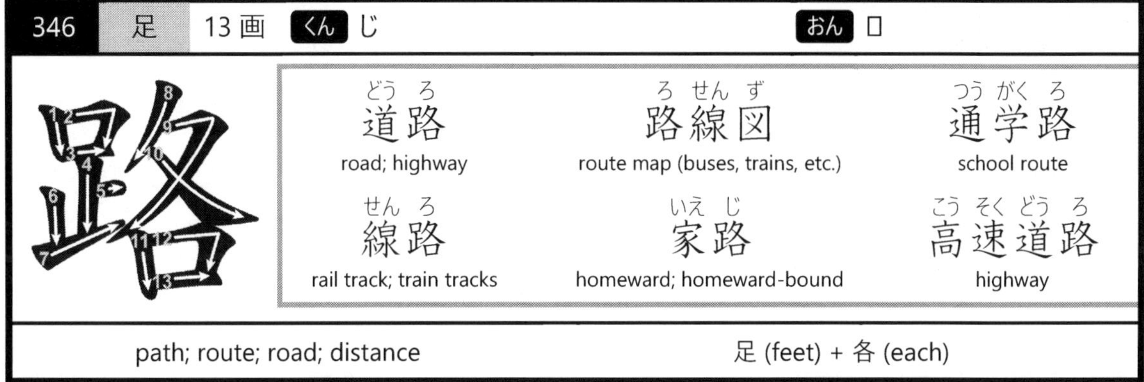

346 | 足 | 13 画 | くん じ | おん ロ

路

どうろ 道路 road; highway	ろせんず 路線図 route map (buses, trains, etc.)	つうがくろ 通学路 school route
せんろ 線路 rail track; train tracks	いえじ 家路 homeward; homeward-bound	こうそくどうろ 高速道路 highway

path; route; road; distance — 足 (feet) + 各 (each)

347 | 广 | 10 画 | くん none | おん コ、ク

庫

そうこ 倉庫 warehouse; storehouse	くり 庫裏 priest's quarters; temple kitchen	れいぞうこ 冷蔵庫 refrigerator
しゃこ 車庫 garage; carport	きんこ 金庫 safe; cashbox; depository	れいとうこ 冷凍庫 freezer

warehouse; storehouse — 广 (dotted cliff) + 車 (wheel)

348 | 弋 | 6 画 | くん none | おん シキ

式

しきじょう 式場 ceremonial hall	しき 式 ceremony; formula; style	すうしき 数式 mathematical formula
かいかいしき 開会式 opening ceremony	そつぎょうしき 卒業式 graduation ceremony	わしき 和式 Japanese style

ceremony; style; system; method — 工 (construction) + 弋 (bird trap)

Kanji Parts used in the New Kanji

者	person	土	soil	广	dotted cliff
阝	large village	反	anti-	車	wheel
鳥	bird	足	feet	工	construction
山	mountain	各	each	弋	bird trap

18 Kanji Memory Tools 漢字記憶術

This section helps you organically memorize kanji readings, meanings, and construction.

都

者 阝
Many persons in a large village make it a "METROPOLIS".

❶京都（きょうと）の❷都（みやこ）ホテルに泊（と）まりました。

I stayed in a ❷Miyako (metropolitan) hotel in ❶Kyoto.

島

鳥 山
The bird flew to the mountain on the "ISLAND".

❶島国（しまぐに）の日本（にほん）には、❷無人島（むじんとう）が六千以上（ろくせんいじょう）あります。

There are over 6,000 ❷uninhabited islands in the ❶island country of Japan.

坂

土 反
Flat soil is the anti-thesis of a "SLOPE".

❶坂道（さかみち）に❷「急坂注意（きゅうはんちゅうい）」の標識（ひょうしき）がありました。

On the ❶sloped road there was "❷steep incline warning" sign ❷steep slopes around my house.

路

足 各
Your feet must each be on the "PATH".

この❶道路（どうろ）の先（さき）は❷袋小路（ふくろこうじ）です。

Ahead of this ❶road is a ❷blind alley.

庫

广 車
Below the dotted cliff there is a wheel "WAREHOUSE".

❶庫裏（くり）にはお坊（ぼう）さんがいて、❷車庫（しゃこ）には車（くるま）があります。

In the ❶priest's quarters is a monk, and in the ❷garage there is a car.

式

工 弋
The construction of the bird trap was my "STYLE".

❶和式（わしき）の❷結婚式（けっこんしき）に❸正式（せいしき）に招待（しょうたい）された。

I've been ❸officially invited to a ❶Japanese style ❷wedding ceremony.

18 Understanding Kanji Parts 漢字部分の理解

● 18-1. The "dotted cliff" radical まだれ (广)

Even though the meaning of this radical is "dotted cliff," it represents a roof on a house. It's often used with kanji related to buildings.

warehouse; storehouse		wide; broad; spacious	
庫 dotted cliff + wheel	きんこ **金庫** safe; cashbox そうこ **倉庫** storehouse; warehouse	広 dotted cliff + MU	ひろ **広い** wide; spacious ひろば **広場** plaza; open space

store; shop		courtyard; garden; yard	
店 dotted cliff + fortune telling	みせ **お店** store; shop; restaurant しょてん **書店** bookshop; bookstore	庭 dotted cliff + court	にわ **庭** garden; yard; courtyard こうてい **校庭** schoolyard; playground

floor; bed; padding		squat; seat; cushion; sit	
床 dotted cliff + tree	ゆか **床** floor ねどこ **寝床** bed; crib; kip	座 dotted cliff + sit	すわ **座る** to sit; to squat こうざ **口座** account (e.g. bank)

bottom; sole; depth		urban prefecture; govt office	
底 dotted cliff + ancient tribe	そこ **底** bottom; sole かいてい **海底** bottom of the ocean; undersea	府 dotted cliff + attach	せいふ **政府** government; administration ふりつ **府立** urban prefecture managed; prefectural

● 18-2. Where you place the village is important こざとへん

In this lesson, we learned 都 which has 阝 as its second part (on the right). We have already learned kanji that have 阝 on the left of the kanji. Depending on where the 阝 is located in the kanji, the name of the part and its meaning are slightly different.

When on the left, 阝 is called こざとへん and means, "small village" and when it's on the right, it's called おおざと meaning "large village". Note that there isn't へん in the name of おおざと.

18 Kanji Usage 漢字の使い方

● 18-3. When and why 大坂 changed to 大阪

First it's important to know that 反 can mean not only "anti-" as a part, but it can also mean "to return" or "go back". 反 is a part the 阪 kanji in the large city 大阪 (おおさか).

Prior to 1968, the city of Osaka 大阪 was written as, 大坂 (おおさか). If you compare the characters, you can see that the left part of the kanji is different.

The original character 坂 (さか), meaning "slope, incline", when broken can mean "returning to the soil" which is symbolic for death. To avoid this meaning, during the Meiji restoration period, the 土 (soil) radical was changed to 阝 (village).

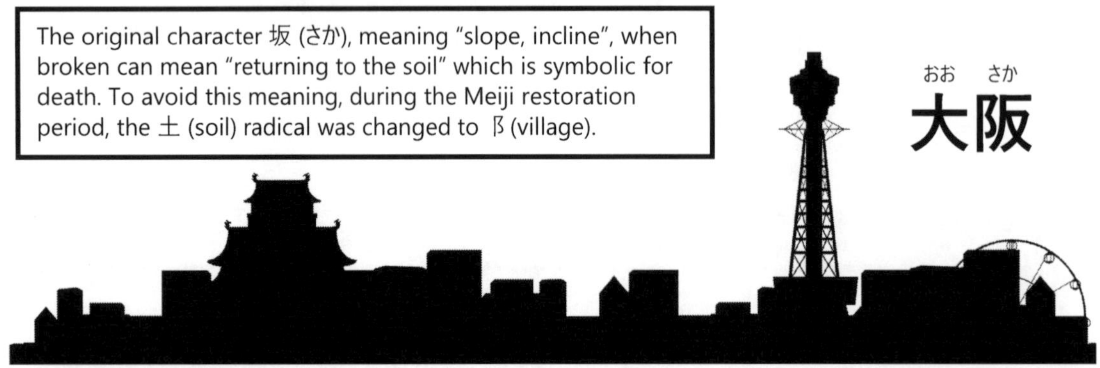

● 18-4. There are more than just prefectures in Japan

You might have heard there are 47 prefectures in Japan. Indeed there are 47 areas that are collectively called 都道府県 (administrative divisions of Japan), but only 43 of them are designated as 県 (prefecture).

Let's look at the 4 classifications:

都 Large Metropolitan Area — Kanji From Zero! ❷ Lesson 18

東京都 is the only area designated as 都 in Japan. 都 is used for "larqe metropolitan area". 都 is part of the words 都市 (city) and 大都市 (metropolis).

道 Road — Kanji From Zero! ❶ Lesson 32

北海道 is the northernmost of the 4 main Japanese islands. 道 means "road". With 東京都 the 都 can be removed and the area still be recognized as simply, 東京 but with 北海道 its designation of 道 is never removed from its name.

府 Urban Prefecture — Kanji From Zero! ❸ Lesson 13

京都府 and 大阪府 are the two remaining 府 in Japan. Before becoming 東京都, 東京 was referred to as 東京府 and before that 江戸府 . In modern Japan, 府 and 県 are similar and both are translated as just "prefecture".

県 Prefecture — Kanji From Zero! ❷ Lesson 16

The remaining 43 areas are all designated as 県, from 青森県 in the north, to 沖縄県 in the most southern reaches of the Japan archipelago.

● 18-5. Small differences, different meanings 鳥

It's fun when kanji follows easy-to-understand storylines. 島 (island) from this lesson and a few others containing 鳥 (bird) are great examples of kanji that make sense.

BIRD
The four bottom strokes of 鳥 represents the folded wings. The horizontal stroke inside of the box represents the eye of the bird.

ISLAND
島 is created with 山 (mountain) and 鳥 (bird). The original meaning was of an ocean bird stopping on a rocky mountain.

CROW; RAVEN
烏 has one stroke less than 鳥 (bird). Due to a crow's black color, the eye can't be seen. It's said that this is why there isn't a visible line in the box part of the kanji.

PIGEON; DOVE
You might ask, why 九 (nine) is in 鳩. For fun we can imagine that the reason is due to a pigeons cry being 「クー」, which is similar to number 9 in Japanese.

TO SING / CRY / CHIRP (BIRDS)
口 (mouth) is added to 鳥 (bird) to create the verb used for a "chirp".

18 Words You Can Write 書ける言葉

首都（しゅと） capital city; metropolis

首 都

都心（としん） city center; urban centre

都 心

半島（はんとう） peninsula

半 島

島国（しまぐに） island country; island nation

島 国

坂道（さかみち） hill road

坂 道

路上（ろじょう） (on the) road; (in the) street

路 上

路線（ろせん） route; line; alignment

路 線

金庫（きんこ） safe; cashbox

金 庫

車庫（しゃこ） garage; depot (trains, buses, etc.)

車庫

式場（しきじょう） ceremonial hall

式場

文庫（ぶんこ） book collection; paperback book

文庫

大都会（だいとかい） big city

大都会

上り坂（のぼりざか） uphill; ascent

上り坂

入学式（にゅうがくしき） entrance ceremony

入学式

東京都（とうきょうと） Tokyo Metropolis; Tokyo metropolitan area

東京都

高速道路（こうそくどうろ） highway; freeway

高速道路

18 Kanji Workbook Activities

● 1. Stroke Order Check 書き順確認

Each kanji has a stroke with an arrow on it. Write its order number below the kanji.

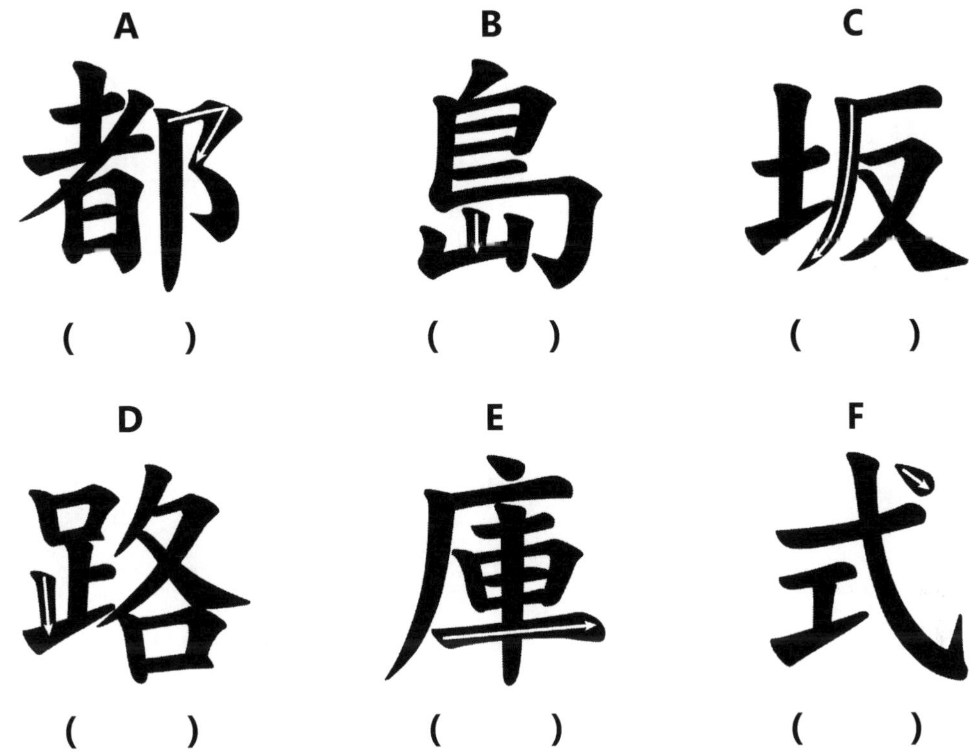

● 2. Kanji Readings

Write FURIGANA above the underlined kanji words.

1. すみませんが、今日は都合が悪いんです。
2. わたしは島育ちで、都会に行ったことがありません。
3. 上り坂はきついけど、下り坂は楽です。
4. わたしは毎日、高速道路を使います。
5. 車を後ろから車庫に入れるのが 苦手です。

● 3. Kanji Meaning Match

Write the following kanji next to its meaning: 畑 式 路 州 島 都 庫 坂 庭

1.____ garden 2. ____ road 3. ____ state

4. ____ storage 5. ____ field 6. ____ slope

7. ____ island 8. ____ ceremony 9. ____ metropolitan

● 4. Fill in the Kanji

Fill in the appropriate kanji in the blanks for each sentence.

だい と かい せい かつ

1. ___ ___ ___ で___ ___してみたいです。

I want to try living in a big city.

に ほん しま ぐに

2. ___ ___ は ___ ___です。

Japan is an island country.

さか みち ころ お

3. ボールが___ ___ を___ がり___ちました。

The ball rolled down the sloped road.

せん ろ ちか あたら

4. ___ ___の___くに___ しいマンションが たちました。

There are new apartments near the train tracks.

かね きん こ い

5. パスポートとお___をホテルの___ ___に___れましょう。

Let's put our passports and money in the hotel safe.

に ほん し がつ にゅう がく しき

6. ___ ___ では、___ ___に ___ ___ ___があります。

In Japan, there are school entrance ceremonies in April.

つう がく ろ くるま おお

7. この___ ___ ___は___が___くて、あぶないです。

This school route is dangerous as there are many cars.

● 5. Kanji Matching

Connect each kanji with an おん or くん reading. Use each reading only ONCE.

式 •	• こ
都 •	• と
庫 •	• しき
配 •	• きゃく
島 •	• とう
客 •	• ろ
路 •	• はい
宿 •	• やど
坂 •	• や
屋 •	• さか

18 Answer Key 答え合わせ

1. Stroke order check (answers)

A) 9　　B) 8　　C) 5
D) 6　　E) 9　　F) 6

3. Kanji meaning match (answers)

1. 庭 garden　2. 路 road　3. 州 state
4. 庫 storage　5. 畑 field　6. 坂 slope
7. 島 island　8. 式 ceremony　9. 都 metropolitan

2. Kanji Readings (answers)

1. すみませんが、今日(きょう)は都合(つごう)が悪(わる)いんです。　Excuse me but today isn't good for me.
2. わたしは島育(しまそだ)ちで、都会(とかい)に行(い)ったことがありません。　Being island-raised, I've never been to a large city.
3. 上(のぼ)り坂(ざか)はきついけど、下(くだ)り坂(ざか)は楽(らく)です。　Uphill is tough, but downhill is easy.
4. わたしは毎日(まいにち)、高速道路(こうそくどうろ)を使(つか)います。　I use the highway every day.
5. 車(くるま)を後(うし)ろから車庫(しゃこ)に入(い)れるのが 苦手(にがて)です。　I'm not good at putting my car in the garage in from the back.

4. Fill in the kanji (answers)

1. 大都会で生活してみたいです。
2. 日本は島国です。
3. ボールが坂道を転がり落ちました。
4. 線路の近くに新しいマンションがたちました。
5. パスポートとお金をホテルの金庫に入れましょう。
6. 日本では、四月に入学式があります。
7. この通学路は車が多くて、あぶないです。

5. Kanji matching (answers)

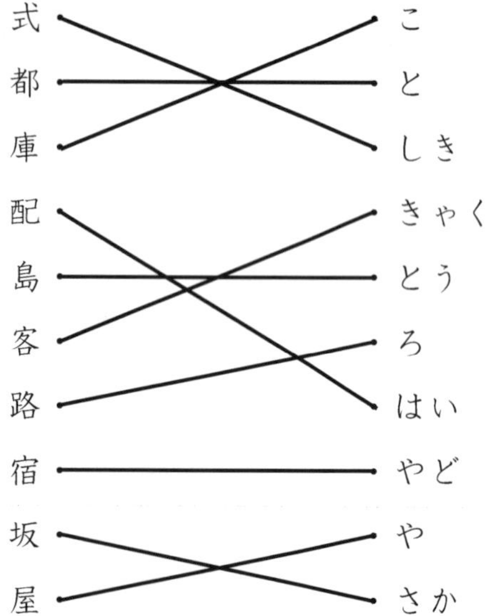

19 Kanji Lesson 19: 度等倍秒部列

349-354

Kanji that can be used as "counter" words

19 New Kanji 新しい漢字

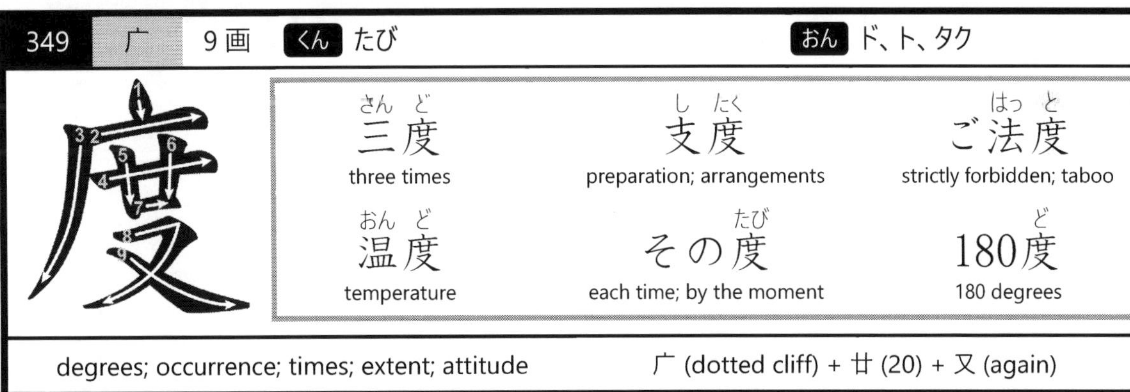

349 | 广 | 9画 | くん たび | おん ド、ト、タク

三度 (さんど) three times
支度 (したく) preparation; arrangements
ご法度 (ごはっと) strictly forbidden; taboo
温度 (おんど) temperature
その度 (そのたび) each time; by the moment
180度 (180ど) 180 degrees

degrees; occurrence; times; extent; attitude
广 (dotted cliff) + 廿 (20) + 又 (again)

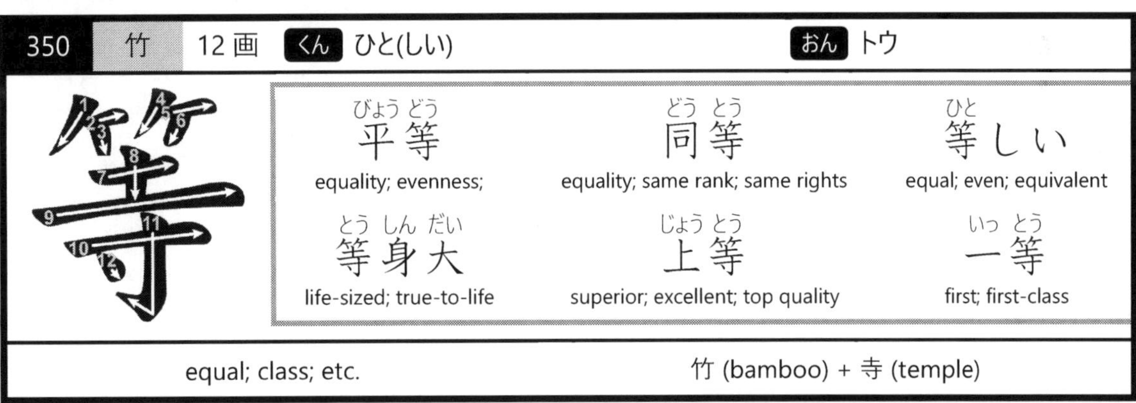

350 | 竹 | 12画 | くん ひと(しい) | おん トウ

平等 (びょうどう) equality; evenness;
同等 (どうとう) equality; same rank; same rights
等しい (ひとしい) equal; even; equivalent
等身大 (とうしんだい) life-sized; true-to-life
上等 (じょうとう) superior; excellent; top quality
一等 (いっとう) first; first-class

equal; class; etc.
竹 (bamboo) + 寺 (temple)

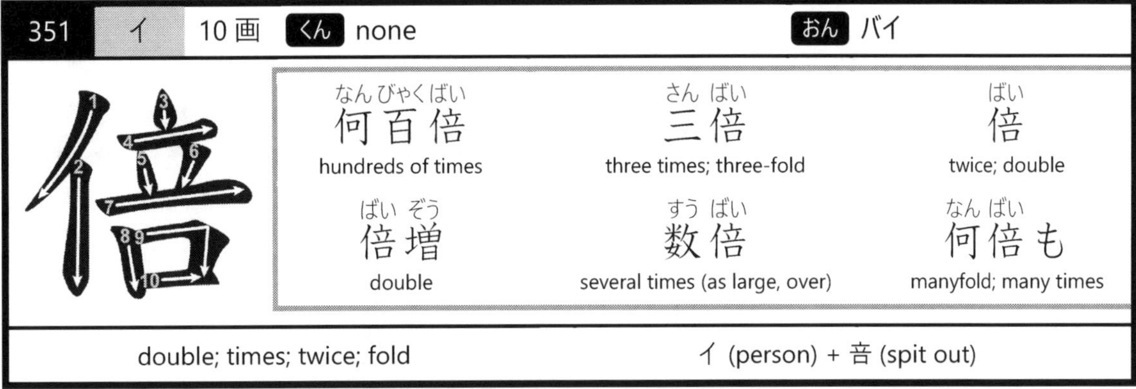

351 | イ | 10画 | くん none | おん バイ

何百倍 (なんびゃくばい) hundreds of times
三倍 (さんばい) three times; three-fold
倍 (ばい) twice; double
倍増 (ばいぞう) double
数倍 (すうばい) several times (as large, over)
何倍も (なんばいも) manyfold; many times

double; times; twice; fold
イ (person) + 咅 (spit out)

352	禾	9 画	くん none	おん ビヨウ

秒

いちびょう 一秒 one second	びょう よ 秒読み countdown; second reading	まいびょう 毎秒 every second
びょうそく 秒速 per second	すうびょう 数秒 several seconds	びょうしん 秒針 second hand of a clock

second (1/60 minute) — 禾 (grain stalk) + 少 (few)

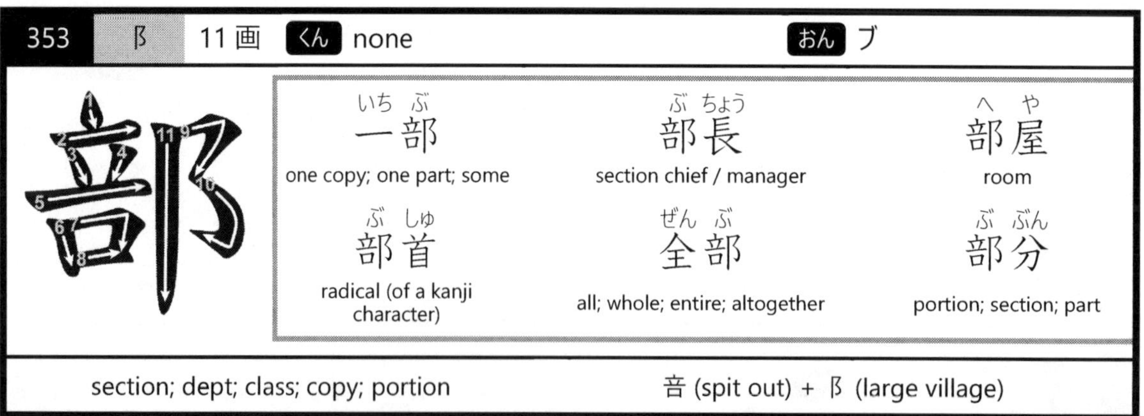

353	阝	11 画	くん none	おん ブ

部

いち ぶ 一部 one copy; one part; some	ぶ ちょう 部長 section chief / manager	へ や 部屋 room
ぶ しゅ 部首 radical (of a kanji character)	ぜん ぶ 全部 all; whole; entire; altogether	ぶ ぶん 部分 portion; section; part

section; dept; class; copy; portion — 音 (spit out) + 阝 (large village)

354	刂	6 画	くん none	おん レツ

列

に れつ 二列 two lines; double file	れっ とう 列島 archipelago; chain of islands	れつ 列 row; line; file
れっ しゃ 列車 railway train	ぎょうれつ 行列 a line; a queue; parade	さい ぜん れつ 最前列 front row

line; row; rank; chain; column — 歹 (bare bone) + 刂 (knife)

Kanji Parts used in the New Kanji

广	dotted cliff	寺	temple	少	few
廿	20	亻	person	阝	large village
又	again	音	spit out	歹	bare bone
竹	bamboo	禾	grain stalk	刂	knife

19 Kanji Memory Tools 漢字記憶術

This section helps you organically memorize kanji readings, meanings, and construction.

度

广 廿 又
The dotted cliff was 20 degrees again. This is the 3rd "**OCCURRENCE**".

旅行(りょこう)の❶支度(したく)をする❷度(たび)に疲(つか)れるから、❸今度(こんど)はしたくない。

❷Every time I ❶prepare for a trip, I get tired so I don't want to do it ❸next time.

等

竹 寺
Bamboo can be at temples "**ETC**".

国民(こくみん)は法(ほう)の下(もと)で❶等(ひと)しく❷平等(びょうどう)です。

Citizens are ❶equally ❷equal under the law.

倍

亻 咅
That person spit out gum three "**TIMES**".

給料(きゅうりょう)が❶二倍(にばい)になったけど、家賃(やちん)も❷倍増(ばいぞう)した。

My salary ❶doubled but my rent also ❷doubled.

秒

禾 少
The grain stalk was invisible for a few "**SECONDS**".

❶数秒前(すうびょうまえ)に❷秒針(びょうしん)が❸三秒間(さんびょうかん)止(と)まった。

A ❶few seconds ago the ❷second hand of the clock stopped for a ❸period of three seconds.

部

咅 阝
Please spit out all of your food in this large village or just a "**PORTION**".

この❶部屋(へや)に必要(ひつよう)な❷部品(ぶひん)が❸全部(ぜんぶ)あります。

❸All of the necessary ❷parts are in this ❶room.

列

歹 刂
The bare bone was next to the knife in a "**ROW**".

❶列車(れっしゃ)で❷日本列島(にほんれっとう)を旅(たび)しました。

I travelled the ❷Japan archipelago by ❶railway train.

19 Kanji Usage 漢字の使い方

● 19-1. Every minute and second counts with kanji 度(ど)・秒(びょう)

Here are some set phrases that used the kanji taught in this lesson. The first phrase, literally means to "exceed a degree."

度(ど)が過(す)ぎる	to go a little too far; to try too hard
度(ど)が過(す)ぎる筋(きん)トレは怪我(けが)をします。 Excessive muscle training will cause injury.	

The next phrase literally means, "fight with each minute and each second".

一分一秒(いっぷんいちびょう)を争(あらそ)う	Every minute counts. We don't have a moment to lose.
消防士(しょうぼうし)の仕事(しごと)は、一分一秒(いっぷんいちびょう)を争(あらそ)います。 Every minute counts for a fireman's job.	

● 19-2. An interesting thing about 倍(ばい) and 二倍(にばい)

In the past 倍(ばい) meant the "same amount" of a specific amount, but in modern Japan, Both 倍(ばい) and 二倍(にばい) mean "double" the amount. As you can see in the examples, the meaning doesn't change whether you use 倍(ばい) or 二倍(にばい)

EXAMPLES USING 倍(ばい)

1. 人数(にんずう)が倍(ばい)になった。
   The amount of people doubled.
2. 去年(きょねん)より給料(きゅうりょう)が倍(ばい)になりました。
   My salary is two times more than last year.

EXAMPLES USING 二倍(にばい)

3. 人数(にんずう)が二倍(にばい)になった。
   The amount of people doubled.
4. 去年(きょねん)より給料(きゅうりょう)が二倍(にばい)になりました。
   My salary is two times more than last year.

is the same as

19-3. Doing more than others with 人一倍

人一倍 means, "(much) more than others; exceedingly; extremely; unusually".

It's used to show how someone or yourself is doing something MUCH MORE than others.

EXAMPLE SENTENCES

1. 彼女は人一倍努力して、今の仕事を得ました。
   She earned this job by working hard way more than others.
2. 私は人一倍、心配性です。
   I'm much more of a worrier than others.
3. 私は北海道生まれで、人一倍寒さに強いです。
   Being born in Hokkaido, I'm extremely strong in the cold.

NOTE: It would feel unnatural to use 二倍 in the examples above.

19-4. Company Departments 部

部 can mean "department" and is used to describe parts of a company. Where as in English we tend to say just "accounting", Japanese will say 経理部 (けいりぶ) (accounting department). Here are some other common "departments" of companies.

general affairs	sales	human resources
そうむぶ 総務部	えいぎょうぶ 営業部	じんじぶ 人事部

operations	development	manufacturing
じぎょうぶ 事業部	かいはつぶ 開発部	せいぞうぶ 製造部

EXAMPLE SENTENCES

1. 経理部の田中です。 I'm Tanaka from accounting.
2. 人事部のスタッフが厳しいです。 The human resources staff are strict.

● 19-5. The many clubs of kanji 部 (ぶ)

部 (ぶ) can also mean "club" and Japanese students are involved in many 部活 (ぶかつ) (extracurricular activities). Here are few you may hear when watching アニメ or attending Japanese school.

baseball club	soccer club
やきゅうぶ 野球部	ぶ サッカー部

dance club	broadcast club
ぶ ダンス部	ほうそうぶ 放送部

debate club	brass band club
べんろんぶ 弁論部	すいそうがくぶ 吹奏楽部

drama club	track and field club
えんげきぶ 演劇部	りくじょうぶ 陸上部

When editing this section we debated about removing 弁論部 (べんろんぶ) (debate club) because it isn't very common in Japan, despite its relative popularity in America and other English speaking countries.

The proposed replacement was 吹奏楽部 (すいそうがくぶ) (brass band club), which I felt was not common in America. The debate was ended with a compromise and brass band club was added and debate club kept.

● 19-6. How can something mean "next time" and "this time" 今度

今度(こんど) can mean, "this time" which makes sense since it's made up of 今 (now) and 度 (occurrence). However, Japanese people often use 今度(こんど) to mean "next time". Consider the phrase また今度(こんど), which is equivalent to "see you next time". Context is everything.

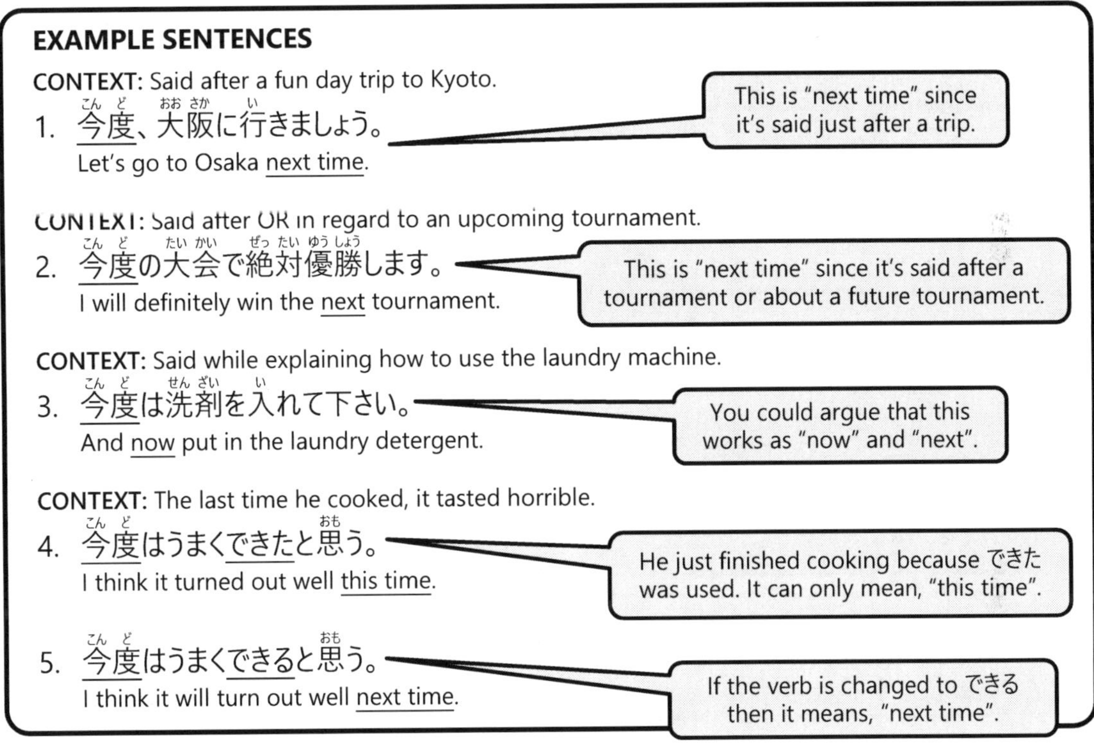

EXAMPLE SENTENCES

CONTEXT: Said after a fun day trip to Kyoto.

1. 今度(こんど)、大阪(おおさか)に行(い)きましょう。
   Let's go to Osaka next time.
   This is "next time" since it's said just after a trip.

CONTEXT: Said after OR in regard to an upcoming tournament.

2. 今度(こんど)の大会(たいかい)で絶対(ぜったい)優勝(ゆうしょう)します。
   I will definitely win the next tournament.
   This is "next time" since it's said after a tournament or about a future tournament.

CONTEXT: Said while explaining how to use the laundry machine.

3. 今度(こんど)は洗剤(せんざい)を入(い)れて下さい。
   And now put in the laundry detergent.
   You could argue that this works as "now" and "next".

CONTEXT: The last time he cooked, it tasted horrible.

4. 今度(こんど)はうまくできたと思(おも)う。
   I think it turned out well this time.
   He just finished cooking because できた was used. It can only mean, "this time".

5. 今度(こんど)はうまくできると思(おも)う。
   I think it will turn out well next time.
   If the verb is changed to できる then it means, "next time".

If you want to be sure you mean, "this time" then you should use, 今回(こんかい) (this time; now).

19 Words You Can Write 書ける言葉

今度（こんど） this time; now; next time; another time

今	度										

何度（なんど） how many times?; how often?

何	度										

上等（じょうとう） of high quality; premium

上	等										

四倍（よんばい） fourfold; quadruple; four times

四	倍										

倍数（ばいすう） multiple

倍	数										

五秒（ごびょう） five seconds

五	秒										

部屋（へや） room

部	屋										

細部（さいぶ） details; particulars

細	部										

配列（はいれつ） arrangement; disposition; array (programming)

配列

整列（せいれつ） array; lining-up

整列

部長（ぶちょう） head of a section or department

部長

会う度（あうたび） every time I see (someone)

会う度

運動等（うんどうとう） exercise etc.; work-out etc.

運動等

等しい（ひとしい） equal; equivalent

等しい

秒読み（びょうよみ） countdown

秒読み

四十度（よんじゅうど） 40 degrees (40°C/104°F)

四十度

19 Kanji Workbook Activities

● 1. Stroke Order Check 書き順確認

Each kanji has a stroke with an arrow on it. Write its order number below the kanji.

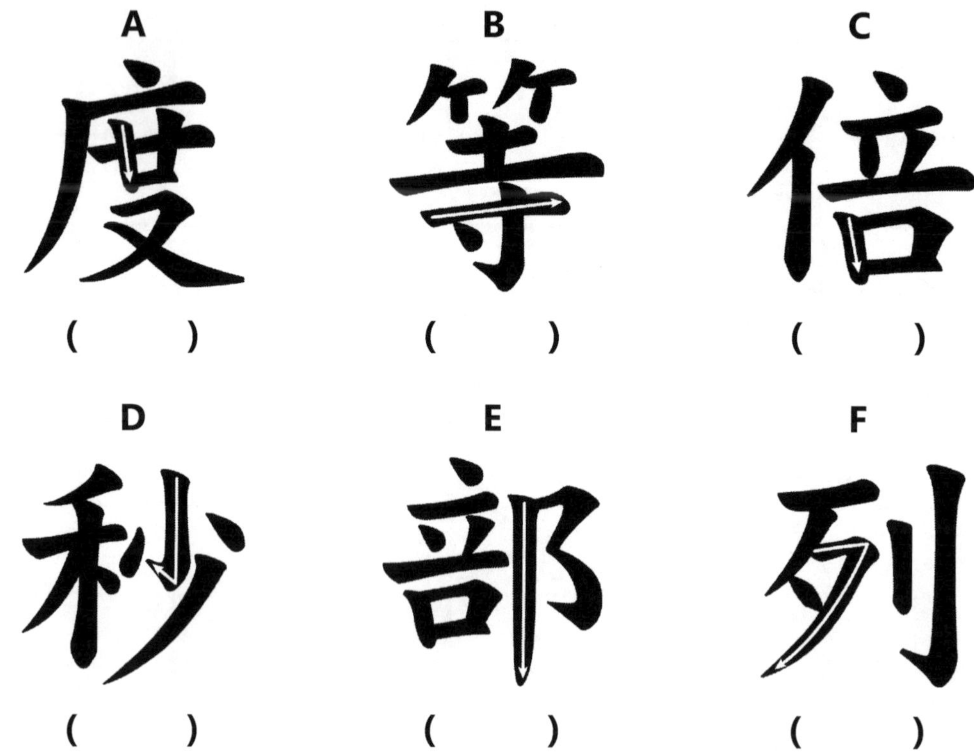

● 2. Kanji Readings

Write FURIGANA above the underlined kanji words.

1. おとなりの赤ちゃんは、会う度に大きくなっています。
2. 上等な神戸牛を食べるために、行列にならびました。
3. たからくじで、一等の三千万円を当てたいです。
4. 二の三倍は、六です。
5. 「湖」の部首は、何ですか。

● 3. Kanji Meaning Match

Write the following kanji next to its meaning: 列 秒 等 度 港 岸 倍 部 橋

1.____ degree 2. ____ second 3. ____ line

4. ____ equal 5. ____ section 6. ____ shore

7. ____ double 8. ____ bridge 9. ____ harbor

● 4. Fill in the Kanji

Fill in the appropriate kanji in the blanks for each sentence.

こん ど きょう と やど や

1. ____ ____、____ ____の____ ____に とまります。

Next time I will be staying in a Kyoto inn.

ひと やっ き くだ

2. このケーキを____ しく、____つに ____って____さい。

Please cut this cake evenly into eight pieces.

とも いえ うち に ばい おお

3. ____ だちの____は、わたしの____ の____ ____ の____きさです。

My friend's house is double the size of my house.

でん し さん じゅう びょう かん あたた

4. このコーヒーを ____ ____ レンジで____ ____ ____ ____、____めてください。

Please warm up this coffee in the microwave for a period of 30 seconds.

いち ぶ くば くだ

5. テストを ____ ____ ずつ、____って____さい。

Please pass out one copy of the test to each.

みせ まえ ぎょう れつ

6. ____ の ____ に____ ____が できています。

There's a line formed in front of the store.

おん ど よん じゅう に ど

7. おふろの____ ____は、____ ____ ____ ____にしています。(42°C = 107.6°F)

I'm keeping the temperature of the bath at 42 degrees.

● 5. Kanji Matching

Connect each kanji with an おん or くん reading. Use each reading only ONCE.

部 •	• ぶ
所 •	• びょう
倍 •	• ど
宿 •	• やど
度 •	• しょ
族 •	• れつ
等 •	• とう
秒 •	• ぞく
列 •	• ばい
打 •	• だ

19 Answer Key 答え合わせ

1. Stroke order check (answers)

A) 5　　B) 10　　C) 8

D) 6　　E) 11　　F) 3

3. Kanji meaning match (answers)

1. 度 degree　　2. 秒 second　　3. 列 line
4. 等 equal　　5. 部 section　　6. 岸 shore
7. 倍 double　　8. 橋 bridge　　9. 港 harbor

2. Kanji Readings (answers)

1. おとなりの赤(あか)ちゃんは、会(あ)う度(たび)に大(おお)きくなっています。 The baby next door gets bigger every time I see them.
2. 上等(じょうとう)な神戸牛(こうべぎゅう)を食(た)べるために、行列(ぎょうれつ)にならびました。 We waited in line to eat the top-quality Kobe beef.
3. たからくじで、一等(いっとう)の三千万円(さんぜんまんえん)を当(あ)てたいです。 I want to win the first prize of 30 million yen in the lottery.
4. 二(に)の三倍(さんばい)は、六(ろく)です。 3 times 2 is 6.
5. 「湖(みずうみ)」の部首(ぶしゅ)は、何(なん)ですか。 What is the radical for "lake"?

4. Fill in the kanji (answers)

1. 今度、京都の宿屋にとまります。
2. このケーキを等しく、八つに切って下さい。
3. 友だちの家は、わたしの家の二倍の大きさです。
4. このコーヒーを電子レンジで三十秒間、温めてください。
5. テストを一部ずつ、配って下さい。
6. 店の前に行列ができています。
7. おふろの温度は、四十二度にしています。

5. Kanji matching (answers)

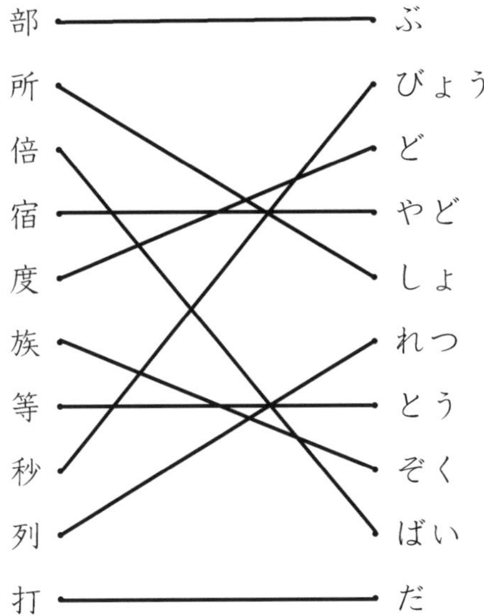

20 Kanji Lesson 20: 階級期号章丁

355-360

Kanji that can be used as "counter" words (part 2)

20 New Kanji 新しい漢字

355 | 阝 | 12 画 | くん none | おん カイ

階

にかい 二階 second floor; upstairs	かいか 階下 downstairs; bottom of stairs	かいだん 階段 stairs; staircase
おんかい 音階 musical scale	かいきゅう 階級 (social) class; rank; grade	だんかい 段階 grade; stage; gradation

stair; floor; story — 阝 (place) + 皆 (everyone)

356 | 糸 | 9 画 | くん none | おん キュウ

級

いっきゅう 一級 first-class; one grade	こうきゅう 高級 high class; high grade; luxury	どうきゅうせい 同級生 classmate; peer
しょきゅう 初級 beginner level	ちゅうきゅう 中級 intermediate level	じょうきゅう 上級 advanced level

class; grade; rank — 糸 (thread) + 及 (to reach)

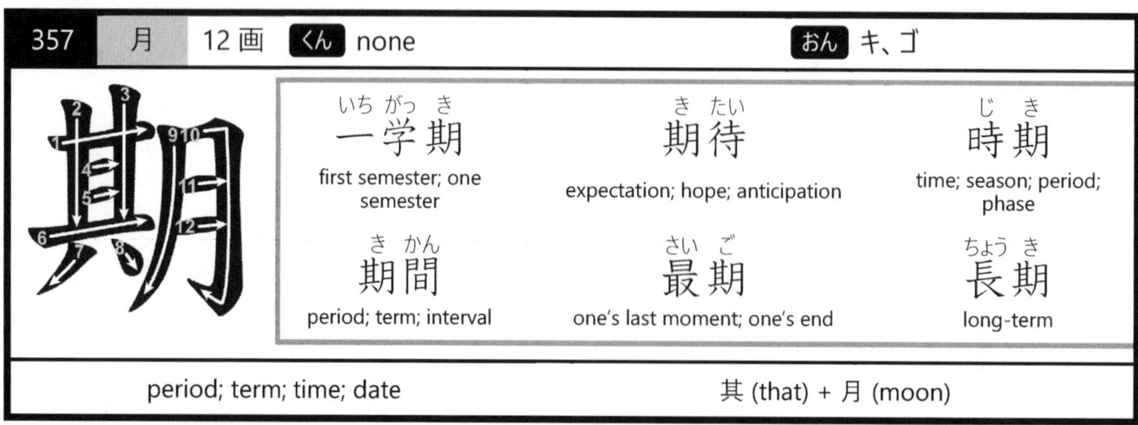

357 | 月 | 12 画 | くん none | おん キ、ゴ

期

いちがっき 一学期 first semester; one semester	きたい 期待 expectation; hope; anticipation	じき 時期 time; season; period; phase
きかん 期間 period; term; interval	さいご 最期 one's last moment; one's end	ちょうき 長期 long-term

period; term; time; date — 其 (that) + 月 (moon)

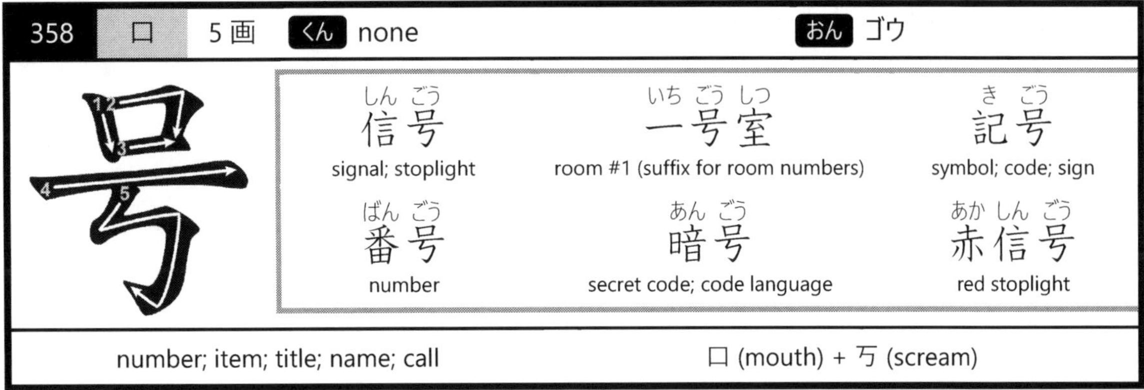

358	口	5 画	くん none	おん ゴウ

しんごう 信号	いちごうしつ 一号室	きごう 記号
signal; stoplight	room #1 (suffix for room numbers)	symbol; code; sign
ばんごう 番号	あんごう 暗号	あかしんごう 赤信号
number	secret code; code language	red stoplight

number; item; title; name; call — 口 (mouth) + 丂 (scream)

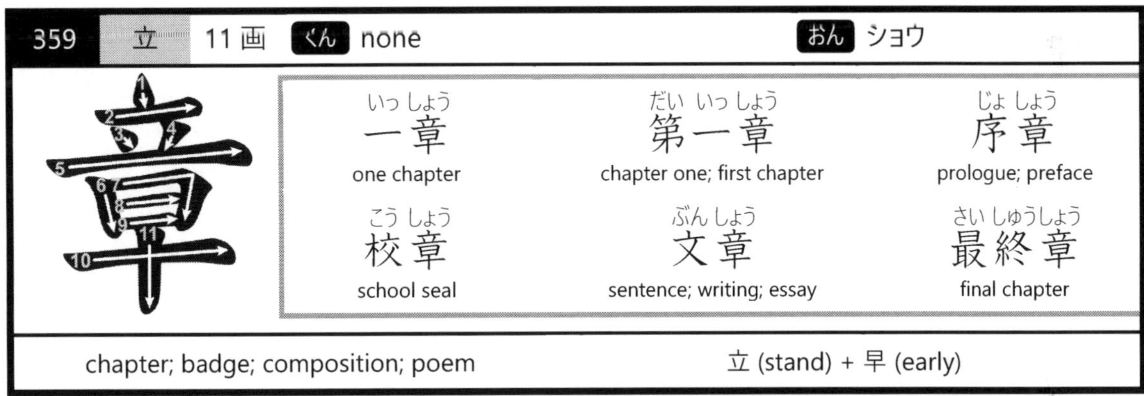

359	立	11 画	くん none	おん ショウ

いっしょう 一章	だいいっしょう 第一章	じょしょう 序章
one chapter	chapter one; first chapter	prologue; preface
こうしょう 校章	ぶんしょう 文章	さいしゅうしょう 最終章
school seal	sentence; writing; essay	final chapter

chapter; badge; composition; poem — 立 (stand) + 早 (early)

360	一	2 画	くん none	おん チョウ、テイ

丁

ていねい 丁寧	いっちょう 一丁	にちょうめ 二丁目
polite; careful; thorough	a pair of scissors; a block of tofu	2-chome (block 2)
ほうちょう 包丁	らくちょう 落丁	ちょうど 丁度
kitchen knife	missing leaf; pages missing	exactly; precisely

counter for sheets; pages; scissors — 丁 (nail)

Kanji Parts used in the New Kanji

阝	small village	其	that	立	stand
皆	everyone	月	moon	早	early
糸	thread	口	mouth	丁	nail
及	and	丂	scream		

20 Kanji Memory Tools 漢字記憶術

This section helps you organically memorize kanji readings, meanings, and construction.

階

阝 皆
This small village is for everyone on the 3rd "**FLOOR**".

この❶階段(かいだん)で❷5階(かい)まで上(あ)がってください。

Please go up to the ❷5th floor on these ❶stairs.

級

糸 及
When this thread is reached, up will go your "**RANK**".

❶同級生(どうきゅうせい)は、まだ❷初級(しょきゅう)レベルなのに、日本語(にほんご)で❸高級車(こうきゅうしゃ)が買(か)えた。

Despite a ❶classmate only being ❸beginner level, they were able to buy a ❷luxury car in Japanese.

期

其 月
That type of moon is rare for this "**PERIOD**".

❶一学期(いちがっき)に❷「一期一会(いちごいちえ)」ということわざを覚(おぼ)えました。

In my ❶first semester, I learned the proverb, ❷"One time one meeting".

号

口 丂
My mouth wants to scream when I think of "**NUMBERS**".

❶五号室(ごごうしつ)の❷電話番号(でんわばんごう)は何(なん)ですか。

What is ❶room 5's ❷phone number?

章

立 早
If I stand and it's early I can finish the "**CHAPTER** ".

❶勲章(くんしょう)をもらった軍人(ぐんじん)が❷15章(しょう)の小説(しょうせつ)を書(か)いた。

The soldier that received a ❶medal wrote a novel with ❷15-chapter novel.

丁

丁
Nail is the "**COUNTER FOR SHEETS, PAGES, AND SCISSORS**".

シェフが❶丁寧(ていねい)に ❷包丁(ほうちょう)の使(つか)い方(かた)を教(おし)えてくれた。

The chef ❶thoroughly taught me out how to use a ❷kitchen knife.

20 Kanji Usage 漢字の使い方

● 20-1. The Japan Kanji Aptitude Test「漢検」

Many students of Japanese are familiar with the 日本語能力試験 (Japanese Language Proficiency Test) which tests Japanese comprehension skill. However, they may not be aware of the 日本漢字能力検定 (Japanese Kanji Aptitude Test) or just 漢検 for short.

The test is split into 10 ranks or, as we learned in this lesson, 級. Around 90% of the test takers range from elementary to high school students. In 2017, approximately 720,000 people took the test, with the most common level tested for being 3級. It's thought that even for Japanese adults 3級 feels difficult.

Rank	Approximate Grade	# of Kanji	Requirements
10 級	1st grade student	80 字	Out of 150 points must get 80% correct
9 級	2nd grade student	240 字	
8 級	3rd grade student	440 字	
7 級	4th grade student	640 字	Out of 200 points must get 70% correct
6 級	5th grade student	825 字	
5 級	6th grade student	1,006 字	
4 級	student attending junior high	1,322 字	
3 級	junior high graduate	1,607 字	
準 2 級	student attending high school	1,940 字	
2 級	high school graduate / college	2,136 字	Out of 200 points must get 80% correct
準 1 級	college	約 3,000 字	
1 級	college	約 6,000 字	

準 (semi-)　字 (characters)　約 (approximately)

For more information visit the official website: **https://www.kanken.or.jp/kanken/**

● 20-2. Same sound, different kanji「さいご」

さいご both mean "the end", but just different types of ends.

end; conclusion; last; final; most recent	one's last moment; one's death; one's end
さいご 最後	さいご 最期
列の最後に並ぶ (line up at the end of the line)	祖父の最期を看取る (care for your grandfather until his last moment)
今年最後のレースだ (it's the final race of the year.)	静かな最期を迎える (approach a quiet death)
最後まで頑張る (do your best until the end)	ナポレオンの最期は謎だった (Napoleon's death was a mystery.)

● 20-3. Counting ships... 号

号 (ごう) means number. However, unlike English, it's added to the end a number. 号 (ごう) is used to identify things from hotel rooms to modes of transportation.

ship / bus / train #	train car # / bus #	room #
～号 (ごう)	～号車 (ごうしゃ)	～号室 (ごうしつ)

EXAMPLE SENTENCES

1. お客様の部屋は101号室でございます。 Your room is room number 101.
2. 3号車にお手洗いがあります。 There are restrooms in car 3.
3. とき301号に乗って、大阪に行きます。 I'll take the TOKI 301 to Osaka.

● 20-4. Japanese addresses

In America addresses start with a number, then the street name, then moves to the larger areas such as city then state. Japan does this in reverse and starts with the big areas and moves to the smaller ending with street.

The following address is for Shibuya Station in Tokyo which is famous for the "Scramble" intersection where intersecting crosswalks are filled with hundreds of people as they "scramble" in between the shopping area on the station.

とうきょうと　しぶやく　どうげんざか　ちょうめ

東京都 渋谷区 道玄坂１丁目

So for the Shibuya station, we start with 東京都(とうきょうと) (Tokyo City) followed by 渋谷区(しぶやく) (Shibuya District) and ending with the street name 道玄坂(どうげんざか) then the "block" is denoted with a kanji we learned in this lesson 1丁目(ちょうめ) (first block).

City blocks are counted using the 丁目 counter. The 目 part is what gives the number its ordinal rank. In other words instead of 二丁目 being "block 2" it's "2nd block".

● 20-5. PROVERB: "One time one meeting" 一期一会

The Japanese proverb 一期一会(いちごいちえ) doesn't have an easy direct translation, but the meaning roughly is, "Cherish each meeting as it might be the only one."

20 Words You Can Write 書ける言葉

三階（さんがい） third floor

三 階

階下（かいか） downstairs

階 下

二級（にきゅう） second-class, secondary

二 級

上級（じょうきゅう） advanced level; high grade; senior

上 級

期間（きかん） period; term; interval

期 間

早期（そうき） early stage

早 期

番号（ばんごう） number

番 号

元号（げんごう） era name

元 号

文章（ぶんしょう） sentence; writing; article; composition

文章

丁重（ていちょう） polite; courteous; hospitable

丁重

級友（きゅうゆう） classmate

級友

長期（ちょうき） long period; long-term

長期

同級生（どうきゅうせい） classmate

同級生

新学期（しんがっき） new school term

新学期

落丁本 (らくちょうぼん) book with missing pages

落丁本

一丁目（いっちょうめ） 1-chome (Block 1)

一丁目

20 Kanji Workbook Activities

● 1. Stroke Order Check 書き順確認

Each kanji has a stroke with an arrow on it. Write its order number below the kanji.

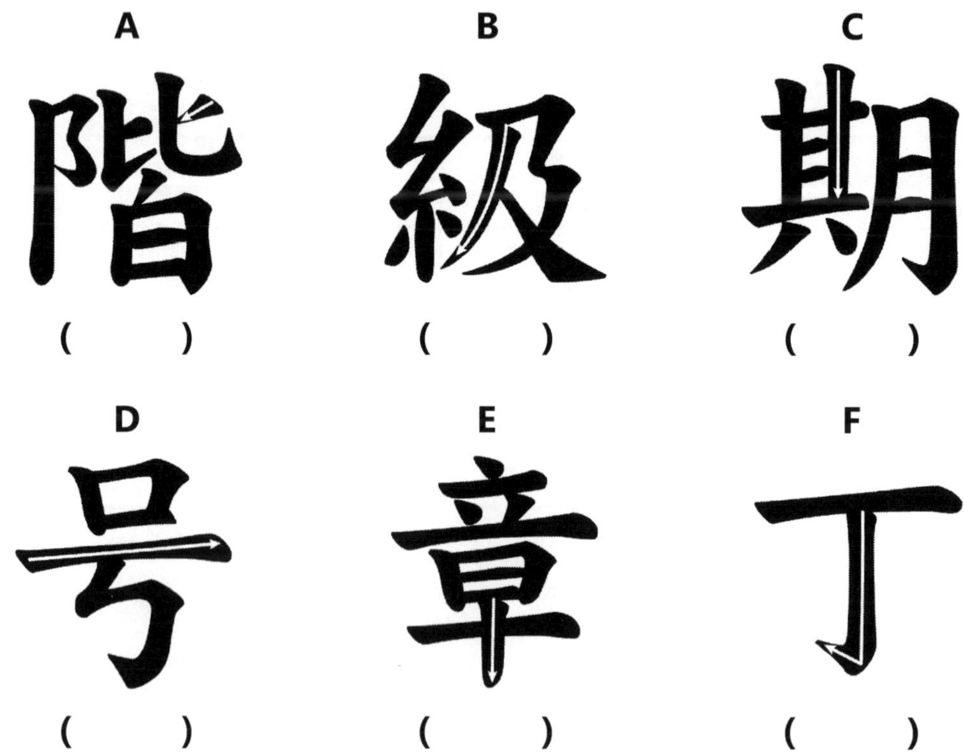

● 2. Kanji Readings

Write FURIGANA above the underlined kanji words.

1. ゲームで階級が上がって、うれしいです。
2. 四月から日本語の上級クラスに入りました。
3. 母に「もう、あなたに何も期待しません」と言われた。
4. 先日、102 号室の方に会いました。
5. 落丁本なので、文章がぜんぶ読めません。

● 3. Kanji Meaning Match

Write the following kanji next to its meaning: 丁 秒 級 章 列 階 号 坂 期

1. ____ floor
2. ____ number
3. ____ chapter
4. ____ grade
5. ____ second
6. ____ slope
7. ____ period
8. ____ scissors
9. ____ line

● 4. Fill in the Kanji

Fill in the appropriate kanji in the blanks for each sentence.

ろく ねん せい きょう しつ さん がい

1. ____ ____ ____の____ ____は ____ ____に あります。

The 6th grade classroom is on the 3rd floor.

あいだ まち どう きゅう せい あ

2. この ____、____で____ ____ ____に____ いました。

The other day I met a classmate in town.

らい ねん ちょう き やす

3. ____ ____、____ ____の____ みを とることに しました。

I decided to take a long-term vacation next year.

あたら でん わ ばん ごう

4. ____しい ____ ____ ____ ____が おぼえられません。

I can't remember my new telephone number.

なが ぶん しょう よ にが て

5. ____い____ ____を____ むのは ____ ____です。

I'm not good at reading long sentences.

に ちょう め こう えん ひろ

6. ____ ____ ____の____ ____は ____いです。

The park on block 2 is wide (big).

しん がっ き とも あ たの

7. ____ ____ ____に____ だちに____うのが____しみです。

I'm looking forward to meeting my friends on the new semester.

● 5. Kanji Matching

Connect each kanji with an おん or くん reading. Use each reading only ONCE.

章 •	• きゅう
神 •	• かん
期 •	• ちょう
館 •	• しょう
階 •	• かい
医 •	• い
級 •	• かみ
号 •	• ごう
丁 •	• こ
庫 •	• き

20 Answer Key 答え合わせ

1. Stroke order check (answers)

A) 6 B) 7 C) 3
D) 4 E) 11 F) 2

3. Kanji meaning match (answers)

1. 階 floor 2. 号 number 3. 章 chapter
4. 級 grade 5. 秒 second 6. 坂 slope
7. 期 period 8. 丁 scissors 9. 列 line

2. Kanji Readings (answers)

1. ゲームで階級が上がって、うれしいです。 I'm happy that I rose rank in the game.
2. 四月から日本語の上級クラスに入りました。 I entered the advanced Japanese class from April.
3. 母に「もう、あなたに何も期待しません」と言われた。 I was told by my mom, "I don't expect anything of you anymore!".
4. 先日、102号室の方に会いました。 The other day I met the person from room 102.
5. 落丁本なので、文章がぜんぶ読めません。 I can't read all the sentences since the book is missing pages.

4. Fill in the kanji (answers)

1. 六年生の教室は三階にあります。
2. この間、町で同級生に会いました。
3. 来年、長期の休みを とることにしました。
4. 新しい電話番号が おぼえられません。
5. 長い文章を読むのは苦手です。
6. 二丁目の公園は広いです。
7. 新学期に友だちに会うのが楽しみです。

5. Kanji matching (answers)

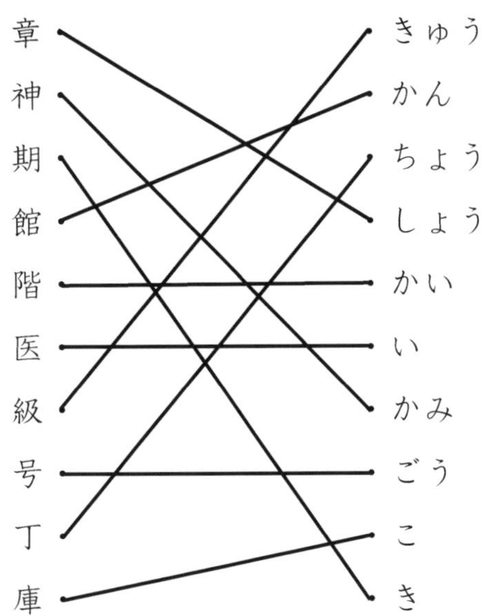

Kanji Lessons 16-20: Super Review 4

From the teacher...

Test your knowledge of the kanji learned in the last 5 lessons.

1. Build-a-Kanji 漢字の組み合わせ

Combine the left and right parts to make seven of the kanji learned in lessons 16-20.

RULES
1. You can use the radical and kanji parts as many times as you want.
2. Some kanji can use two kanji parts.

部首 (Radical)		
匚	氵	广
辶	阝	亻
立	糸	田
宀	禾	ネ

Other Kanji Parts		
少	メ	月
火	一	白
比	早	古
車	申	者

SAMPLE	1	2	3	4	5	6	7
階							

● 2. Okurigana drill 送り仮名ドリル

Circle the correct 漢字 + 送り仮名 combination.

1. やどる	・宿る	・宿どる
2. やくだつ	・役く立つ	・役立つ
3. かかる	・係かる	・係る
4. あらわす	・表す	・表らわす
5. とれる	・取れる	・取る
6. つかう	・使かう	・使う

● 3. Kanji selection 漢字の選択

Select the best kanji to replace the underlined section of the sentence.

1. サンフランシスコの空____から、日本へしゅっぱつしました。
   A. 所　B. 州　C. 港　D. 院

2. すみませんが、コピーを 10____、とって来て下さい。
   A. 度　B. 部　C. 等　D. 号

3. 日本は____国で、海にかこまれています。
   A. 都　B. 港　C. 畑　D. 島

4. 今度、新しい住____を教えて下さい。
   A. 所　B. 局　C. 県　D. 区

● 4. Kanji reading selection 読みの選択

Select the best reading for the underlined kanji.

1. 一年に一度、むかしの同級生と集まります。
   A. と　B. ど　C. たび　D. かい

2. 新年まで秒読みですね。
   A. ひょう　B. びょう　C. ぴょう　D. じょう

3. 明日の都合はどうですか。
   A. つ　B. と　C. みやこ　D. づ

4. この上り坂を上がるのは、たいへんです。
   A. はん　B. ばん　C. さか　D.ざか

● 5. Compound kanji word puzzle 熟語パズル

Fill in the correct kanji based on the list below the puzzle.

	1)	2)	3)
4)	5)	6)	7)
8)	9)		
	10)	11)	

Down ↓	
English meaning	**Hiragana**
3) long term	ちょうき
4) archipelago	れっとう
6) school district	がっく
7) expectation; hope	きたい
8) island country	しまぐに
Left to Right →	
5) first semester, one semester	いちがっき
9) area, district, division	ちく
10) detail	さいぶ
11) room	へや

← Right to Left	
English meaning	**Hiragana**
1) road	どうろ
2) sloping road	さかみち
5) one line	いちれつ

SR4 Answer Key 答え合わせ

1. Build-a-Kanji (answers) (order can vary)

SAMPLE 階 1) 区 2) 湖 3) 畑 4) 都 5) 庫 6) 秒 7) 章

2. Okurigana drill (answers)

1. やどる	**・宿る**	・宿どる	4. あらわす	**・表す**	・表らわす
2. やくだつ	・役く立つ	**・役立つ**	5. とれる	**・取れる**	・取る
3. かかる	・係かる	**・係る**	6. つかう	・使かう	**・使う**

3. Kanji selection (answers)

1. C – 空港(くうこう) I departed from the San Francisco airport to Japan.
2. B – 10部(ぶ) Excuse me, but please get 10 copies.
3. D – 島国(しまぐに) Japan, being an island country, is surrounded by the ocean.
4. A – 住所(じゅうしょ) Tell me your new address next time.

4. Kanji reading selection (answers)

1. B – 一度(いちど) Once a year my old classmates get together.
2. B – 秒読み(びょうよ) It's a countdown until the new year.
3. A – 都合(つごう) What are you doing tomorrow? (What are you circumstances tomorrow?)
4. D – 上り坂(のぼ ざか) It's hard to go up this incline.

5. Compound kanji word puzzle (answers)

路	道	坂	長
列	一	学	期
島	地	区	待
国	細	部	屋

21 Kanji Lesson 21: 仕事委員研究

361-366

Work related kanji

21 New Kanji 新しい漢字

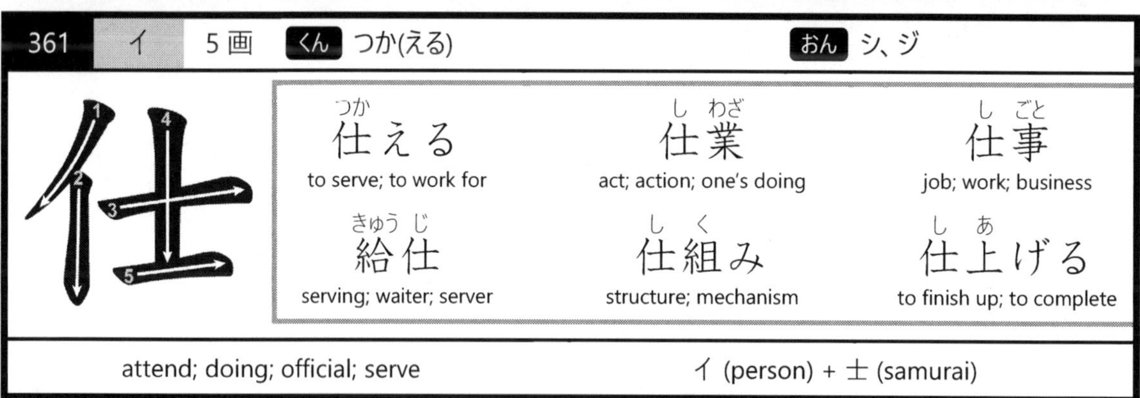

361 | 亻 | 5画 | くん つか(える) | おん シ、ジ

仕える (つか) to serve; to work for	仕業 (しわざ) act; action; one's doing	仕事 (しごと) job; work; business
給仕 (きゅうじ) serving; waiter; server	仕組み (しくみ) structure; mechanism	仕上げる (しあ) to finish up; to complete

attend; doing; official; serve — 亻 (person) + 士 (samurai)

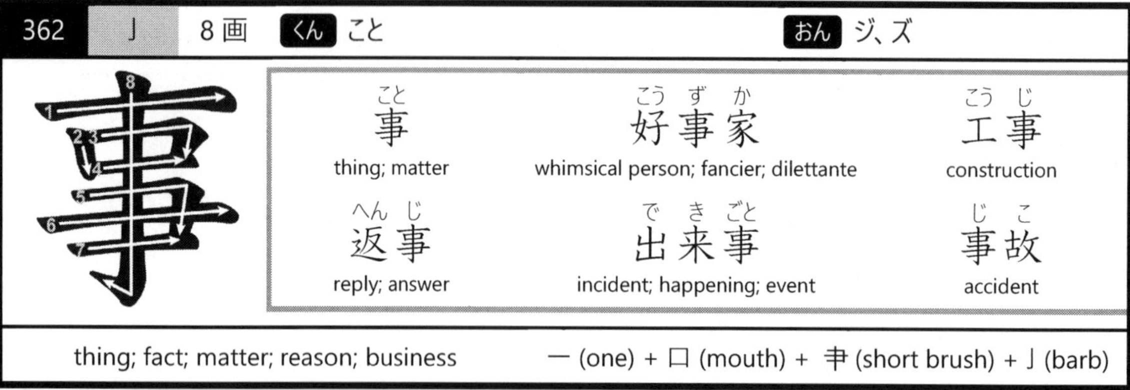

362 | 亅 | 8画 | くん こと | おん ジ、ズ

事 (こと) thing; matter	好事家 (こうずか) whimsical person; fancier; dilettante	工事 (こうじ) construction
返事 (へんじ) reply; answer	出来事 (できごと) incident; happening; event	事故 (じこ) accident

thing; fact; matter; reason; business — 一 (one) + 口 (mouth) + 彐 (short brush) + 亅 (barb)

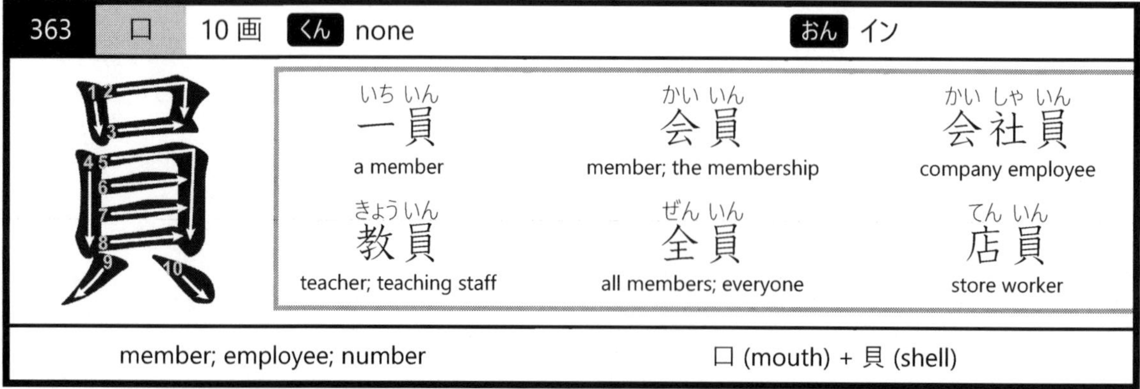

363 | 口 | 10画 | くん none | おん イン

一員 (いちいん) a member	会員 (かいいん) member; the membership	会社員 (かいしゃいん) company employee
教員 (きょういん) teacher; teaching staff	全員 (ぜんいん) all members; everyone	店員 (てんいん) store worker

member; employee; number — 口 (mouth) + 貝 (shell)

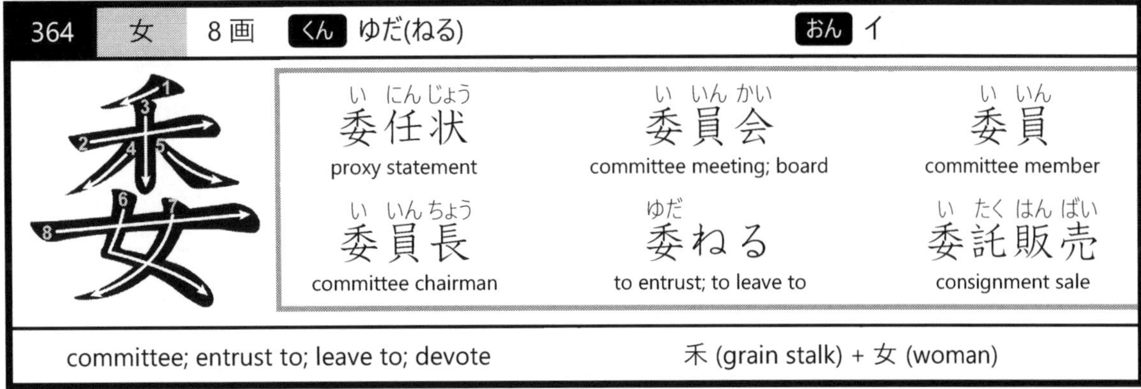

364 | 女 | 8 画 | くん ゆだ(ねる) | おん イ

いにんじょう 委任状 proxy statement	いいんかい 委員会 committee meeting; board	いいん 委員 committee member
いいんちょう 委員長 committee chairman	ゆだ 委ねる to entrust; to leave to	いたくはんばい 委託販売 consignment sale

committee; entrust to; leave to; devote — 禾 (grain stalk) + 女 (woman)

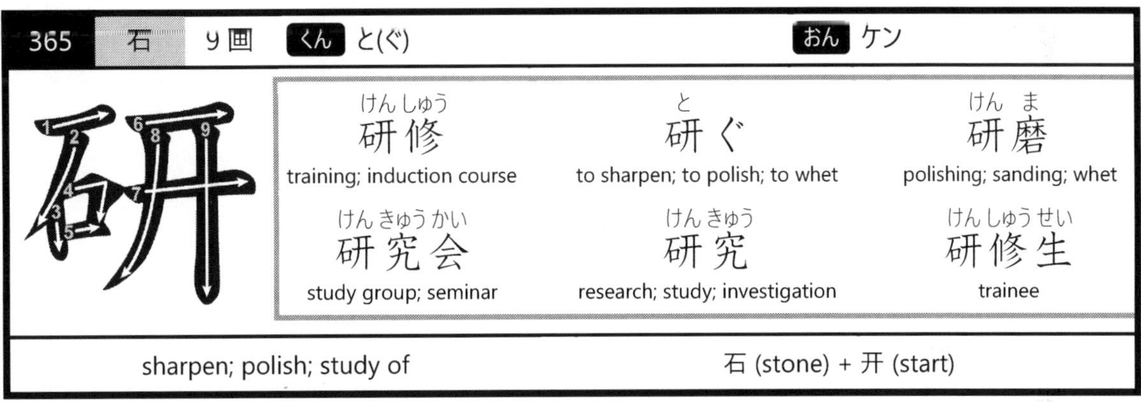

365 | 石 | 9 画 | くん と(ぐ) | おん ケン

けんしゅう 研修 training; induction course	と 研ぐ to sharpen; to polish; to whet	けんま 研磨 polishing; sanding; whet
けんきゅうかい 研究会 study group; seminar	けんきゅう 研究 research; study; investigation	けんしゅうせい 研修生 trainee

sharpen; polish; study of — 石 (stone) + 开 (start)

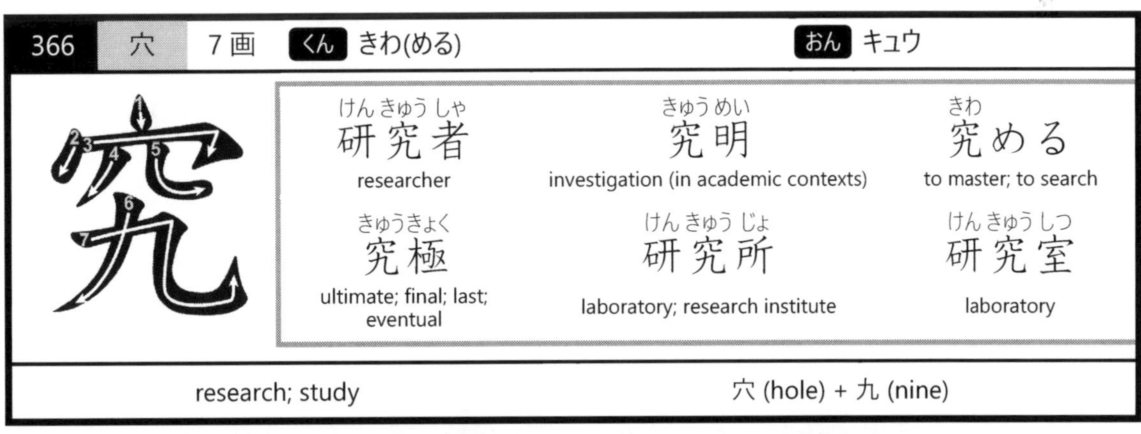

366 | 穴 | 7 画 | くん きわ(める) | おん キュウ

けんきゅうしゃ 研究者 researcher	きゅうめい 究明 investigation (in academic contexts)	きわ 究める to master; to search
きゅうきょく 究極 ultimate; final; last; eventual	けんきゅうじょ 研究所 laboratory; research institute	けんきゅうしつ 研究室 laboratory

research; study — 穴 (hole) + 九 (nine)

Kanji Parts used in the New Kanji

亻	person	丿	barb	开	start
士	samurai	禾	grain stalk	穴	hole
一	one	女	woman	九	nine
口	mouth	貝	shell		
聿	short brush	石	stone		

21 Kanji Memory Tools 漢字記憶術

This section helps you organically memorize kanji readings, meanings, and construction.

仕

イ 士
When a person is asked by a samurai they must "**ATTEND**".

私(わたし)は人(ひと)に❶仕(つか)える❷仕事(しごと)が苦手(にがて)です。
I'm not good at ❷work that ❶serves people.

事

一 口 ⼹ 亅
One mouth and a short brush can poke a barb into the "**MATTER**".

この❶事故(じこ)は、❷なかった事(こと)にしましょう。
Let's act like this ❶accident ❷didn't happen.

員

口 貝
Put your mouth on this shell to reach a "**MEMBER**".

父(ちち)は❶会社員(かいしゃいん)、母(はは)は❷教員(きょういん)、僕(ぼく)はただの家族(かぞく)の❸一員(いちいん)です。
My father is a ❶company employee, my mother is ❷teaching staff, and I'm just a ❸member of the family.

委

禾 女
The grain stalk is carried by a woman I have "**ENTRUST(ED) TO**".

❶委員会(いいんかい)では、❷委員長(いいんちょう)に全(すべ)てを❸委(ゆだ)ねてはいけません。
We can't ❸entrust everything to the ❷committee chairman at the ❶committee meeting.

研

石 开
This stone will start to "**SHARPEN**".

私(わたし)は米(こめ)の❶研究者(けんきゅうしゃ)ですが、お米(こめ)の❷研(と)ぎ方(かた)を知(し)りません。
I'm a rice ❶researcher, but I don't know how to ❷wash rice.

究

穴 九
The hole in the number nine would be weird to "**RESEARCH**".

❶研究者(けんきゅうしゃ)としての❷道(みち)を究(きわ)めることにした。
I decided to ❷find my way as a ❶researcher.

21 Understanding Kanji Parts 漢字部分の理解

● 21-1. How kanji is made

This section is purposely put late into the book so you can benefit from your experience of looking at many kanji constructions. We also assume you have looked at other sources teaching kanji and have been sometimes surprised to see a completely different meaning assigned to a part of the kanji than we have learned in this book. The way kanji were made is called 漢字の成り立ち (かんじの なりたち) in Japanese. The なりたち (composition) of kanji for any kanji is easily accessible on the internet from multiple sources.

Kanji were not created in one day or with a masterplan. They were added to the language over time by different people and groups and over time were rearranged, strokes added and or dropped. And even origins forgotten or misinterpret. As a result, kanji are not uniform in their design.

Let's look at our basic understanding of the kanji radical. We already learned that a radical is the "main" part of the kanji character. It's how the kanji is grouped and indexed. For example, fish related kanji tend to have 魚 (fish) radical and many water related kanji have the 水 (water) radical.

Examples of kanji using さんずいへん "water radical"			
さんずいへん	いけ (pond)	あぶら (oil)	あら(う) (to wash)
氵 →	池	油	洗

Examples of kanji using つちへん "soil radical"			
つちへん	ち (ground)	しろ (castle)	ば (place)
土 →	地	城	場

Other kanji parts are also often chosen due to the meaning so as to create a logical story for that character. There are four categories that kanji are divided. Let's look at each one, starting with the easiest to understand.

NOTE: Don't focus on the English or Japanese naming classification for the four categories. It's more important to understand the concept behind them.

1. **Pictographic Characters 象形文字 (しょうけいもじ)**
   These characters are essentially drawings of the item they represent. These are the easiest to understand since they often look like the thing they represent.

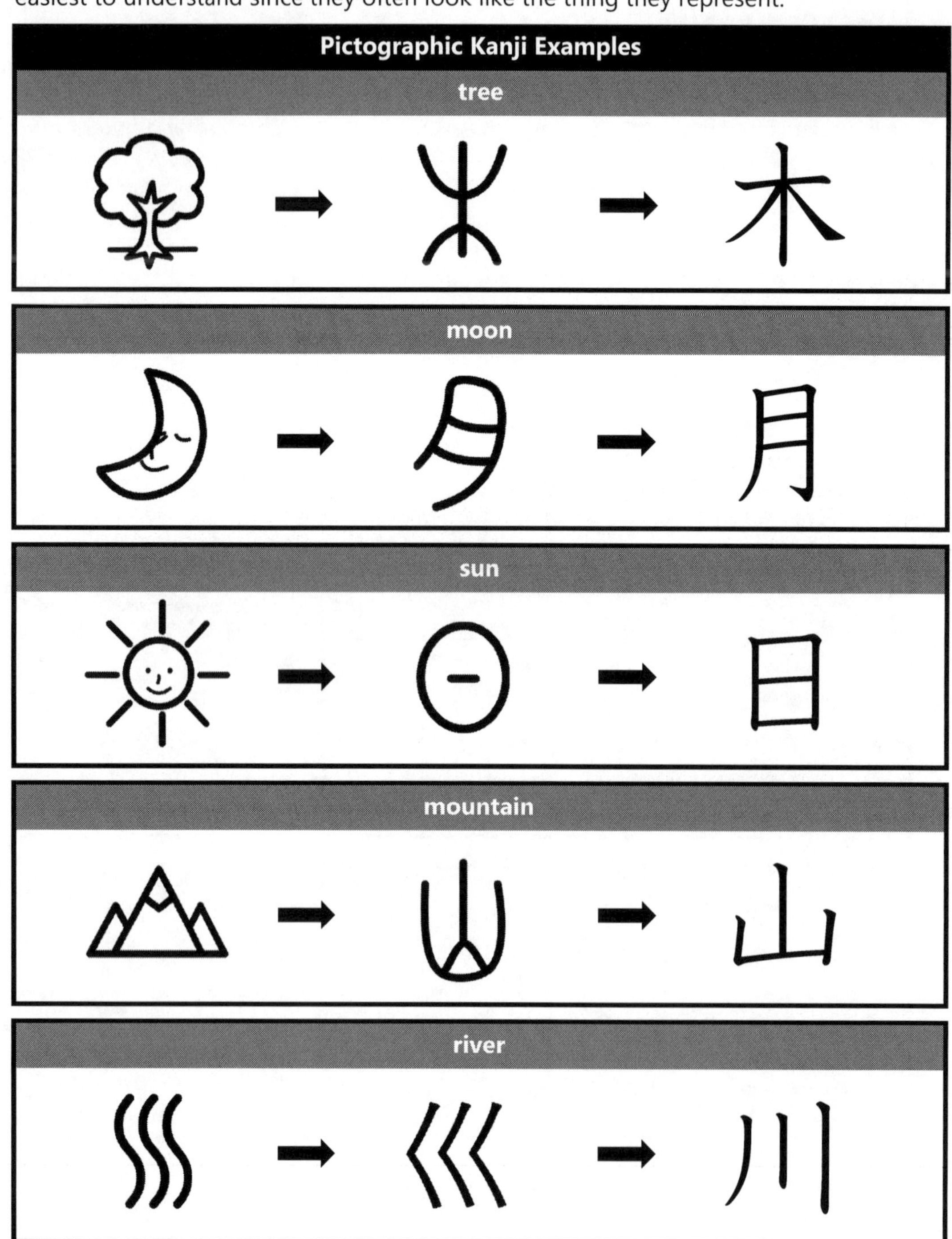

NOTE: These are just conceptual transformations from the object to the current kanji. There are often more steps in between.

2. **Indicative Characters 指事文字 (しじもじ)**
   This is the least common type of construction. These kanji are designed using dots and lines to represent things that are hard to represent.

Indicative Kanji Examples	
up; above	
→	上
down; under	
→	下
inside; center	
→	中

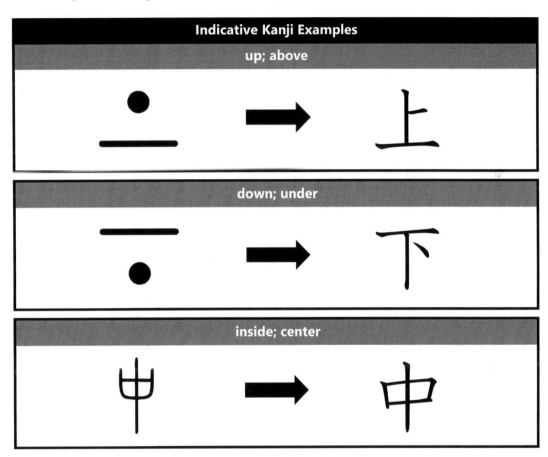

3. **Ideographic Characters 会意文字 (かいいもじ)**
   These are kanji that are made with parts that are also stand-alone kanji chosen based on the underlying meaning of the parts and how they work together to build a story. Together they form a new meaning.

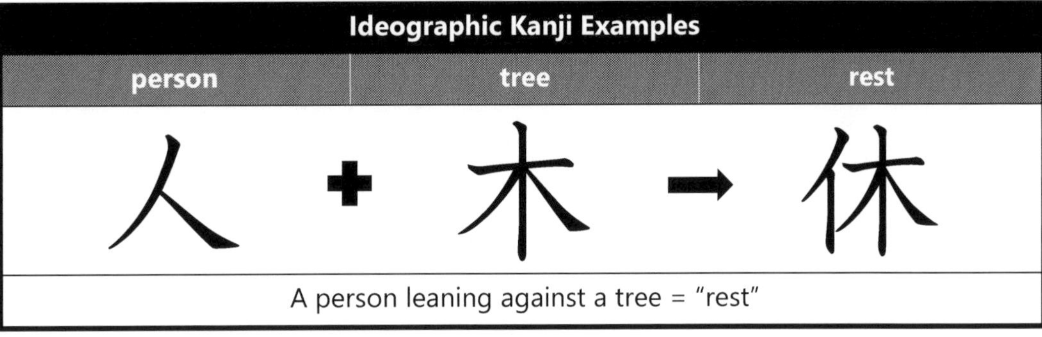

Ideographic Kanji Examples		
person	tree	rest
人 +	木 →	休
A person leaning against a tree = "rest"		

mouth	bird	chirp; cry; sound
口 +	鳥 →	鳴
The mouth of a bird makes a "chirp"		

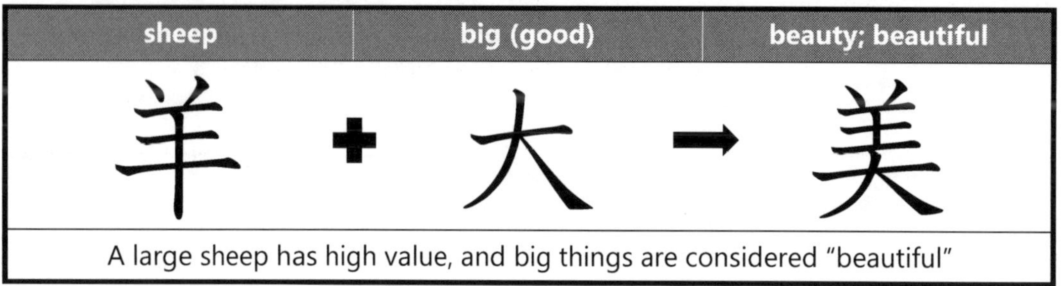

sheep	big (good)	beauty; beautiful
羊 +	大 →	美
A large sheep has high value, and big things are considered "beautiful"		

4. **Semasio-Phonetic Characters 形声文字 (けいせいもじ)**
   These kanji are typically made up of two parts, one representing a sound, and one representing a meaning. Often the part representing a sound was chosen because it was the sound desired for that kanji.

Semasio-Phonetic Kanji Examples		
meaning	**sound (reading)**	**Semasio-Phonetic**
rice	ふん	**flour; powder (ふん)**
米 +	分 →	粉
mouth	もん	**question (もん)**
口 +	門 →	問
sun	せい	**clear up, sunny (せい)**
日 +	青 →	晴

21-2. The problem with kanji dictionary kanji breakdowns

We touched on this topic in the beginning of the book and in the prior section, but let's go a bit deeper into inconsistent or seemingly nonsensical kanji constructions.

If all kanji were ideographic (made with parts based on meaning) we would be able to just learn all the base parts and then easily and logically imagine most of the meanings of each character. But as discussed in the prior section, sometimes parts are chosen based on the *desired sound*, and sometimes a part is chosen just because it had the *right look* to make a better visual story.

And unfortunately, because all kanji weren't created the same way, it means that making a coherent story that is uniform between all kanji isn't possible. In this book we chose broad interpretations of each part and avoid "pictographic" meanings often sited in Japanese sources.

However, even in this book we have assigned meaning to kanji parts based on looks, often when there were no other meanings available. For example, we have this part 𠂉 which we called "high heels" because it looks like a "high heel".

For consistency across multiple kanji, each kanji part in this book has *only one meaning*, no matter what kanji it's used in.

Now here is where you might face some difficulty. When looking at Japanese kanji dictionary breakdowns, they will often not have the same definition for some parts. This is because they seem to favor a more pictographic approach in explaining each character. This might be because the books teaching kanji are often for elementary school children.

Because of this, you might be taught that in one kanji a certain part means, "big" and in another it means, "right hand". But this is just the case of a kanji part being assigned a meaning to match the kanji being taught, while the parts actual meaning might be completely unrelated.

It's fine to learn this way, but it also means you will have to learn multiple unconnected meanings for each part. And these parts, when used in another kanji, might be assigned a completely different meaning. As a result, you might end up thinking your brain is broken or that you really are bad at kanji. Of course, most likely this isn't the case.

The final thought on the troublesome mnemonics (story telling) of kanji is this: As long as you know kanji itself isn't consistent, you shouldn't feel so bad when your own understanding of kanji isn't consistent. Keep on pushing! There are only 12 more lessons in this book! Make sure to take a break before moving to book 3!

● 21-3. A cheat code to guessing a kanji's おんよみ

It's estimated that up to 85% of kanji have a part that was used simply because the sound of the part matched a desired sound for that kanji (in Chinese reading).

Therefore, it's often safe to assume that the おんよみ (Chinese reading) of a kanji, is the same as one of its parts. You will be right more than wrong using this method to guess a reading.

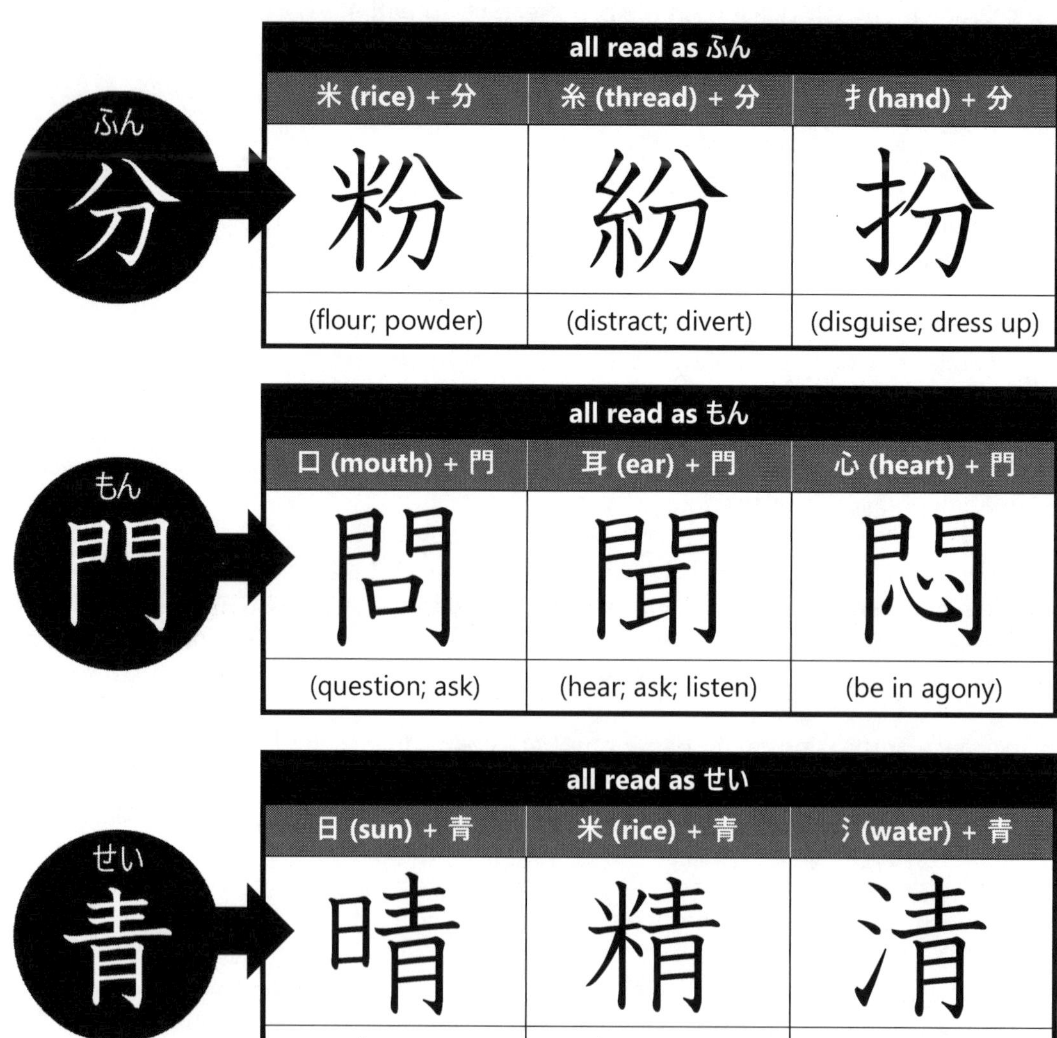

ふん
分
all read as ふん
米 (rice) + 分
糸 (thread) + 分
扌(hand) + 分
粉
紛
扮
(flour; powder)
(distract; divert)
(disguise; dress up)
もん
門
all read as もん
口 (mouth) + 門
耳 (ear) + 門
心 (heart) + 門
問
聞
悶
(question; ask)
(hear; ask; listen)
(be in agony)
せい
青
all read as せい
日 (sun) + 青
米 (rice) + 青
氵(water) + 青
晴
精
清
(clear up)
(refined; energy)
(pure; purify)

21 Kanji Usage 漢字の使い方

● 21-4. Same kanji word, different reading and meaning 大事

I once made a video titled, "Japanese is trying to kill you". For part 2, I could make one called, "Kanji is trying to kill you". Here is some hard proof of my theory! Look at these following words that look EXACTLY the same but are not read the same.

important; valuable; precious	serious matter; major incident; crisis
だい じ 大事	おお ごと 大事
彼女(かのじょ)は大事(だいじ)な人(ひと)です。 My girlfriend / she is a precious person.	大事(おおごと)にしたくないです。 I don't want to make it a big deal.
今(いま)は仕事(しごと)が大事(だいじ)です。 My current work is important.	大事(おおごと)にならなくてよかったです。 I'm glad it didn't turn into a crisis.

personnel affairs; human resources; HR	other people's affairs; somebody else's problem
じん じ 人事	ひと ごと 人事
私(わたし)は人事(じんじ)の原(はら)です。 I'm Hara of human resources (at the company).	これは人事(ひとごと)じゃなくて、皆(みんな)の事(こと)です。 This isn't someone else's problem, it's everyone's.
毎週金曜日(まいしゅうきんようび)は人事(じんじ)チームと会議(かいぎ)します。 Every Friday we have meetings with the HR team.	人事(ひとごと)みたいな顔(かお)をしないで下(くだ)さい！ Don't make a face like it's someone else's issue!

You will often see 他(ほか) (other) added to 人事(ひとごと), making it 他人事(ひとごと), in order to avoid it being read as, 人事(じんじ). Further proving that kanji is trying to kill you is the fact that 他人事(ひとごと), can also be read as 他人事(たにんごと), but luckily, in this case, it still means, "other people's affairs".

● 21-5. Origin story of 事

The mnemonic parts used for 事 is probably not as good as its two other origin stories.

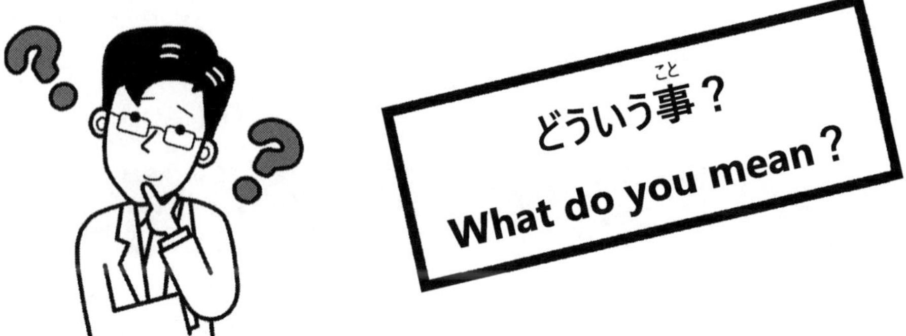

Origin Story #1

事 is thought to represent the written prayer words that have been tied to a tree branch or hung in the shrine.

漢字が理解できますように！
I hope to be able to understand Kanji!

In Japan, Japanese people write their wishes and dreams on a small wooden board called 神馬 (えま) and then hang them at shrines.

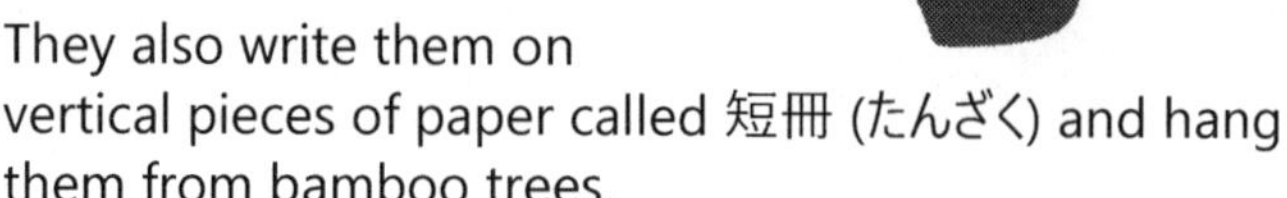

They also write them on vertical pieces of paper called 短冊 (たんざく) and hang them from bamboo trees.

You can also purchase your "fortune" or as it's called in Japanese, おみくじ which will tell you whether you have good luck or not. If you draw "good fortune", 大吉 (だいきち) you are supposed to tie the おみくじ to a tree to insure that you actually get the fortune promised.

Origin Story #2

It's also said that 事 could originate from the image of a hand holding a flag on the end of a pole.

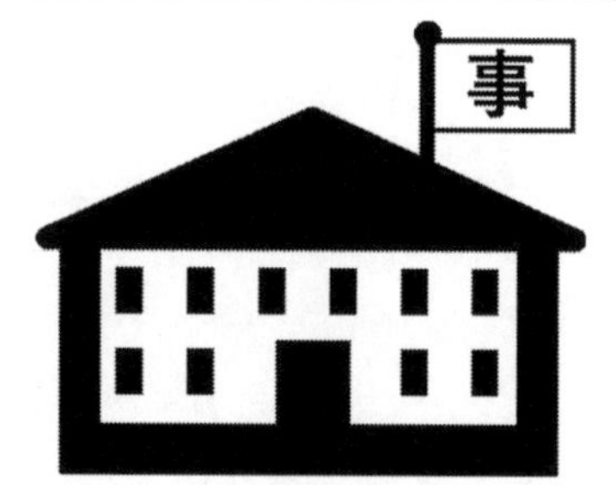

事 can represent the flags put up designating places where work was done, such as a government office.

● 21-6. Why do you "polish" rice?（研ぐ）

Depending on the context, 研ぐ means, "to sharpen or to polish". So, we can say 刀を研ぐ (sharpen a sword), or ヤスリで研ぐ (polish with sandpaper). Before cooking, Japanese people "wash" rice. However, instead 洗う (wash), they use 米を研ぐ (sharpen or polish rice).

Prior to modern processing of rice, bags of rice contained a lot of leftover 米ぬか (rice bran) after removing the rice husks. The rice needed to be sufficiently washed to remove the excess 米ぬか. Now that rice polishing technology has advanced, rice only needs to be lightly "polished".

According to co-author Kanako, many Japanese people use improper techniques to polish their rice. To avoid similar mistakes, let's look at the *dos and don'ts* of "polishing" rice.

How to make tasty rice (THE DOS)

1) Because the rice absorbs the water, you should use quality water.
2) With spread fingers, gently stir up to 4 times, then quickly pour out the water.
3) Next, for 2 or 3 cycles, stir up to 8 times with clean water and remove the water.
4) Let the rice soak for up to an hour in quality water.
5) Now you can cook the rice!

What to avoid! (THE DON'TS)

1) Scrubbing the rice.
2) Putting the rice in a draining basket. (the rice will crack)
3) Polishing until the rice becomes transparent. (it won't taste good)

21 Words You Can Write 書ける言葉

仕事（しごと） job; work

仕事

仕方(しかた) way; method; means

仕方

食事（しょくじ） meal

食事

記事（きじ） article; news story; report

記事

火事（かじ） fire

火事

駅員（えきいん） station worker

駅員

店員（てんいん） store clerk

店員

研究（けんきゅう） research; study

研究

委員（いいん） committee member

委	員										

社員（しゃいん） company employee; member of a corporation

社	員										

大事（だいじ） important

大	事										

究める (きわめる) to master; to search

究	め	る									

委ねる (ゆだねる) to entrust (a matter) to; to devote oneself to

委	ね	る									

研究所 (けんきゅうしょ) research institute; laboratory

研	究	所									

仕上げる（しあげる） to finish up; to complete; to polish off

仕	上	げ	る								

学級委員（がっきゅういいん） class representative

学	級	委	員								

21 Kanji Workbook Activities

● 1. Stroke Order Check 書き順確認

Each kanji has a stroke with an arrow on it. Write its order number below the kanji.

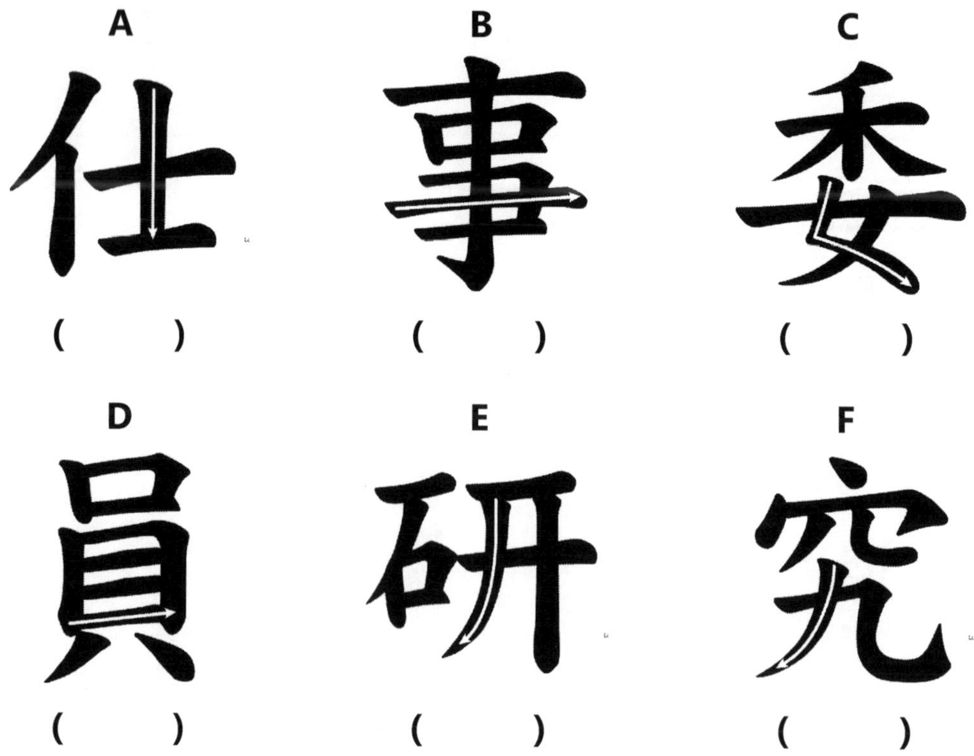

● 2. Kanji Readings

Write FURIGANA above the underlined kanji words.

1. レポートを仕上げる時間がひつようです。
2. 今日、びっくりする出来事がありました。
3. 中学で学級委員をしていました。
4. わたしは、刀を研ぐ仕事をしています。
5. わたしの研究所は三階にあります。

3. Kanji Meaning Match

Write the following kanji next to its meaning: 仕 究 階 事 章 研 員 期 委

1.____ thing 2. ____ committee 3. ____ sharpen

4. ____ serve 5. ____ member 6. ____ chapter

7. ____ research 8. ____ stairs 9. ____ period

4. Fill in the Kanji

Fill in the appropriate kanji in the blanks for each sentence.

け らい おう さま つか

1. ___ ___は ___ ___に___えます。

Servants serve the king.

いち にち さん かい しょく じ

2. わたしは___ ___ に___ ___、___ ___をします。

I eat three times in a day.

がっ こう い いん ちょう

3. ___ ___で ___ ___ ___にえらばれました。

I was chosen as the committee chairman at school.

ちち えき いん

4. ___ は ___ ___ として、はたらいています。

My father works as a station worker.

ほし けん きゅう と く

5. ___の ___ ___に___ り ___んでいます。

I am working hard on star research.

みち きわ おも

6. わたしはシェフの___を___めたいと___います。

I think I want to pursue the path to (being a) chef.

がっ きゅう い いん へん じ

7. ___ ___ ___ ___ から ___ ___ が とどきました。

A response has arrived from the class representative.

● 5. Kanji Matching

Connect each kanji with an おん or くん reading. Use each reading only ONCE.

究 •	• と
員 •	• こと
倍 •	• こ
仕 •	• し
坂 •	• い
事 •	• けん
委 •	• ばい
庫 •	• いん
研 •	• さか
都 •	• きゅう

21 Answer Key 答え合わせ

1. Stroke order check (answers)

A) 4 B) 6 C) 6

D) 8 E) 8 F) 6

3. Kanji meaning match (answers)

1. 事 thing 2. 委 committee 3. 研 sharpen

4. 仕 serve 5. 員 member 6. 章 chapter

7. 究 research 8. 階 stairs 9. 期 period

2. Kanji Readings (answers)

1. レポートを仕上(しあ)げる時間(じかん)がひつようです。 I need time to finish the report.
2. 今日(きょう)、びっくりする出来事(できごと)がありました。 There was a surprising event today.
3. 中学(ちゅうがく)で学級委員(がっきゅういいん)をしていました。 I was the class officer in junior high school.
4. わたしは、刀(かたな)を研(と)ぐ仕事(しごと)をしています。 My job is sharpening swords.
5. わたしの研究所(けんきゅうじょ)は三階(さんがい)にあります。 My laboratory is on the third floor.

4. Fill in the kanji (answers)

1. 家来は王様に仕えます。
2. わたしは一日に三回、食事をします。
3. 学校で委員長にえらばれました。
4. 父は駅員として、はたらいています。
5. 星の研究に取り組んでいます。
6. わたしはシェフの道を究めたいと思います。
7. 学級委員から返事が とどきました。

5. Kanji matching (answers)

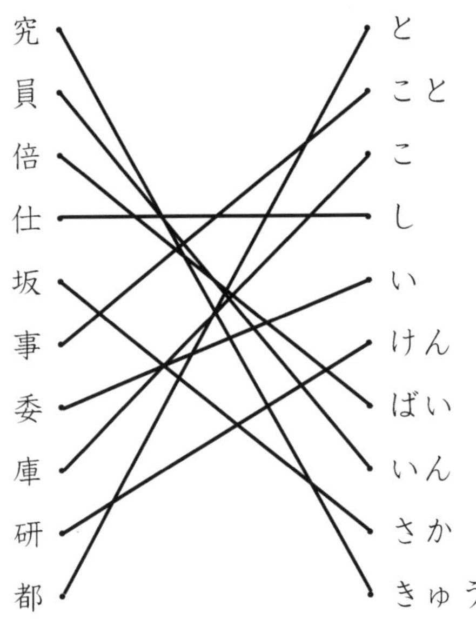

22 Kanji Lesson 22: 炭柱笛板筆皿

367-372

Kanji related to tools

22 New Kanji 新しい漢字

367	火	9 画	くん すみ	おん タン

炭

すみ 炭 charcoal	たん さん 炭酸 carbonated water; carbonic acid	すみ び 炭火 charcoal fire
せき たん 石炭 coal; pit coal	たん すい か ぶつ 炭水化物 carbohydrate	たん そ 炭素 carbon

charcoal; coal — 山 (mountain) + 厂 (cliff) + 火 (fire)

368	木	9 画	くん はしら	おん チュウ

柱

はしら 柱 pillar; post; support	はしら ど けい 柱時計 wall clock; grandfather clock	ちゃ ばしら 茶柱 upright-floating tea stalk
でん ちゅう 電柱 power pole; utility pole	だい こく ばしら 大黒柱 central pillar; main provider	せき ちゅう 石柱 stone pillar

pillar; post; cylinder; support — 木 (tree) + 主 (master)

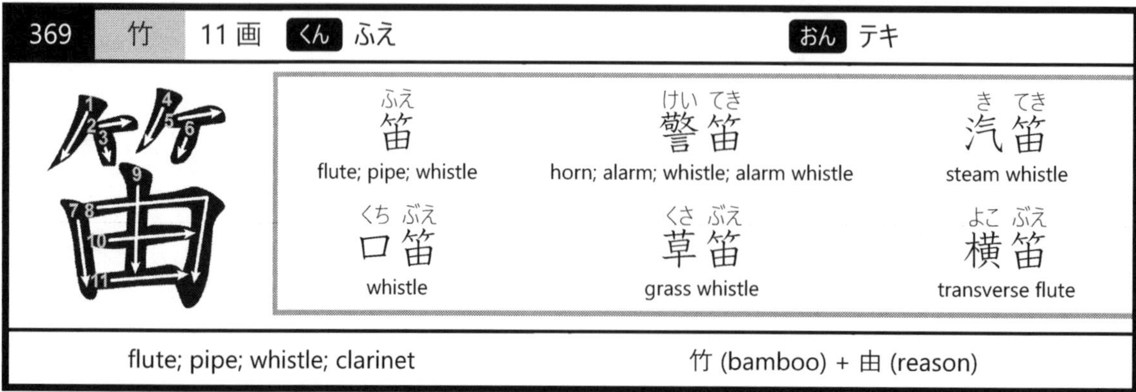

369	竹	11 画	くん ふえ	おん テキ

笛

ふえ 笛 flute; pipe; whistle	けい てき 警笛 horn; alarm; whistle; alarm whistle	き てき 汽笛 steam whistle
くち ぶえ 口笛 whistle	くさ ぶえ 草笛 grass whistle	よこ ぶえ 横笛 transverse flute

flute; pipe; whistle; clarinet — 竹 (bamboo) + 由 (reason)

370	木	8 画	くん いた	おん ハン、バン

板

いた 板 board; plank	ごう はん 合板 veneer board; joint publication	いた まな板 cutting board
こく ばん 黒板 blackboard	かん ばん 看板 signboard; sign; doorplate	はん が 版画 woodblock print

board; plank; plate; stage — 木 (tree) + 反 (anti-)

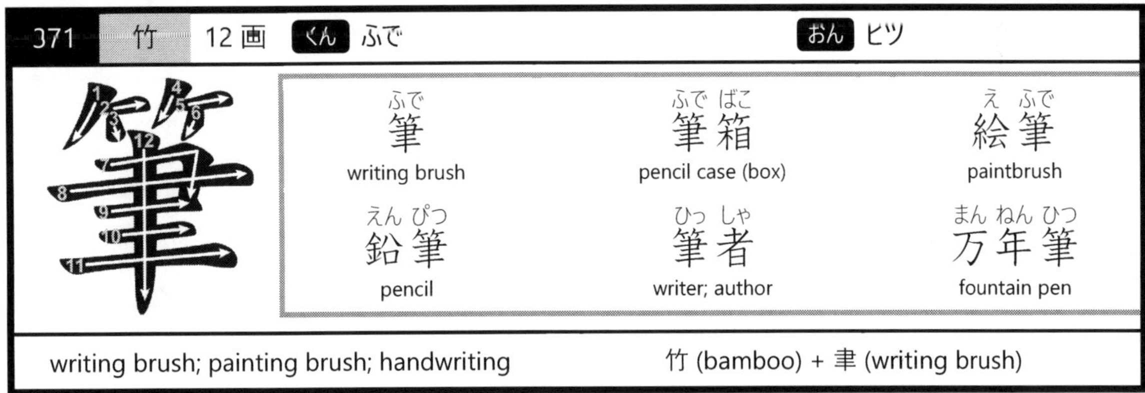

371	竹	12 画	くん ふで	おん ヒツ

筆

ふで 筆 writing brush	ふで ばこ 筆箱 pencil case (box)	え ふで 絵筆 paintbrush
えん ぴつ 鉛筆 pencil	ひっ しゃ 筆者 writer; author	まん ねん ひつ 万年筆 fountain pen

writing brush; painting brush; handwriting — 竹 (bamboo) + 聿 (writing brush)

372	皿	5 画	くん さら	おん none

皿

さら 皿 dish; plate; serving	さら あら 皿洗い washing-up; dish-washing	こ ざら 小皿 small dish
はい ざら 灰皿 ashtray	ひと さら 一皿 one plate	う ざら 受け皿 saucer

dish; plate — 皿 (dish)

Kanji Parts used in the New Kanji

山	mountain	主	master	聿	writing brush
厂	cliff	竹	bamboo	皿	dish
火	fire	由	reason		
木	tree	反	anti-		

22 Kanji Memory Tools 漢字記憶術

This section helps you organically memorize kanji readings, meanings, and construction.

炭

山 厂 火
The mountain on the cliff is on fire due to " **COAL**".

すみ び やきにく た とき たんさんいんりょう の
❶炭火焼肉を食べる時は、❷炭酸飲料が飲みたくなる。

When I eat ❶charcoal grilled meat, I want to drink a ❷carbonated drink.

柱

木 主
The tree is the master of all "**PILLAR(S)**".

いえ はしら ねんだい でんちゅう つく
この家の❶柱は 1900年代の❷電柱で作られています。

The ❶pillars of this house are made out of 1900's ❷power poles.

笛

竹 由
Being made by bamboo is the reason I wanted this "**FLUTE**".

でんしゃ けいてき くちぶえ おと き
電車の❶警笛で❷口笛の音が聞こえない。

I can't hear the ❶whistling because of the train ❷horn.

板

木 反
A tree is the anti-thesis of a "**BOARD**".

いた かんばん つく
❶板で❷看板を作った。

I made a ❷sign with a ❶board.

筆

竹 聿
Bamboo is used to make writing brush and "**PAINTING BRUSH**".

わたし まんねんひつ えんぴつ ふでばこ い
私の❶万年筆と❷鉛筆を❸筆箱に入れた。

I put my ❶fountain pen and ❷pencil in the ❸pencil case.

皿

皿
A dish is also a "**PLATE**".

さらあら おおざら わ
❶皿洗いのバイトで、❷大皿を割ってしまいました。

At my ❶dishwashing part time job I accidently broke a ❷platter.

22 Understanding Kanji Parts 漢字部分の理解

● 22-1. The "bamboo" radical たけかんむり (竹)

Let's look at some kanji that have たけかんむり (bamboo radical).

flute; clarinet; pipe; whistle		writing brush; painting brush	
笛	くちぶえ 口笛 whistle	筆	ふで 筆 writing brush
bamboo + reason	きてき 汽笛 steam whistle	bamboo + writing brush	ひっしゃ 筆者 writer; author

solution; answer		calculate; number; divining	
答	こた 答え answer; reply; response	算	さんすう 算数 arithmetic
bamboo + suited	くちごた 口答え back talk; backchat	bamboo + eye + 20	けいさん 計算 calculation; count

ordinal number; residence		etc.; and so forth; class; equal	
第	だいいっぽ 第一歩 first step	等	びょうどう 平等 equality; evenness; fair
bamboo + condolences + NO	だいさんしゃ 第三者 third person; third party	bamboo + temple	いっとう 一等 first-class; first-rank

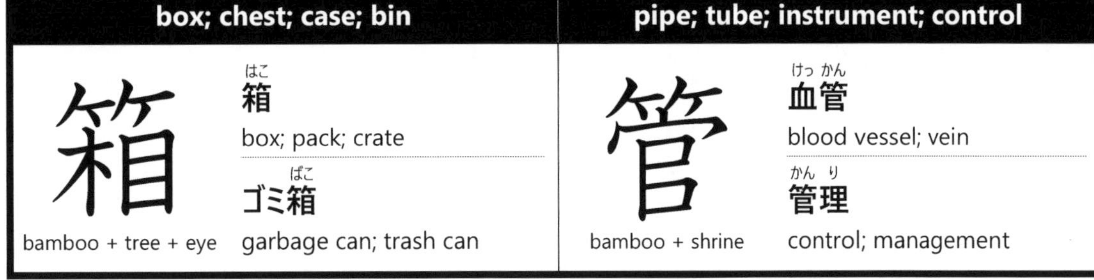

box; chest; case; bin		pipe; tube; instrument; control	
箱	はこ 箱 box; pack; crate	管	けっかん 血管 blood vessel; vein
bamboo + tree + eye	ばこ ゴミ箱 garbage can; trash can	bamboo + shrine	かんり 管理 control; management

22 Kanji Usage 漢字の使い方

● 22-2. Good fortune from upright-floating tea stalks? 柱

For a 茶柱 (tea stalk) to float upright in tea, many conditions must be met.

1) The 茎 (stalk) must still be attached to the 茶葉 (tea leaf), which is rare!
2) The 茶こし (tea strainer) must have allowed a relatively thick 茎 (stalk, stem) through the strainer mesh.
3) The 茎 (stalk) must have absorbed water to be heavy, while one portion must be light to allow it to stand.

It's considered 珍しい (unusual; rare) or めったにない (rare) when all three of these conditions are met. And めったにない events are thought to be 縁起が良い (a good omen; good fortune).

● 22-3. Useful set phrases using 板

Here are some set phrases using 板 from this lesson.

板につく	to get used to one's work; to become accustomed to one's position
結婚して、主婦の生活が板についてきました。 After getting married, (she) became accustomed to her lifestyle as a housewife.	
退職して、主夫の生活が板についてきました。 After retiring, (he) became accustomed to his lifestyle as a house husband.	

NOTE: In both a new role was taken after a life change. しゅふ means both "housewife" and "house-husband" just by changing the kanji. This phrase can be used for anyone in a new role or job. However, it should not be used when talking to someone above you in status.

板挟みになる	to be stuck between a rock and a hard place; to be torn between conflicting demands
係長の私は、上司と部下の板挟みになって大変です。 As the chief of staff, I have a hard time getting caught between my boss and my subordinates.	

22 Words You Can Write 書ける言葉

石炭（せきたん） coal

石炭

炭火(すみび) charcoal fire

炭火

電柱(でんちゅう) power pole; utility pole

電柱

汽笛(きてき) steam whistle

汽笛

草笛(くさぶえ) grass whistle

草笛

黒板(こくばん) blackboard

黒板

毛筆(もうひつ) ink brush

毛筆

絵筆(えふで) paintbrush

絵筆

大皿（おおざら） large plate; platter

大皿

登板（とうばん） taking the mound; pitching a game

登板

筆先（ふでさき） tip of brush

筆先

自筆（じひつ） one's own handwriting; autograph

自筆

木炭画（もくたんが） charcoal drawing

木炭画

柱時計（はしらどけい） wall clock

柱時計

大黒柱（だいこくばしら） central pillar; main provider

大黒柱

板の間（いたのま） a room with a wooden floor

板の間

22 Kanji Workbook Activities

● 1. Stroke Order Check 書き順確認

Each kanji has a stroke with an arrow on it. Write its order number below the kanji.

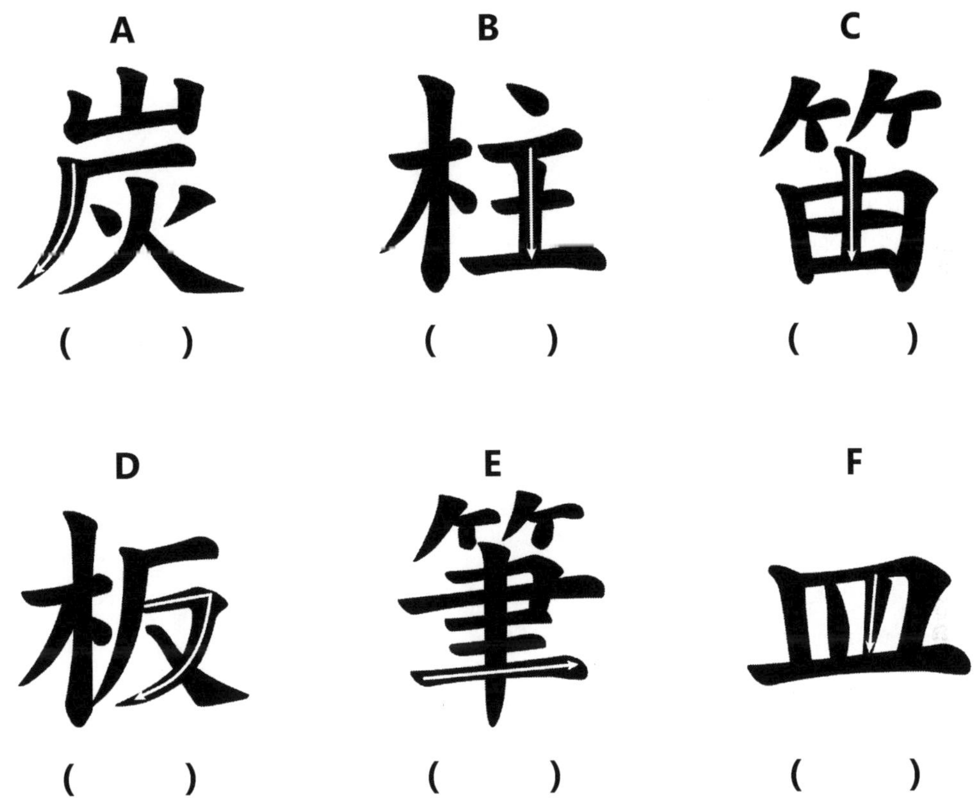

● 2. Kanji Readings

Write FURIGANA above the underlined kanji words.

1. あれは石炭を運ぶ列車です。
2. 先日、車をお神社の石柱にぶつけてしまいました。
3. 遠くから汽笛の音が聞こえます。
4. 日本の多くの小学校では、黒板が使われています。
5. 筆で字を書く時は、筆先を整えて下さい。

● 3. Kanji Meaning Match

Write the following kanji next to its meaning: 員 笛 仕 究 皿 筆 板 炭 柱

1.____ pillar　　2. ____ charcoal　　3. ____ whistle

4. ____ board　　5. ____ brush　　6. ____ dish

7. ____ serve　　8. ____ member　　9. ____ research

● 4. Fill in the Kanji

Fill in the appropriate kanji in the blanks for each sentence.

すみ　び

1. ____ ____やきのチキンは おいしいです。

Charcoal fired chicken is delicious.

か　ぞく　だい　こく　ばしら　ちち　はは

2. うちの ____ ____の____ ____ ____は ____ではなく、____ です。

The central pillar of our family is not my father, but my mother.

おとうと　くち　ぶえ　ある

3. ____ は よく____ ____をふきながら____きます。

My younger brother often walks while he whistles.

へ　や　いた　ま

4. わたしの____ ____は____の____だから ゆかが いつも つめたいです。

Since my room has a wooden floor, the floor is always cold.

あか　ふで　も

5. むすめは ____ い____ ばこを____っています。

My daughter has a red pencil case.

まい　にち　さら　て

6. ____ ____、お____ あらいを____つだいます。

I help with dish washing every day.

うち　ふる　はしら　ど　けい

7. ____に おじいさんの ____い____ ____ ____ があります。

My grandfather's old wall clock is in our house.

● 5. Kanji Matching

Connect each kanji with an おん or くん reading. Use each reading only ONCE.

筆 •	• ひつ
橋 •	• こと
笛 •	• たん
炭 •	• さか
畑 •	• はた
皿 •	• ふえ
板 •	• さら
坂 •	• はし
柱 •	• ちゅう
事 •	• いた

22 Answer Key 答え合わせ

1. Stroke order check (answers)

A) 5 B) 7 C) 9
D) 7 E) 11 F) 4

3. Kanji meaning match (answers)

1. 柱 pillar 2. 炭 charcoal 3. 笛 whistle
4. 板 board 5. 筆 brush 6. 皿 dish
7. 仕 serve 8. 員 member 9. 究 research

2. Kanji Readings (answers)

1. あれは石炭(せきたん)を運(はこ)ぶ列車(れっしゃ)です。 That's a train that transports coal.
2. 先日(せんじつ)、車(くるま)をお神社(じんじゃ)の石柱(せきちゅう)にぶつけてしまいました。 The other day I crashed my car into the stone pillar of a shrine.
3. 遠(とお)くから汽笛(きてき)の音(おと)が聞(き)こえます。 The sound of a steam whistle can be heard from far away.
4. 日本(にほん)の多(おお)くの小学校(しょうがっこう)では、黒板(こくばん)が使(つか)われています。 Blackboards are used in many elementary schools in Japan.
5. 筆(ふで)で字(じ)を書(か)く時(とき)は、筆先(ふでさき)を整(ととの)えて下(くだ)さい。 When writing with a brush, please prepare the tip of the brush.

4. Fill in the kanji (answers)

1. 炭火やきのチキンは、おいしいです。
2. うちの家族の大黒柱は父ではなく、母です。
3. 弟は よく口笛をふきながら歩きます。
4. わたしの部屋は板の間だから、ゆかが いつも つめたいです。
5. むすめは 赤い筆ばこを持っています。
6. 毎日、お皿あらいを手つだいます。
7. 家におじいさんの古い柱時計があります。

5. Kanji matching (answers)

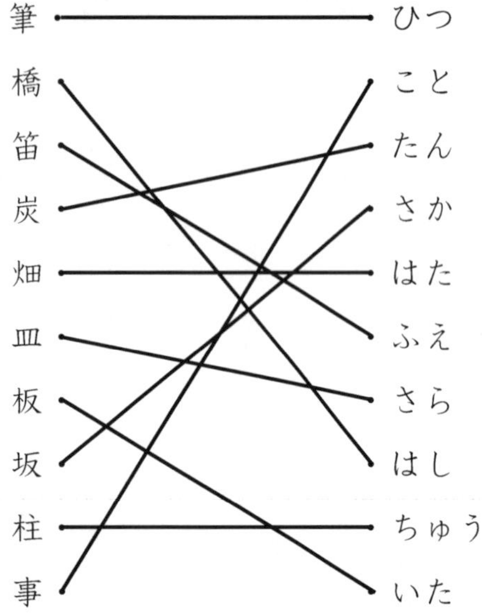

23 Kanji Lesson 23: 品服物薬箱帳

373-378

Kanji use to describe "things"

23 New Kanji 新しい漢字

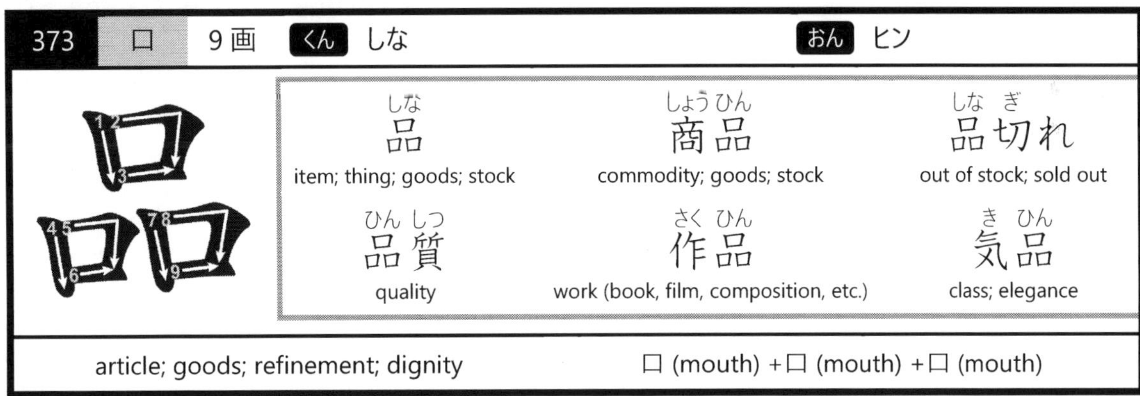

373 | 口 | 9 画 | くん しな | おん ヒン

品

品 (しな) item; thing; goods; stock	商品 (しょうひん) commodity; goods; stock	品切れ (しなぎ) out of stock; sold out
品質 (ひんしつ) quality	作品 (さくひん) work (book, film, composition, etc.)	気品 (きひん) class; elegance

article; goods; refinement; dignity — 口 (mouth) +口 (mouth) +口 (mouth)

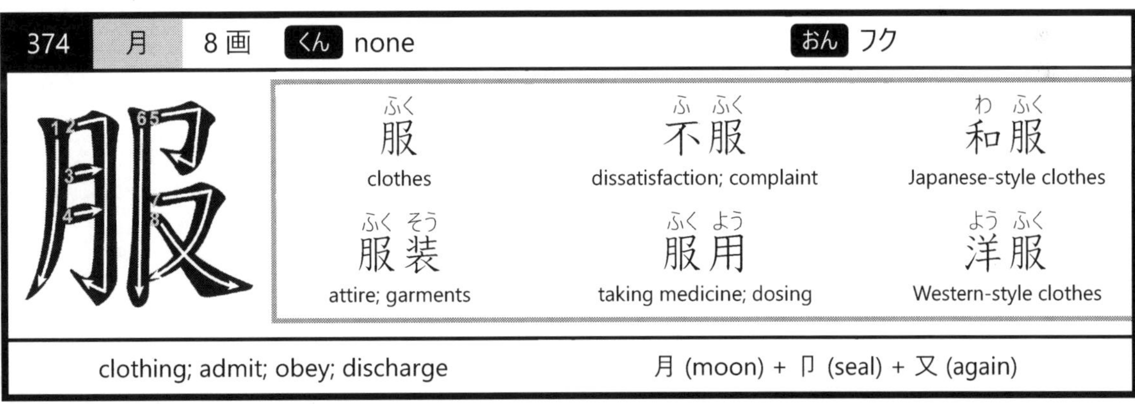

374 | 月 | 8 画 | くん none | おん フク

服

服 (ふく) clothes	不服 (ふふく) dissatisfaction; complaint	和服 (わふく) Japanese-style clothes
服装 (ふくそう) attire; garments	服用 (ふくよう) taking medicine; dosing	洋服 (ようふく) Western-style clothes

clothing; admit; obey; discharge — 月 (moon) + 卩 (seal) + 又 (again)

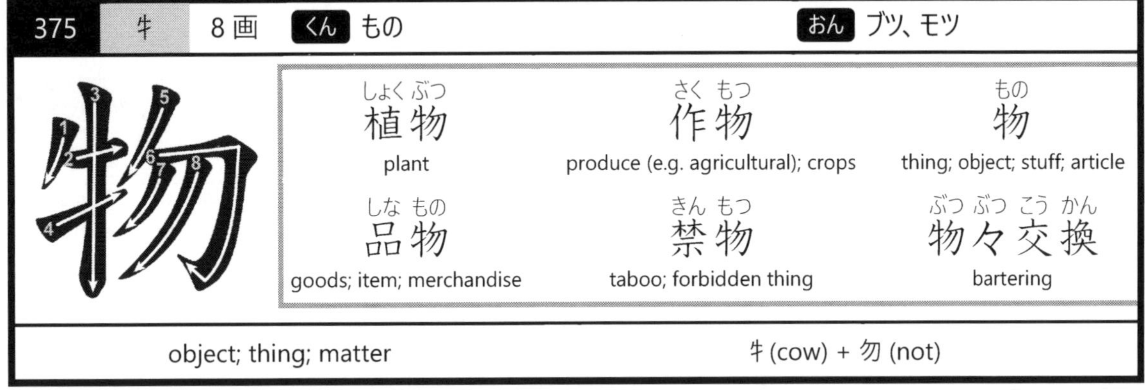

375 | 牛 | 8 画 | くん もの | おん ブツ、モツ

物

植物 (しょくぶつ) plant	作物 (さくもつ) produce (e.g. agricultural); crops	物 (もの) thing; object; stuff; article
品物 (しなもの) goods; item; merchandise	禁物 (きんもつ) taboo; forbidden thing	物々交換 (ぶつぶつこうかん) bartering

object; thing; matter — 牛 (cow) + 勿 (not)

376	艹	16 画	くん くすり	おん ヤク

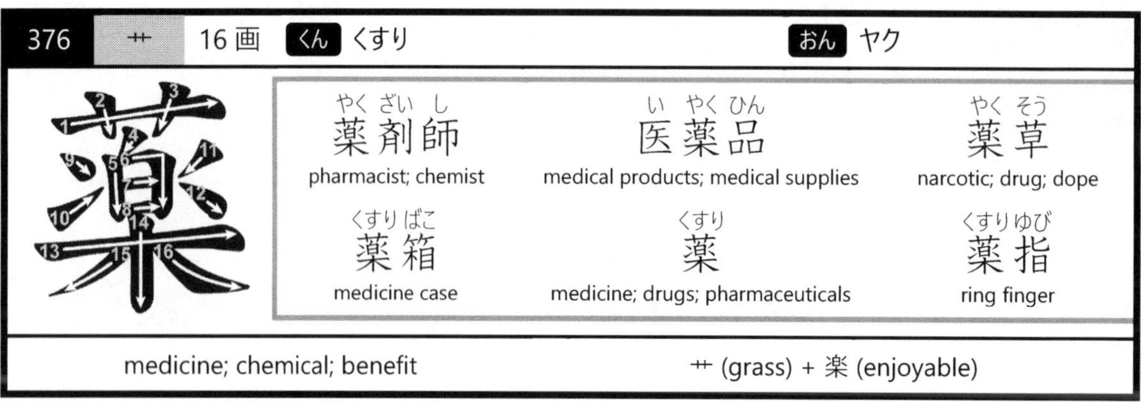

やく ざい し 薬剤師 pharmacist; chemist	い やく ひん 医薬品 medical products; medical supplies	やく そう 薬草 narcotic; drug; dope
くすり ばこ 薬箱 medicine case	くすり 薬 medicine; drugs; pharmaceuticals	くすり ゆび 薬指 ring finger

medicine; chemical; benefit — 艹 (grass) + 楽 (enjoyable)

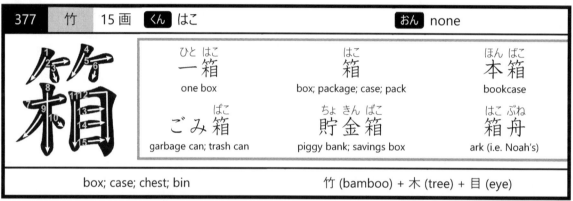

377	竹	15 画	くん はこ	おん none

ひと はこ 一箱 one box	はこ 箱 box; package; case; pack	ほん ばこ 本箱 bookcase
ばこ ごみ箱 garbage can; trash can	ちょ きん ばこ 貯金箱 piggy bank; savings box	はこ ぶね 箱舟 ark (i.e. Noah's)

box; case; chest; bin — 竹 (bamboo) + 木 (tree) + 目 (eye)

378	巾	11 画	くん none	おん チョウ

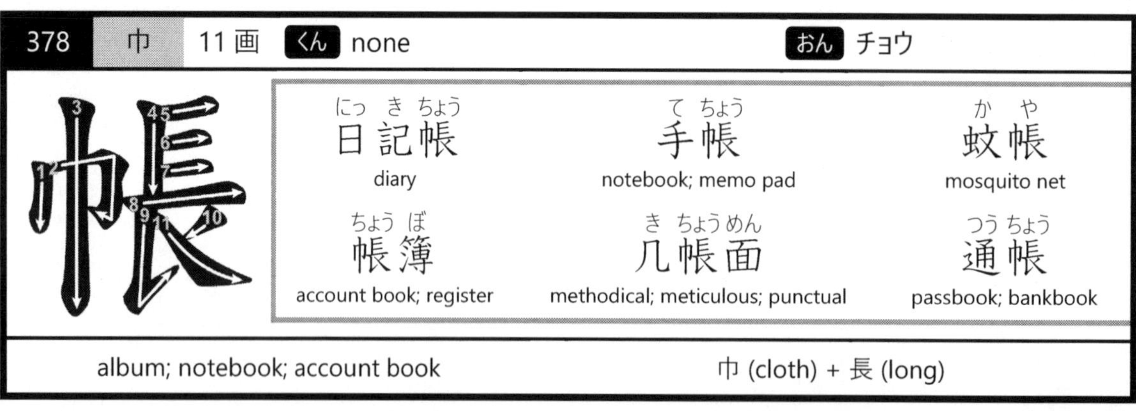

にっ き ちょう 日記帳 diary	て ちょう 手帳 notebook; memo pad	か や 蚊帳 mosquito net
ちょう ぼ 帳簿 account book; register	き ちょう めん 几帳面 methodical; meticulous; punctual	つう ちょう 通帳 passbook; bankbook

album; notebook; account book — 巾 (cloth) + 長 (long)

Kanji Parts used in the New Kanji

口	mouth	勿	not	目	eye
月	moon	艹	grass	巾	cloth
卩	seal	楽	enjoyable	長	long
又	again	竹	bamboo		
牛	cow	木	tree		

23 Kanji Memory Tools 漢字記憶術

This section helps you organically memorize kanji readings, meanings, and construction.

品

口 口 口
My mouth, your mouth and his mouth can use many "**GOODS**".

欲しい❶商品は、全て❷品切れでした。
All of the ❶products I want are ❷sold out.

服

月 卩 又
There is a moon on my seal and again on my "**CLOTHING**".

❶服を着替えたら❷一服しましょう。
After we change our ❶clothes, let's ❷take a break.

物

牛 勿
The cow is not an "**OBJECT**".

❶動物は動く❷生き物だ。
❶Animals are ❷living things that move.

薬

艹 楽
This grass was enjoyable "**MEDICINE**".

❶薬局で❷薬剤師さんから❸薬を買いました。
I bought the ❸medicine from the ❷pharmacist at the ❶pharmacy.

箱

竹 木 目
The bamboo tree has its eye on that "**BOX**".

❶貯金箱を❷箱に入れました。
I put my ❶piggy bank in a ❷box.

帳

巾 長
A cloth that's really long is in my "**ACCOUNT BOOK**".

❶几帳面な人は❷手帳にたくさんメモを書く。
A ❶methodical person writes many memos in their ❷notebook.

23 Kanji Usage 漢字の使い方

● 23-1. Same kanji, different reading/meaning 品

Often when a kanji is used by itself, it's read with the 訓読み(くんよみ) (Japanese reading), and when combined with other kanji to make a 熟語(じゅくご) (compound kanji word), it tends to be 音読み(おんよみ) (Chinese reading). Of course this rule doesn't always work, as some kanji like 品 show us.

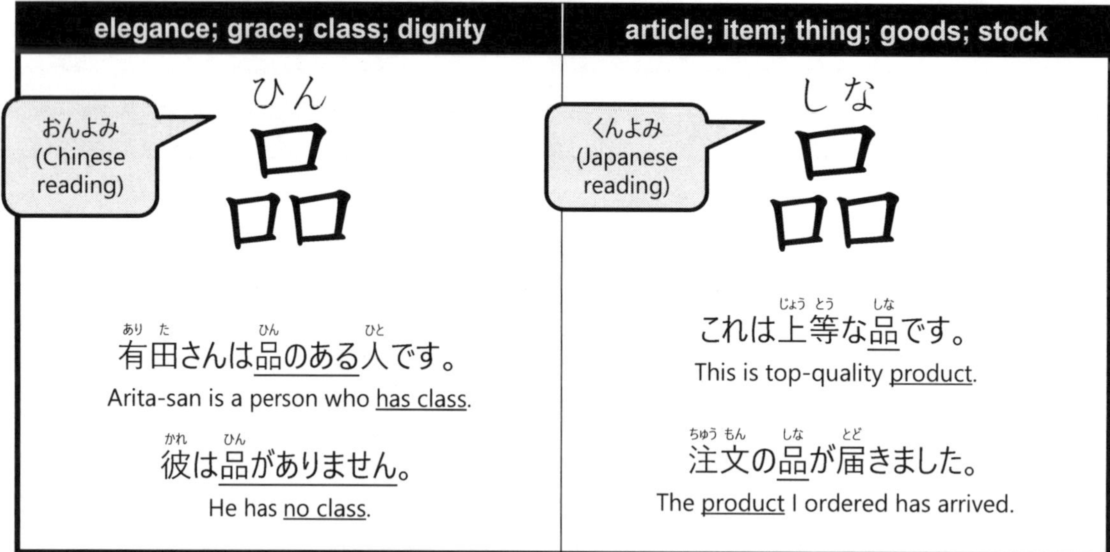

elegance; grace; class; dignity
おんよみ (Chinese reading)
ひん
品
有田(ありた)さんは品(ひん)のある人(ひと)です。
Arita-san is a person who has class.
彼(かれ)は品(ひん)がありません。
He has no class.
article; item; thing; goods; stock
くんよみ (Japanese reading)
しな
品
これは上等(じょうとう)な品(しな)です。
This is top-quality product.
注文(ちゅうもん)の品(しな)が届(とど)きました。
The product I ordered has arrived.

Here are some other words using 品.

品質(ひんしつ)	quality	商品(しょうひん)	merchandise
手品(てじな)	magic; illusion	下品(げひん)	vulgar; indecent

You probably noticed that all the words above, except one, have 品 as ひん. While normally compound kanji tend to use the 音読み (おんよみ) "Chinese reading", it isn't always the case. Here are some other words using 品 that break the quick rule about which reading to use.

goods; article; thing	sold out; out of stock
しな もの 品物	しな ぎ 品切れ

● 23-2. People in the box 箱

箱入り娘 is a term that directly translates to “daughter in a box”. It comes from the Edo period in Japan when items of value were stored or moved in boxes. It can either mean that the daughter, normally from a wealthy family, is treated as special or that she has lived a sheltered life. The interpretation is different from person to person. In modern times, other things are called 箱入りの______ (a treasured ______) to show that the item is a treasured item.

“Trash can” in Japanese is ゴミ箱. However, there is another interesting box. The Japanese have a custom of buying お札 (talisman) at temples for good luck in a variety of categories ranging from finding love to healing a pain in their lower back. At the beginning of the year, the talisman is returned to the temple and put into the お祓い箱 (purification box). This act has been co-opted into the act of removing things from your life that aren’t needed with お払い箱 using the kanji 払 (pay, clear out) instead of 祓 (purify). It can also be used in a very negative way to say you got dumped or fired with the phrase, お払い箱になる.

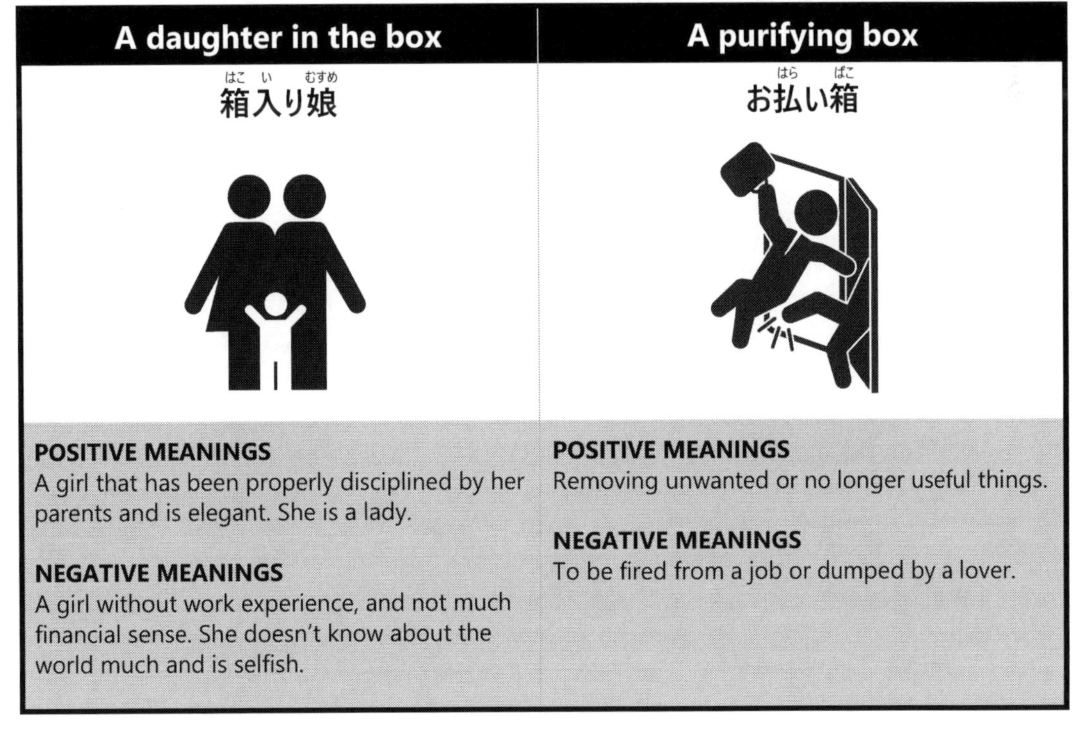

A daughter in the box
箱入り娘
POSITIVE MEANINGS
A girl that has been properly disciplined by her parents and is elegant. She is a lady.
NEGATIVE MEANINGS
A girl without work experience, and not much financial sense. She doesn’t know about the world much and is selfish.
A purifying box
お払い箱
POSITIVE MEANINGS
Removing unwanted or no longer useful things.
NEGATIVE MEANINGS
To be fired from a job or dumped by a lover.

● 23-3. Compound words using 物

Be careful to note that the reading of 物 changes depending on the word.

Compound	Meaning of the first kanji	English
生物（せいぶつ）	生 = life; genuine; birth	living thing; creature; biology
動物（どうぶつ）	動 = move; motion; shift	animal
名物（めいぶつ）	名 = name; noted; reputation	famous product; specialty
着物（きもの）	着 = wear; clothing; arrive	kimono; clothes
本物（ほんもの）	本 = book; true; main; origin; real	real thing; genuine article
建物（たてもの）	建 = build	building
宝物（たからもの）	宝 = treasure; wealth; valuables	treasure; treasured item
禁物（きんもつ）	禁 = prohibition; ban; forbid	taboo; forbidden thing
荷物（にもつ）	荷 = baggage; load; cargo	luggage; baggage; package

23 Words You Can Write 書ける言葉

上品（じょうひん） elegant; refined; polished

上品

下品（げひん） vulgar; indecent; crude

下品

夏服（なつふく） summer clothes

夏服

冬服（ふゆふく） winter clothes

冬服

動物（どうぶつ） animal

動物

物語（ものがたり） story; tale; legend

物語

薬屋（くすりや） drug store

薬屋

薬品（やくひん） medicine; chemicals

薬品

筆箱（ふでばこ） pencil box; pencil case

筆	箱										

木箱（きばこ） wooden box

木	箱										

通帳（つうちょう） bankbook

通	帳										

食品（しょくひん） food; food products

食	品										

書物（しょもつ） book; volume

書	物										

電話帳（でんわちょう） telephone directory

電	話	帳									

物知り（ものしり） well-informed person; walking dictionary

物	知	り									

空き箱（あきばこ） empty box

空	き	箱									

23 Kanji Workbook Activities

● 1. Stroke Order Check 書き順確認

Each kanji has a stroke with an arrow on it. Write its order number below the kanji.

● 2. Kanji Readings

Write FURIGANA above the underlined kanji words.

1. <u>社長</u>のおくさんは、<u>上品</u>できれいな<u>方</u>です。

2. <u>今</u>は、かぜ<u>薬</u>だけ<u>服用</u>しています。

3. <u>兄</u>は<u>本</u>をたくさん<u>読</u>んでいて、<u>物知</u>りです。

4. <u>空</u>き<u>箱</u>があったら、<u>一箱</u>ください。

5. <u>新</u>しい<u>日記帳</u>を<u>買</u>いました。

● 3. Kanji Meaning Match

Write the following kanji next to its meaning: 服 薬 帳 炭 委 品 物 箱 階

1.____ album　2. ____ box　3. ____ object

4. ____ medicine　5. ____ stairs　6. ____ committee

7. ____ charcoal　8. ____ clothes　9. ____ goods

● 4. Fill in the Kanji

Fill in the appropriate kanji in the blanks for each sentence.

もう　いま　しな　ぎ

1. ____ しわけありません。____、____ ____れです。

I apologize, we are currently out of stock.

さむ　ふゆ　ふく　だ

2. ____ くなったから、____ ____ を____します。

I'm going to take out winter clothes since it got cold.

こ　とき　いろ　もの　がたり　よ

3. ____ どもの____ 、____ んな____ ____を____みました。

I read a variety of stories (tales) when I was a kid.

い　やく　ひん　やっ　きょく　か

4. この____ ____ ____は、____ ____で ____えます。

You can buy this medicine at the pharmacy.

くすり　ばこ　め　ぐすり　と　くだ

5. あの____ ____から ____ ____を____ って____さい。

Please take some eye drops from that medicine box over there.

て　ちょう　か

6. ____ ____ に よていを ____ いておきます。

I'll write my plans in my notebook (planner).

みせ　しな　もの

7. このお____ には、いい ____ ____がたくさん あります。

There are a lot of good products in this store.

● 5. Kanji Matching

Connect each kanji with an おん or くん reading. Use each reading only ONCE.

品 •	• ひん
等 •	• やく
薬 •	• とう
帳 •	• やど
宿 •	• いん
湖 •	• ちょう
服 •	• ぶつ
物 •	• こ
院 •	• はこ
箱 •	• ふく

23 Answer Key 答え合わせ

1. Stroke order check (answers)

A) 8 B) 6 C) 7

D) 8 E) 12 F) 5

2. Kanji Readings (answers)

1. 社長(しゃちょう)のおくさんは、上品(じょうひん)できれいな方(かた)です。
The company president's wife is an elegant and pretty person.
2. 今(いま)は、かぜ薬(ぐすり)だけ服用(ふくよう)しています。
Right now, I'm only taking cold medicine.
3. 兄(あに)は本(ほん)をたくさん読(よ)んでいて、物知(ものし)りです。
My older brother reads a lot of books and knows a lot.
4. 空(あ)き箱(ばこ)があったら、一箱(ひとはこ)ください。
If you have any empty boxes, please give me one.
5. 新(あたら)しい日記帳(にっきちょう)を買(か)いました。
I bought a new diary book.

3. Kanji meaning match (answers)

1. 帳 album 2. 箱 box 3. 物 object
4. 薬 medicine 5. 階 stairs 6. 委 committee
7. 炭 charcoal 8. 服 clothes 9. 品 goods

4. Fill in the kanji (answers)

1. 申しわけありません。今、品切れです。
2. 寒くなったから、冬服を出します。
3. 子どもの時、色んな物語を読みました。
4. この医薬品は、薬局で買えます。
5. あの薬箱から目薬を取って下さい。
6. 手帳によていを書いておきます。
7. このお店には、いい品物がたくさんあります。

5. Kanji matching (answers)

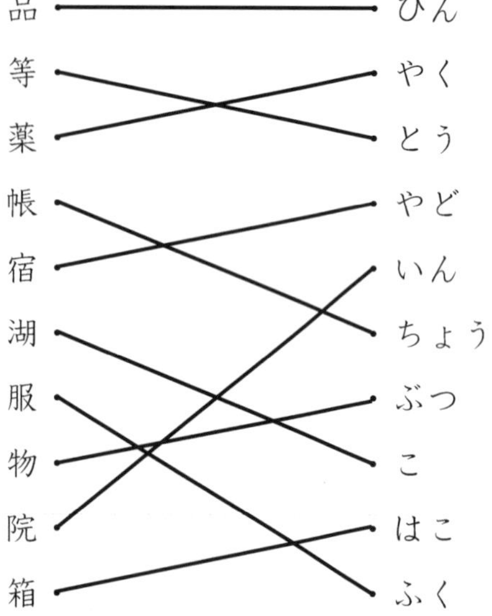

24 Kanji Lesson 24: 詩漢題予勉礼

379-384

Kanji related to "studying"

24 New Kanji 新しい漢字

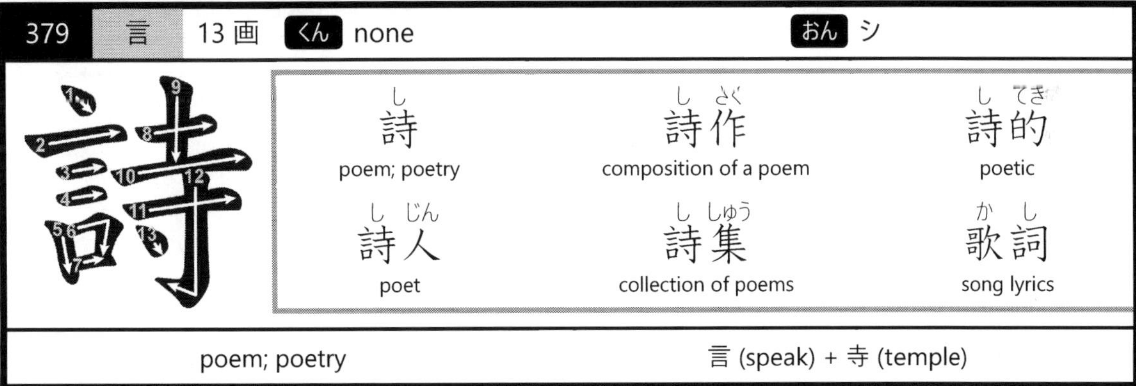

379 | 言 | 13 画 | くん none | おん シ

し 詩 poem; poetry	し さく 詩作 composition of a poem	し てき 詩的 poetic
し じん 詩人 poet	し しゅう 詩集 collection of poems	か し 歌詞 song lyrics

poem; poetry — 言 (speak) + 寺 (temple)

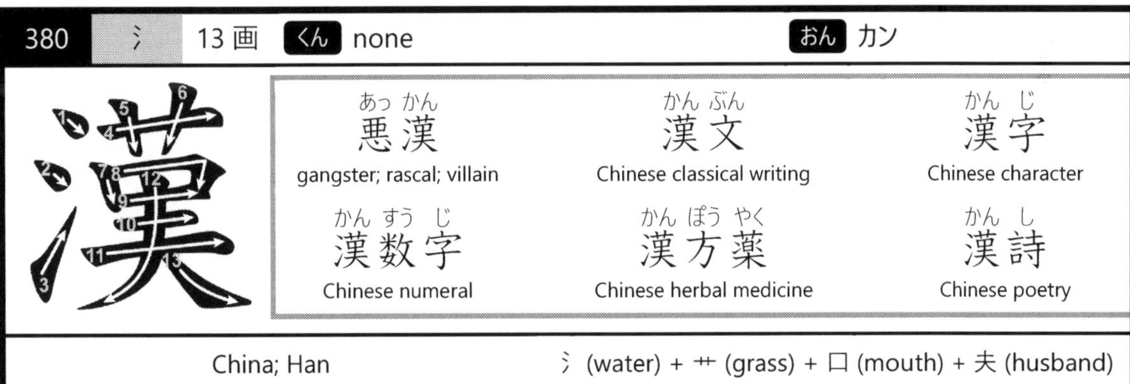

380 | 氵 | 13 画 | くん none | おん カン

あっ かん 悪漢 gangster; rascal; villain	かん ぶん 漢文 Chinese classical writing	かん じ 漢字 Chinese character
かん すう じ 漢数字 Chinese numeral	かん ぽう やく 漢方薬 Chinese herbal medicine	かん し 漢詩 Chinese poetry

China; Han — 氵 (water) + 艹 (grass) + 口 (mouth) + 夫 (husband)

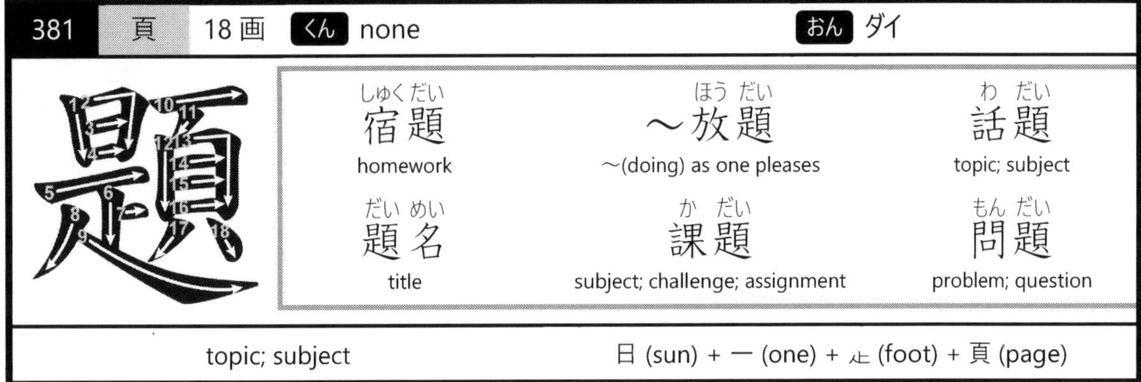

381 | 頁 | 18 画 | くん none | おん ダイ

しゅく だい 宿題 homework	ほう だい ～放題 ～(doing) as one pleases	わ だい 話題 topic; subject
だい めい 題名 title	か だい 課題 subject; challenge; assignment	もん だい 問題 problem; question

topic; subject — 日 (sun) + 一 (one) + 止 (foot) + 頁 (page)

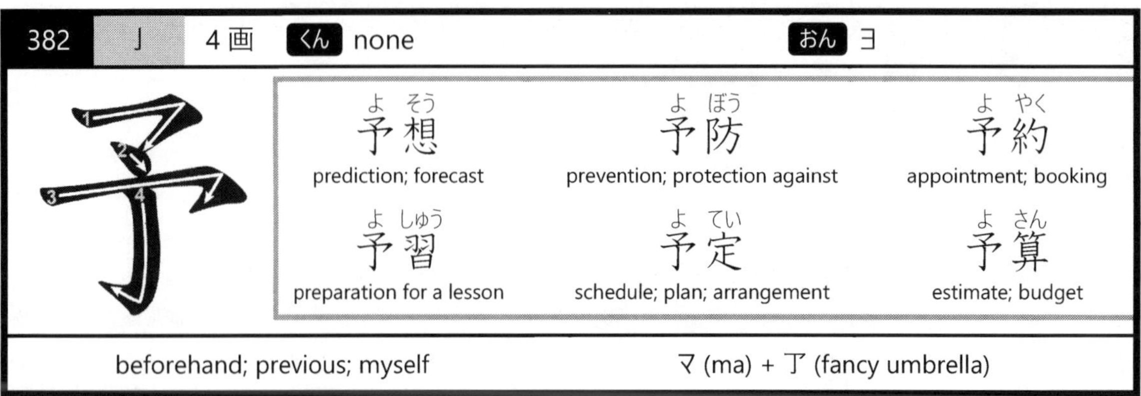

382 | 亅 | 4 画 | くん none | おん ヨ

よそう 予想	よぼう 予防	よやく 予約
prediction; forecast	prevention; protection against	appointment; booking
よしゅう 予習	よてい 予定	よさん 予算
preparation for a lesson	schedule; plan; arrangement	estimate; budget

beforehand; previous; myself — マ (ma) + 了 (fancy umbrella)

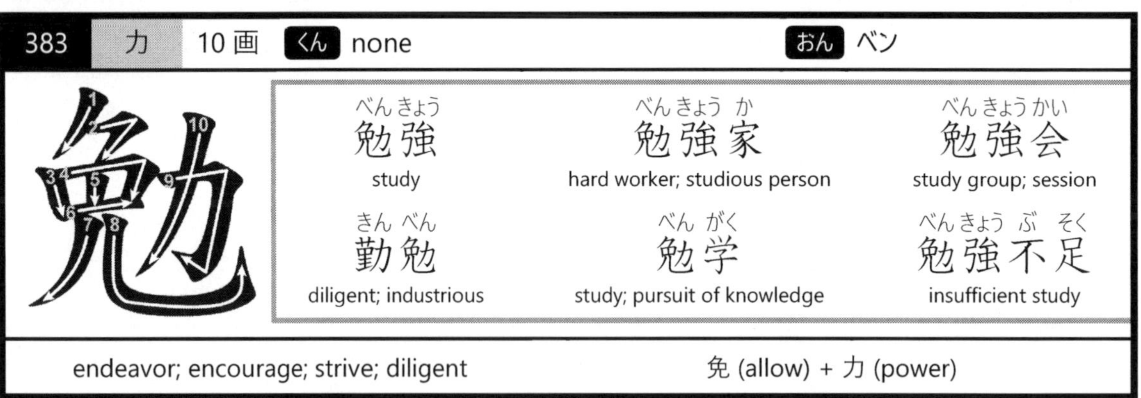

383 | 力 | 10 画 | くん none | おん ベン

べんきょう 勉強	べんきょうか 勉強家	べんきょうかい 勉強会
study	hard worker; studious person	study group; session
きんべん 勤勉	べんがく 勉学	べんきょうぶそく 勉強不足
diligent; industrious	study; pursuit of knowledge	insufficient study

endeavor; encourage; strive; diligent — 免 (allow) + 力 (power)

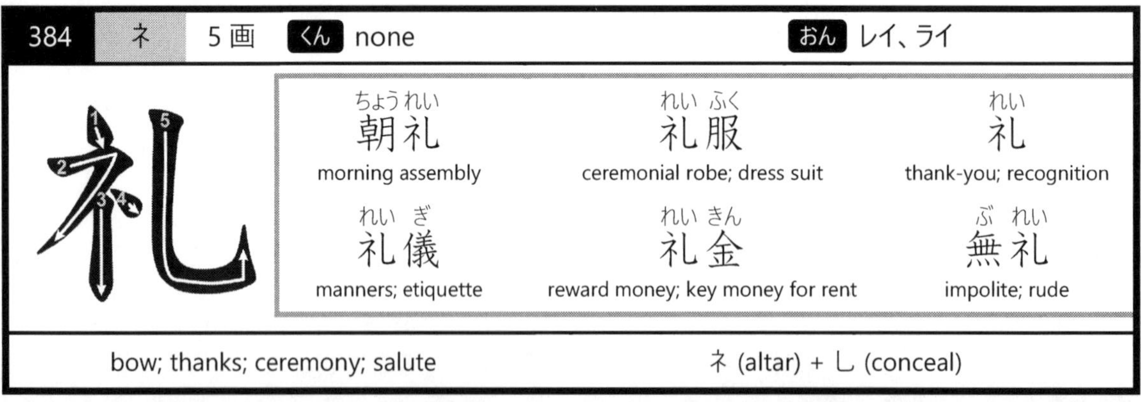

384 | ネ | 5 画 | くん none | おん レイ、ライ

ちょうれい 朝礼	れいふく 礼服	れい 礼
morning assembly	ceremonial robe; dress suit	thank-you; recognition
れいぎ 礼儀	れいきん 礼金	ぶれい 無礼
manners; etiquette	reward money; key money for rent	impolite; rude

bow; thanks; ceremony; salute — ネ (altar) + し (conceal)

Kanji Parts used in the New Kanji

言	speak	日	sun	免	allow
寺	temple	一	one	力	power
氵	water	止	foot	ネ	altar
艹	grass	頁	page	し	conceal
口	mouth	マ	katakana MA		
夫	husband	了	fancy umbrella		

24 Kanji Memory Tools 漢字記憶術

This section helps you organically memorize kanji readings, meanings, and construction.

詩

言 寺
You can speak at the temple your "**POEM**".

この曲(きょく)の❶歌詞(かし)は❷詩的(してき)です。

The ❶lyrics of this song are ❷poetic.

漢

氵 艹 口 夫
Water and grass sustains the mouth of your husband in "**CHINA**".

❶漢和辞典(かんわじてん)で❷漢字(かんじ)を調(しら)べました。

I looked up a ❶Chinese character in a ❷Chinese character dictionary.

題

日 一 龰 頁
The sun has one foot on the page for this "**SUBJECT**".

❶宿題(しゅくだい)が終わったら、お菓子(かし)が❷食(た)べ放題(ほうだい)だよ。

When you finish your ❶homework, snacks are ❷all you can eat.

予

マ 丁
I wrote a katakana ma on my fancy umbrella "**BEFOREHAND**".

インフルエンザの❶予防接種(よぼうせっしゅ)の❷予約(よやく)をしています。

I have an ❷appointment for an influenza ❶vaccination.

勉

免 力
Allow me to use my power and I'll be "**DILIGENT**".

うちの娘(むすめ)はいつも❶勤勉(きんべん)に❷勉強(べんきょう)しています。

My daughter always ❶diligently ❷studies.

礼

ネ し
At the altar there is nothing to conceal, just say "**THANKS**".

日本(にほん)では❶礼(れい)を返(かえ)さないと、❷失礼(しつれい)です。

In Japan, if you don't return a ❶bow, it's ❷ rude.

24 Understanding Kanji Parts 漢字部分の理解

● 24-1. The "speech" radical ごんべん (言)

ごんべん is a handy radical to know since it's used in so many kanji.

say; word	plot; plan; scheme; measure
言 speak	計 speak + 10
い 言う to say; to declare	けい かく 計画 plan; schedule; project
こと ば 言葉 language; words	けい さん 計算 calculation; count

scribe; account; narrative	talk; tale
記 speak + self	話 speak + tongue
き にゅう 記入 filling in; entry (in a form)	はなし 話 talk; speech; chat
き しゃ 記者 reporter	でん わ 電話 telephone; phone call

read	word; speech; language
読 speak + sell	語 speak + 5 + mouth
よ 読む to read	げん ご 言語 language
どく しゃ 読者 reader (e.g., book; article)	に ほん ご 日本語 Japanese (language)

poem; poetry	tune; tone; investigate; prepare
詩 speak + temple	調 speak + perimeter
し 詩 poem; verse of poetry	しら 調べる to examine; to look up
きん だい し 近代詩 modern poetry	ちょう せい 調整 adjustment; coordination

24 Kanji Usage 漢字の使い方

● 24-2. Japanese Manners 礼

I'd like to have some "words" about your manners!

courteous; polite

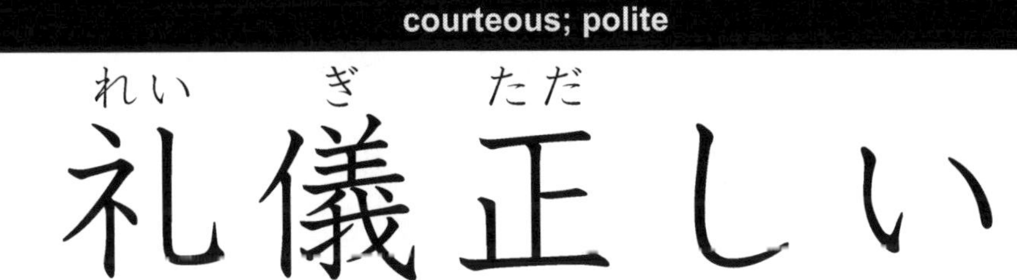

This is literally, "manners correct". It's someone that correctly follows proper etiquette.

同僚(どうりょう)の緑(みどり)さんは、いつも礼儀正(れいぎただ)しいです。

My co-worker Midori is always courteous.

rude

しつ れい
失礼

失礼(しつれい) is made "loss" and "thanks". Someone who has "lost thanks" is rude. When leaving you can say, 失礼(しつれい)します (literally, "I will be rude") even though you weren't actually rude, it can be thought to be rude to leave first especially from work. But it's just a phrase so don't think too deep on it.

緑(みどり)さんと違(ちが)って、山下(やました)さんは結構(けっこう)失礼(しつれい)な人(ひと)です。

Unlike Midori-san, Yamashita-san is a pretty rude person.

In Japanese school in the morning the teacher will tell the students to stand, then bow, and then go back to sitting. This is done with three commands:

1. STAND	2. BOW	3. SIT
起立(きりつ)	礼(れい)	着席(ちゃくせき)
meaning: rise and stand	meaning: bow / thanks	meaning: arrive at seat

● 24-3. Bad and, not-so-bad manners in Japan 日本の礼儀

Tipping in Japan is said to be insulting. Here are some other bad food related manners.

eating on a train	eating while walking	eating before checkout

Eating on a subway, local or crowded train is considered bad manners. It dirties the train for everyone. A major exception are trains with back-of-seat trays designed for food. On many long-distance trains, you will even be offered food for purchase from a food cart going through the train.	During festivals, it's OK to walk while eating food that doesn't require chopsticks or other utensils. If something can be eaten without causing a mess, then it MIGHT be okay to eat while walking. A single hamburger might be okay, but not a messy big mac. Eating while shopping is definitely bad manners.	Even if this may be acceptable where you're from, eating before you have purchased items in a grocery store (even one grape) would be surprisingly bad manners in Japan. People will look at you coldly! Let's be honest though... this is bad manners in most countries! You heathen!

Some things considered rude in other countries are perfectly acceptable in Japan.

making slurping noises	sniffling	silence after a sneeze

In Japan, when eating soup, ramen, spaghetti, or anything that can be slurped, it's okay to slurp. According to co-author Kanako, this is especially common for men! Once you get used to slurping your hot coffee, you won't be able to go back. I promise!	Sniffling isn't a big deal in Japan. In fact, it's considered more embarrassing to blow your nose in public. The practice of blowing your nose into a handkerchief in other countries is thought unsanitary by many in Japan. It is kind of disgusting, isn't it?	In the English-speaking world when someone sneezes, we reflectively say, "bless you". In Japan, when you sneeze, you aren't required to say, "excuse me" and don't expect to hear anyone say, "bless you" because the proper response to a sneeze in Japan is silence.

24 Words You Can Write 書ける言葉

詩人（しじん） poet

詩	人										

漢詩（かんし） Chinese poetry

漢	詩										

漢字（かんじ） Chinese character

漢	字										

宿題(しゅくだい) homework

宿	題										

問題（もんだい） question; problem

問	題										

話題（わだい） theme; topic

話	題										

予定（よてい） schedule; plan

予	定										

予想（よそう） prediction; anticipation; expectation

予	想										

礼服（れいふく） full-dress suit; ceremonial clothes

礼服

朝礼（ちょうれい） morning assembly

朝礼

予算（よさん） estimate; budget

予算

礼金（れいきん） key money; reward

礼金

一礼（いちれい） a bow (salute, greeting)

一礼

漢方薬（かんぽうやく） Chinese herbal medicine

漢方薬

勉強家（べんきょうか） hard worker, studious person

勉強家

勉強中（べんきょうちゅう） while studying; in the middle of studying

勉強中

24 Kanji Workbook Activities

● 1. Stroke Order Check 書き順確認

Each kanji has a stroke with an arrow on it. Write its order number below the kanji.

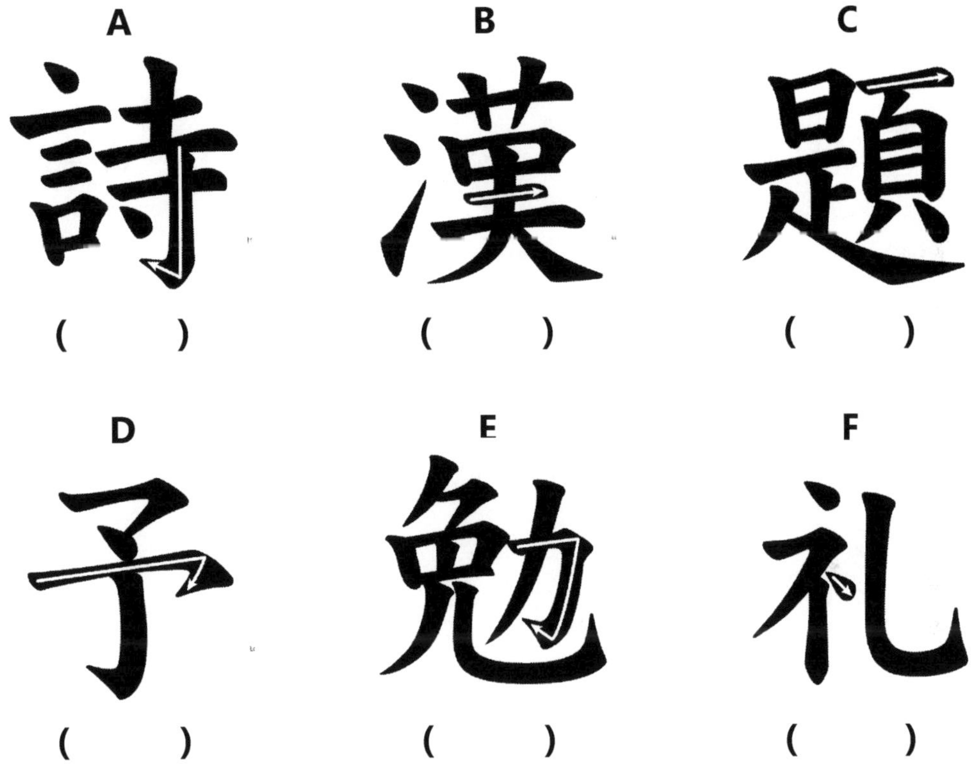

● 2. Kanji Readings

Write FURIGANA above the underlined kanji words.

1. 学生の時は、詩人になりたいと思っていました。
2. 今、漢方薬について勉強しています。
3. テスト問題を予想して勉強しました。
4. 予習をすることは、大切です。
5. 学校の朝礼は、8 時 45 分に始まります。

● 3. Kanji Meaning Match

Write the following kanji next to its meaning: 筆 題 予 板 物 勉 漢 礼 詩

1.____ poem   2. ____ previous   3. ____ bow

4. ____ Han, China   5. ____ strive   6. ____ board

7. ____ subject   8. ____ brush   9. ____ object

● 4. Fill in the Kanji

Fill in the appropriate kanji in the blanks for each sentence.

し か はじ

1. さいきん、___ を___ き___ めました。

Recently, I've started writing poems.

かん じ らく

2. ___ ___ をおぼえるのは、___ じゃありません。

It's not easy to remember the kanji.

しん ゆう わ だい

3. ___ ___ とは いつも ___ ___がつきません。

With my best friend, we never run out of topics.

あ した よ てい

4. ___ ___は どんな___ ___ですか。

What kind of plans do you have for tomorrow?

きん よう び べん きょう かい い

5. ___ ___ ___の___ ___ ___に___きますか。

Are you going to the Friday study group?

せん せい れい て がみ か

6. ___ ___に お ___の___ ___を___きましょう。

Let's write a thank you letter to the teacher.

で よ そう べん きょう

7. テストに___ るところを___ ___して ___ ___します。

I will study the parts that I predict will be on the test.

● 5. Kanji Matching

Connect each kanji with an おん or くん reading. Use each reading only ONCE.

礼 •	• だい
帳 •	• し
勉 •	• べん
箱 •	• ちょう
詩 •	• かん
漢 •	• はこ
予 •	• よ
服 •	• ふく
題 •	• れい
笛 •	• ふえ

24 Answer Key 答え合わせ

1. Stroke order check (answers)

A) 12　B) 10　C) 10

D) 3　E) 9　F) 4

3. Kanji meaning match (answers)

1. 詩 poem　2. 予 previous　3. 礼 bow
4. 漢 Han, China　5. 勉 strive　6. 板 board
7. 題 subject　8. 筆 brush　9. 物 object

2. Kanji Readings (answers)

1. 学生(がくせい)の時(とき)は、詩人(しじん)になりたいと思(おも)っていました。
   When I was a student, I thought I wanted to become a poet.
2. 今(いま)、漢方薬(かんぽうやく)について勉強(べんきょう)しています。
   I'm learning about Chinese herbal medicine now.
3. テスト問題(もんだい)を予想(よそう)して、勉強(べんきょう)しました。
   I anticipating the test questions and studied them.
4. 予習(よしゅう)をすることは、大切(たいせつ)です。
   It's important to prepare (prior to a lesson).
5. 学校(がっこう)の朝礼(ちょうれい)は、8 時(じ)45分(ふん)に始(はじ)まります。
   The school's morning assembly starts at 8:45.

4. Fill in the kanji (answers)

1. さいきん、詩を書き始めました。
2. 漢字をおぼえるのは、楽じゃありません。
3. 親友とは いつも話題がつきません。
4. 明日はどんな予定ですか。
5. 金曜日の勉強会に行きますか。
6. 先生に お礼の手紙を書きましょう。
7. テストに出るところを予想して 勉強します。

5. Kanji matching (answers)

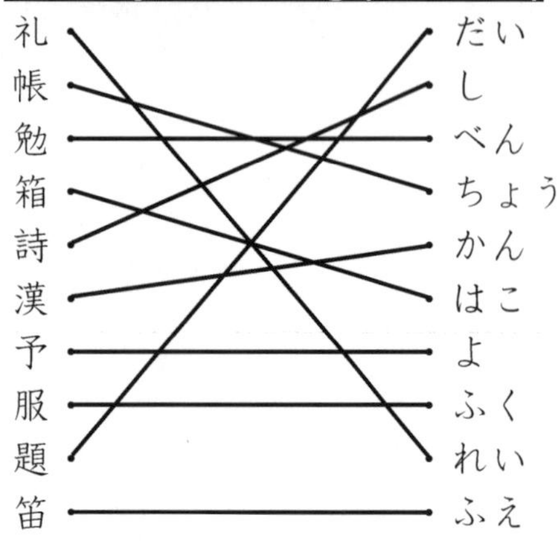

25 Kanji Lesson 25: 農羊緑豆葉根

385-390

Kanji related to agriculture and nature

25 New Kanji 新しい漢字

385	辰	13 画	くん none	おん ノウ

農

のうじょう 農場 farm (agriculture)	のうさくぶつ 農作物 agricultural produce; crops	のうやく 農薬 agricultural chemical
のうぎょう 農業 agriculture	のうか 農家 farmer; farming family	のうそん 農村 farm village

agriculture; farmers — 曲 (tune) + 辰 (dragon)

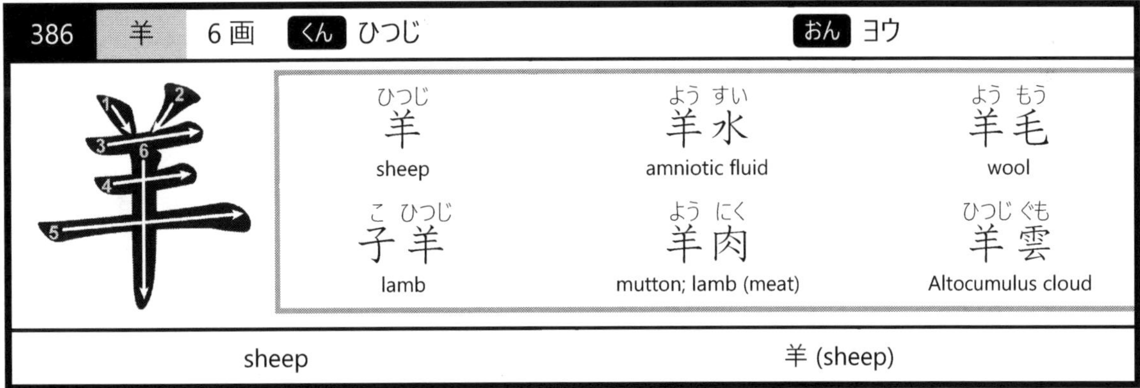

386	羊	6 画	くん ひつじ	おん ヨウ

羊

ひつじ 羊 sheep	ようすい 羊水 amniotic fluid	ようもう 羊毛 wool
こひつじ 子羊 lamb	ようにく 羊肉 mutton; lamb (meat)	ひつじぐも 羊雲 Altocumulus cloud

sheep — 羊 (sheep)

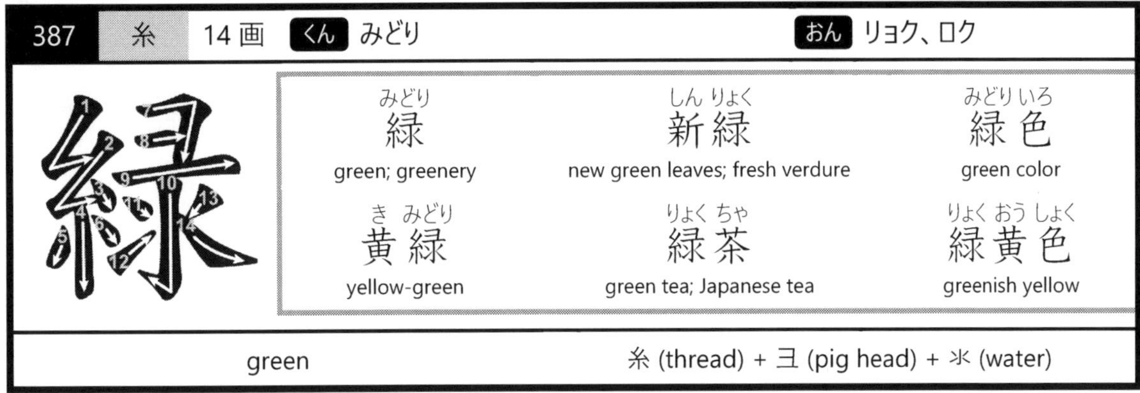

387	糸	14 画	くん みどり	おん リョク、ロク

緑

みどり 緑 green; greenery	しんりょく 新緑 new green leaves; fresh verdure	みどりいろ 緑色 green color
きみどり 黄緑 yellow-green	りょくちゃ 緑茶 green tea; Japanese tea	りょくおうしょく 緑黄色 greenish yellow

green — 糸 (thread) + ヨ (pig head) + 氺 (water)

388	豆	7 画	くん まめ	おん トウ、ズ

だい ず 大豆 soybean	えだ まめ 枝豆 edamame (green soybeans)	まめ 豆 beans; peas
とう にゅう 豆乳 soy milk	とう ふ 豆腐 tofu; bean curd	なっ とう 納豆 fermented beans

beans; pea; midget — 豆 (bean)

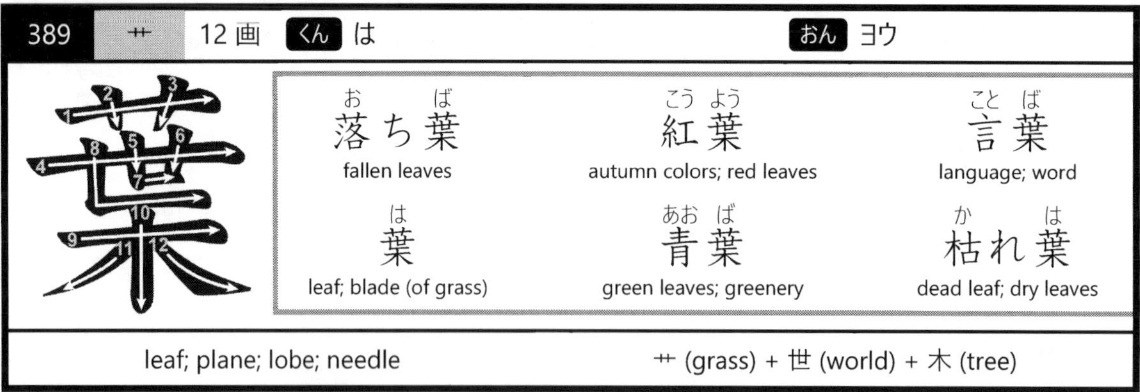

389	艹	12 画	くん は	おん ヨウ

お ば 落ち葉 fallen leaves	こう よう 紅葉 autumn colors; red leaves	こと ば 言葉 language; word
は 葉 leaf; blade (of grass)	あお ば 青葉 green leaves; greenery	か は 枯れ葉 dead leaf; dry leaves

leaf; plane; lobe; needle — 艹 (grass) + 世 (world) + 木 (tree)

390	木	10 画	くん ね	おん コン

だい こん 大根 daikon; radish	こん き 根気 patience; persistence; energy	や ね 屋根 roof
き ね 木の根 root of a tree	ね もと 根元 root; stool; base	こん きょ 根拠 basis; grounds

root; source; basis — 木 (tree) + 艮 (stay still)

Kanji Parts used in the New Kanji

曲	tune	ヨ	pig head	世	world
辰	dragon	氺	water	木	tree
羊	sheep	豆	bean	艮	stay still
糸	thread	艹	grass		

25 Kanji Memory Tools 漢字記憶術

This section helps you organically memorize kanji readings, meanings, and construction.

農

曲 辰

The tune of the dragon is good for "**AGRICULTURE**".

❶農薬(のうやく)なしで育(そだ)った❷農産物(のうさんぶつ)がこの❸農村(のうそん)の名物(めいぶつ)です。

❷Agricultural products grown without ❶pesticides are a specialty of this ❸farming village.

羊

羊

Even sheep are sometimes "**SHEEP**".

一頭(いっとう)の❶羊(ひつじ)で、❷羊毛(ようもう)のセーターが三枚(さんまい)編(あ)めます。

Three ❷wool sweaters can be knit with one ❶sheep.

緑

糸 ヨ 氺

The thread holding the pig head over the water is "**GREEN**".

❶緑茶(りょくちゃ)は❷緑(みどり)です。

❶Green tea is ❷green.

豆

豆

A bean is merely a "**BEAN**".

❶豆腐(とうふ)は❷「大豆(だいず)」という❸豆(まめ)で作(つく)ります。

❶Tofu is made from ❷beans called ❸"soybeans".

葉

艹 世 木

All the grass in the world for a tree or a "**LEAF**".

❶「紅葉(こうよう)」という❷言葉(ことば)は、「紅(くれない)」と❸「葉(は)」で出来(でき)ています。

The ❷word, ❶"autumn colors" is made up of "deep red" and ❸"leaf".

根

木 艮

A tree always stays still because of its "**ROOT(S)**".

いたずらっ子(こ)が❶屋根(やね)に❷大根(だいこん)を投(な)げた。

A mischievous child threw a ❷radish on the ❶roof.

25 Understanding Kanji Parts 漢字部分の理解

● 25-1. More kanji with the "thread" radical, いとへん (糸)

In Kanji From Zero! book 1 Lesson 16 we covered this same radical, but there are even more kanji that have the いとへん radical.

promise; approximately		grandchild; descendants	
約	やくそく **約束** a promise	終	お **終わり** the end
thread + ladle	けいやく **契約** a contract	thread + winter	しゅうてん **終点** last stop (train, bus etc.)

distract; mistaken for		association; unite; cooperate	
紛	ふんしつ **紛失** loss; going missing	組	くみあい **組合** union; association; guild
thread + divide	まぎ **紛らわしい** easily mixed up / mistaken	thread + also	そしき **組織** organization

longitude; pass thru		tie; bind; join; fasten	
経	けいど **経度** longitude	結	けっこん **結婚** marriage
thread + again + soil	けいざい **経済** economy; economics	thread + joy	けっか **結果** result; consequence

shrink; contract		crimson; deep red	
縮	ちぢ **縮まる** to shrink	紅	くれない **紅** deep red; rouge; lipstick
thread + inn	あっしゅく **圧縮** compression; compaction	thread + craft	こうちゃ **紅茶** black tea

25 Kanji Usage 漢字の使い方

● 25-2. Food and seasonings made with soybean 大豆 (だいず)

Soybeans are an important part of the Japanese diet.

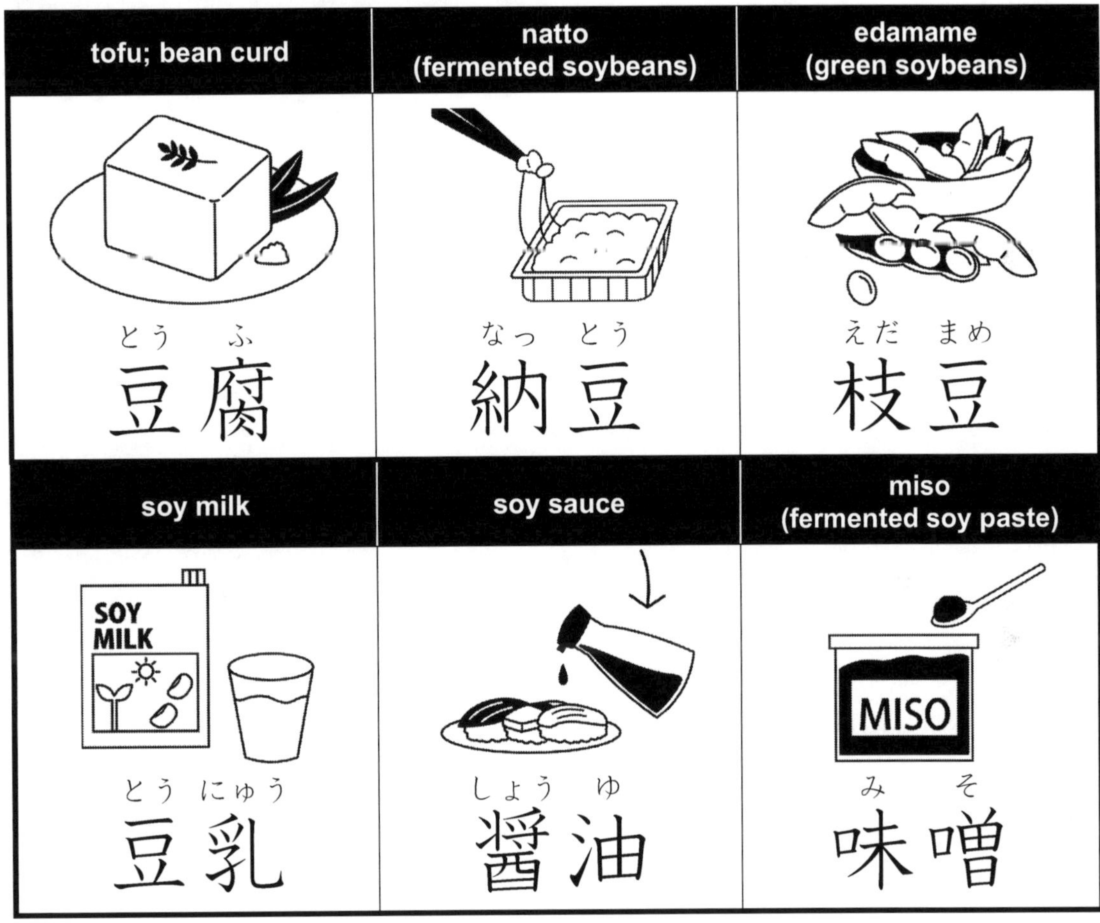

tofu; bean curd
とうふ
豆腐
natto (fermented soybeans)
なっとう
納豆
edamame (green soybeans)
えだまめ
枝豆
soy milk
SOY MILK
とうにゅう
豆乳
soy sauce
しょうゆ
醤油
miso (fermented soy paste)
MISO
みそ
味噌

My introduction to 納豆 (なっとう)

When I was in high school in Japan, one of the first times I stayed in a Japanese family's home I was introduced to なっとう (fermented soy beans) at dinner. To me it smelled horrible and just looked like beans soaked in snot. Anyways... the father told me that they only rarely eat なっとう and that it was special because of how expensive it is. So, even though it smelled bad, I ate all of it while focusing on not throwing up vowing never to eat it again.

A few years later I was walking with my Japanese girlfriend in a Japanese supermarket and she suggested we get なっとう to eat. I was a bit taken aback since I hated なっとう and it was WAY too expensive for my budget. When I told her this, she informed me that なっとう was only 100 yen (about a dollar). Initially I was amazed at how cheap なっとう had gotten over the years since my first time eating it. Then I realized the father had played an amazing joke on me! Although I don't like なっとう, I suggest you try it and find out for yourself.

● 25-3. What's wrong with 大根(だいこん) (Japanese radish)?

While Japanese radishes might be delicious, they are part of some negative words.

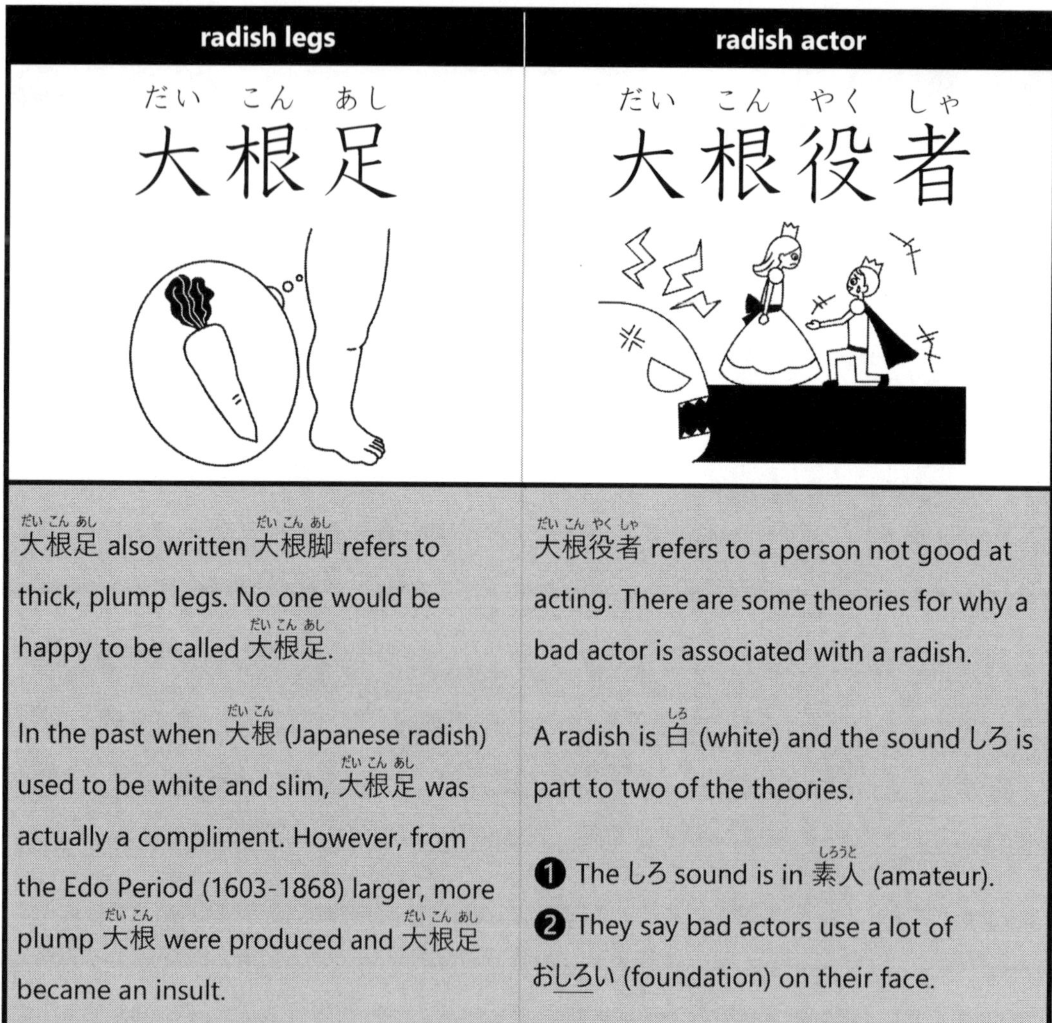

radish legs	radish actor
だい こん あし 大根足	だい こん やく しゃ 大根役者
大根足(だいこんあし) also written 大根脚(だいこんあし) refers to thick, plump legs. No one would be happy to be called 大根足(だいこんあし). In the past when 大根(だいこん) (Japanese radish) used to be white and slim, 大根足(だいこんあし) was actually a compliment. However, from the Edo Period (1603-1868) larger, more plump 大根(だいこん) were produced and 大根足(だいこんあし) became an insult.	大根役者(だいこんやくしゃ) refers to a person not good at acting. There are some theories for why a bad actor is associated with a radish. A radish is 白(しろ) (white) and the sound しろ is part to two of the theories. ❶ The しろ sound is in 素人(しろうと) (amateur). ❷ They say bad actors use a lot of おしろい (foundation) on their face.

25 Words You Can Write 書ける言葉

農場（のうじょう） farm (agriculture)

農場

子羊（こひつじ） lamb

子羊

羊毛（ようもう） wool

羊毛

緑地（りょくち） green tract of land

緑地

緑茶（りょくちゃ） green tea

緑茶

大豆（だいず） soybean

大豆

黒豆（くろまめ） black soy bean

黒豆

言葉（ことば） language; word

言葉

屋根（やね） roof

屋	根										

根気（こんき） persistence; patience

根	気										

黄緑（きみどり） pea green; yellow-green

黄	緑										

小豆（あずき） azuki bean (Vigna angularis)

小	豆										

葉っぱ（はっぱ） a leaf; leaves

葉	っ	ぱ									

農作物（のうさくぶつ） agricultural produce

農	作	物									

羊小屋（ひつじごや） sheepfold

羊	小	屋									

落ち葉（おちば） fallen leaves

落	ち	葉									

25 Kanji Workbook Activities

● 1. Stroke Order Check 書き順確認

Each kanji has a stroke with an arrow on it. Write its order number below the kanji.

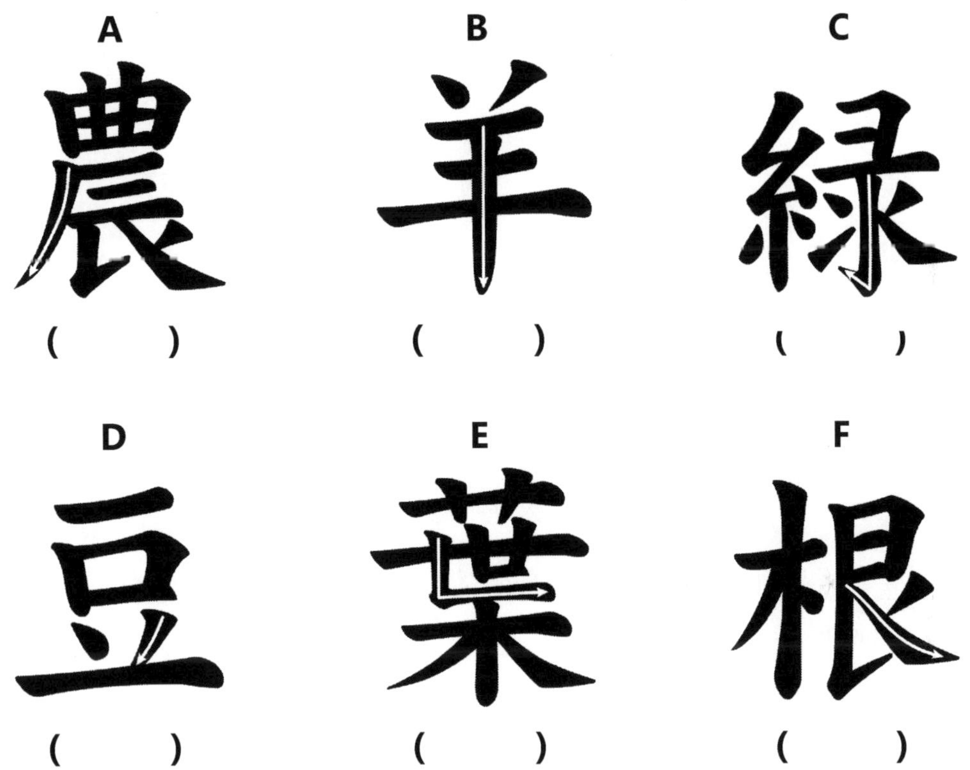

● 2. Kanji Readings

Write FURIGANA above the underlined kanji words.

1. この<u>食品</u>は、<u>農薬</u>を<u>使</u>っていません。

2. <u>野原</u>に<u>大</u>きい<u>羊</u>が<u>五頭</u>、います。

3. けんこうのために、<u>緑茶</u>を<u>飲</u>んでいます。

4. <u>大根</u>の<u>葉</u>っぱも<u>食</u>べられますか。

5. わたしはえだ<u>豆</u>がすきで、よくスーパーで<u>買</u>います。

● 3. Kanji Meaning Match

Write the following kanji next to its meaning: 葉 根 礼 章 豆 緑 駅 羊 農

1. ____ agriculture
2. ____ bow
3. ____ station
4. ____ sheep
5. ____ beans
6. ____ leaf
7. ____ green
8. ____ chapter
9. ____ root

● 4. Fill in the Kanji

Fill in the appropriate kanji in the blanks for each sentence.

(のう そん う)
1. わたしは____ ____で____ まれました。

I was born in a farm village.

(よう もう か おも)
2. ____ ____のセーターを____ おうと____っています。

I'm thinking of buying a wool sweater.

(こう えん みどり)
3. ____ ____の____がきれいです。

The park greenery is pretty.

(まめ つか だい)
4. わたしは、____を____った りょうりが____すきです。

I really like cooking that incorporates (uses) beans.

(こと ば き)
5. ____ ____には____をつけましょう。

Let's be careful with our words.

(や ね ふる あま)
6. ____ ____が____ いので、____もりしています。

Since the roof is old, it's leaking rain.

(のう じょう ひつじ み)
7. ニュージーランドの____ ____で ____を____ました。

I saw a sheep at a New Zealand farm.

● 5. Kanji Matching

Connect each kanji with an おん or くん reading. Use each reading only ONCE.

葉 •	• ちゅう
緑 •	• かん
柱 •	• は
農 •	• のう
号 •	• こん
根 •	• ごう
豆 •	• まめ
館 •	• な
羊 •	• よう
投 •	• りょく

25 Answer Key 答え合わせ

1. Stroke order check (answers)

A) 8　B) 6　C) 10

D) 6　E) 8　F) 10

2. Kanji meaning match (answers)

1. 農 agriculture 2. 礼 bow 3. 駅 station
4. 羊 sheep 5. 豆 beans 6. 葉 leaf
7. 緑 green 8. 章 chapter 9. 根 root

3. Kanji Readings (answers)

1. この食品(しょくひん)は、農薬(のうやく)を使(つか)っていません。 — These food products don't use agrochemicals.
2. 野原(のはら)に大(おお)きい羊(ひつじ)が五頭(ごとう)、います。 — There are five large sheep in the field.
3. けんこうのために、緑茶(りょくちゃ)を飲(の)んでいます。 — I drink green tea for my health.
4. 大根(だいこん)の葉(は)っぱも食(た)べられますか。 — Can you also eat the leaves of radishes?
5. わたしはえだ豆(まめ)がすきで、よくスーパーで買(か)います。 — I like EDAMAME so I often buy them at the supermarket.

4. Fill in the kanji (answers)

1. わたしは[農村]で[生]まれました。
2. [羊毛]のセーターを[買]おうと[思]っています。
3. [公園]の[緑]がきれいです。
4. わたしは、[豆]を[使]ったりょうりが[大]すきです。
5. [言葉]には[気]をつけましょう。
6. [屋根]が[古]いので、[雨]もりしています。
7. ニュージーランドの[農場]で[羊]を[見]ました。

5. Kanji matching (answers)

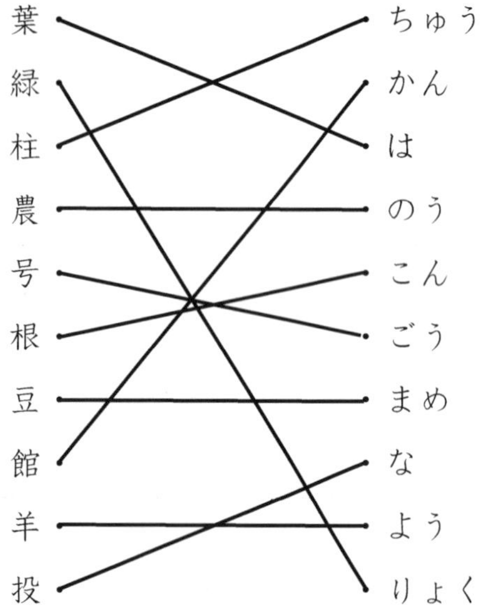

Kanji Lessons 21-25:

Super Review 5

From the teacher...

Test your knowledge of the kanji learned in the last 5 lessons.

● 1. Build-a-Kanji 漢字の組み合わせ

Combine the left and right parts to make seven of the kanji learned in lessons 21-25.

RULES
1. You can use the radical and kanji parts as many times as you want.
2. Some kanji can use two kanji parts.

部首 (Radical)		
言	氵	广
辶	木	亻
立	口	艹
巾	辰	礻

Other Kanji Parts		
楽	長	反
曲	士	白
比	早	主
車	寺	貝

SAMPLE	1	2	3	4	5	6	7
仕							

● 2. Okurigana drill 送り仮名ドリル

Circle the correct 漢字 + 送り仮名 combination.

1. つかえる	・仕える	・仕かえる
2. ゆだねる	・委る	・委ねる
3. きわめる	・究める	・究る

● 3. Kanji selection 漢字の選択

Select the best kanji to replace the underlined section of the sentence.

1. パズルをする時は、____気がいります。
   A. 勉　B. 根　C. 予　D. 研

2. あの新しいゲームは人気があるので、すぐ____切れになりました。
   A. 物　B. 箱　C. 品　D. 有

3. 来週の予定は、____帳に書いておきます。
   A. 通　B. 役　C. 日　D. 手

4. 外を歩いている時、電____にぶつかってしまいました。
   A. 話　B. 板　C. 柱　D. 坂

● 4. Kanji reading selection 読みの選択

Select the best reading for the underlined kanji.

1. 薬局でかぜ薬を買ってきます。
   A. くすり　B. やく　C. やっ　D. らく

2. 家の庭で、植物をそだてています。
   A. もの　B. ぶつ　C. ふつ　D. もつ

3. 大豆は体にとてもいいです。
   A. とう　B. ず　C. まめ　D. こん

4. 毎日、緑黄色やさいを食べましょう。
   A. りょく　B. ろく　C. えん　D. みどり

● 5. Compound kanji word puzzle 熟語パズル

Fill in the correct kanji based on the list below the puzzle.

1)	2)		3)
4)		5)	6)
7)	8)		
	9)		10)

Down ↓

English meaning	Hiragana
1) roof	やね
2) medicine box	くすりばこ
3) Chinese poem	かんし
4) patience; persistence	こんき
5) writer; author	ひっしゃ
6) collection of poems	ししゅう
7) elegance; grace	きひん

Left to Right →

English meaning	Hiragana
8) batter; hitter	だしゃ
9) bankbook; passbook	つうちょう

← Right to Left

English meaning	Hiragana
2) drug store	くすりや
3) Chinese herbal medicine	かんぽうやく
5) pencil box	ふでばこ
10) datebook; pocket planner	てちょう

SR5 Answer Key 答え合わせ

1. Build-a-Kanji (answers) (order can vary)

SAMPLE 仕 1) 員 2) 柱 3) 農 4) 板 5) 薬 6) 詩 7) 帳

2. Okurigana drill (answers)

1. つかえる	**・仕える**	・仕かえる
2. ゆだねる	・委る	**・委ねる**
3. きわめる	**・究める**	・究る

3. Kanji selection (answers)

1. B – 根気(こんき) You need perseverance when you do puzzles.
2. C – 品切れ(しなぎ) Since that game was popular, it sold out right away.
3. D – 手帳(てちょう) I'll write in my notebook (memo pad) next week's schedule.
4. C – 電柱(でんちゅう) When walking outside, I bumped into an electric pole.

4. Kanji reading selection (answers)

1. C – 薬局(やっきょく) I'll go ahead and buy some medicine at the pharmacy.
2. B – 植物(しょくぶつ) I'm growing plants in my house's yard.
3. B – 大豆(だいず) Soybeans are really good for the body.
4. A – 緑黄色野菜(りょくおうしょくやさい) Let's eat (greenish-yellow) vegetables high in beta-carotene every day.

5. Compound kanji word puzzle (answers)

屋	薬	方	漢
根	箱	筆	詩
気	打	者	集
品	通	帳	手

26 Kanji Lesson 26: 商業世界実球

391-396

Kanji that is related to business and the world

26 New Kanji 新しい漢字

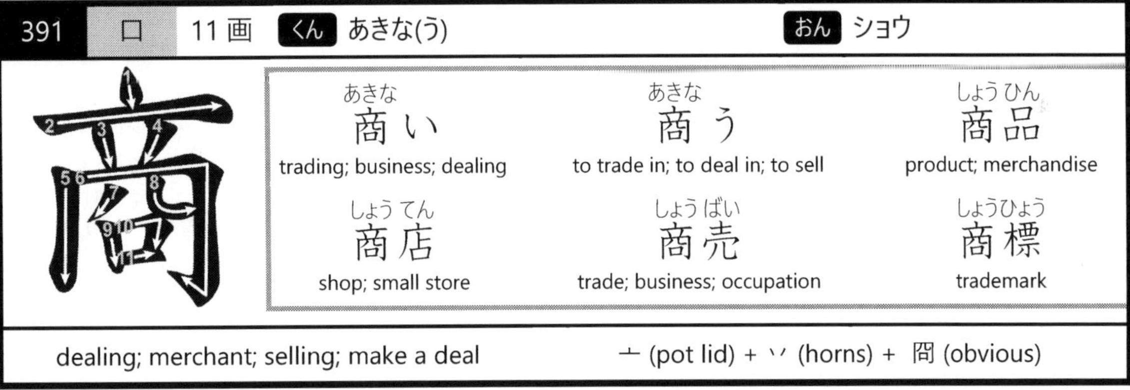

391 | 口 | 11 画 | くん あきな(う) | おん ショウ

商

あきな 商い trading; business; dealing	あきな 商う to trade in; to deal in; to sell	しょうひん 商品 product; merchandise
しょうてん 商店 shop; small store	しょうばい 商売 trade; business; occupation	しょうひょう 商標 trademark

dealing; merchant; selling; make a deal | 亠 (pot lid) + ソ (horns) + 冏 (obvious)

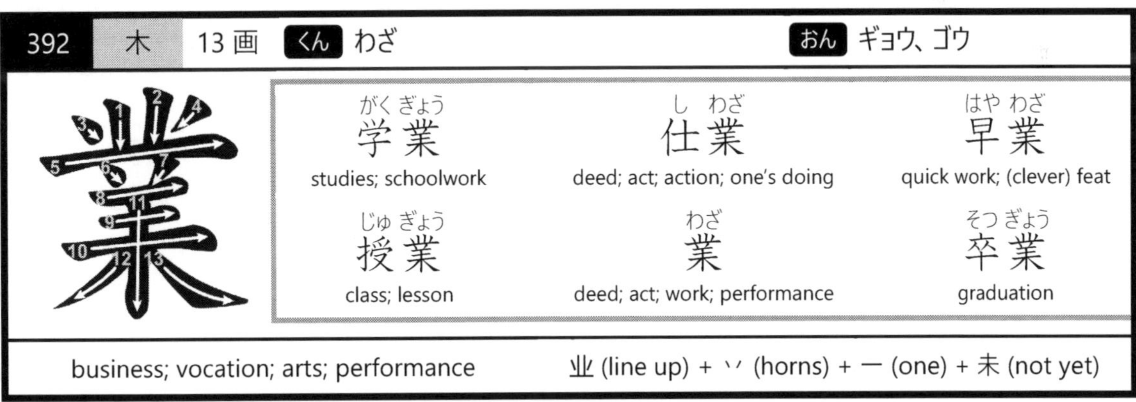

392 | 木 | 13 画 | くん わざ | おん ギョウ、ゴウ

業

がくぎょう 学業 studies; schoolwork	しわざ 仕業 deed; act; action; one's doing	はやわざ 早業 quick work; (clever) feat
じゅぎょう 授業 class; lesson	わざ 業 deed; act; work; performance	そつぎょう 卒業 graduation

business; vocation; arts; performance | 业 (line up) + ソ (horns) + 一 (one) + 未 (not yet)

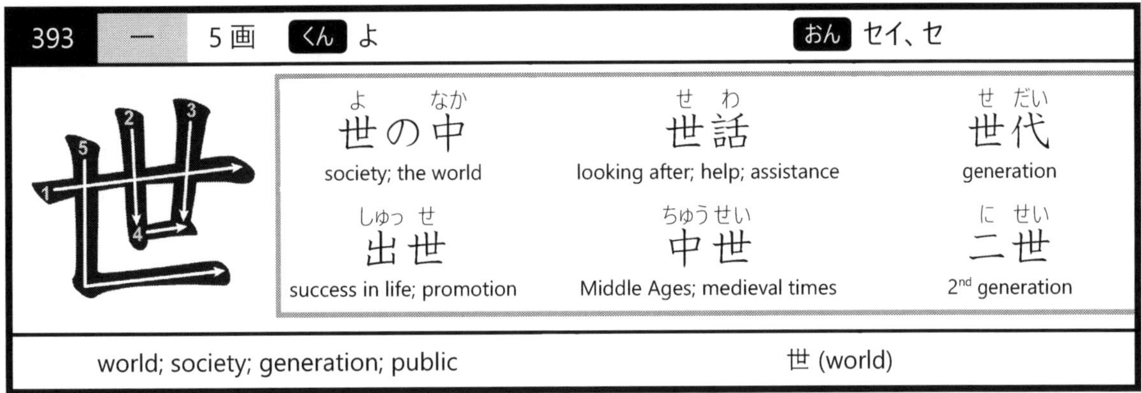

393 | 一 | 5 画 | くん よ | おん セイ、セ

世

よ なか 世の中 society; the world	せわ 世話 looking after; help; assistance	せだい 世代 generation
しゅっせ 出世 success in life; promotion	ちゅうせい 中世 Middle Ages; medieval times	にせい 二世 2nd generation

world; society; generation; public | 世 (world)

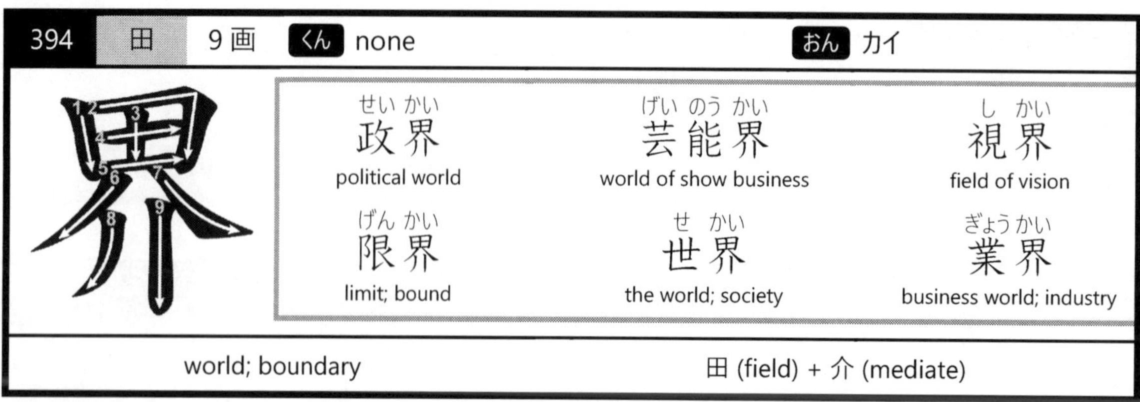

394 | 田 | 9 画 | くん none | おん カイ

せい かい 政界 political world	げい のう かい 芸能界 world of show business	し かい 視界 field of vision
げん かい 限界 limit; bound	せ かい 世界 the world; society	ぎょう かい 業界 business world; industry

world; boundary — 田 (field) + 介 (mediate)

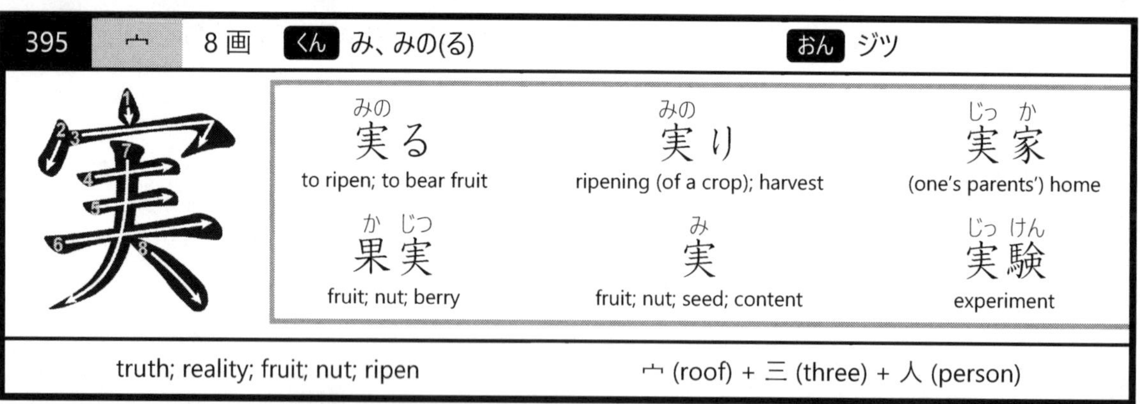

395 | 宀 | 8 画 | くん み、みの(る) | おん ジツ

みの 実る to ripen; to bear fruit	みの 実り ripening (of a crop); harvest	じっ か 実家 (one's parents') home
か じつ 果実 fruit; nut; berry	み 実 fruit; nut; seed; content	じっ けん 実験 experiment

truth; reality; fruit; nut; ripen — 宀 (roof) + 三 (three) + 人 (person)

396 | 王 | 11 画 | くん たま | おん キュウ

球

たま 球 ball (in sports); bulb	きゅうじょう 球場 baseball stadium	や きゅう 野球 baseball
でん きゅう 電球 light bulb	ち きゅう 地球 the earth; the globe	にし はん きゅう 西半球 western hemisphere

sphere; ball — 王 (king) + 求 (demand)

Kanji Parts used in the New Kanji

亠	pot lid	未	not yet	三	three
⺌	horns	世	world	人	person
冏	obvious	田	field	王	king
业	line up	介	mediate	求	demand
一	one	宀	roof		

26 Kanji Memory Tools 漢字記憶術

This section helps you organically memorize kanji readings, meanings, and construction.

商

Having a pot lid (亠) with horns (丷), it's obvious (冏) he's a "**MERCHANT**".

❶商店街(しょうてんがい)の寿司屋(すしや)に❷「商(あきな)い中(ちゅう)」の看板(かんばん)が出(で)ています。

There's an ❷"open for business" sign on the sushi place in the ❶shopping street.

業

People line up (业) for horns (丷) although one (一) said it's not yet (未) a "**BUSINESS**".

一年(いちねん)で大学(だいがく)を❶卒業(そつぎょう)できる❷早業(はやわざ)はないだろうか。

I wonder if there is ❷quick work to ❶be able to graduate college in one year.

世

The world (世) is just the "**WORLD**".

❶世紀末(せいきまつ)に❷世界中(せかいじゅう)で❸世論調査(よろんちょうさ)が行(おこな)われた。

At the ❶end of the century ❸opinion polls were conducted ❷around the world.

界

This field (田) is mediated (介) by the "**WORLD**".

この❶業界(ぎょうかい)には❷限界(げんかい)がある。

There are ❷limits to this ❶industry.

実

That this roof (宀) was made by a three (三) person (人) team is the "**TRUTH**".

来週(らいしゅう)❶確実(かくじつ)に❷実家(じっか)のリンゴの❸実(み)が❹実(みの)るはずだ。

Next week ❶for sure, my ❷parents' apple trees should ❹bear ❸fruit.

球

The king (王) made a demand (求) for his "**BALL**".

❶野球部(やきゅうぶ)の一年目(いちねんめ)は、❷球拾(たまひろ)いだけでした。

My first year on the ❶baseball team, was just ❷picking up balls.

26 Kanji Usage 漢字の使い方

● 26-1. The difference between 玉 and 球

In book 1, we learned 玉(たま) (ball). Now in this lesson with learn 球(たま) which also means "ball" and "sphere". They both have the same readings of たま and きゅう, so how are they different?

玉 is used to express items considered beautiful, excellent, or to have value such as 宝石(ほうせき) (jewels, gems), or 鉱石(こうせき) (minerals, crystals). And even though 玉(たま) means "ball," it doesn't mean the item must be perfectly round. If there is a general roundness, the 玉(たま) can be used.

Words using 玉

1\. 水玉(みずたま)
polka dots

2\. 百円玉(ひゃくえんだま)
100-yen coin

3\. ビー玉(だま)
marbles

4\. 毛玉(けだま)
pilling; lint; hairball

5\. シャボン玉(だま)
soap bubble

6\. 玉座(ぎょくざ)
throne

球(たま) is used for round shaped items, or items that are spherical, however it doesn't mean that something is beautiful or that it has value. The word "ball" uses the 球(たま).

Words using 球

1\. 球技(きゅうぎ)
ball game

2\. 卓球(たっきゅう)
table tennis; ping-pong

2\. 水球(すいきゅう)
water polo

4\. 電球(でんきゅう)
light bulb

5\. 赤血球(せっけっきゅう)
red blood cell

5\. 眼球(がんきゅう)
eyeball

● 26-2. Kanji industries 業

Here are some industries using 業 in them.

Kanji	Meaning of the other kanji	English
ほんぎょう 本業	本 = book; present; main; real	principal occupation; core business
ふくぎょう 副業	副 = vice-; assistant; duplicate	side job; subsidiary business
りんぎょう 林業	林 = grove; forest	forestry industry
のうぎょう 農業	農 = agriculture; farmers	agriculture
こうぎょう 工業	工 = craft; construction	(manufacturing) industry
えいぎょう 営業	営 = occupation; camp; build	business; trade; sales
じえいぎょう 自営業	自 = oneself	independent or self-owned business
ざんぎょう 残業	残 = remainder; leftover; balance	overtime (work)
しつぎょう 失業	失 = lose; error; fault; loss	unemployment; losing one's job
きゅうぎょう 休業	休 = rest; day off; retire; sleep	closed; shutdown; holiday
かいぎょう 開業	開 = open; unseal; unfold	establishment of one's own business
がくぎょう 学業	学 = study; learning; science	studies; schoolwork

26 Words You Can Write 書ける言葉

商社（しょうしゃ） trading company; firm

商 社

商人（しょうにん） trade; business

商 人

農業（のうぎょう） agriculture

農 業

世界（せかい） the world; society

世 界

世話（せわ） looking after; assistance

世 話

業界（ぎょうかい） business world; industry

業 界

実行（じっこう） practice; performance

実 行

実力（じつりょく） ability; true strength

実 力

実は（じつは） as a matter of fact; to tell you the truth

実	は										

球根（きゅうこん） plant bulb

球	根										

気球（ききゅう） balloon; blimp

気	球										

商業（しょうぎょう） commerce; trade; business

商	業										

前世（ぜんせ） previous existence; previous life

前	世										

始業式（しぎょうしき） opening ceremony

始	業	式									

世界一（せかいいち） best in the world

世	界	一									

商い中（あきないちゅう） in business; open

商	い	中									

26 Kanji Workbook Activities

● 1. Stroke Order Check 書き順確認

Each kanji has a stroke with an arrow on it. Write its order number below the kanji.

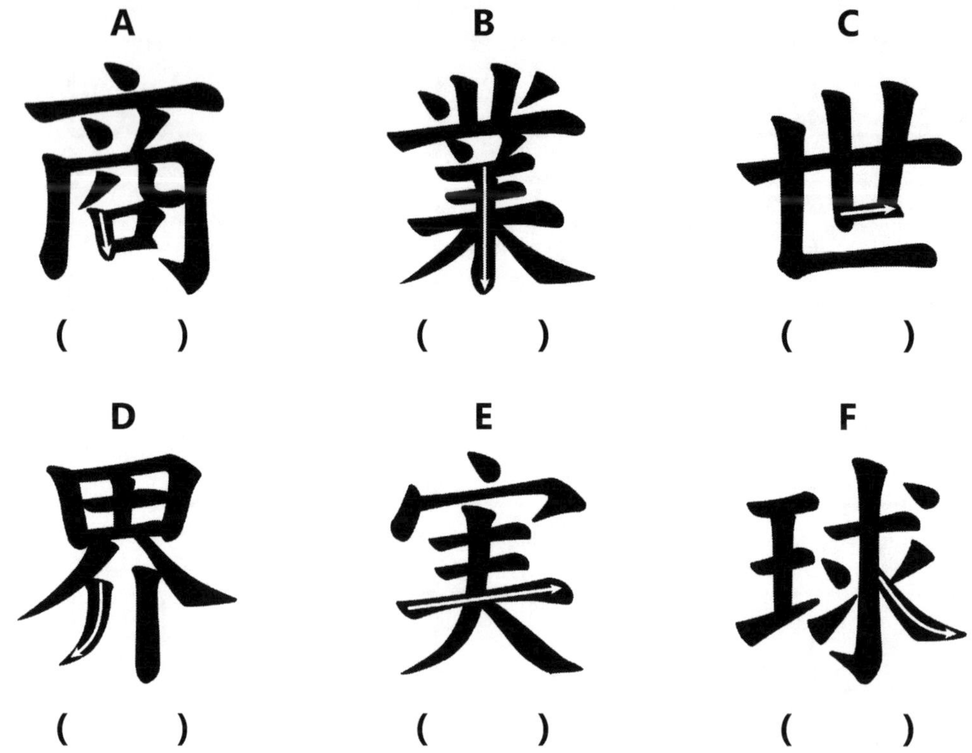

● 2. Kanji Readings

Write FURIGANA above the underlined kanji words.

1. わたしは、コンビニに<u>商品</u>を<u>配送</u>する<u>仕事</u>をしています。

2. <u>今</u>は<u>学業</u>をがんばりたいと<u>思</u>います。

3. わたしは<u>早</u>く<u>出世</u>したいです。

4. もっと<u>色</u>んな<u>世界</u>を<u>見</u>たほうがいいです。

5. <u>実</u>は<u>高校生</u>の<u>時</u>、<u>野球</u>をしていました。

● 3. Kanji Meaning Match

Write the following kanji next to its meaning: 実 世 羊 商 球 服 界 業 皿

1.____ merchant 2. ____ world 3. ____ boundary

4. ____ business 5. ____ sphere 6. ____ clothes

7. ____ fruit 8. ____ plate 9. ____ sheep

● 4. Fill in the Kanji

Fill in the appropriate kanji in the blanks for each sentence.

しょう ばい はじ

1. さいきん、____ ____を____めました。

I recently started a business.

おん がく ぎょう かい

2. ____ ____ ____ ____ は、とてもきびしいです。

The music business is really strict.

せん せい せ わ

3. ____ ____には、お____ ____になりました。

I'm indebted to my teacher.

はは せ かい いち

4. ____ のりょうりは、____ ____ ____です。

My mother's cooking is the best in the world.

みの あき

5. ____ りの____ になりました。

It's a fruitful autumn.

あいだ きゅう こん う

6. この____、チューリップの____ ____を____えました。

The other day I planted a tulip bulb.

しょう がつ じっ か かえ

7. お___ ___に、___ ___に___りました。

On New Year's, I returned to my parent's house.

● 5. Kanji Matching

Connect each kanji with an おん or くん reading. Use each reading only ONCE.

商 •	• しょう
世 •	• ぎょう
路 •	• きゅう
神 •	• じん
業 •	• よ
界 •	• しょ
実 •	• じつ
球 •	• ろ
所 •	• かい
者 •	• しゃ

26 Answer Key 答え合わせ

1. Stroke order check (answers)

A) 9 B) 11 C) 4

D) 8 E) 6 F) 10

2. Kanji meaning match (answers)

1. 商 merchant 2. 世 world 3. 界 boundary
4. 業 business 5. 球 sphere 6. 服 clothes
7. 実 fruit 8. 皿 plate 9. 羊 sheep

3. Kanji Readings (answers)

1. わたしは、コンビニに商品(しょうひん)を配送(はいそう)する仕事(しごと)をしています。 I work delivering goods to convenience stores.
2. 今(いま)は学業(がくぎょう)をがんばりたいと思(おも)います。 I want to do my best in my studies.
3. わたしは早(はや)く出世(しゅっせ)したいです。 I want to move up the ladder soon.
4. もっと色(いろ)んな世界(せかい)を見(み)たほうがいいです。 You should see more variety of worlds.
5. 実(じつ)は高校生(こうこうせい)の時(とき)、野球(やきゅう)をしていました。 Actually, when I was in high school I played baseball.

4. Fill in the kanji (answers)

1. さいきん、商売を始めました。
2. 音楽業界は、とてもきびしいです。
3. 先生には、お世話になりました。
4. 母のりょうりは、世界一です。
5. 実りの秋になりました。
6. この間、チューリップの球根を植えました。
7. お正月に、実家に帰りました。

5. Kanji matching (answers)

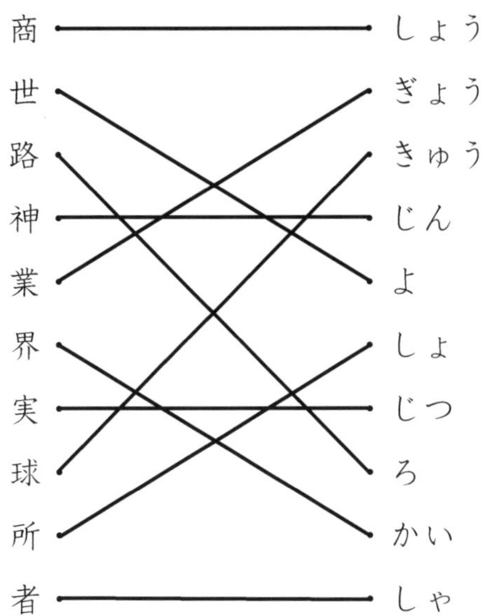

27 Kanji Lesson 27: 397- 402

反対全両面命

Kanji related to phrases, aspects, and sides

27 New Kanji 新しい漢字

397	又	4 画	くん そ(る、らす)	おん ハン、タン、ホン

反

はんたい 反対 opposition; resistance	そ 反らす to warp; to curve; to bend (transitive)	たんもの 反物 fabric; cloth; textiles
むほん 謀反 rebellion; treason	そ 反る to warp; to curve; to bend (intransitive)	はんせい 反省 introspection; reflection

anti-; opposite; variable measure of fabric — 反 (anti-)

398	寸	7 画	くん none	おん タイ、ツイ

対

いっつい 一対 a pair; a couple	たいりつ 対立 confrontation; opposition	たいとう 対等 equality; equivalence
たいわ 対話 dialogue; discussion	いったいいち 一対一 one-to-one; one-on-one	いぬたいねこ 犬対猫 dogs versus cats

opposite; versus; even; anti-; compare — 文 (sentence) + 寸 (measurement)

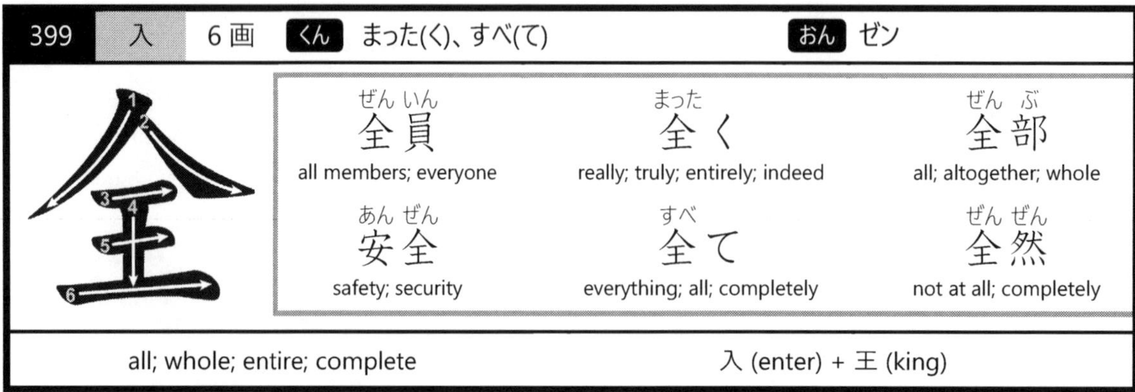

399	入	6 画	くん まった(く)、すべ(て)	おん ゼン

全

ぜんいん 全員 all members; everyone	まった 全く really; truly; entirely; indeed	ぜんぶ 全部 all; altogether; whole
あんぜん 安全 safety; security	すべ 全て everything; all; completely	ぜんぜん 全然 not at all; completely

all; whole; entire; complete — 入 (enter) + 王 (king)

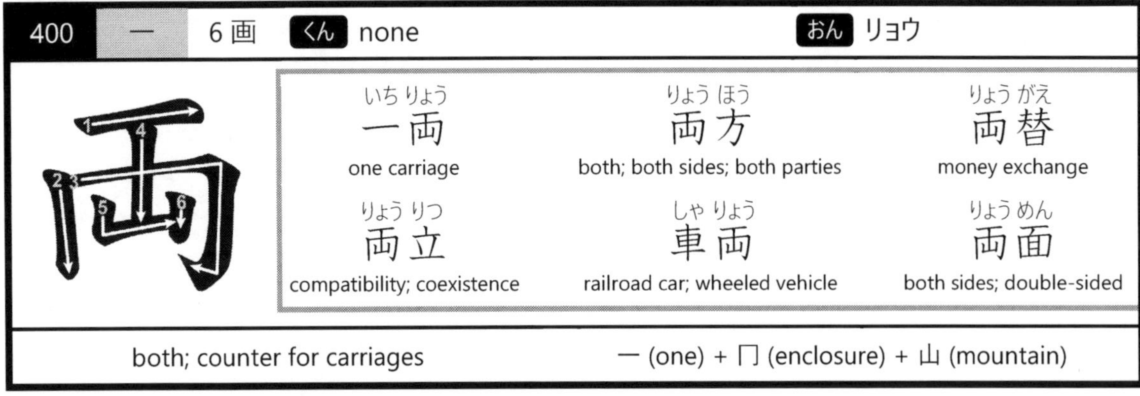

400	一	6 画	くん none	おん リョウ

両

いち りょう 一両 one carriage	りょう ほう 両方 both; both sides; both parties	りょう がえ 両替 money exchange
りょう りつ 両立 compatibility; coexistence	しゃ りょう 車両 railroad car; wheeled vehicle	りょう めん 両面 both sides; double-sided

both; counter for carriages — 一 (one) + 冂 (enclosure) + 山 (mountain)

401	面	9 画	くん おも、おもて、つら	おん メン

面

しち めんちょう 七面鳥 turkey	が めん 画面 screen (PC/phone); picture; scene	そと づら 外面 outward appearance
おも しろ 面白い Interesting; funny	こわ おもて 強面 fierce look; tough look	めん せつ 面接 interview (for a job)

face; surface; mask; aspect; side — 面 (surface)

402	口	8 画	くん いのち	おん メイ、ミョウ

命

いのち 命 life; lifetime	し めい 使命 mission; errand; task; duty	じゅ みょう 寿命 life span
うん めい 運命 fate; destiny	めい 命じる to order; to command	めい れい 命令 an order; command

life; destiny; fate; command; decree — 人 (person) + 一 (one) + 叩 (thrash)

Kanji Parts used in the New Kanji

反	anti-	王	king	面	surface
文	sentence	一	one	人	person
寸	measurement	冂	enclosure	叩	thrash
入	enter	山	mountain		

27 Kanji Memory Tools 漢字記憶術

This section helps you organically memorize kanji readings, meanings, and construction.

反

反

The anti-thesis is the "**ANTI-**".

❶反(そ)らした板(いた)に白(しろ)い❷反物(たんもの)を張(は)って「❸謀反(むほん) ❹反対(はんたい)」と書(か)いた。

I put white ❶fabric on the ❷warped board, and wrote "❹against ❸rebellion".

対

文 寸

Sentence measurement must include the word, "**VERSUS**".

日本(にほん)で❶一対(いっつい)の茶碗(ちゃわん)を❷絶対(ぜったい)買(か)います。

I'm will ❷definitely buy ❶a pair of bowls in Japan.

全

入 王

Enter the king to be "**WHOLE**".

❶全員(ぜんいん)が❷全(まった)く休憩(きゅうけい)なしで❸全(すべ)てのごみを拾(ひろ)った。

❶Everybody picked up ❸all the trash without any break ❷at all.

両

一 冂 山

One enclosure on the mountain is enough for "**BOTH**".

❶両親(りょうしん)と同(おな)じ❷車両(しゃりょう)に乗(の)っています。

I'm riding on the same ❶train car as my ❷parents.

面

面

The surface is the "**SURFACE**".

彼(かれ)は❶外面(そとづら)が❷強面(こわおもて)だけど、❸内面(ないめん)は優(やさ)しくて❹面白(おもしろ)いです。

His ❶outward appearance is ❷tough looking, but on the ❸inside he is kind and ❹funny.

命

人 一 叩

A person needs just one thrash to know the value of "**LIFE**".

「❶寿命(じゅみょう)が尽(つ)きるまで王子(おうじ)の❷命(いのち)を守(まも)れ」と❸命令(めいれい)された。

I ❸was ordered, "Protect the ❷life of the prince until your ❶lifespan is exhausted".

27 Kanji Usage 漢字の使い方

● 27-1. Subtle Differences, Big Changes

Here are some kanji that might easily be mistaken for each other.

anti-; opposite		return; answer; fade; repay	
反 anti-	はん 反する to be contrary to; to oppose はん たい 反対 opposition; objection	返 anti- + road	かえ 返す to return; to put back へん じ 返事 reply; answer; response

plank; board; plate; stage		slope; incline; hill	
板 anti- + tree	いた 板 board; plank; pane こく ばん 黒板 blackboard	坂 anti- + soil	さか 坂 slope; hill くだ ざか 下り坂 descent; downhill

● 27-2. Japanese proverbs using 両 and 面

If you ever find yourself standing between two lovely Japanese women, you can flatter them with this Japanese proverb. I never miss an opportunity to flatter, and it works!

りょう て はな 両手に花 Flowers in both hands.	A lady on each arm. Two blessings at once.
	To monopolize two beautiful things and good things at the same time. OR a man that has two women by his side.
な つら はち 泣きっ面に蜂 A bee into a crying face.	**When it rains, it pours. Rub salt into a wound.**
	Bad things tend to pile up. When a crying face swells up, if a bee stings, it will be swell up even more.

● 27-3. Completely and not at all 全

When I learned Japanese, I was taught that 全然 (not at all) could only be used with negative words or negative conjugations of adjectives and verbs.

EXAMPLE SENTENCES (全然 + NEGATIVE)

1. この映画は、全然面白くないです。
   This moving isn't interesting at all.
2. 人が全然いないです。
   There aren't any people at all.
3. 全然ダメです。
   I not good at all.
4. このピザは全然美味しくないです。
   This pizza is totally tastes good!

Despite what used to be taught, Japanese language researchers determined that 全然 is not limited to just negative conjugations. In modern Japan, 全然 is often also used with positives to mean "completely". So, feel free to use 全然 with positives despite what your teacher might say.

EXAMPLE SENTENCES (全然 + POSITIVE)

1. 唯さんは、全然綺麗です。
   Yui is totally pretty.
2. この宝石は思ったより全然いいです。
   This jewel is so much better than I thought.
3. 全然大丈夫です！
   It's totally okay!
4. これは思ったより全然美味しいです。
   This is so much tastier than I thought.

● 27-4. A pair of Japanese words 一対

Even though 一対 (いっつい) means, "a pair" it's not the same as how English uses a "pair". In English we can have a pair of scissors, pairs of pants, pairs of glasses. But in Japanese only things that are disconnected can be a "pair". So, you can't say "pair of scissors" etc.

NOTE パンツ in Japanese, means "underwear", so be careful!
In Japanese "pants" are actually called, ずぼん.

● 27-5. More words with 対

対 is used in more important words than we could fit in the initial introduction, so here are a few more you can definitely use.

absolute; definite	opposite; against; reverse	compatible
ぜったい 絶対	はんたい 反対	たいおう 対応

絶対に is a common adverb meaning, "definitely".

EXAMPLE SENTENCES

1. 今日中(きょうじゅう)に絶対(ぜったい)に宿題(しゅくだい)を終(お)わらせます。
   Before the end of today, I'm definitely going to finish my homework.

2. 私(わたし)は動物実験(どうぶつじっけん)に反対(はんたい)です。
   I'm against animal experiments.

3. 今朝(けさ)、シャツを反対(はんたい)に着(き)てしまった。
   This morning I put my shirt on backwards.

4. このアプリはWindows 11に対応(たいおう)していますか。
   Is this app compatible with Windows 11?

● 27-6. Best of both worlds 両

両 means, "both" and is part of many 熟語 (じゅくご) "compound words".

both hands	both feet; both legs	both legs
りょうて 両手	りょうあし 両足	りょうあし 両脚

both arms	both sides	both parents; parents
りょううで 両腕	りょうがわ 両側	りょうしん 両親

27 Words You Can Write 書ける言葉

反対（はんたい） opposition; objection

反対

反感（はんかん） antipathy; animosity; ill feeling

反感

対面（たいめん） interview; meeting; facing; confronting

対面

対岸（たいがん） opposite shore

対岸

全国（ぜんこく） countrywide; whole country

全国

全力（ぜんりょく） all one's power; whole energy

全力

車両（しゃりょう） rolling stock; railroad cars

車両

両足（りょうあし） both legs

両足

地面（じめん） ground

地面

面長（おもなが） oval-faced; long-faced

面長

赤面（せきめん） blushing; getting red in the face

赤面

命中（めいちゅう） (direct) hit; hitting the mark

命中

命日（めいにち） death anniversary

命日

命がけ（いのちがけ） risking one's life; desperate

命がけ

命拾い（いのちびろい） narrow escape from death

命拾い

反する（はんする） to be contrary to; to oppose; to rebel

反する

27 Kanji Workbook Activities

● 1. Stroke Order Check 書き順確認

Each kanji has a stroke with an arrow on it. Write its order number below the kanji.

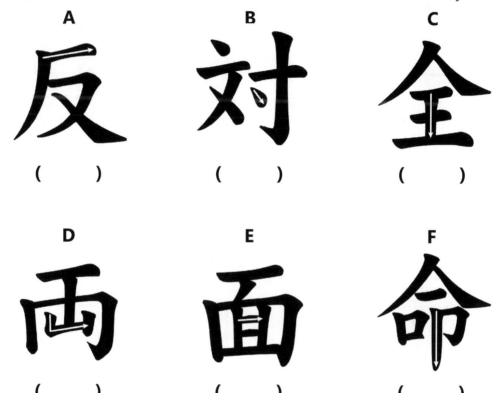

A	B	C
反	対	全
( )	( )	( )

D	E	F
両	面	命
( )	( )	( )

● 2. Kanji Meaning Match

Write the following kanji next to its meaning: 命 両 対 根 反 業 全 面 実

1. ____ fruit
2. ____ business
3. ____ root
4. ____ life
5. ____ versus
6. ____ both
7. ____ anti-
8. ____ all
9. ____ surface

● 3. Kanji Readings

Write FURIGANA above the underlined kanji words.

1. 家にある反物で、スカートを作ってみました。

2. 去年 習った漢字は、全部おぼえていません。

3. 両親は、北海道に住んでいます。

4. 友人は、とても面白い人です。

5. 明日はおじいちゃんの命日です。

● 4. Fill in the Kanji

Fill in the appropriate kanji in the blanks for each sentence.

1. (りょう しん / はん たい)
わたしは___ ___に けっこんを___ ___されました。
My marriage was opposed by my parents.

2. (うち / こ / ひと / たい わ / にが て)
___の ___は、___ と___ ___するのが___ ___です。
My child is not good at having dialogue with people.

3. (うん どう かい / ぜん りょく / はし)
___ ___ ___では、___ ___で___りました。
At the sports day event, I ran with my full power.

4. (でん しゃ / に りょう め / の)
わたしはいつも___ ___の___ ___ ___に___ります。
I always ride on the second car of the train.

5. (が めん / くら / み)
___ ___が___くて、よく___ えません。
I can't see well since the screen is so dark.

6. ___ が まとに___ ___しました。
(furigana: や / めい ちゅう)
The arrow hit the target.

7. ___ ___ がいたくて、___けませんでした。
(furigana: りょう あし / うご)
Both of my feet hurt, so I couldn't move.

● 5. Kanji Matching

Connect each kanji with an おん or くん reading. Use each reading only ONCE.

反 •	• へん
命 •	• はん
返 •	• けん
対 •	• たい
全 •	• いのち
県 •	• こ
両 •	• りょう
面 •	• ぜん
期 •	• おも
庫 •	• き

27 Answer Key 答え合わせ

1. Stroke order check (answers)

A) 1 B) 7 C) 4

D) 5 E) 7 F) 8

2. Kanji meaning match (answers)

1. 実 fruit 2. 業 business 3. 根 root

4. 命 life 5. 対 versus 6. 両 both

7. 反 anti- 8. 全 all 9. 面 surface

3. Kanji Readings (answers)

1. 家(うち)(家(いえ))にある反物(たんもの)で、スカートを作(つく)ってみました。 I made a skirt of fabric I had at home (my house).
2. 去年(きょねん)習(なら)った漢字(かんじ)は、全部(ぜんぶ)おぼえていません。 I don't remember all the kanji I learned last year.
3. 両親(りょうしん)は、北海道(ほっかいどう)に住(す)んでいます。 My parents live in Hokkaido.
4. 友人(ゆうじん)は、とても面白(おもしろ)い人(ひと)です。 My friend is a very interesting person.
5. 明日(あした)はおじいちゃんの命日(めいにち)です。 Tomorrow is the anniversary of my grandfather's death.

4. Fill in the kanji (answers)

1. わたしは[両親]にけっこんを[反対]されました。
2. [家]の[子]は、[人]と[対話]するのが[苦手]です。
3. [運動会]では、[全力]で[走]りました。
4. わたしはいつも[電車]の[二両目]に[乗]ります。
5. [画面]が[暗]くて、よく[見]えません。
6. [矢]がまとに[命中]しました。
7. [両足]がいたくて、[動]けませんでした。

5. Kanji matching (answers)

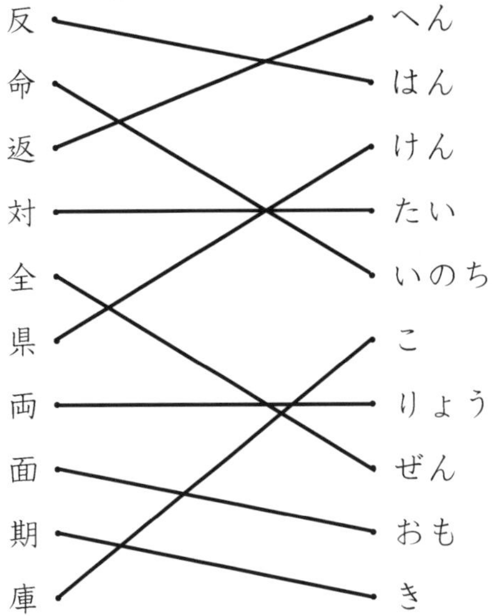

28 Kanji Lesson 28: 旅荷味具由発

403-408

Kanji related to travel

28 New Kanji 新しい漢字

403 方 10画 くん たび おん リョ

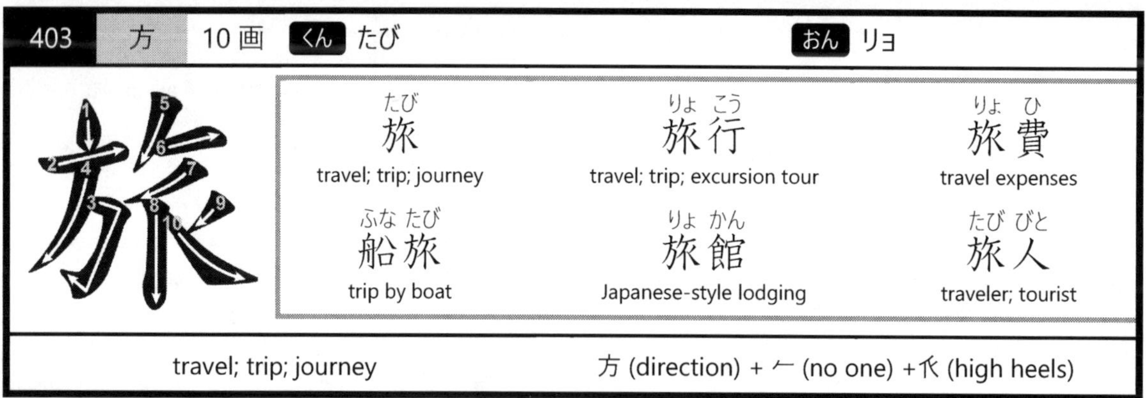

travel; trip; journey — 方 (direction) + 𠂉 (no one) + 㐅 (high heels)

404 艹 10画 くん に おん カ

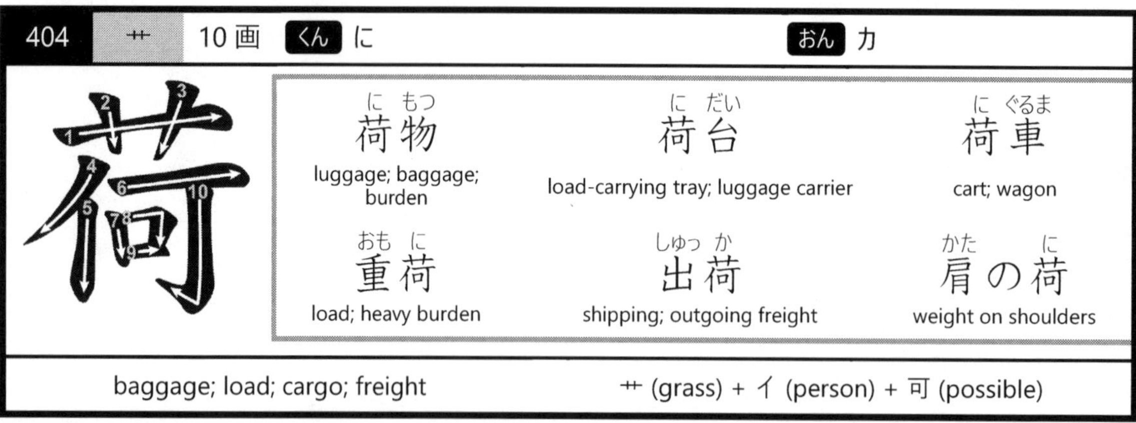

baggage; load; cargo; freight — 艹 (grass) + イ (person) + 可 (possible)

405 口 8画 くん あじ、あじ(わう) おん ミ

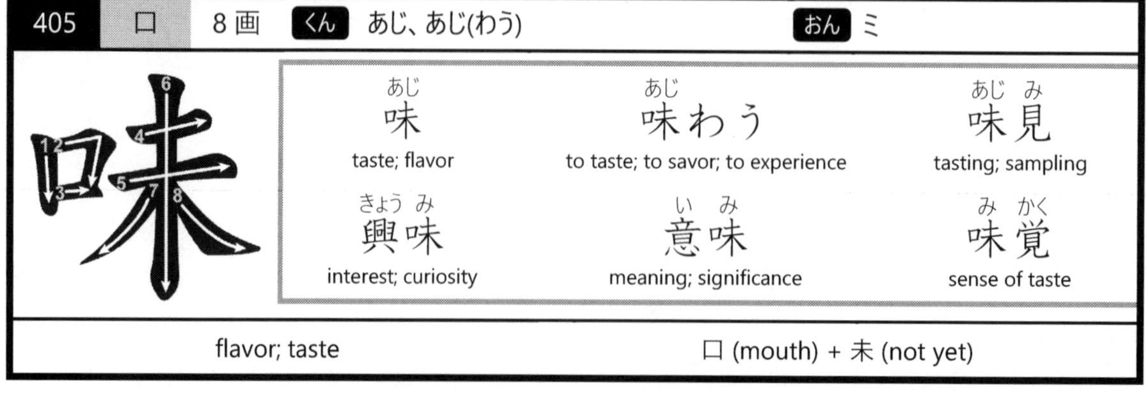

flavor; taste — 口 (mouth) + 未 (not yet)

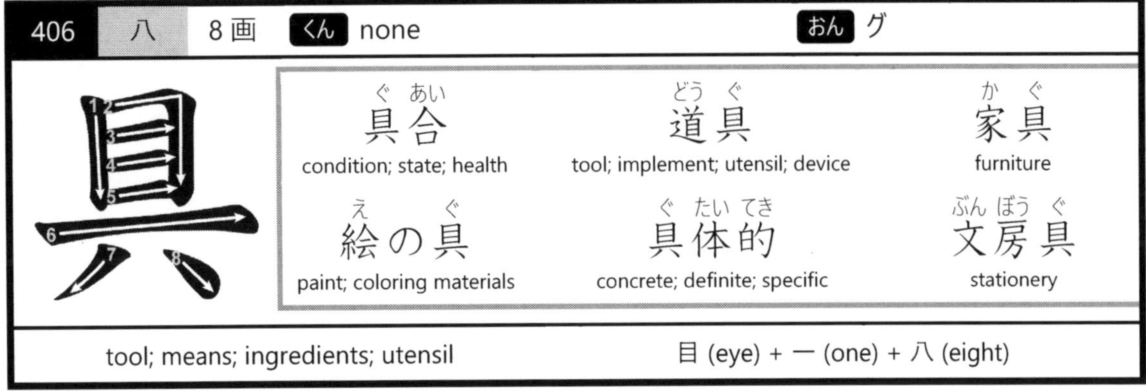

406
八
8画
くん none
おん グ
具
ぐあい 具合 condition; state; health
どうぐ 道具 tool; implement; utensil; device
かぐ 家具 furniture
えのぐ 絵の具 paint; coloring materials
ぐたいてき 具体的 concrete; definite; specific
ぶんぼうぐ 文房具 stationery
tool; means; ingredients; utensil
目 (eye) + 一 (one) + 八 (eight)

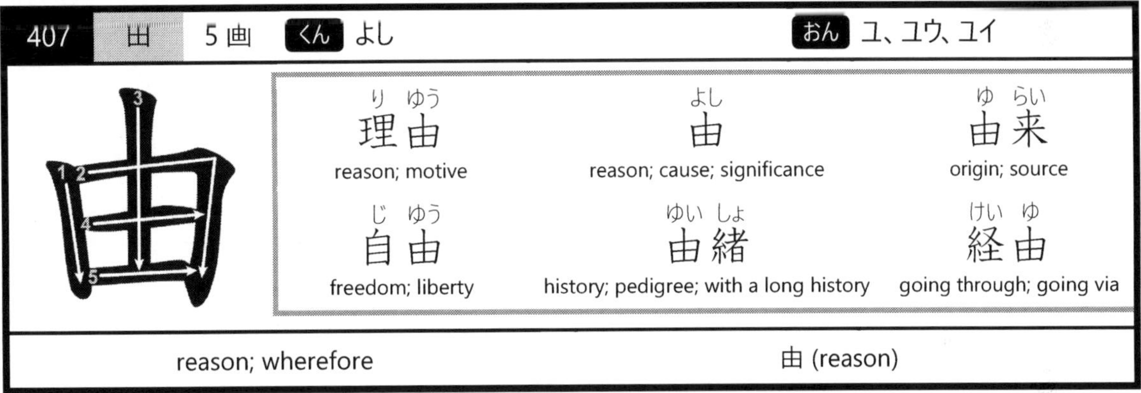

407
田
5画
くん よし
おん ユ、ユウ、ユイ
由
りゆう 理由 reason; motive
よし 由 reason; cause; significance
ゆらい 由来 origin; source
じゆう 自由 freedom; liberty
ゆいしょ 由緒 history; pedigree; with a long history
けいゆ 経由 going through; going via
reason; wherefore
由 (reason)

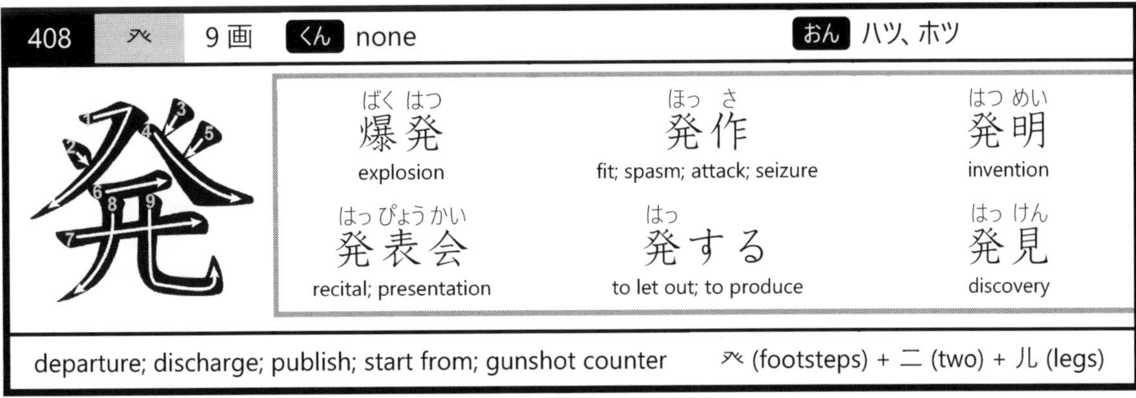

408
癶
9画
くん none
おん ハツ、ホツ
発
ばくはつ 爆発 explosion
ほっさ 発作 fit; spasm; attack; seizure
はつめい 発明 invention
はっぴょうかい 発表会 recital; presentation
はっする 発する to let out; to produce
はっけん 発見 discovery
departure; discharge; publish; start from; gunshot counter
癶 (footsteps) + 二 (two) + 儿 (legs)

Kanji Parts used in the New Kanji

方	direction	可	possible	八	eight
𠂉	no one	口	mouth	由	reason
𧘇	high heels	未	not yet	癶	footsteps
艹	grass	目	eye	二	two
イ	person	一	one	儿	legs

28 Kanji Memory Tools 漢字記憶術

This section helps you organically memorize kanji readings, meanings, and construction.

旅

方 𠂉 𠅃
This direction, no-one wearing high heels can "**TRAVEL**".

りょこう ひとり たび いちばん す
❶旅行は、❷一人旅が一番好きです。
As for ❶travelling, I like ❷travelling alone the most.

荷

艹 亻 可
Having grass on my person is possible or in my "**BAGGAGE**".

ぜんぶ しょうひん しゅっか かた に お
全部の商品を❶出荷して、❷肩の荷が下りました。
Having ❶shipped all the products, a ❷weight was lifted off my shoulders.

味

口 未
My mouth can not yet appreciate the "**FLAVOR; TASTE**".

あじ きょうみしんしん
どんな❶味がするか❷興味深々です。
I'm ❷very interested as to what it ❶tastes like.

具

目 一 八
The eye had one pupil and eight "**TOOLS**".

ぶんぼうぐてん え ぐ か
❶文房具店で、❷絵の具を買いました。
I bought ❷paint at the ❶stationery shop.

由

由
The reason is this "**REASON**".

ゆいしょ じんじゃ いちじへいさ りゆう し よし
❶由緒ある神社が一時閉鎖した❷理由を❸知る由もなかった。
I had ❸no way of knowing the ❷reason for the ❶venerable shrine was temporarily closed.

発

癶 二 儿
The footsteps of two legs mean, "**DEPARTURE**".

しゅっぱつ まえ しんぞうほっさ お
❶出発の前にパイロットが❷心臓発作を起こした。
Before ❶departure, the pilot had a ❷heart attack.

28 Kanji Usage 漢字の使い方

● 28-1. “Departure” and “Origin” 発

Here are some words you can use every day while using transportation in Japan.

departure	first departure (of day)	departure (of a train etc.)
しゅっぱつ 出発	しはつ 始発	はっしゃ 発車

発 can also come after a TIME or a LOCATION to say that a train or bus departs at a certain time or from a certain location. It can also be used to show the origin of people and things.

EXAMPLES

1. 10時(じ)15分(ふん)発(はつ)の電車(でんしゃ)
   the train departing at 10:15
2. 成田(なりた)発(はつ)、サンフランシスコ行(ゆ)き
   departing Narita, to San Francisco
3. 東京(とうきょう)発(はつ)のバンド
   a band from Tokyo
4. 台湾(たいわん)発(はつ)のタピオカ・ドリンク
   a tapioca drink from Taiwan

● 28-2. Kinds of taste using 味

In America, we are used to chip flavors such as “cheese”, “ranch”, and “barbeque”. Japan has some unique flavors that you might be surprised to see.

EXAMPLES

1. うすしお味(あじ)
   lightly salted flavor
2. コンソメ味(あじ)
   consommé flavor
3. フレンチサラダ味(あじ)
   French salad flavor

4. しょうゆマヨ味(あじ)
   soy sauce mayonnaise flavor
5. バターしょうゆ味(あじ)
   butter soy sauce flavor
6. 関西(かんさい)だししょうゆ味(あじ)
   Kansai fish / kelp stock soy sauce

● 28-3. Useful set phrases using 荷 and 由

Here are some more set phrases using kanji from this lesson.

肩(かた)の荷(に)が下(お)りる	to feel the weight being lifted off my shoulders / that's a relief.

この仕事(しごと)が終(お)わって、<u>肩(かた)の荷(に)が下(お)りました</u>。

The <u>weight's off my shoulders</u> now that this work is done.

荷(に)が重(おも)い	to be under pressure / to feel too much responsibility

学級委員長(がっきゅういいんちょう)になるのは、<u>荷(に)が重(おも)い</u>です。

Becoming the class representative is a <u>heavy burden</u>.

知(し)る由(よし)もない	to have no way of knowing that / to be completely ignorant of

無口(むくち)な山田君(やまだくん)が、こんなにいい人(ひと)だったなんて、<u>知(し)る由(よし)もなかった</u>。

I <u>had no way of knowing that</u> the untalkative Yamada was this good of a person.

28 Words You Can Write 書ける言葉

旅先（たびさき） destination; goal (of travel)

旅	先										

入荷（にゅうか） arrival of goods; goods received

入	荷										

荷物（にもつ） luggage; baggage

荷	物										

後味（あとあじ） after taste

後	味										

味方（みかた） friend; ally; supporter; standing by; backing up

味	方										

家具（かぐ） furniture

家	具										

遊具（ゆうぐ） play equipment; playground equipment

遊	具										

自由（じゆう） freedom; liberty

自	由										

理由（りゆう） reason; motive

理	由										

活発（かっぱつ） vigor; active; lively

活	発										

地味（じみ） plain; simple; sober; modest; quiet

地	味										

雨具（あまぐ） rain gear

雨	具										

発車（はっしゃ） departure (of a train, car, etc.); leaving

発	車										

一人旅（ひとりたび） traveling alone; solitary journey

一	人	旅									

発電所（はつでんしょ） power station; power plant

発	電	所									

旅行会社（りょこうがいしゃ） travel agent; travel agency

旅	行	会	社								

28 Kanji Workbook Activities

● 1. Stroke Order Check 書き順確認

Each kanji has a stroke with an arrow on it. Write its order number below the kanji.

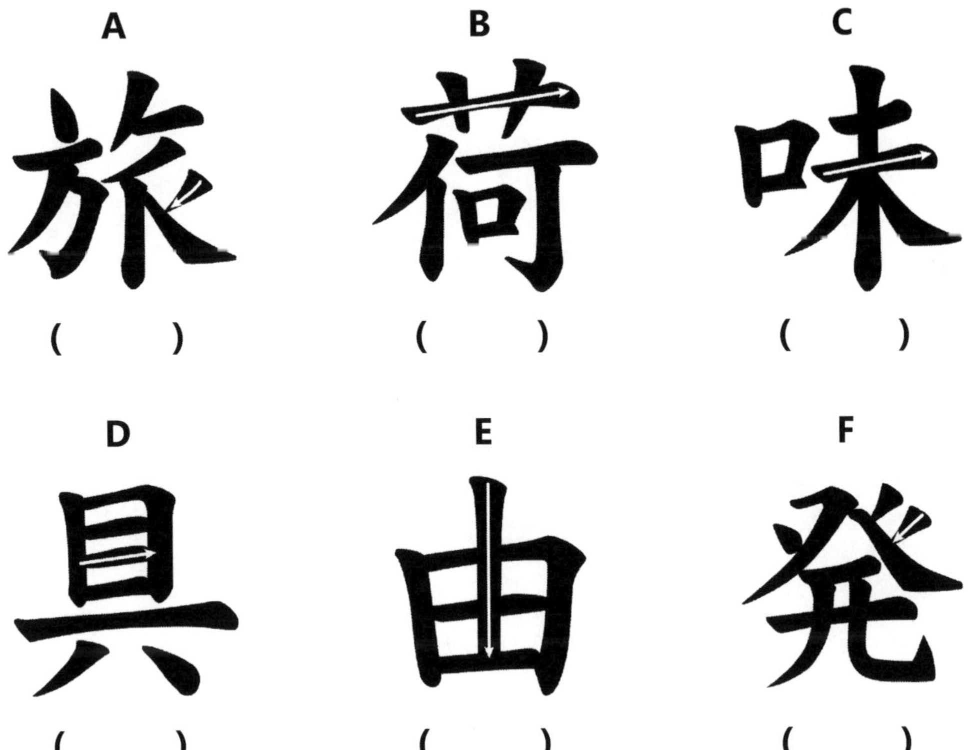

● 2. Kanji Meaning Match

Write the following kanji next to its meaning: 旅 味 豆 由 発 実 反 荷 具

1.____ beans
2. ____ truth
3. ____ anti-
4. ____ travel
5. ____ flavor
6. ____ reason
7. ____ baggage
8. ____ ingredients
9. ____ departure

● 3. Kanji Readings

Write FURIGANA above the underlined kanji words.

1. 十日間の船旅は、とても楽しかったです。

2. 今日、商品を出荷しました。

3. カレーライスを作ったので、味見して下さい。

4. 新しい家具を買うことにしました。

5. きのう、学校へ来なかった理由は何ですか。

● 4. Fill in the Kanji

Fill in the appropriate kanji in the blanks for each sentence.

1. (たび)___ (さき)___ で (ゆう)___ (じん)___ に (あ)___ いました。
   I met a friend at my trip destination.

2. この (はこ)___ を (に)___ (だい)___ につみましょう。
   Let's pack this box into the luggage carrier.

3. お (ねえ)___ ちゃんは、いつでもわたしの (み)___ (かた)___ です。
   My oldest sister is always my ally.

4. (せん)___ (しゅう)___ は (ぐ)___ (あい)___ が (わる)___ くて、(やす)___ んでいました。
   I took off last week since my condition was so bad.

5. (じ)___ (ぶん)___ の (な)___ (まえ)___ の (ゆ)___ (らい)___ を (し)___ っています。
   I know the origin of my own name.

きょ う はっ ぴょう かい

6. ___ ___ は、ピアノの___ ___ ___があります。

Today there is a piano recital.

ひと り たび おも

7. ヨーロッパに___ ___ ___しようと___ っています。

I'm thinking of travelling alone to Europe.

● 5. Kanji Matching

Connect each kanji with an おん or くん reading. Use each reading only ONCE.

荷 •	• に
具 •	• りょ
羊 •	• は
発 •	• はつ
旅 •	• ゆう
住 •	• ぐ
味 •	• み
由 •	• す
葉 •	• よう
物 •	• ぶつ

28 Answer Key 答え合わせ

1. Stroke order check (answers)

A) 9 B) 1 C) 5

D) 4 E) 3 F) 5

2. Kanji meaning match (answers)

1. 豆 beans 2. 実 truth 3. 反 anti-
4. 旅 travel 5. 味 flavor 6. 由 reason
7. 荷 baggage 8. 具 ingredients 9. 発 departure

3. Kanji Readings (answers)

1. 十日間(とおかかん)の船旅(ふなたび)は、とても楽(たの)しかったです。 The 10-day boat trip was very fun.
2. 今日(きょう)、商品(しょうひん)を出荷(しゅっか)しました。 Today we shipped the products.
3. カレーライスを作(つく)ったので、味見(あじみ)して下(くだ)さい。 I made curry rice so please taste it.
4. 新(あたら)しい家具(かぐ)を買(か)うことにしました。 I decided to by new furniture.
5. きのう、学校(がっこう)へ来(こ)なかった理由(りゆう)は何(なん)ですか。 What's the reason you didn't come to school yesterday?

4. Fill in the kanji (answers)

1. 旅先で友人に会いました。
2. この箱を荷台につみましょう。
3. お姉ちゃんは、いつでもわたしの味方です。
4. 先週は具合が悪くて、休んでいました。
5. 自分の名前の由来を知っています。
6. 今日は、ピアノの発表会があります。
7. ヨーロッパに一人旅しようと思っています。

5. Kanji matching (answers)

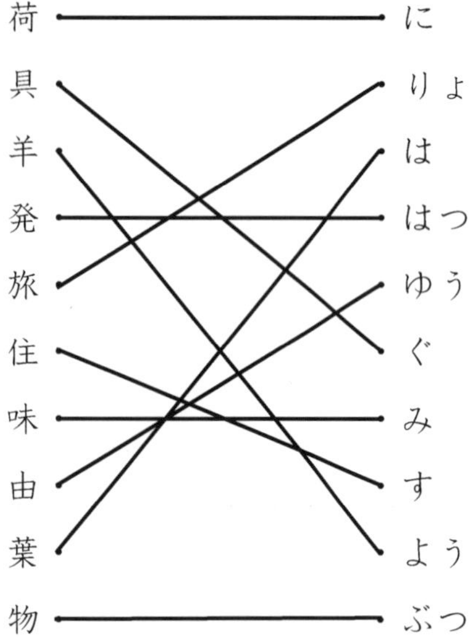

29 Kanji Lesson 29: 酒祭昔福昭和

409-414

Kanji related to festivals and era

29 New Kanji 新しい漢字

409 酉 10画 くん さけ、さか おん シュ

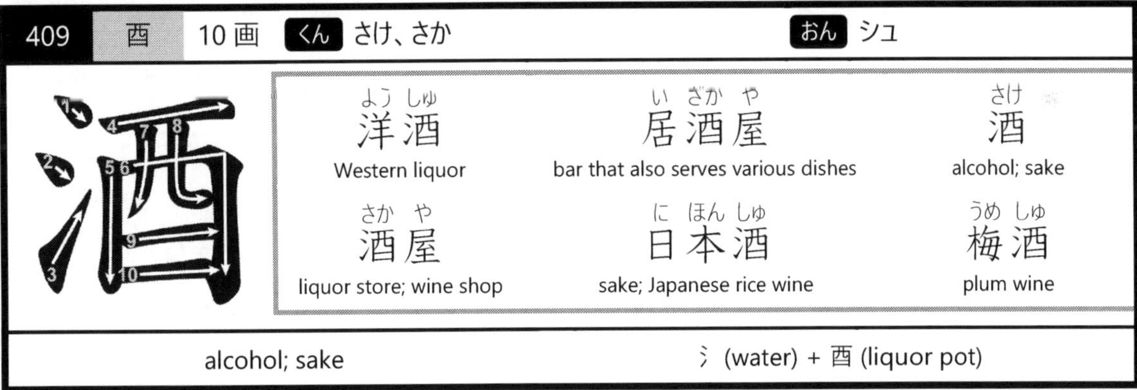

ようしゅ 洋酒 Western liquor	いざかや 居酒屋 bar that also serves various dishes	さけ 酒 alcohol; sake
さかや 酒屋 liquor store; wine shop	にほんしゅ 日本酒 sake; Japanese rice wine	うめしゅ 梅酒 plum wine

alcohol; sake — 氵 (water) + 酉 (liquor pot)

410 示 11画 くん まつ(る、り) おん サイ

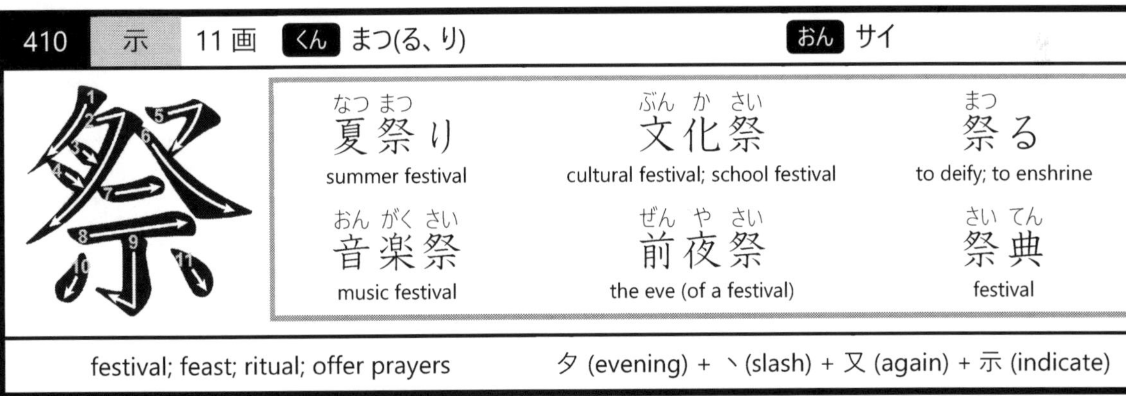

なつまつ 夏祭り summer festival	ぶんかさい 文化祭 cultural festival; school festival	まつ 祭る to deify; to enshrine
おんがくさい 音楽祭 music festival	ぜんやさい 前夜祭 the eve (of a festival)	さいてん 祭典 festival

festival; feast; ritual; offer prayers — 夕 (evening) + 丶 (slash) + 又 (again) + 示 (indicate)

411 日 8画 くん むかし おん セキ、シャク

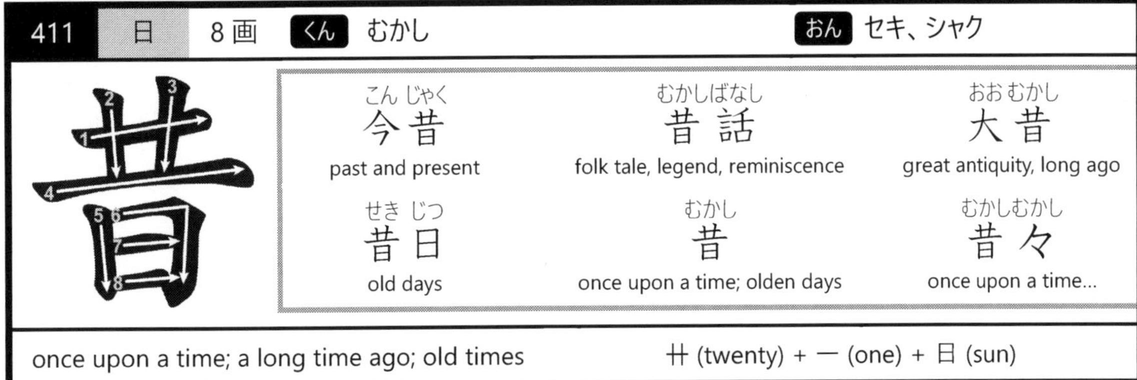

こんじゃく 今昔 past and present	むかしばなし 昔話 folk tale, legend, reminiscence	おおむかし 大昔 great antiquity, long ago
せきじつ 昔日 old days	むかし 昔 once upon a time; olden days	むかしむかし 昔々 once upon a time...

once upon a time; a long time ago; old times — 卄 (twenty) + 一 (one) + 日 (sun)

412	ネ	13 画	くん none	おん フク

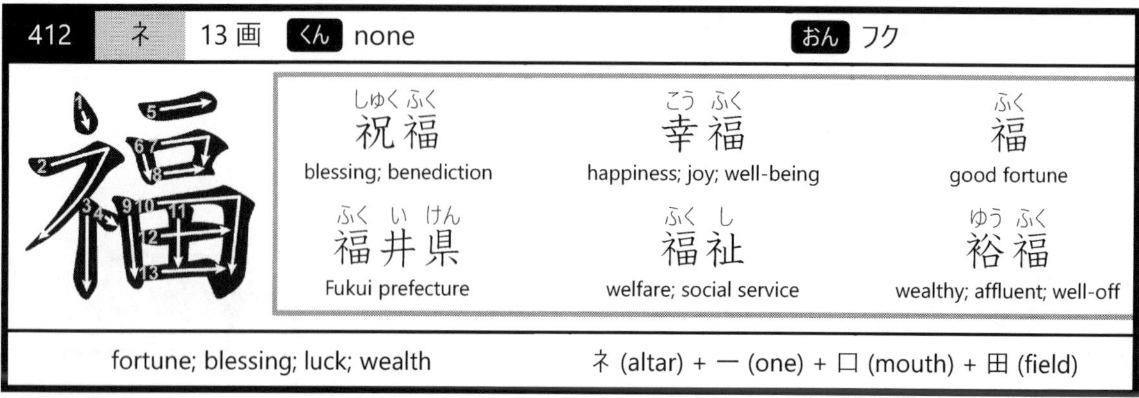

しゅくふく 祝福 blessing; benediction	こうふく 幸福 happiness; joy; well-being	ふく 福 good fortune
ふくいけん 福井県 Fukui prefecture	ふくし 福祉 welfare; social service	ゆうふく 裕福 wealthy; affluent; well-off

fortune; blessing; luck; wealth — ネ (altar) + 一 (one) + 口 (mouth) + 田 (field)

413	日	9 画	くん none	おん ショウ

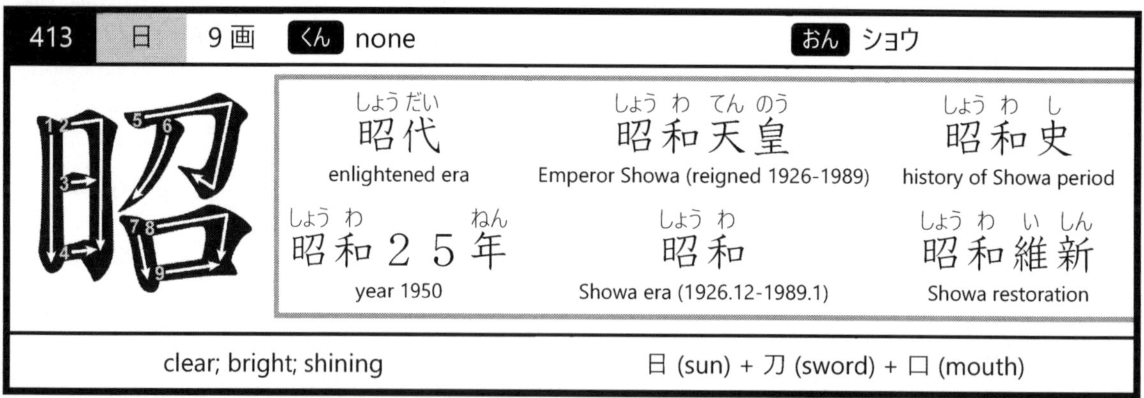

しょうだい 昭代 enlightened era	しょうわてんのう 昭和天皇 Emperor Showa (reigned 1926-1989)	しょうわし 昭和史 history of Showa period
しょうわ ねん 昭和２５年 year 1950	しょうわ 昭和 Showa era (1926.12-1989.1)	しょうわいしん 昭和維新 Showa restoration

clear; bright; shining — 日 (sun) + 刀 (sword) + 口 (mouth)

414	口	8 画	くん やわ(らぐ、らげる)、なご(む、やか)	おん ワ、オ

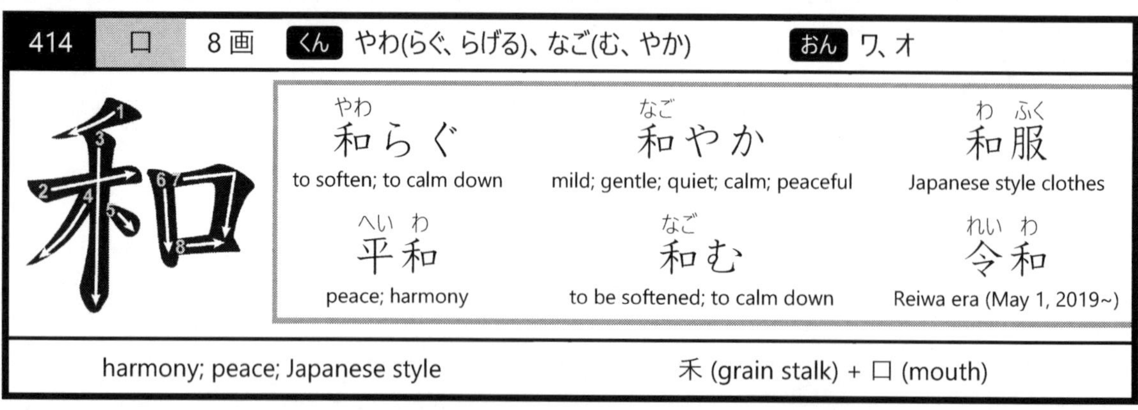

やわ 和らぐ to soften; to calm down	なご 和やか mild; gentle; quiet; calm; peaceful	わふく 和服 Japanese style clothes
へいわ 平和 peace; harmony	なご 和む to be softened; to calm down	れいわ 令和 Reiwa era (May 1, 2019~)

harmony; peace; Japanese style — 禾 (grain stalk) + 口 (mouth)

Kanji Parts used in the New Kanji

氵	water	示	indicate	口	mouth
酉	liquor pot	廿	twenty	田	field
夕	evening	一	one	刀	sword
丶	slash	日	sun	禾	grain stalk
又	again	ネ	altar		

29 Kanji Memory Tools 漢字記憶術

This section helps you organically memorize kanji readings, meanings, and construction.

酒

氵 酉

The water in this liquor pot is actually "**ALCOHOL**".

い ざか や　に ほん しゅ　いろいろ　さけ　の

❶居酒屋ではワインや❷日本酒など色々な❸お酒が飲めます。

In ❶Japanese pubs you can drink a variety of ❷alcohol like wine or ❸Japanese liquor.

祭

夕 丶 又 示

An evening where we slash again indicates a "**FESTIVAL**".

がくえんさい　がっ こう ない　おこな　まつ

❶学園祭は学校内で行う❷祭りです。

A ❶school festival is a ❷festival held inside of a school.

昔

廾 一 日

There were twenty one suns "**A LONG TIME AGO**".

おおむかし　か　こんじゃくものがたりしゅう　さっ か　わ

❶大昔に書かれた「❷今昔物語集」の作家は分かりません。

The writer of the "❷Konjaku Monogatarishuu" (Stories of Past and Present Collection), written ❶long ago, is not known.

福

礻 一 口 田

At the altar, one mouth gave the field its "**BLESSING**".

こ ども　こう ふく　ねが　ふく こ　な づ

子供の❶幸福を願って❷福子と名付けた。

Wishing for my child's ❷happiness, I named her ❶Fukuko (blessed child).

昭

日 刀 口

The sun cast its sword into the mouth and is "**SHINING**".

しょう わ う　しょう わ てん のう　おぼ

❶昭和生まれですが、❷昭和天皇のことをあまり覚えていません。

I was ❶born in Showa (era), but I don't remember much about the ❷Emperor Showa.

和

禾 口

The grain stalk's mouth spoke of "**HARMONY**".

わ ふく　き　こころ　なご

❶和服を着ると、心が❷和みます。

When I wear ❶Japanese style clothing, my heart ❷calms down.

29 Understanding Kanji Parts 漢字部分の理解

● 29-1. A better breakdown of 祭 and 福

To make remembering the kanji easier, we have had to make compromises when breaking down each kanji into its individual parts. To avoid overwhelming the student with parts, we tend to choose the broadest meaning for each of the parts.

Unfortunately, this means that some kanji have much more interesting or more memorable stories. Let's look what is a more natural breakdown of 祭 into its original parts:

The "better" breakdown of 祭		
祭	祭	祭
Here the 夕 (with an extra line) signifies the "meat of the sacrifice" to be made.	Here 又 can also mean "right hand" signifying the hand putting the sacrifice on the altar.	And here 示 can mean "a platform" or an "altar" where the offering is made.

福 also has a more interesting breakdown than our pragmatic one:

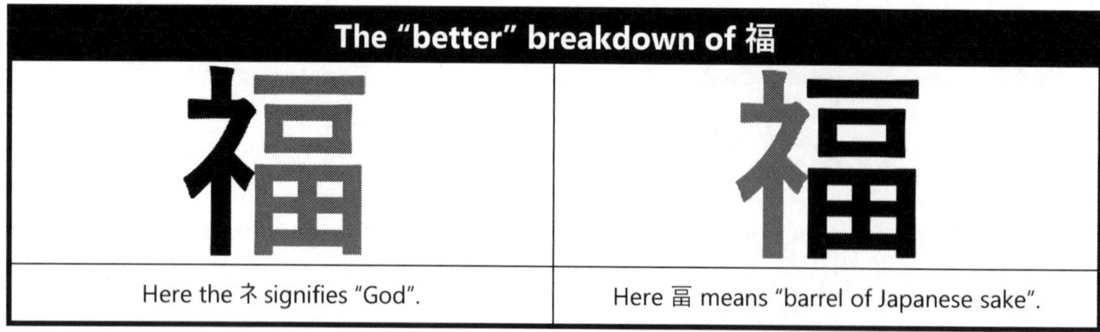

The "better" breakdown of 福	
福	福
Here the ネ signifies "God".	Here 畐 means "barrel of Japanese sake".

The problem with learning this way is that it's time intensive to learn specialized meanings of each part that might only apply to one kanji. And on the flip side, learning one meaning for each part that spans multiple kanji is more efficient, but sometimes provides a less memorable mnemonic.

● 29-2. The "mouth" radical くち (口)

Here are some kanji that contain the くち radical.

Meaning	Kanji	Components	Word 1	Reading	English	Word 2	Reading	English
mouth; opening	口	mouth	蛇口	じゃ ぐち	water faucet	人口	じん こう	population
right	右	NO + one + mouth	右手	みぎ て	right hand	右折	う せつ	turning to the right
old	古	10 + mouth	古い	ふる	old; aged	古代	こ だい	ancient times
pedestal; a stand	台	MU + mouth	台	だい	stand; rack; table	台所	だいどころ	kitchen
fit; suit; join	合	gather + mouth	合う	あ	to fit; to match	試合	し あい	match; game; contest
name; noted; reputation	名	evening + mouth	名前	な まえ	name; full name	有名	ゆう めい	famous; fame
goods; refinement; dignity	品	three mouths	品物	しな もの	goods; article; thing	食品	しょく ひん	food; food products
harmony; Japanese style	和	two branch tree + mouth	平和	へい わ	peace; harmony	和食	わ しょく	Japanese food

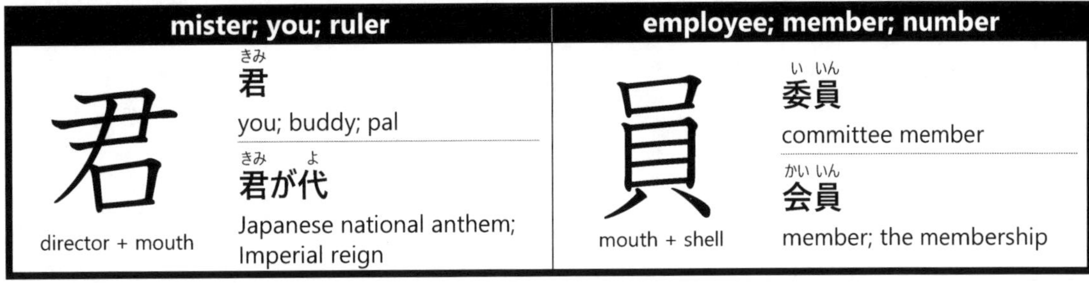

Meaning	Kanji	Components	Word 1	Reading	English	Word 2	Reading	English
mister; you; ruler	君	director + mouth	君	きみ	you; buddy; pal	君が代	きみ よ	Japanese national anthem; Imperial reign
employee; member; number	員	mouth + shell	委員	い いん	committee member	会員	かい いん	member; the membership

29 Kanji Usage 漢字の使い方

● 29-3. Which one do you like, Japanese or Western? (和 and 洋)

和 is used for many words referring to Japanese specific things. 洋 is used for Western things. We learn 洋 in lesson 30.

Japanese 和	Western 洋
わ しき **和式** Japanese style	よう しき **洋式** Western style; foreign style
わ ふく **和服** Japanese clothes	よう ふく **洋服** Western-style clothes
わ しつ **和室** Japanese-style room	よう しつ **洋室** Western-style room
わ しょく **和食** Japanese food	よう しょく **洋食** Western-style food
わ が し **和菓子** Japanese sweets	よう が し **洋菓子** Western sweets

● 29-4. Famous Japanese festivals 祭

You won't want to miss out on some of the most famous Japanese festivals.

Festival	Why it's famous	Location / Dates
さっ ぽろ ゆき まつ **札幌雪祭り** Sapporo Snow Festival	Large-scale snow and ice sculptures from artists around the world. Music guest on snow stages and many winter events.	Sapporo City January, February
あお もり まつり **青森ねぶた祭** Aomori Nebuta Festival	Large lantern floats and parades, live music. Ends with a huge firework display on the final day.	Aomori City August
あわ おど **阿波踊り** Awa Dance Festival	Largest dance festival in all of Japan. Taiko drums and other traditional Japanese music instrument performances.	Tokushima Prefecture August
せん だい たなばた まつ **仙台七夕祭り** Sendai Tanabata Festival	Large multi-colored hanging decorations covering over shopping streets. Music, food, shopping.	Many cities / Sendai City July
ぎ おん まつり **祇園祭** Gion Festival	Billed as the most famous festival in Japan. Many events including large traditional float parades.	Kyoto (Yasaka Shrine) July

● 29-5. Japanese eras

In Japan there is a separate way of counting years from the one we are used to in the west. The years are based on the reign of the emperor. Japan is currently in the 令和 era which began on May 1, 2019 after the abdication of the 平成天皇 (Heisei era emperor). One of the longest eras was 昭和 which was from December, 1926 to January 1989.

Japanese people will fondly remember each of the eras similarly to how the west will remember the "70s" or "80s". Also, their birth year is also often expressed was the year of the era. For example, I was born in 1972, so I can say I was born 昭和４７年 and someone born in 2002 would be 平成１４年. Children born in 2022 are born in 令和4年.

Era Name (meaning)	Years	Emperor Name
明治 (wishing for a bright era)	1868-1912	睦仁
大正 (big justice)	1912-1926	嘉仁
昭和 (shining peace)	1926-1989	裕仁
平成 (everlasting peace)	1989-2019	明仁
令和 (beautiful harmony)	2019-	徳仁

While they emperors are alive they are referred to as their name plus 天皇, but after death they are referred to as the name of their era plus 天皇. This means that when 博仁天皇 passed he became 昭和天皇.

29 Words You Can Write 書ける言葉

酒屋（さかや） liquor store

酒 屋

祭日（さいじつ） national holiday

祭 日

昔話（むかしばなし） folklore; legend

昔 話

昔風（むかしふう） old fashioned

昔 風

昭和（しょうわ） Showa era

昭 和

和紙（わし） Japanese paper

和 紙

和室（わしつ） Japanese-style room

和 室

和食（わしょく） Japanese-style meal

和 食

酒場（さかば） bar; pub; tavern

酒 場

祭り（まつり） festival

祭	り										

幸福（こうふく） happiness; joy; well-being

幸	福										

昔人間（むかしにんげん） old-fashioned person; old-timer

昔	人	間									

前夜祭（ぜんやさい） the eve (of a festival)

前	夜	祭									

福引き（ふくびき） lottery; drawing

福	引	き									

和らぐ（やわらぐ） to soften; to calm down

和	ら	ぐ									

飲酒運転（いんしゅうんてん） drunken driving; drinking and driving

飲	酒	運	転								

29 Kanji Workbook Activities

● 1. Stroke Order Check 書き順確認

Each kanji has a stroke with an arrow on it. Write its order number below the kanji.

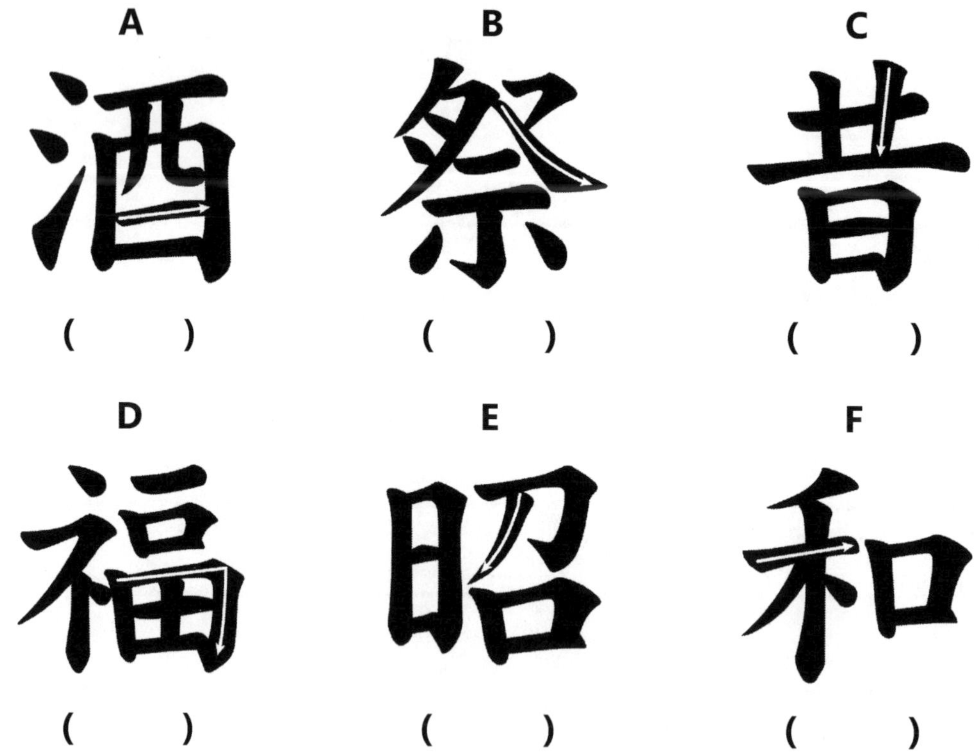

● 2. Kanji Readings

Write FURIGANA above the underlined kanji words.

1. 飲酒運転をしてはいけません。
2. この神社は子どもの神様を祭っています。
3. 昔話はたくさん読みました。
4. 田中さんは、幸福な家庭で育ちました。
5. 父は昭和 生まれで、昔人間です。

● 3. Kanji Meaning Match

Write the following kanji next to its meaning: 和 福 荷 祭 反 酒 昔 昭 命

1.____ alcohol 2. ____ old times 3. ____ shining

4. ____ festival 5. ____ fortune 6. ____ Japanese-style

7. ____ baggage 8. ____ anti- 9. ____ life

● 4. Fill in the Kanji

Fill in the appropriate kanji in the blanks for each sentence.

1. わたしは ワインより____ ____ ____のほうがすきです。（に ほん しゅ）

I like Japanese rice wine more than wine.

2. ____ ____りで ゆかたを ____ ました。（なつ まつ / き）

I wore a yukata at the summer festival.

3. ____ は、よく____ ____しましたが、____ はしません。（むかし / うん どう / いま）

A long time ago, I often exercised, but now I don't.

4. ____ ____きで、____ ____が____たりました。（ふく び / いっ とう / あ）

At the drawing, I won the first prize.

5. ____ は____ ____ ____ ____ ____ ____まれです。（はは / しょう わ ご じゅう ねん う）

My mother was born Showa year 50.

6. ____ はいつも____ ____ですが、ときどきピザも____べます。（うち / わ しょく / た）

We always eat Japanese food, but sometimes we eat pizza.

7. ____ ____ でお____を____むと、____が____みます。（わ しつ / ちゃ / の / こころ / なご）

If you drink tea in a Japanese style room, your heart will be soothed.

● 5. Kanji Matching

Connect each kanji with an おん or くん reading. Use each reading only ONCE.

酒 •	• み
昔 •	• むかし
味 •	• しゅ
昭 •	• さい
由 •	• ゆう
和 •	• わ
祭 •	• しょう
福 •	• はしら
界 •	• かい
柱 •	• ふく

29 Answer Key 答え合わせ

1. Stroke order check (answers)

A) 9　B) 6　C) 3
D) 10　E) 6　F) 2

3. Kanji meaning match (answers)

1. 酒 alcohol　2. 昔 old times　3. 昭 shining
4. 祭 festival　5. 福 fortune　6. 和 Japanese-style
7. 荷 baggage　8. 反 anti-　9. 命 life

2. Kanji Readings (answers)

1. 飲酒(いんしゅ)運転(うんてん)をしてはいけません。 You shouldn't drink and drive.
2. この神社(じんじゃ)は子(こ)どもの神様(かみさま)を祭(まつ)っています。 This shrine is dedicated to the "God of children".
3. 昔話(むかしばなし)はたくさん読(よ)みました。 I read a lot of folktales.
4. 田中(たなか)さんは、幸福(こうふく)な家庭(かてい)で育(そだ)ちました。 Tanaka grew up in a happy family.
5. 父(ちち)は昭和(しょうわ) 生(う)まれで、昔人間(むかしにんげん)です。 My dad, born in the Showa-era, is old-fashioned.

4. Fill in the kanji (answers)

1. わたしはワインより日本酒のほうがすきです。
2. 夏祭りで ゆかたを着ました。
3. 昔は、よく運動しましたが、今はしません。
4. 福引きで、一等が当たりました。
5. 母は昭和五十年生まれです。
6. 家はいつも和食ですが、ときどきピザも食べます。
7. 和室でお茶を飲むと、心が和みます。

5. Kanji matching (answers)

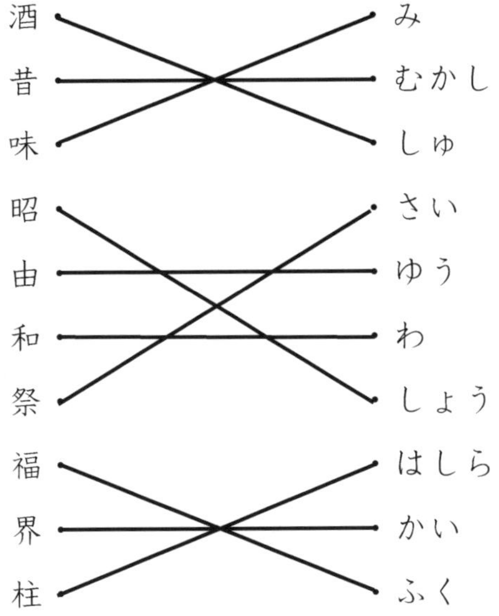

30 Kanji Lesson 30: 氷波湯油注洋

415-420

Kanji with the water radical

30 New Kanji 新しい漢字

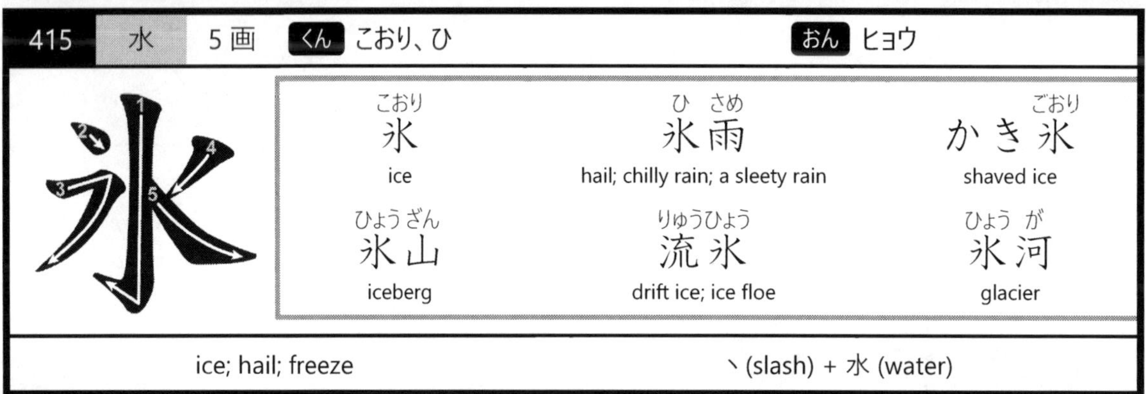

415 | 水 | 5 画 | くん こおり、ひ | おん ヒョウ

氷

こおり 氷 ice	ひ さめ 氷雨 hail; chilly rain; a sleety rain	ごおり かき氷 shaved ice
ひょうざん 氷山 iceberg	りゅうひょう 流氷 drift ice; ice floe	ひょう が 氷河 glacier

ice; hail; freeze — 丶(slash) + 水 (water)

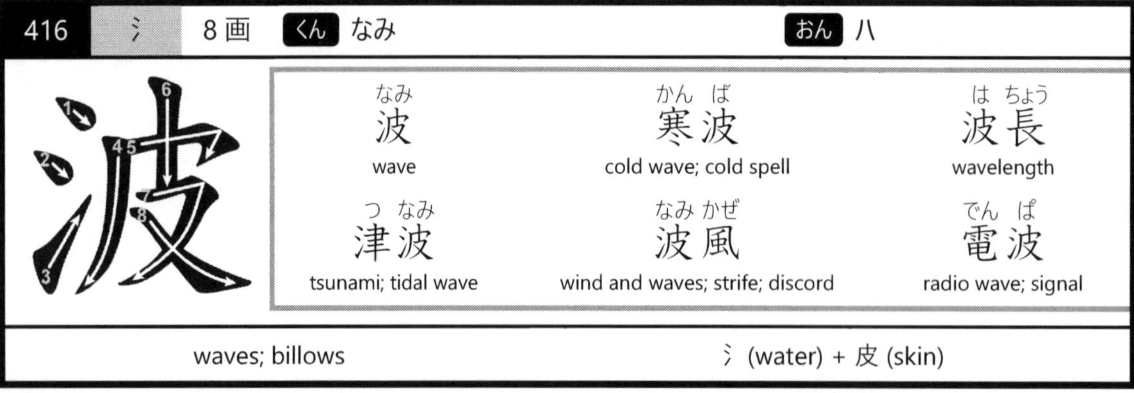

416 | 氵 | 8 画 | くん なみ | おん ハ

波

なみ 波 wave	かん ぱ 寒波 cold wave; cold spell	は ちょう 波長 wavelength
つ なみ 津波 tsunami; tidal wave	なみ かぜ 波風 wind and waves; strife; discord	でん ぱ 電波 radio wave; signal

waves; billows — 氵 (water) + 皮 (skin)

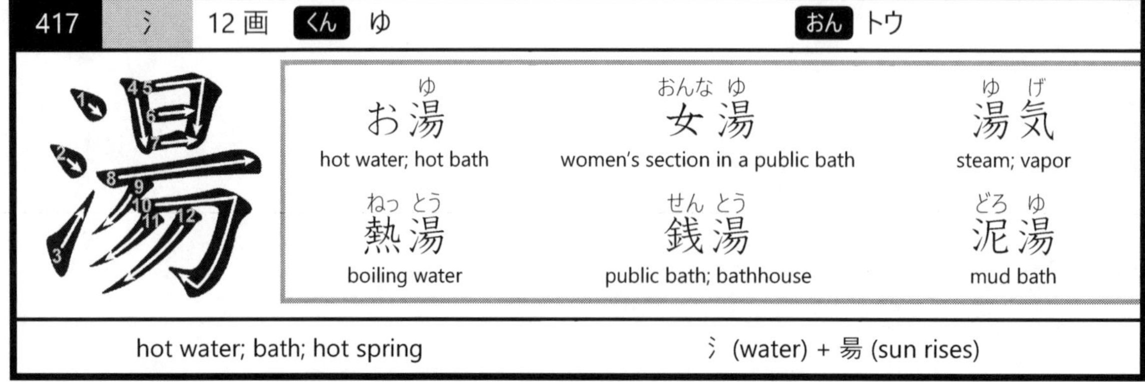

417 | 氵 | 12 画 | くん ゆ | おん トウ

湯

ゆ お湯 hot water; hot bath	おんな ゆ 女湯 women's section in a public bath	ゆ げ 湯気 steam; vapor
ねっ とう 熱湯 boiling water	せん とう 銭湯 public bath; bathhouse	どろ ゆ 泥湯 mud bath

hot water; bath; hot spring — 氵 (water) + 昜 (sun rises)

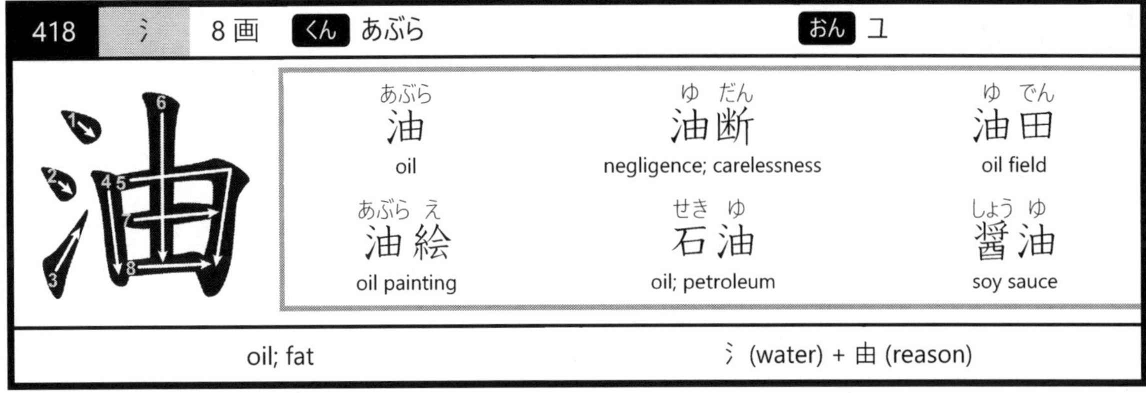

418 | 氵 | 8 画 | くん あぶら | おん ユ

油	油断	油田
あぶら	ゆ だん	ゆ でん
oil	negligence; carelessness	oil field
油絵 (あぶら え)	石油 (せき ゆ)	醤油 (しょう ゆ)
oil painting	oil; petroleum	soy sauce

oil; fat — 氵 (water) + 由 (reason)

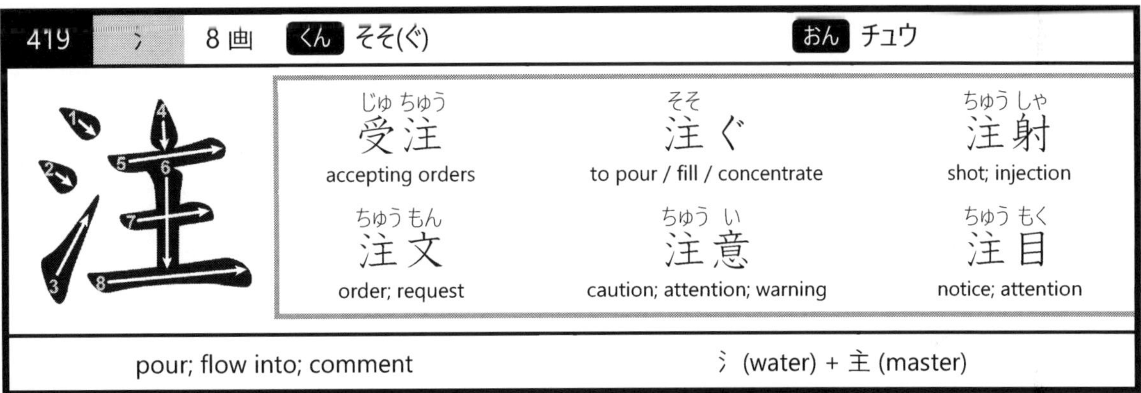

419 | 氵 | 8 画 | くん そそ(ぐ) | おん チュウ

受注	注ぐ	注射
じゅ ちゅう	そそ	ちゅう しゃ
accepting orders	to pour / fill / concentrate	shot; injection
注文 (ちゅう もん)	注意 (ちゅう い)	注目 (ちゅう もく)
order; request	caution; attention; warning	notice; attention

pour; flow into; comment — 氵 (water) + 主 (master)

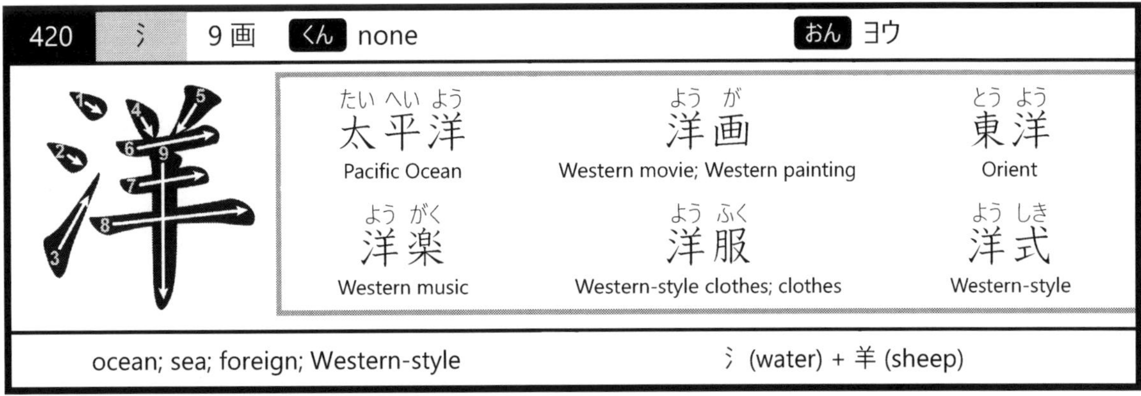

420 | 氵 | 9 画 | くん none | おん ヨウ

太平洋	洋画	東洋
たい へい よう	よう が	とう よう
Pacific Ocean	Western movie; Western painting	Orient
洋楽 (よう がく)	洋服 (よう ふく)	洋式 (よう しき)
Western music	Western-style clothes; clothes	Western-style

ocean; sea; foreign; Western-style — 氵 (water) + 羊 (sheep)

Kanji Parts used in the New Kanji

丶	slash	皮	skin	主	master
水	water	昜	sun rises	羊	sheep
氵	water	由	reason		

30 Kanji Memory Tools 漢字記憶術

This section helps you organically memorize kanji readings, meanings, and construction.

氷

丶 水

Slash the water to make "**ICE**".

❶氷山(ひょうざん)の❷氷(こおり)で❸かき氷(ごおり)を作(つく)った。

I made a ❸snow cone with the ❷ice of an ❶iceberg's.

波

氵 皮

The water splashed on my skin forming "**WAVES**".

❶波止場(はとば)は❷津波(つなみ)で破壊(はかい)された。

The ❶wharf was destroyed by the ❶tidal wave (tsunami).

湯

氵 昜

water + sun rises = "**HOT WATER**".

❶銭湯(せんとう)で、❷男湯(おとこゆ)と❸女湯(おんなゆ)を間違(まちが)えた。

At the ❶bathhouse I mistook the ❷men's bath and the ❸women's bath.

油

氵 由

Water for some reason, doesn't mix with "**OIL** ".

❶油絵(あぶらえ)に❷醤油(しょうゆ)をこぼした。

I spilled ❷soy sauce on an ❶oil painting.

注

氵 主

Water on your master you should "**POUR**".

ネット販売(はんばい)に❶力(ちから)を注(そそ)いだら、❷注文(ちゅうもん)が増(ふ)えてきた。

❷Orders increased ❶when we concentrated our efforts on web sales.

洋

氵 羊

Using water to bathe your sheep is "**WESTERN STYLE**".

❶東洋人(とうようじん)が❷洋服(ようふく)を脱(ぬ)いで❸太平洋(たいへいよう)に飛(と)び込(こ)んだ。

The Asian person took of their ❶clothes and jumped into ❷the Pacific Ocean.

30 Kanji Usage 漢字の使い方

● 30-1. Useful set phrases using 波 and 油

Here are some set phrases you might find useful using some kanji from this lesson.

波風(なみかぜ)を立(た)てる	to rock the boat; to make waves

職場(しょくば)では、波風(なみかぜ)を立(た)てないようにしましょう。

Let's try to not rock the boat at the workplace.

波長(はちょう)が合(あ)う	to get along well; to be on the same wavelength

ルームメイトの持田君(もちだくん)とは、波長(はちょう)が合(あ)います。

I get along well with my roommate Mochida.

波(なみ)に乗(の)る	to ride a wave of; to go with the times

今(いま)まで現金主義(げんきんしゅぎ)でしたが、やっとキャッシュレスの波(なみ)に乗(の)りました。

Up until now we were cash based, but finally we got on board with cashless.

油(あぶら)を売(う)る	to loaf (particularly on the job); to idle one's time away

油(あぶら)を売(う)っていないで、仕事(しごと)をして下(くだ)さい。

Stop loafing around and do some work.

油(あぶら)をしぼる	to scold; to give a sound scolding; to reprimand severely

今月(こんげつ)の成績(せいせき)が悪(わる)かったので、上司(じょうし)に油(あぶら)をしぼられました。

Since our results were bad this month, I got reprimanded severely by my boss.

30-2. Subtle Differences, Big Changes (Part 1)

Here are some kanji that are easy to confuse if you don't pay attention to the parts.

water	icicle; ice; hail; freeze
水 みず **水** water; fluid すい でん **水田** (water-filled) paddy field	氷 こおり **氷** ice ひょう ざん **氷山** iceberg

eternity; long; lengthy	swim
永 えい えん **永遠** eternity; permanence えいじゅう **永住** permanent residence	泳 およ **泳ぐ** to swim すい えい **水泳** swimming

request; want; wish for; demand	spring; fountain
求 もと **求める** to want; to wish for きゅう じん **求人** recruiting; job offer	泉 いずみ **泉** spring; fountain おん せん **温泉** hot spring

30-3. Subtle Differences, Big Changes (Part 2)

Ready for more? Here are some OTHER kanji that have only slight changes.

hot water; bath; hot spring	location; place
湯 water + sun rises ゆ **お湯** hot water ねっ とう **熱湯** boiling water	場 soil + sun rises ば しょ **場所** place; location; spot こう じょう **工場** factory; workshop

sunshine; positive; daytime	
陽 place + sun rises	太陽(たいよう) sun 陽気(ようき) cheerful; merry; lively

intestines; guts; bowels	
腸 flesh + sun rises	胃腸(いちょう) stomach and intestines; digestive organs 大腸(だいちょう) large intestine

raise; elevate; fry	
揚 hand + sun rises	揚(あ)げる to raise; to deep-fry 抑揚(よくよう) intonation; accent; modulation

wound; hurt; injury; cut	
傷 person + sun rises	傷(きず) wound; injury; cut; scar 重傷(じゅうしょう) serious wound; serious injury

● 30-4. Modern Japanese words with 洋

In modern Japan words containing 洋(よう), to denote "western" origin, don't carry the same meaning as they had prior to the war when things from the west were not common.

Since 洋服(ようふく) "western style clothing" are the norm in Japan, when modern Japanese people say 服(ふく) (clothes) they most often mean, 洋服(ようふく) such as slacks, jeans, blouses, etc. common in the western world. Prior to World War 2 Japanese people wore 和服(わふく) (Japanese clothes) such as 着物(きもの)、浴衣(ゆかた) etc., but now 和服(わふく) are often just worn for ceremonies and special events.

In modern Japan, often instead of saying, 洋楽(ようがく) one might just say ポップ, ロック to mean "western music". For Japanese rock or pop music JPOP or JROCK is commonly used.

In a store selling Blu-ray they might have separate 洋画(ようが) (Western movie) 邦画(ほうが) (Japanese movie) sections. If someone has a specific taste in movies they might use 洋画(ようが) or 邦画(ほうが) to denote the genre they like, but generally speaking, 映画(えいが) (movie) is used for all movie types.

洋間(ようま) (western-style room) is a room that doesn't have tatami mats on the floor. A 洋式(ようしき)トイレ (western-style toilet) is a toilet you sit on versus a 和式(わしき)トイレ (Japanese-style toilet) that you squat over.

30 Words You Can Write 書ける言葉

氷水（こおりみず） ice water

氷水

電波（でんぱ） radio wave; reception; signal

電波

大波（おおなみ） billow; big wave

大波

湯気（ゆげ） steam; vapour

湯気

湯船（ゆぶね） bathtub

湯船

原油（げんゆ） crude oil

原油

軽油（けいゆ） diesel oil; gas oil; light oil

軽油

注目（ちゅうもく） notice; attention; observation

注目

注文（ちゅうもん） order; request

注	文										

洋風（ようふう） Western-style

洋	風										

西洋（せいよう） the west; Western countries

西	洋										

男湯（おとこゆ） men's bath; men's section in a public bath

男	湯										

氷点下（ひょうてんか） below freezing

氷	点	下									

太西洋（たいせいよう） Atlantic Ocean

太	西	洋									

湯のみ（ゆのみ） teacup

湯	の	み									

波止場（はとば） wharf; landing-stage; jetty

波	止	場									

30 Kanji Workbook Activities

● 1. Stroke Order Check 書き順確認

Each kanji has a stroke with an arrow on it. Write its order number below the kanji.

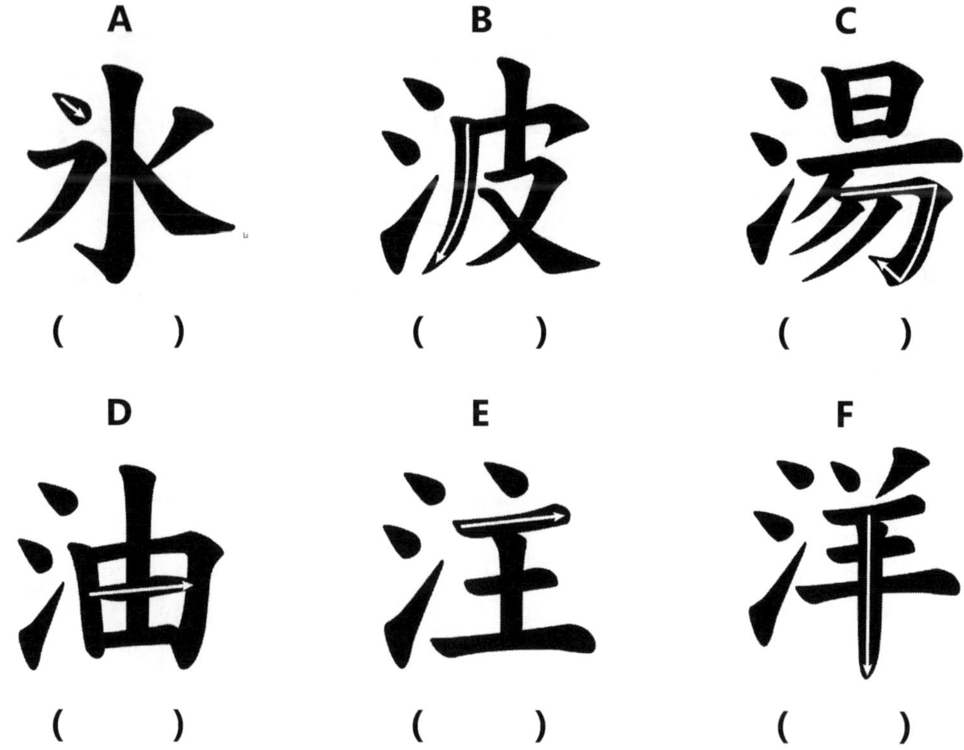

● 2. Kanji Readings

Write FURIGANA above the underlined kanji words.

1. いちご味のかき氷を注文しました。
2. 波止場にある青い船が、わたしのです。
3. 湯気が出ていないコーヒーは、飲みたくないです。
4. 冬は石油ストーブを使っています。
5. わたしは東洋医学を勉強していました。

● 3. Kanji Meaning Match

Write the following kanji next to its meaning: 氷 洋 旅 波 面 注 湯 油 葉

1. ____ leaf
2. ____ travel
3. ____ surface
4. ____ ice
5. ____ hot water
6. ____ oil
7. ____ wave
8. ____ pour
9. ____ Western-style

● 4. Fill in the Kanji

Fill in the appropriate kanji in the blanks for each sentence.

こん や き おん ひょう てん か さ

1. ___ ___は___ ___ が___ ___ ___ に ___がります。

This evening the temperature is going to lower to below freezing.

あ す かん ぱ く

2. ___ ___は、___ ___がやって___るでしょう。

Tomorrow a cold wave will likely come along.

とき ゆ ぶね

3. つかれている ___ は、___ ___につかります。

When I'm tired I soak in the bathtub.

きん よう び あぶら え と

4. ___ ___ ___に___ ___のクラスを___っています。

On Fridays I take an oil painting class.

し ごと ぜん りょく そそ

5. ___ ___に ___ ___を___ いでいます。

I pour my full energy into my work.

むかし よう ふく も

6. ___は たくさん___ ___を___っていました。

A long time ago I had a lot of clothes.

あつ ひ こおり みず

7. ___い___ は ___ ___がほしくなります。

On a hot day I want ice water.

● 5. Kanji Matching

Connect each kanji with an おん or くん reading. Use each reading only ONCE.

氷 •	• よう
洋 •	• とう
油 •	• ちゅう
消 •	• け
波 •	• こう
漢 •	• かん
注 •	• あぶら
湯 •	• こ
港 •	• こおり
湖 •	• なみ

30 Answer Key 答え合わせ

1. Stroke order check (answers)

A) 2 B) 4 C) 10

D) 7 E) 5 F) 9

3. Kanji meaning match (answers)

1. 葉 leaf 2. 旅 travel 3. 面 surface
4. 氷 ice 5. 湯 hot water 6. 油 oil
7. 波 wave 8. 注 pour 9. 洋 Western-style

2. Kanji Readings (answers)

1. いちご味(あじ)のかき氷(ごおり)を注文(ちゅうもん)しました。 I ordered a strawberry flavor shaved ice.
2. 波止場(はとば)にある青(あお)い船(ふね)が、わたしのです。 The blue boat at the wharf is mine.
3. 湯気(ゆげ)が出(で)ていないコーヒーは、飲(の)みたくないです。 I don't want to drink coffee that isn't steaming.
4. 冬(ふゆ)は石油(せきゆ)ストーブを使(つか)っています。 In the winter we use oil heaters.
5. わたしは東洋医学(とうよういがく)を勉強(べんきょう)していました。 I was studying oriental medicine.

4. Fill in the kanji (answers)

1. 今夜は気温が氷点下に下がります。
2. 明日は、寒波がやって来るでしょう。
3. つかれている時は、湯船につかります。
4. 金曜日に油絵のクラスを取っています。
5. 仕事に全力を注いでいます。
6. 昔は たくさん洋服を持っていました。
7. 暑い日は 氷水がほしくなります。

5. Kanji matching (answers)

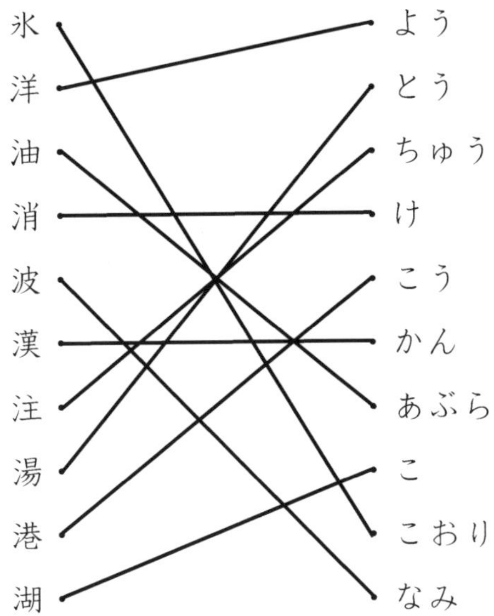

SR6

Kanji Lessons 26-30:
Super Review 6

From the teacher...

Test your knowledge of the kanji learned in the last 5 lessons.

● 1. Build-a-Kanji 漢字の組み合わせ

Combine the left and right parts to make seven of the kanji learned in lessons 26-30.

RULES

1. You can use the radical and kanji parts as many times as you want.
2. Some kanji can use two or three kanji parts.

部首 (Radical)		
日	氵	广
辶	木	亻
立	口	艹
巾	王	ネ

Other Kanji Parts		
一	口	未
何	皮	田
比	羊	主
求	刀	貝

SAMPLE	1	2	3	4	5	6	7
球							

● 2. Okurigana drill 送り仮名ドリル

Circle the correct 漢字 + 送り仮名 combination.

1. あきない	・商ない	・商い
2. そらす	・反す	・反らす
3. まったく	・全たく	・全く
4. そそぐ	・注ぐ	・注そぐ

● 3. Kanji selection 漢字の選択

Select the best kanji to replace the underlined section of the sentence.

1. わたしは日本酒より____酒のほうをよく飲みます。
   A. 和　B. 湯　C. 祭　D. 洋

2. カレーを作ったんですが、____見してもらえますか。
   A. 味　B. 食　C. 飲　D. 調

3. ちょっと____合が悪いので、家に帰ります。
   A. 体　B. 具　C. 薬　D. 動

4. ____面コピーを取ってきて下さい。
   A. 全　B. 反　C. 両　D. 部

● 4. Kanji reading selection 読みの選択

Select the best reading for the underlined kanji.

1. 主人と出会ったのは、運命だったと思います。
   A. いのち　B. めい　C. みょう　D. せい

2. 田中さんは面白くて、やさしい人です。
   A. めん　B. つら　C. おもて　D. おも

3. 体を後ろに反らしてみましょう。
   A. そ　B. は　C. た　D. こ

4. 先生のやさしい言葉で、気持ちが和らぎました。
   A. わ　B. お　C. やわ　D. なご

● 5. Compound kanji word puzzle 熟語パズル

Fill in the correct kanji based on the list below the puzzle.

1)	2)	3)	4)
		5)	
6)	7)	8)	9)
10)		11)	

Down ↓	
English meaning	**Hiragana**
1) electro-magnetic wave	でんぱ
2) baseball stadium	きゅうじょう
4) both sides; double-sided	りょうめん
6) shipping; outgoing freight	しゅっか
7) goods; article; thing	しなもの
9) business world; industry	ぎょうかい
Left to Right →	
1) light bulb	でんきゅう
5) screen; scene; picture	がめん
8) commerce; trade; business	しょうぎょう
10) luggage; baggage	にもつ
11) world; society	せかい

← Right to Left	
English meaning	**Hiragana**
3) the earth; the globe	ちきゅう
8) goods; stock; merchandise	しょうひん

SR6 Answer Key 答え合わせ

1. Build-a-Kanji (answers) (order can vary)

SAMPLE 球 1) 洋 2) 荷 3) 味 4) 福 5) 昭 6) 波 7)注

2. Okurigana drill (answers)

1. あきない	・商ない	**[・商い]**
2. そらす	・反す	**[・反らす]**
3. まったく	・全たく	**[・全く]**
4. そそぐ	**[・注ぐ]**	・注そぐ

3. Kanji selection (answers)

1. D – 洋酒（ようしゅ） I drink more western liquor than Japanese liquor.
2. A – 味見（あじみ） I made curry, can I have you taste test it for me?
3. B – 具合（ぐあい） I'm going to return home since my condition (state of health) is a bit bad.
4. C – 両面（りょうめん） Please go take a copy of both sides.

4. Kanji reading selection (answers)

1. B – 運命（うんめい） I think meeting my husband was fate.
2. D – 面白くて（おもしろ） Tanaka-san is an interesting and kind person.
3. A – 反らして（そ） Let's try to bend our body backwards.
4. C – 和らぎました（やわ） My feelings calmed with my teacher's kind words.

5. Compound kanji word puzzle (answers)

電	球	地	両
波	場	画	面
出	品	商	業
荷	物	世	界

31 Kanji Lesson 31: 真意銀鉄第陽

421-426

Some random unrelated kanji

31 New Kanji 新しい漢字

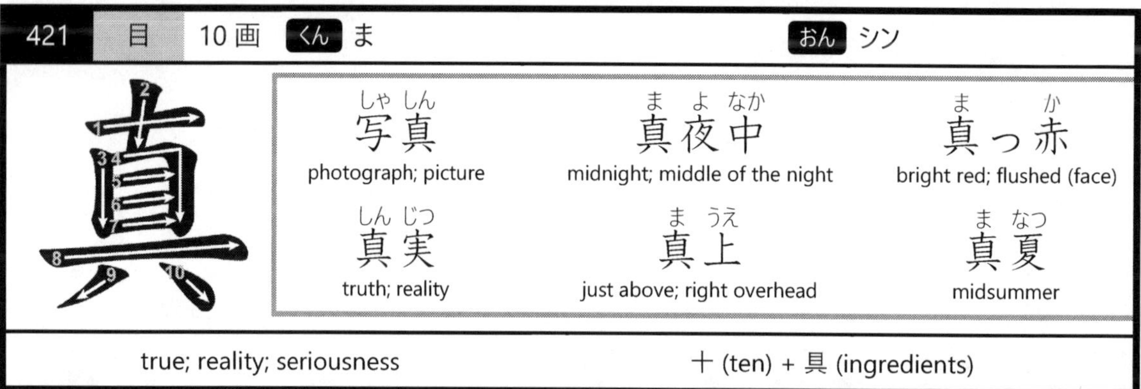

421 | 目 | 10 画 | くん ま | おん シン

しゃしん 写真 photograph; picture	まよなか 真夜中 midnight; middle of the night	まっか 真っ赤 bright red; flushed (face)
しんじつ 真実 truth; reality	まうえ 真上 just above; right overhead	まなつ 真夏 midsummer

true; reality; seriousness | 十 (ten) + 具 (ingredients)

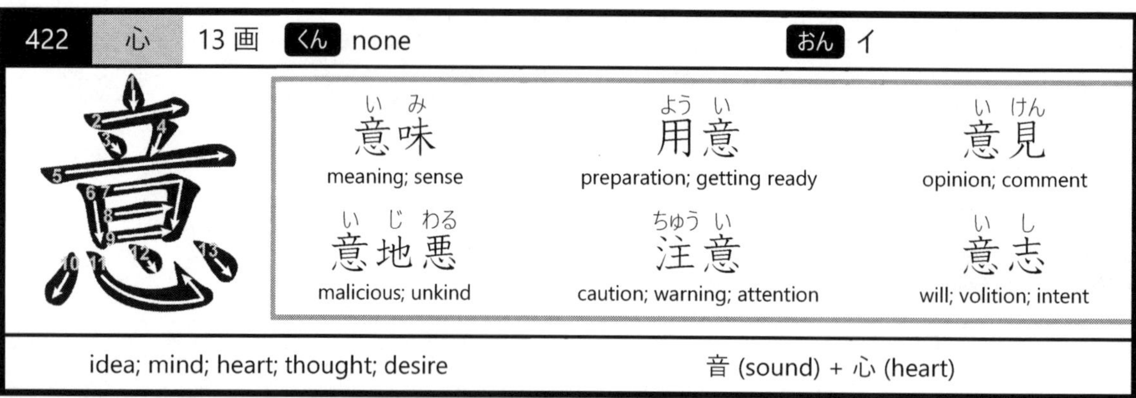

422 | 心 | 13 画 | くん none | おん イ

いみ 意味 meaning; sense	ようい 用意 preparation; getting ready	いけん 意見 opinion; comment
いじわる 意地悪 malicious; unkind	ちゅうい 注意 caution; warning; attention	いし 意志 will; volition; intent

idea; mind; heart; thought; desire | 音 (sound) + 心 (heart)

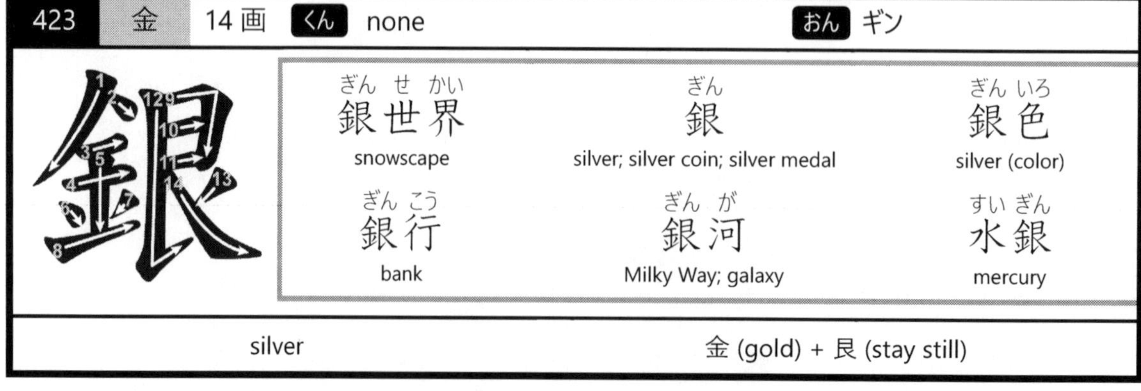

423 | 金 | 14 画 | くん none | おん ギン

ぎんせかい 銀世界 snowscape	ぎん 銀 silver; silver coin; silver medal	ぎんいろ 銀色 silver (color)
ぎんこう 銀行 bank	ぎんが 銀河 Milky Way; galaxy	すいぎん 水銀 mercury

silver | 金 (gold) + 艮 (stay still)

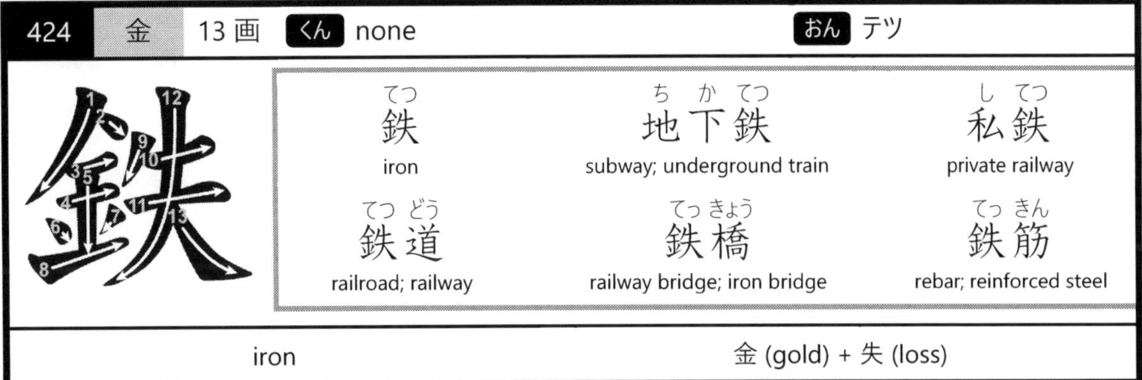

424	金	13 画	くん none	おん テツ

鉄

鉄（てつ） iron	地下鉄（ちかてつ） subway; underground train	私鉄（してつ） private railway
鉄道（てつどう） railroad; railway	鉄橋（てっきょう） railway bridge; iron bridge	鉄筋（てっきん） rebar; reinforced steel

iron — 金 (gold) + 失 (loss)

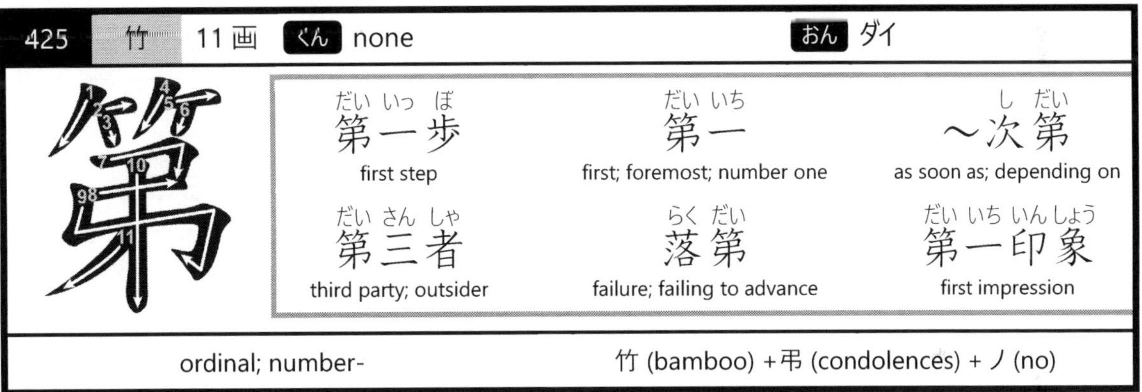

425	竹	11 画	くん none	おん ダイ

第

第一歩（だいいっぽ） first step	第一（だいいち） first; foremost; number one	～次第（しだい） as soon as; depending on
第三者（だいさんしゃ） third party; outsider	落第（らくだい） failure; failing to advance	第一印象（だいいちいんしょう） first impression

ordinal; number- — 竹 (bamboo) + 弔 (condolences) + ノ (no)

426	阝	12 画	くん none	おん ヨウ

陽

太陽（たいよう） sun	陽極（ようきょく） plus terminal; positive pole	陽性（ようせい） positivity; positive
陽気（ようき） cheerful; lively	陽光（ようこう） sunshine; sunlight	落陽（らくよう） setting sun

sunshine; positive; daytime — 阝 (small village) + 昜 (sun rises)

Kanji Parts used in the New Kanji

十	ten	金	gold	弔	condolences
具	ingredients	艮	stay still	ノ	no
音	sound	失	loss	阝	small village
心	heart	竹	bamboo	昜	sun rises

31 Kanji Memory Tools 漢字記憶術

This section helps you organically memorize kanji readings, meanings, and construction.

真

十 具

These <u>ten</u> <u>ingredients</u> are "**TRUE**".

❶真夜中(まよなか)に海(うみ)で❷写真(しゃしん)を撮(と)ったら、❸真(ま)っ黒(くろ)だった。

When I took a ❷photograph at the ocean in ❶the middle of the night it was ❸pitch black.

意

立 目 心

As I <u>stand</u> here, my <u>eye</u> and <u>heart</u> differ on "**DESIRE**".

先生(せんせい)は❶意地悪(いじわる)だと思(おも)ったけど、❷意外(いがい)といい人(ひと)でした。

I thought the teacher was ❶ill-tempered, but he/she is an ❷unexpectedly good person.

銀

金 艮

<u>Gold</u> when <u>stays still</u> becomes "**SILVER**".

雪(ゆき)は❶銀色(ぎんいろ)じゃないのに、どうして❷銀世界(ぎんせかい)と言(い)いますか。

Why do we say ❷snowscape (literally, "silver world"), despite snow not being ❶silver color?

鉄

金 失

<u>Gold</u> is a <u>loss</u> compared to "**IRON**".

❶地下鉄(ちかてつ)で❷鉄砲(てっぽう)が見(み)つかった。

A ❷gun was found on ❶the subway.

第

竹 弔 ノ

The <u>bamboo</u> will give its <u>condolences</u> to <u>no</u> = "**NUMBER-**".

❶第一印象(だいいちいんしょう)は最初(さいしょ)の挨拶(あいさつ)❷次第(しだい)で決(き)まります。

A ❶first impression is determined ❷by (depending on) the first greeting.

陽

阝 昜

This <u>small village</u>, as the <u>sun rises</u>, fills with "**SUNSHINE**".

❶太陽(たいよう)の光(ひかり)に当(あ)たると、❷陽気(ようき)な気分(きぶん)になる。

When the light of the ❶sun hits me, I get a ❷cheerful feeling.

31 Kanji Usage 漢字の使い方

● 31-1. The Yin-Yang of kanji 陽

The Chinese concept of Yin-Yang is 陰陽(いんよう) in Japanese. Without getting into too much detail, 陰陽(いんよう) is about light and dark, positive and negative, good and evil, or basically anything that are opposing forces. The first kanji 陰(かげ) means, "shade" while 陽(よう) means "sunshine".

The only reason I bring up the concept here is to introduce two words. The Covid-19 pandemic started in 2020 and affected the entire world during the writing of this book.

Due to Japan's proximity to the origin of the virus that causes Covid-19, it was one of the earliest countries affected. I hope that future readers of this book are living a life without masks and lockdowns. I also hope you don't need to know the Japanese words for "positive" and "negative" in regards to testing for Covid or any other disease.

positive	negative
陽性(ようせい)	陰性(いんせい)

● 31-2. Useful set phrases using 真

Is there more room in your brain for some set phrases? You have no choice! Here are some set phrases using the kanji in this lesson.

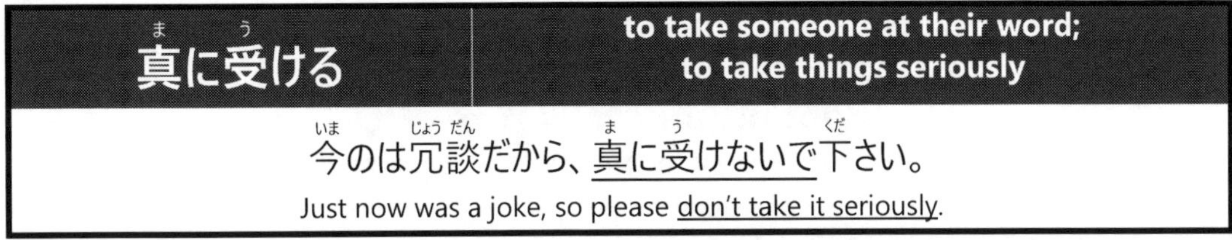

真(ま)に受(う)ける	to take someone at their word; to take things seriously

今(いま)のは冗談(じょうだん)だから、<u>真(ま)に受(う)けないで</u>下(くだ)さい。

Just now was a joke, so please <u>don't take it seriously</u>.

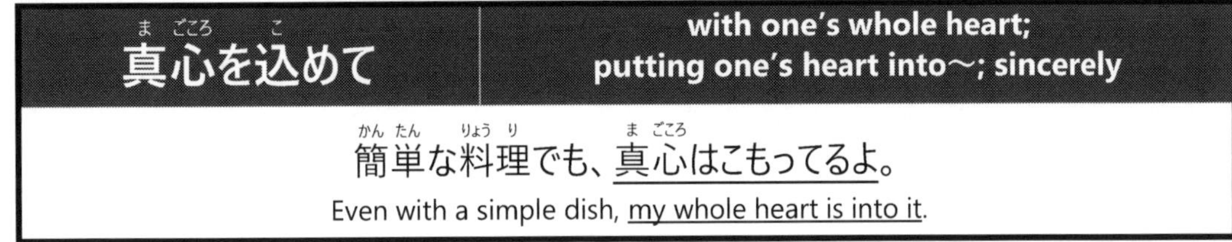

真心(まごころ)を込(こ)めて	with one's whole heart; putting one's heart into～; sincerely

簡単(かんたん)な料理(りょうり)でも、<u>真心(まごころ)はこもってるよ</u>。

Even with a simple dish, <u>my whole heart is into it</u>.

● 31-3. Describing one's state of mind using 意

意 means, "mind", "desire" etc. You can see how it's incorporated into many words showing a person's intentions.

Japanese	Meaning of the first kanji	English meaning
悪意 (あくい)	悪 = bad; false; evil; wrong	evil intention; ill will
善意 (ぜんい)	善 = virtuous; good; goodness	good intention; positive mindset
好意 (こうい)	好 = fond; pleasing; like something	kindness; liking; favor
決意 (けつい)	決 = decide; fix; agree upon	decision; determination
故意 (こい)	故 = happenstance; reason; cause	intent; intention; purpose; guilty mind
合意 (ごうい)	合 = fit; suit; join	mutual understanding; agreement; consent
同意 (どうい)	同 = same; agree; equal	same opinion; same view; agreement; consent
辞意 (じい)	辞 = resign; word; expression	intention to resign
誠意 (せいい)	誠 = sincerity; truth; fidelity	sincerity; good faith
不意 (ふい)	不 = negative; non-; bad	sudden; unexpected; unforeseen

● 31-4. Your Japanese level is up to you! ～次第

The kanji 第 (だい) is used primarily in front of numbers to make "first, second, third" etc. However, it's also part of the word 次第 (しだい) which can be used some important ways.

(NOUN) + 次第
depending on / up to (NOUN)

EXAMPLE SENTENCES (NOUN + 次第)

1. あなた次第です。
   It's up to you!
2. 新車を買うかは値段次第です。
   If I buy a new car depends on the price.
3. 人生は自分次第です。
   Your life is up to yourself.
4. 天気次第で中止になるかも知れない。
   Depending on the weather it might be cancelled.

次第 can also be used with verbs:

(VERB) + 次第
as soon as (VERB)

The verb must be in its い form. The verb can't be a direct action (IE: As soon as I do X~). It must be part of a condition change.

EXAMPLE SENTENCES (いFORM VERB + 次第)

1. わかり次第連絡します。
   As soon as I know I'll contact you.
2. 荷物が届き次第確認します。
   I'll check as soon as the package arrives.
3. 仕事が終わり次第出られます。
   I can leave as soon as work ends.
4. 雪がやみ次第出発します。
   We will depart as soon as the snow stops.

次第に can also be used as an adverb meaning, "gradually; in sequence". It's used when describing a gradual change in a condition or state. It can't be used with a direct action to say something such as, "I will gradually do X".

EXAMPLE SENTENCES (次第に VERB)

1. 次第に晴れそうです。
   It looks like it will gradually get sunny.
2. 私たちは次第に仲良くなった。
   We gradually became friends.
3. 次第に文化が変わった。
   The culture changed gradually.
4. 学校が次第に楽しくなってきている。
   School is getting gradually more fun.

31 Words You Can Write 書ける言葉

真心（まごころ） sincerity; true heart; devotion

真 心

決意（けつい） decision; determination

決 意

真顔（まがお） serious look (on one's face); straight face

真 顔

意外（いがい） unexpected; surprising

意 外

銀行(ぎんこう) bank

銀 行

水銀(すいぎん) mercury

水 銀

鉄分（てつぶん） iron (content)

鉄 分

鉄板（てっぱん） iron plate

鉄 板

落第（らくだい） failure; dropping out of a class

落 第

太陽（たいよう） sun

太 陽

陽気（ようき） cheerful; weather

陽 気

真っ白（まっしろ） pure white

真 っ 白

真っ黒（まっくろ） pitch black

真 っ 黒

第六感（だいろっかん） the sixth sense; hunch

第 六 感

安全第一(あんぜんだいいち) safety first

安 全 第 一

第一人者（だいいちにんしゃ） leading person

第 一 人 者

31 Kanji Workbook Activities

● 1. Stroke Order Check 書き順確認

Each kanji has a stroke with an arrow on it. Write its order number below the kanji.

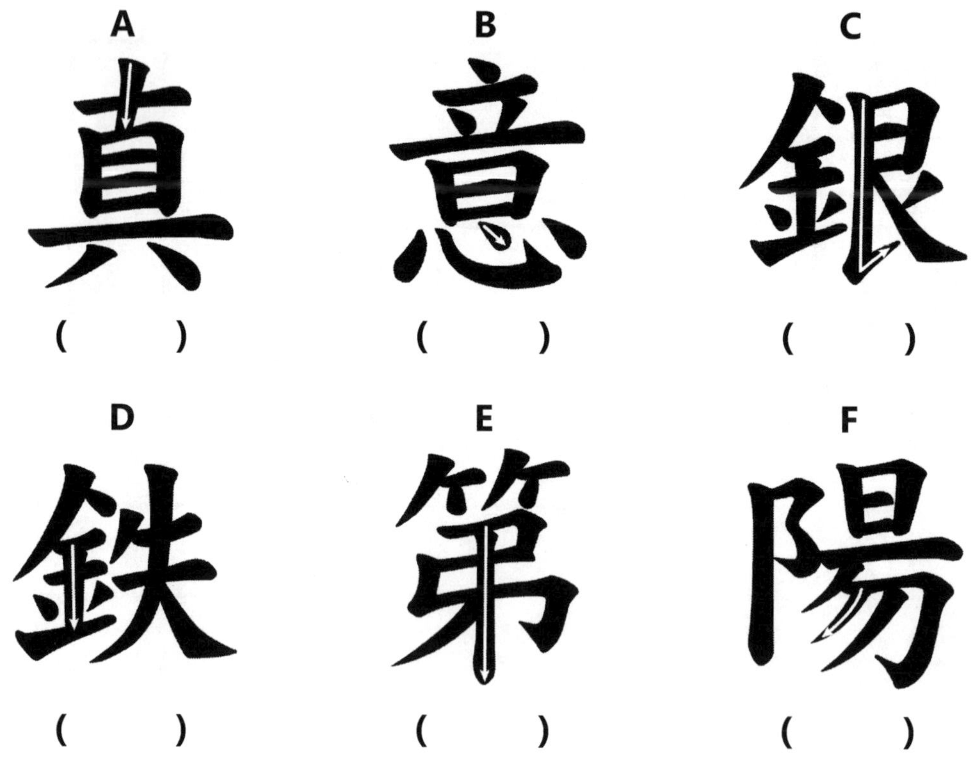

● 2. Kanji Readings

Write FURIGANA above the underlined kanji words.

1. 父は、お酒を少し飲んだだけで、真っ赤になります。
2. 魚を多く食べる人は水銀ちゅうどくがしんぱいです。
3. さくらんぼは、鉄分が多いと言われています。
4. 第三者の意見も聞きたいです。
5. 太陽の光がまぶしいので、サングラスをします。

● 3. Kanji Meaning Match

Write the following kanji next to its meaning: 陽 鉄 波 意 昭 第 銀 氷 真

1.____ true   2. ____ silver   3. ____ iron

4. ____ idea, mind   5. ____ wave   6. ____ sunshine

7. ____ number-   8. ____ ice   9. ____ shining

● 4. Fill in the Kanji

Fill in the appropriate kanji in the blanks for each sentence.

ほん　おも　しろ　ま　よ　なか　よ

1. ___ が___ ___ くて、___ ___ ___まで___んでいました。

The book was so interesting, I read it until the middle of the night.

で　よう　い

2. ___かける ___ ___をしましょう。

Let's make preparations to go out.

そと　ぎん　せ　かい

3. ___ は___ ___ ___で、とてもきれいでした。

Outside, being a snowscape, was very pretty.

ち　か　てつ　つう　がく

4. ___ ___ ___で___ ___しています。

I commute to school on the subway.

だい　いち　げつ　よう　び　さい　じつ

5. ___ ___ ___ ___ ___は ___ ___ です。

The first Monday is a national holiday.

あね　よう　き　ひと

6. ___ は、とても___ ___な___です。

My older sister is a very cheerful person.

もん　だい　い　み　わ

7. この ___ ___の___ ___が___ かりません。

I don't understand the meaning of this question (problem).

● 5. Kanji Matching

Connect each kanji with an おん or くん reading. Use each reading only ONCE.

真 •	• よう
銀 •	• ぎん
注 •	• ふく
第 •	• だい
陽 •	• しん
祭 •	• はつ
鉄 •	• てつ
福 •	• い
意 •	• ちゅう
発 •	• さい

31 Answer Key 答え合わせ

1. Stroke order check (answers)

A) 2 B) 12 C) 12
D) 5 E) 10 F) 11

2. Kanji meaning match (answers)

1. 真 true 2. 銀 silver 3. 鉄 iron
4. 意 idea 5. 波 wave 6. 陽 sunshine
7. 第 number- 8. 氷 ice 9. 昭 shining

3. Kanji Readings (answers)

1. 父(ちち)は、お酒(さけ)を少(すこ)し飲(の)んだだけで、真(ま)っ赤(か)になります。
   My dad gets red drinking just a little alcohol.
2. 魚(さかな)を多(おお)く食(た)べる人(ひと)は水銀(すいぎん)ちゅうどくがしんぱいです。
   People who eat a lot of fish need to be concerned about mercury poisoning.
3. さくらんぼは、鉄分(てつぶん)が多(おお)いと言(い)われています。
   It's said that cherries have a lot of iron.
4. 第三者(だいさんしゃ)の意見(いけん)も聞(き)きたいです。
   I would also like to hear a third party's opinion.
5. 太陽(たいよう)の光(ひかり)がまぶしいので、サングラスをします。
   I'm going to wear sunglasses since the sunlight is bright.

4. Fill in the kanji (answers)

1. [本]が[面白]くて、[真夜中]まで[読]んでいました。
2. [出]かける[用意]をしましょう。
3. [外]は[銀世界]で、とてもきれいでした。
4. [地下鉄]で[通学]しています。
5. [第一月曜日]は[祭日]です。
6. [姉]は、とても[陽気]な[人]です。
7. この[問題]の[意味]が[分]かりません。

5. Kanji matching (answers)

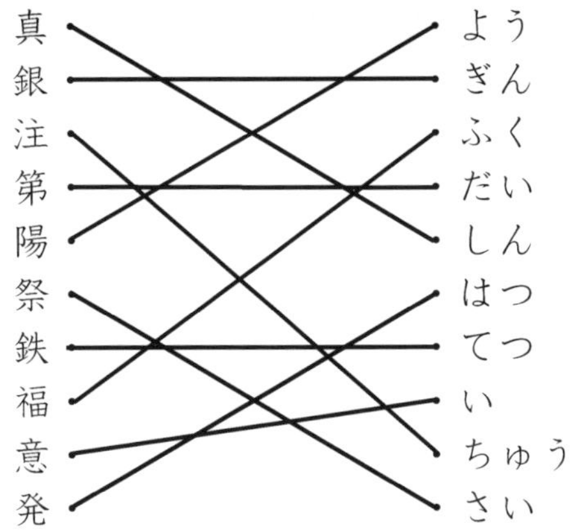

32 Kanji Lesson 32:

427-433

血指歯身鼻皮息

Kanji related to the body

32 New Kanji 新しい漢字

427	血	6画	くん ち	おん ケツ

しゅっけつ 出血 bleeding	けつあつ 血圧 blood pressure	ち 血 blood
けつえき 血液 blood	けんけつ 献血 blood donation	きゅうけつき 吸血鬼 vampire; bloodsucker

blood — ノ (NO) + 皿 (dish)

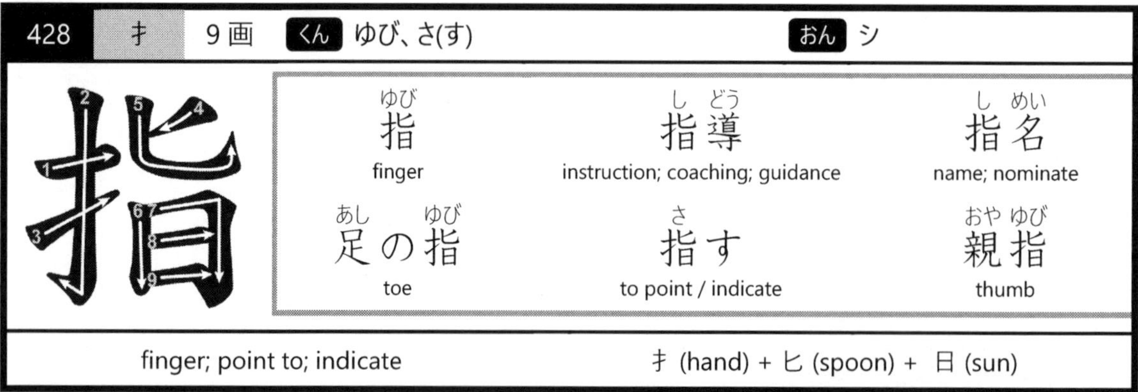

428	扌	9画	くん ゆび、さ(す)	おん シ

ゆび 指 finger	しどう 指導 instruction; coaching; guidance	しめい 指名 name; nominate
あしのゆび 足の指 toe	さ 指す to point / indicate	おやゆび 親指 thumb

finger; point to; indicate — 扌 (hand) + 匕 (spoon) + 日 (sun)

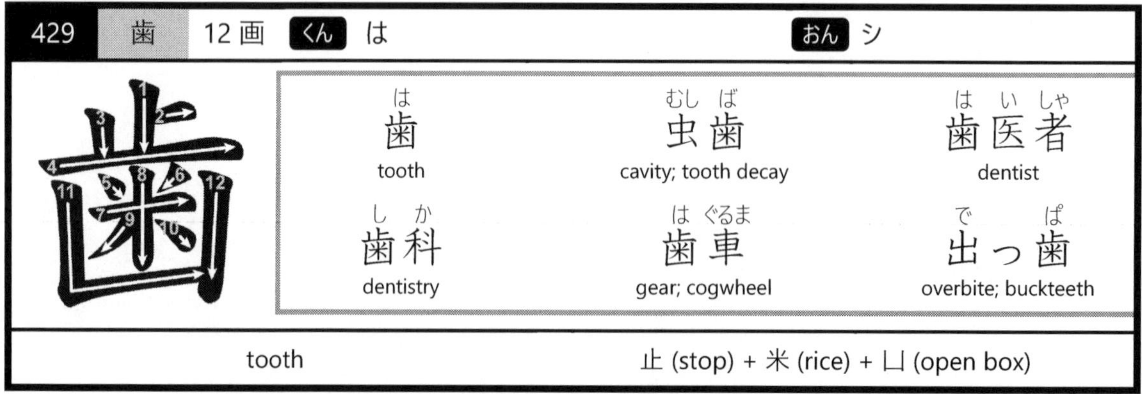

429	歯	12画	くん は	おん シ

は 歯 tooth	むしば 虫歯 cavity; tooth decay	はいしゃ 歯医者 dentist
しか 歯科 dentistry	はぐるま 歯車 gear; cogwheel	でっぱ 出っ歯 overbite; buckteeth

tooth — 止 (stop) + 米 (rice) + 凵 (open box)

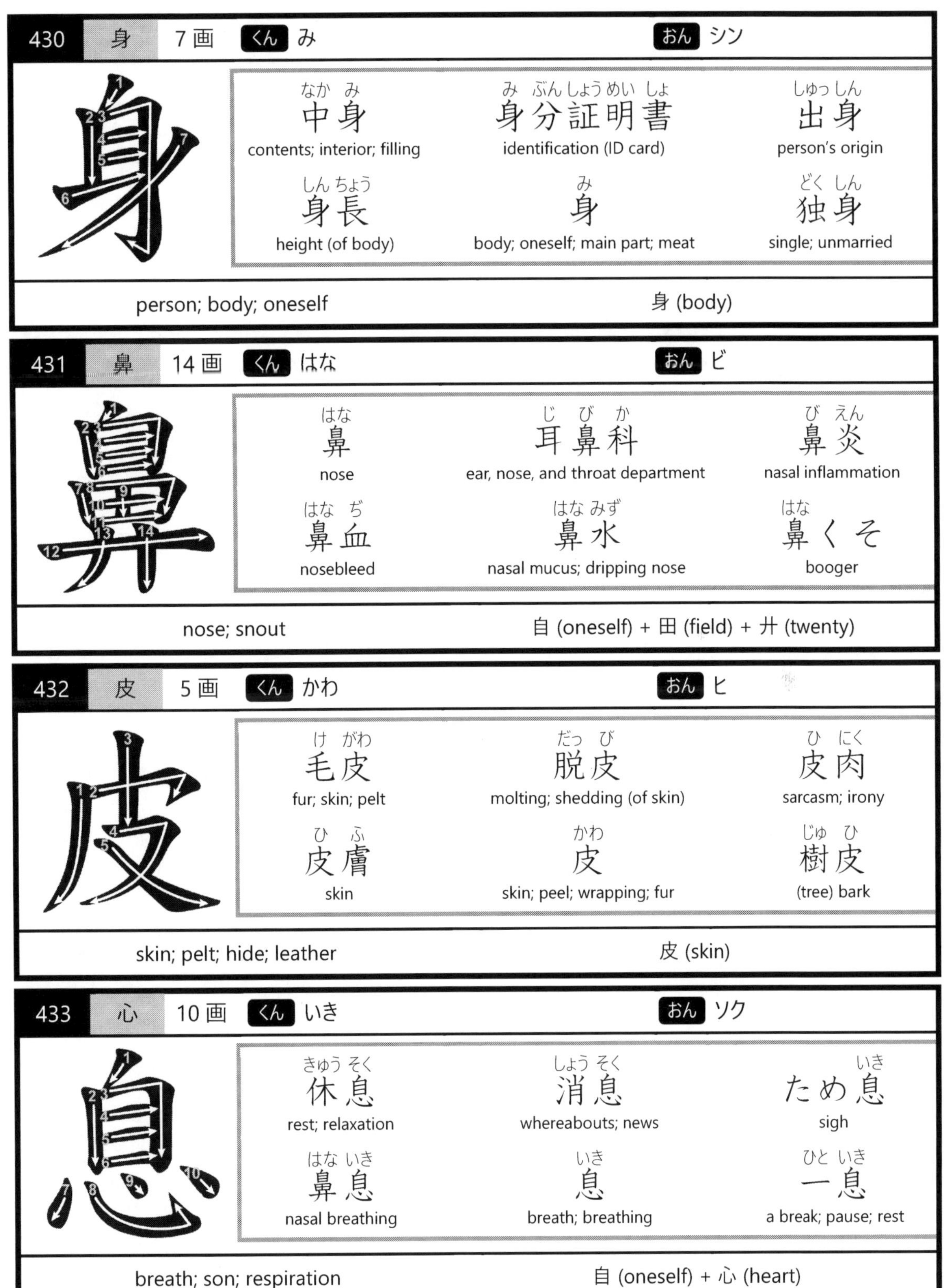

430 | 身 | 7画 | くん み | おん シン

なかみ 中身 contents; interior; filling	みぶんしょうめいしょ 身分証明書 identification (ID card)	しゅっしん 出身 person's origin
しんちょう 身長 height (of body)	み 身 body; oneself; main part; meat	どくしん 独身 single; unmarried

person; body; oneself — 身 (body)

431 | 鼻 | 14画 | くん はな | おん ビ

はな 鼻 nose	じびか 耳鼻科 ear, nose, and throat department	びえん 鼻炎 nasal inflammation
はなぢ 鼻血 nosebleed	はなみず 鼻水 nasal mucus; dripping nose	はな 鼻くそ booger

nose; snout — 自 (oneself) + 田 (field) + 廾 (twenty)

432 | 皮 | 5画 | くん かわ | おん ヒ

けがわ 毛皮 fur; skin; pelt	だっぴ 脱皮 molting; shedding (of skin)	ひにく 皮肉 sarcasm; irony
ひふ 皮膚 skin	かわ 皮 skin; peel; wrapping; fur	じゅひ 樹皮 (tree) bark

skin; pelt; hide; leather — 皮 (skin)

433 | 心 | 10画 | くん いき | おん ソク

きゅうそく 休息 rest; relaxation	しょうそく 消息 whereabouts; news	いき ため息 sigh
はないき 鼻息 nasal breathing	いき 息 breath; breathing	ひといき 一息 a break; pause; rest

breath; son; respiration — 自 (oneself) + 心 (heart)

Kanji Parts used in the New Kanji					
ノ	NO	止	stop	田	field
皿	dish	凵	open box	廾	twenty
扌	hand	米	rice	皮	skin
ヒ	spoon	身	body	心	heart
日	sun	自	oneself		

32 Kanji Memory Tools 漢字記憶術

血

ノ 皿
NO plate should have "**BLOOD**".

❶吸血鬼(きゅうけつき)は❷血(ち)を吸(す)います。

❶Vampires suck ❷blood.

指

扌 ヒ 日
My hand held the spoon while the sun shone on my "**FINGER**".

❶足(あし)の指(ゆび)にも❷指紋(しもん)がありますか。

Do even ❶toes have ❷fingerprints?

歯

止 米 凵
Stop! The rice in the open box chipped my "**TOOTH**".

❶虫歯(むしば)と❷歯石(しせき)は❸歯磨(はみが)きで防(ふせ)げます。

❶Cavities and ❷tartar can be prevented by ❸toothbrushing.

身

身
My body is always just a "**BODY**".

日本(にほん)の❶身分証明書(みぶんしょうめいしょ)には❷身長(しんちょう)がありません。

❷Height isn't on Japanese ❶identification cards.

鼻

自 田 廾
Oneself in a field with twenty others should plug their "**NOSE**".

❶鼻炎(びえん)のせいで、❷鼻水(はなみず)が止(と)まりません。

Due to ❶nasal inflammation, my ❷nose dripping (snot) won't stop.

皮
皮
Skin is just "SKIN".
❶毛皮(けがわ)のコートで❷皮膚(ひふ)がかゆくなります。
❶Fur coats make my ❷skin itchy.

息

自 心
Think of oneself with your heart and take a "**BREATH**".

❶休息(きゅうそく)が取(と)れなくて、❷ため息(いき)をついています。

Unable to take a ❶rest, ❷I'm sighing.

32 Kanji Usage 漢字の使い方

● 32-1. Names of fingers 指

Contrary to what I've said on YouTube, the "middle finger" is not called, フ&$%指(ゆび). Forgive the crude joke! It was suggested by my co-author that junior high school students would read this book and we should remove this joke... but I think we can agree even junior high students have a sense of humor. Let's learn the proper names for Japanese fingers.

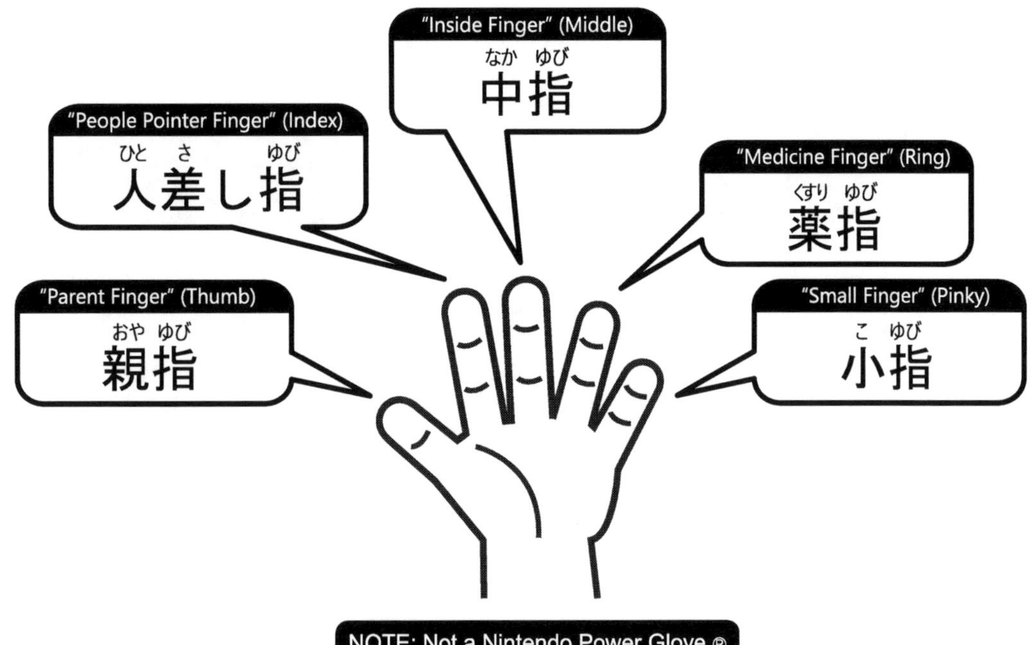

● 32-2. Useful set phrases using 歯, 鼻 and 息

What? MORE useful phrases?! Will they ever run out?

歯が立たない	To be no match for someone: to be unable to compete with someone
ビデオゲームでは、友達に歯が立ちません。 I'm unable to compete against my friend in video games.	

歯車が狂う	to fall to pieces; to be out of control
彼女と遠距離恋愛になってから、歯車が狂い始めました。 Things have begun to fall apart since becoming a long-distance love with my girlfriend.	

鼻が高い	to be proud of oneself / to be proud
長男が医者になって、親として鼻が高いです。 As a parent, I'm proud that my eldest son became a doctor.	

鼻であしらう	to treat with contempt; to turn up one's nose (at someone/something)
モデルのオーディションに行ったら、鼻であしらわれました。 When I went to the model audition, I was treated with contempt.	

息が合う	to be in sync; to be in tune with ～
あの二人の漫才師は、息が合っています。 Those two comedians are in sync.	

息をのむ	to catch one's breath; to have one's breath taken away; to gulp; to gasp
ノルウェーのフィヨルドは、息をのむほど美しいです。 The fjords of Norway are so beautiful that they take your breath away.	

● 32-3. Kinds of teeth using 歯

Here are Japanese teeth words that might help you when you are at the dentist in Japan.

Teeth	Meaning of the other kanji	English
まえ ば 前歯	前 = in front; before	front teeth
おく ば 奥歯	奥 = inner part; interior; back	molars; back teeth
や え ば 八重歯	八重 = multilayered; doubled	double tooth; protruding tooth; high canine
むし ば 虫歯	虫 = insect; bug; temper	cavity; tooth decay
えいきゅう し 永久歯	永久 = eternity; permanence	permanent tooth
にゅう し 乳歯	乳 = milk; breasts	baby tooth; milk tooth
けん し 犬歯	犬 = dog	eyetooth; cuspid; canine
もん し 門歯	門 = gate	incisor; incisive tooth
ばっ し 抜歯	抜 = slip out; extract; pull out	tooth extraction
おや し 親知らず	親 = parent; relative 知らず = without knowing	wisdom tooth
し せき 歯石	石 = stone	dental calculus; tartar
は きょうせい 歯を矯正する	矯 = straighten 正 = correct	to get braces

32 Words You Can Write 書ける言葉

血行（けっこう）blood circulation

血 行

一息（ひといき） one breath; pause; rest

一 息

親指（おやゆび） thumb

親 指

薬指（くすりゆび） ring finger; fourth finger

薬 指

指先（ゆびさき） fingertip

指 先

歯石（しせき） dental calculus; tartar (of the teeth)

歯 石

虫歯（むしば） cavity; tooth decay

虫 歯

自身（じしん） by oneself; personally

自 身

身近（みぢか） near oneself; close to one; familiar

身	近										

鼻声（はなごえ） nasal voice

鼻	声										

鼻歌（はなうた） humming; crooning

鼻	歌										

皮肉（ひにく） sarcasm; irony

皮	肉										

毛皮（けがわ） fur; skin

毛	皮										

息子(むすこ) son

息	子										

歯科医（しかい） dentist

歯	科	医									

息苦しい（いきぐるしい） breathing hard; choking; suffocating

息	苦	し	い								

32 Kanji Workbook Activities

● 1. Stroke Order Check 書き順確認

Each kanji has a stroke with an arrow on it. Write its order number below the kanji.

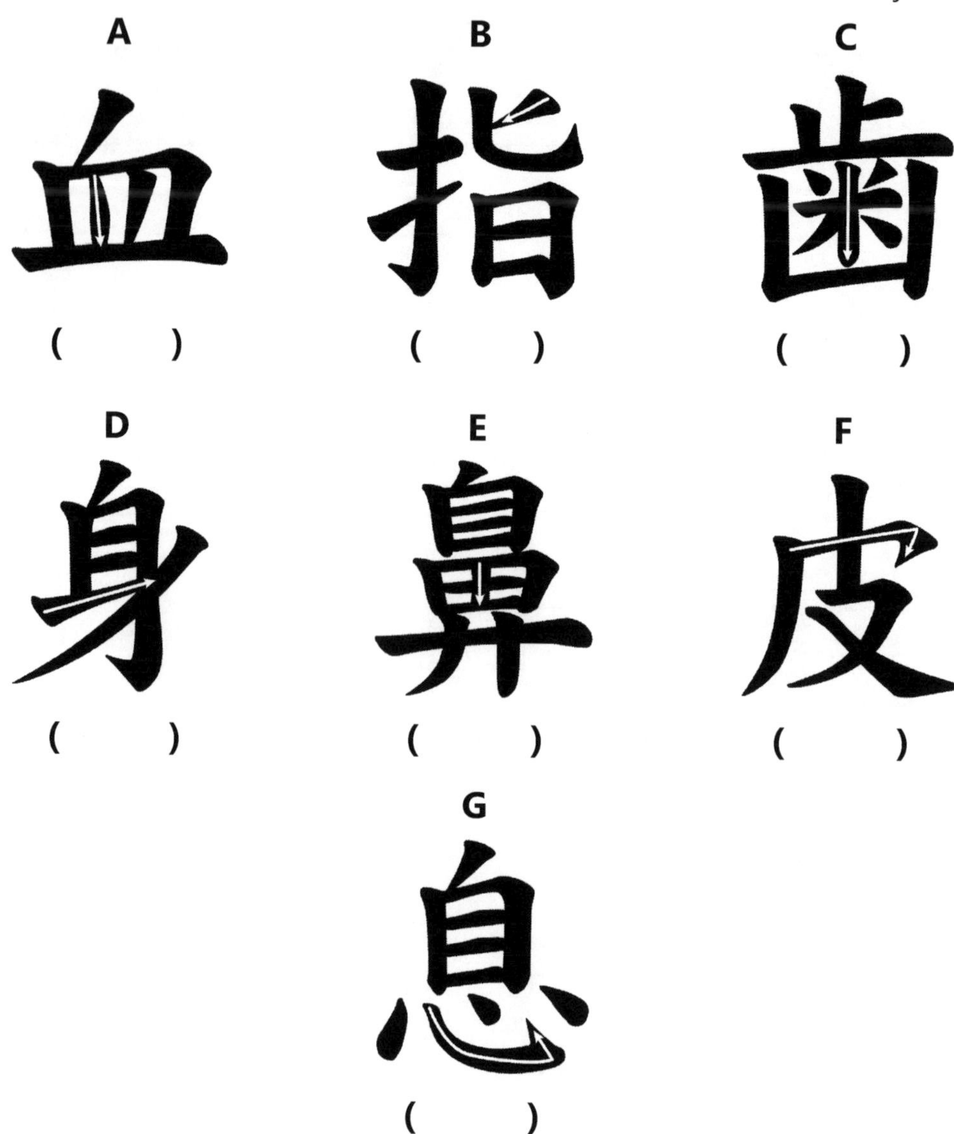

● 2. Kanji Meaning Match

Write the following kanji next to its meaning: 息 鼻 歯 第 血 皿 指 身 皮

1.____ blood	2. ____ tooth	3. ____ nose
4. ____ breath	5. ____ number-	6. ____ plate
7. ____ finger	8. ____ body	9. ____ skin

● 3. Kanji Readings

Write FURIGANA above the underlined kanji words.

1. 歯ぐきから血が出ていたので、歯医者に行きました。
2. 時計が十二時を指しています。
3. 魚の皮と身がうまく分けられません。
4. 今から耳鼻科に行ってきます。
5. 鼻水が出すぎて、息苦しいです。

● 4. Fill in the Kanji

Fill in the appropriate kanji in the blanks for each sentence.

しゅっ けつ と

1. けがをして、しばらく_______が___まりませんでした。

I got injured and for a while the bleeding wouldn't stop.

と しょ がかり し めい

2. わたしは、___ ___ ___に___ ___されました。

I was nominated as the librarian.

うち こ むし ば よん ほん

3. ___の___は、___ ___が___ ___あります。

Our child has four cavities.

とう きょう しゅっ しん

4. わたしは、___ ___ ___ ___です。

I was born in Tokyo.

いもうと はな うた うた

5. ___ は、いつも___ ___を___っています。

My younger sister is always humming.

かわ た

6. りんごの___ は、むいて___ べます。

I peel off the skin of the apple then eat it.

ひと り むす こ いま かい がい

7. うちの___ ___ ___ ___は___ 、___ ___にいます。

Our only son is currently abroad.

● 5. Kanji Matching

Connect each kanji with an おん or くん reading. Use each reading only ONCE.

指 •	• み
身 •	• ひろ
皮 •	• は
拾 •	• はな
息 •	• ゆび
鼻 •	• だい
歯 •	• めい
題 •	• いき
血 •	• ち
命 •	• ひ

32 Answer Key 答え合わせ

1. Stroke order check (answers)

A) 4 B) 4 C) 8
D) 6 E) 9 F) 2
G) 8

3. Kanji meaning match (answers)

1. 血 blood 2. 歯 tooth 3. 鼻 nose
4. 息 breath 5. 第 number- 6. 皿 plate
7. 指 finger 8. 身 body 9. 皮 skin

2. Kanji Readings (answers)

1. 歯(は)ぐきから血(ち)が出(で)ていたので、歯医者(はいしゃ)に行(い)きました。 I went to the dentist since my gums were bleeding.
2. 時計(とけい)が十二時(じゅうにじ)を指(さ)しています。 The clock is pointing to 12 o'clock.
3. 魚(さかな)の皮(かわ)と身(み)がうまく分(わ)けられません。 I can't skillfully separate the skin and body of a fish.
4. 今(いま)から耳鼻科(じびか)に行(い)ってきます。 I'm going to the ear nose doctor (ENT) now.
5. 鼻水(はなみず)が出(で)すぎて、息苦(いきぐる)しいです。 My nose is running so much it's difficult to breathe.

4. Fill in the kanji (answers)

1. けがをして、しばらく出血が止まりませんでした。
2. わたしは、図書係に指名されました。
3. 家の子は、虫歯が四本あります。
4. わたしは、東京出身です。
5. 妹は、いつも鼻歌を歌っています。
6. りんごの皮は、むいて食べます。
7. うちの一人息子は今、海外にいます。

5. Kanji matching (answers)

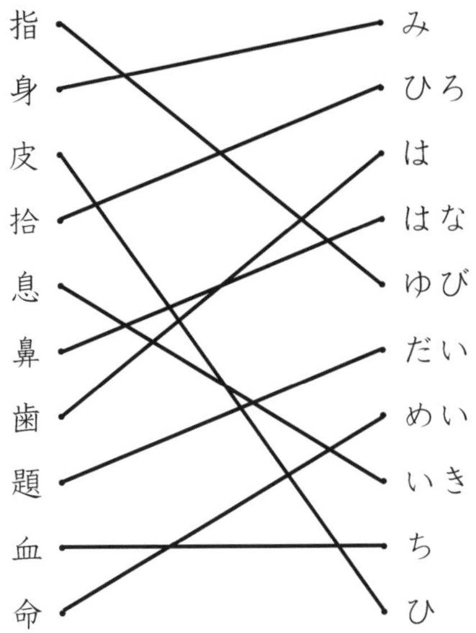

33 Kanji Lesson 33:

434-440

横次化央病平談

The last set of kanji are random of course :-)

33 New Kanji 新しい漢字

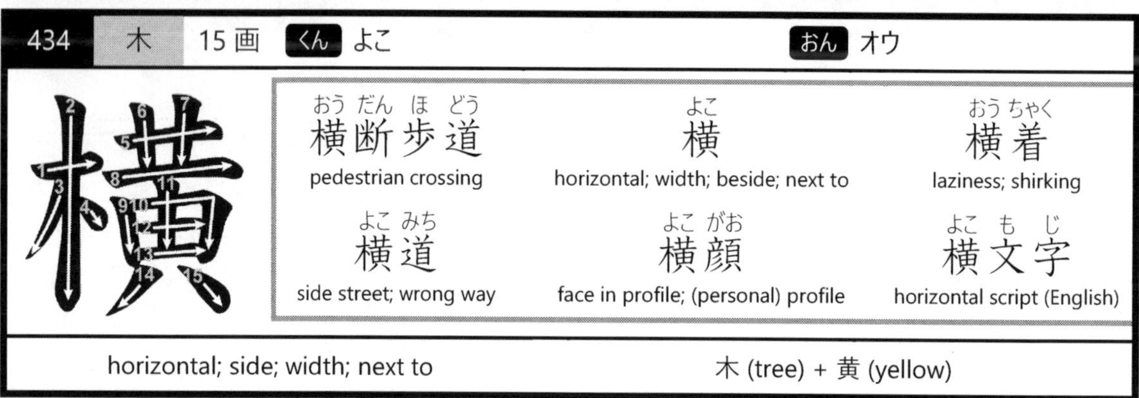

434 | 木 | 15 画 | くん よこ | おん オウ

横断歩道 (おうだんほどう) pedestrian crossing	横 (よこ) horizontal; width; beside; next to	横着 (おうちゃく) laziness; shirking
横道 (よこみち) side street; wrong way	横顔 (よこがお) face in profile; (personal) profile	横文字 (よこもじ) horizontal script (English)

horizontal; side; width; next to — 木 (tree) + 黄 (yellow)

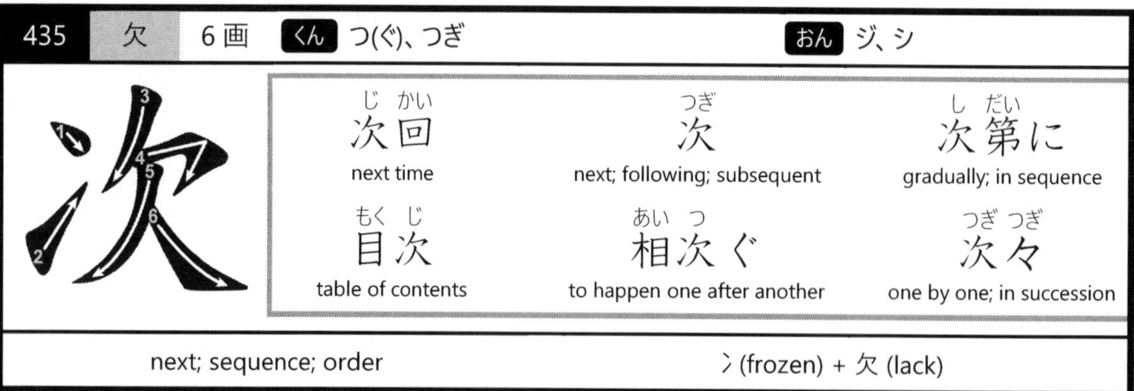

435 | 欠 | 6 画 | くん つ(ぐ)、つぎ | おん ジ、シ

次回 (じかい) next time	次 (つぎ) next; following; subsequent	次第に (しだいに) gradually; in sequence
目次 (もくじ) table of contents	相次ぐ (あいつぐ) to happen one after another	次々 (つぎつぎ) one by one; in succession

next; sequence; order — 冫 (frozen) + 欠 (lack)

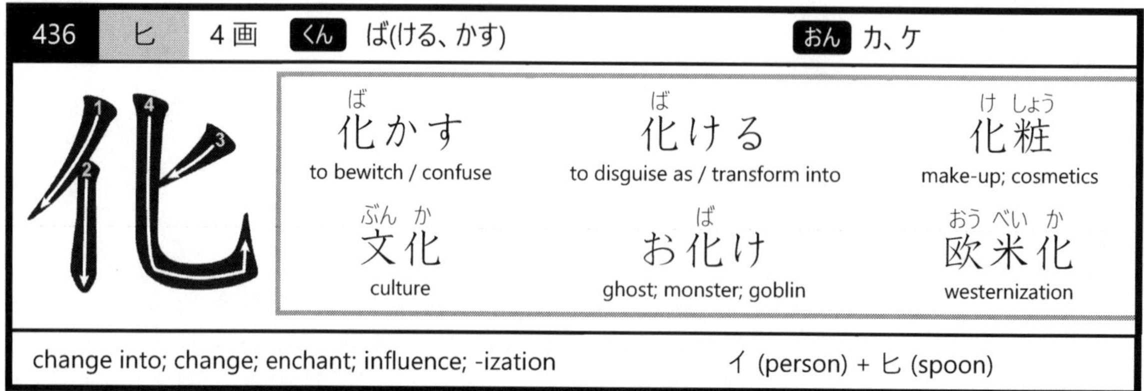

436 | 匕 | 4 画 | くん ば(ける、かす) | おん カ、ケ

化かす (ばかす) to bewitch / confuse	化ける (ばける) to disguise as / transform into	化粧 (けしょう) make-up; cosmetics
文化 (ぶんか) culture	お化け (おばけ) ghost; monster; goblin	欧米化 (おうべいか) westernization

change into; change; enchant; influence; -ization — イ (person) + 匕 (spoon)

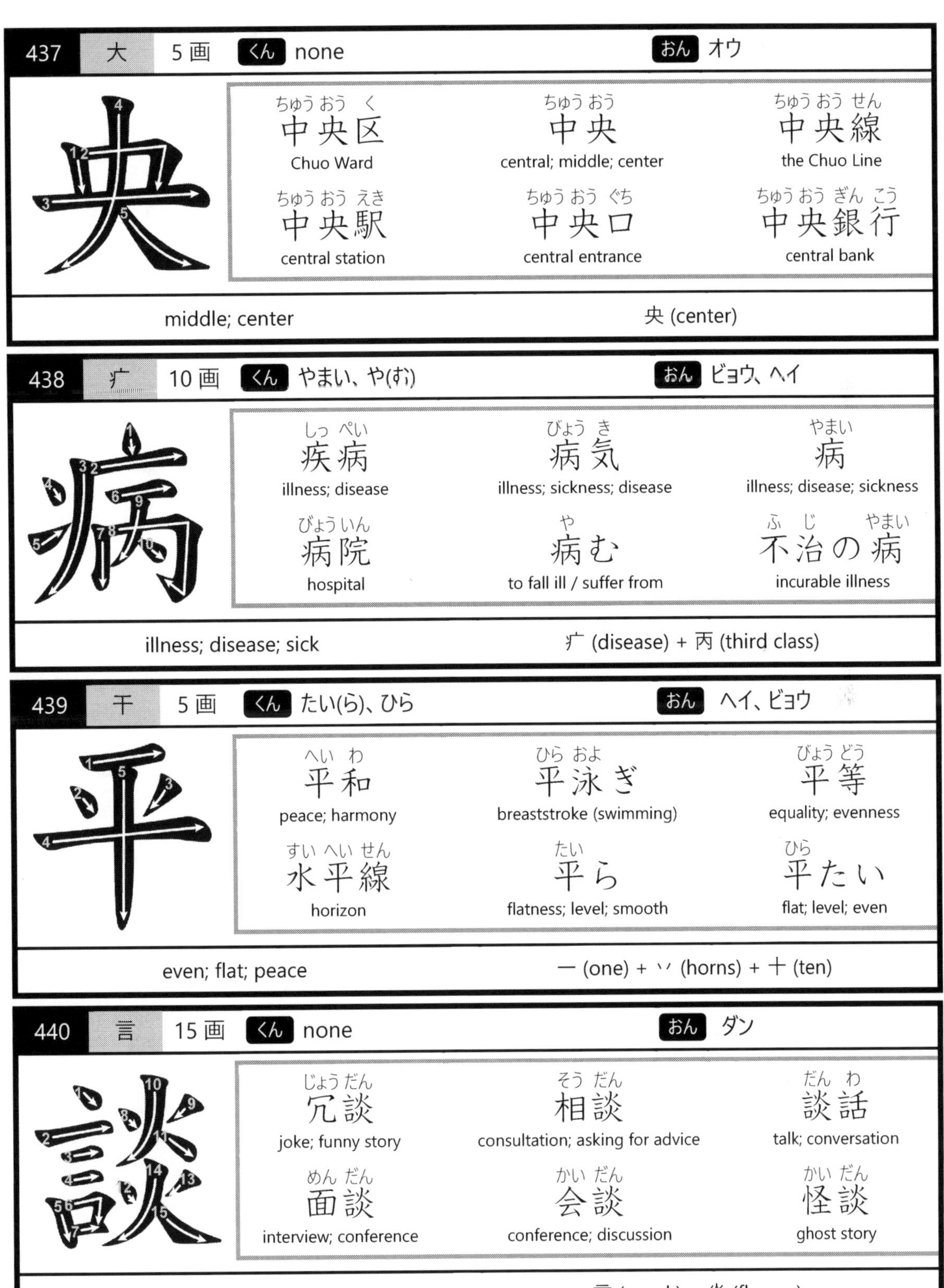

437	大	5 画	くん none	おん オウ

央

ちゅう おう く 中央区 Chuo Ward	ちゅう おう 中央 central; middle; center	ちゅう おう せん 中央線 the Chuo Line
ちゅう おう えき 中央駅 central station	ちゅう おう ぐち 中央口 central entrance	ちゅう おう ぎん こう 中央銀行 central bank

middle; center — 央 (center)

438	疒	10 画	くん やまい、や(む)	おん ビョウ、ヘイ

病

しっ ぺい 疾病 illness; disease	びょう き 病気 illness; sickness; disease	やまい 病 illness; disease; sickness
びょう いん 病院 hospital	や 病む to fall ill / suffer from	ふ じ やまい 不治の病 incurable illness

illness; disease; sick — 疒 (disease) + 丙 (third class)

439	干	5 画	くん たい(ら)、ひら	おん ヘイ、ビョウ

平

へい わ 平和 peace; harmony	ひら およ 平泳ぎ breaststroke (swimming)	びょう どう 平等 equality; evenness
すい へい せん 水平線 horizon	たい 平ら flatness; level; smooth	ひら 平たい flat; level; even

even; flat; peace — 一 (one) + ハ (horns) + 十 (ten)

440	言	15 画	くん none	おん ダン

談

じょう だん 冗談 joke; funny story	そう だん 相談 consultation; asking for advice	だん わ 談話 talk; conversation
めん だん 面談 interview; conference	かい だん 会談 conference; discussion	かい だん 怪談 ghost story

talk; discuss — 言 (speak) + 炎 (flames)

Kanji Parts used in the New Kanji					
木	tree	匕	spoon	ヽノ	horns
黄	yellow	央	center	十	ten
冫	frozen	疒	disease	言	speak
欠	lack	丙	third class	炎	flames
亻	person	一	one		

33 Kanji Memory Tools 漢字記憶術

横

The tree (木) with a yellow (黄) ribbon is on its "**SIDE**".

❶横断歩道(おうだんほどう)の❷横(よこ)に子供(こども)が立(た)っている。

There is a child standing ❷beside ❶the crosswalk.

次

I'm frozen (冫) and lack (欠) a plan for what is "**NEXT**".

❶相次(あいつ)ぐ欠席(けっせき)で❷次男(じなん)の成績(せいせき)は❸次(つぎ)のテスト❹次第(しだい)です。

Due to a ❶string of absences, my ❷second son's grade is ❹up to the ❸next text.

化

A person (亻) with a spoon (匕) is something I can "**CHANGE INTO**".

❶化学(かがく)の先生(せんせい)が❷化粧(けしょう)をして、別人(べつじん)に❸化(ば)けました。

My ❶chemistry teacher put on ❷makeup and ❸transformed into a different person.

央

The center (央) is the "**CENTER**".

❶JR中央線(ちゅうおうせん)の新宿駅(しんじゅくえき)の❷中央口(ちゅうおうぐち)で会(あ)いましょう。

Let's meet at the ❷central exit of the Shinjuku station of the ❶JR central line.

病

This disease (疒) is a third class (丙) "**ILLNESS**".

恋(こい)の❶病(やまい)は、❷病院(びょういん)では治(なお)せません。

Love ❶sickness can't be cured at a ❷hospital.

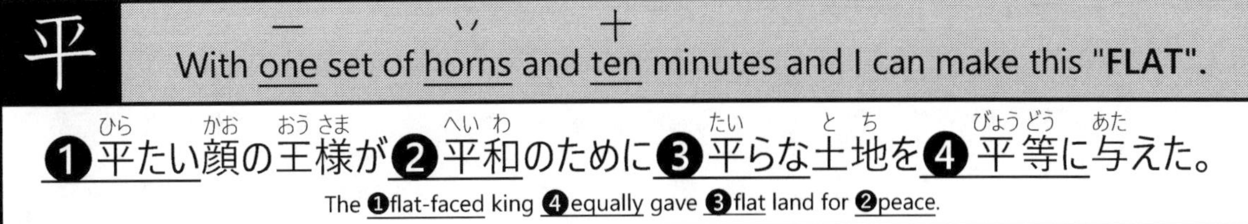

平
一 丷 十
With one set of horns and ten minutes and I can make this "**FLAT**".
❶平(ひら)たい顔(かお)の王様(おうさま)が❷平和(へいわ)のために❸平(たい)らな土地(とち)を❹平等(びょうどう)に与(あた)えた。
The ❶flat-faced king ❹equally gave ❸flat land for ❷peace.

言 炎
We will speak about the flames when we "**DISCUSS**".

❶面談(めんだん)で❷相談(そうだん)しました。

I ❷asked for advice at the ❶conference.

33 Kanji Usage 漢字の使い方

● 33-1. The "-ization" of things 化

Years ago, when I was still a tour guide for Japanese tourists in Las Vegas, another guide was explaining how more and more residential skyscrapers were being built in Las Vegas. He used the word マンハッタン化(か) (Manhattanization / Manhattanizing). This word doesn't officially exist in English nor Japanese, but it was understood by all the customers listening. Here are some other "-ization" words.

Westernization	digitalization
欧米化 (おうべいか)	デジタル化 (か)
The adoption of the practices and culture of western Europe by non-European societies.	Conversion of analog information into formats viewable on a PC or other electronic device.

politicization	optimization
政治問題化 (せいじもんだいか)	最適化 (さいてきか)
Making an issue that affects everyone into an "us vs them" political issue.	The act of making a process run more efficiently, so that it uses less time or resources.

● 33-2. Japanese proverbs using 化 and 病

Here are some Japanese proverbs using kanji from this lesson.

病(やまい)は気(き)から	Disease starts in mind./ It's all mental./ Your mind controls your body.

「病(やまい)は気(き)から」と言(い)うから、あまり心配(しんぱい)しない方(ほう)がいいですよ。

They say that "disease starts in the mind", so you shouldn't worry too much.

化(ば)けの皮(かわ)がはがれる	To strip the wolf of its sheep skin; To show one's true colors

彼女(かのじょ)の化(ば)けの皮(かわ)がはがれて、ショックを受(う)けました。

I was shocked when my girlfriend showed her true colors.

● 33-3. Types of illness 病

Heaven forbid you ever need to use these words in Japan. But just in case let's learn some illness related words.

Illness	Meaning of the first kanji	English
じびょう **持病**	持 = hold; have	chronic disease
たいびょう **大病**	大 = large; big	serious illness; dangerous disease
じゅうびょう **重病**	重 = heavy; important; pile up	serious illness
なんびょう **難病**	難 = difficult; trouble; impossible	incurable disease
きゅうびょう **急病**	急 = hurry; emergency; sudden	sudden illness
はつびょう **発病**	発 = departure; discharge; publish	onset of disease; pathogeny
けびょう **仮病**	仮 = sham; temporary; assumed	feigned illness
とうびょう **闘病**	闘 = fight; war	fighting against an illness
かんびょう **看病**	看 = watch over; see	nursing (a patient)

33 Words You Can Write 書ける言葉

横目（よこめ） sidelong glance

横目

横着（おうちゃく） laziness; dishonesty

横着

次男（じなん） second son

次男

次女（じじょ） second daughter

次女

化石(かせき) fossil

化石

消化（しょうか） digestion

消化

中央（ちゅうおう） central; middle

中央

病人（びょうにん） sick person; patient

病人

病名（びょうめい） name of a disease

病	名										

平気（へいき） all right; fine; okay; coolness; calmness

平	気										

平日（へいじつ） weekday; ordinary days (i.e. non-holiday)

平	日										

商談（しょうだん） business discusion; negotiation

商	談										

化学（かがく） chemistry

化	学										

横書き（よこがき） writing horizontally

横	書	き									

太平洋（たいへいよう） Pacific Ocean

太	平	洋									

談話室（だんわしつ） conversation lounge; common room

談	話	室									

33 Kanji Workbook Activities

● 1. Stroke Order Check 書き順確認

Each kanji has a stroke with an arrow on it. Write its order number below the kanji.

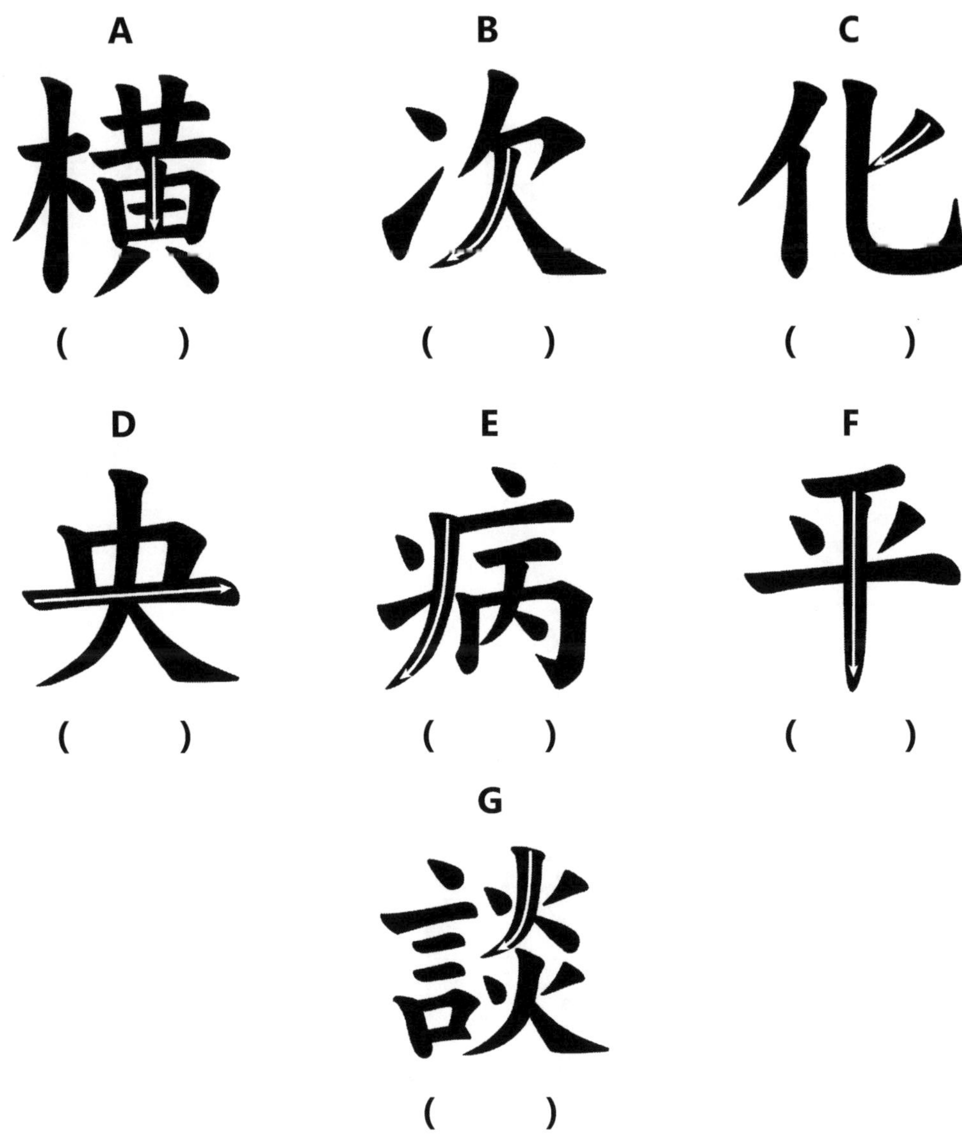

● 2. Kanji Meaning Match

Write the following kanji next to its meaning: 談 病 歯 化 横 皮 次 央 平

1.____ horizontal 2. ____ -ization 3. ____ illness

4. ____ next 5. ____ middle 6. ____ flat

7. ____ discuss 8. ____ tooth 9. ____ skin

● 3. Kanji Readings

Write FURIGANA above the underlined kanji words.

1. うちの横着なねこは、だれとも遊ぼうとしません。
2. 注文が相次いでキャンセルされました。
3. 化石を調べて十年になります。
4. わたしは東京都中央区に住んでいます。
5. 病院に行かなくても平気です。

● 4. Fill in the Kanji

Fill in the appropriate kanji in the blanks for each sentence.

さく ぶん よこ が か くだ

1. ___ ___は、___ ___きで___いて___さい。

Please write our essay with horizontal writing.

あね つぎ ひ

2. ___とけんかをしても、___ の___には なかよくなります。

Even if I fight with my older sister, we make up on the next day.

しょう か もの た

3. いつも___ ___にいい___を___ べています。

I always eat food that's good for digestion.

えき ちゅう おう ぐち ま あ

4. ___ の___ ___ ___で___ち___わせをしましょう。

Let's meet up at the station's central exit.

きょう びょう き がっ こう やす

5. ___ ___ は___ ___で、___ ___を___ みました。

Due to being sick I took a day off of school.

ゆう じん ひら およ じょう ず

6. ___ ___は___ ___ぎが___ ___です。

My friend is skilled at the breaststroke.

に じ せん せい めん だん

7. ___ ___に___ ___ と___ ___があります。

A 2 o'clock I have an interview with the teacher.

● 5. Kanji Matching

Connect each kanji with an おん or くん reading. Use each reading only ONCE.

横 •	• い
化 •	• か
病 •	• びょう
意 •	• よこ
第 •	• いん
談 •	• だん
平 •	• へい
員 •	• だい
次 •	• じ
央 •	• おう

33 Answer Key 答え合わせ

1. Stroke order check (answers)

A) 11　B) 5　C) 3
D) 3　E) 3　F) 5
G) 10

2. Kanji meaning match (answers)

1. 横 horizontal　2. 化 -ization　3. 病 illness
4. 次 next　5. 央 middle　6. 平 flat
7. 談 discuss　8. 歯 tooth　9. 皮 skin

3. Kanji Readings (answers)

1. うちの横着(おうちゃく)なねこは、だれとも遊(あそ)ぼうとしません。 Our lazy cat doesn't try to play with anyone.
2. 注文(ちゅうもん)が相次(あいつ)いでキャンセルされました。 Orders were cancelled one after another.
3. 化石(かせき)を調(しら)べて十年(じゅうねん)になります。 I've been investigating fossils for 10 years.
4. わたしは東京都(とうきょうと)中央区(ちゅうおうく)に住(す)んでいます。 I live in Chuo-ward, Tokyo.
5. 病院(びょういん)に行(い)かなくても平気(へいき)です。 I'm fine not going to the hospital.

4. Fill in the kanji (answers)

1. 作文は、横書きで書いて下さい。
2. 姉とけんかをしても、次の日には なかよくなります。
3. いつも消化にいいもの物を食べています。
4. 駅の中央口で待ち合わせをしましょう。
5. 今日は病気で、学校を休みました。
6. 友人は平泳ぎが上手です。
7. 二時に先生と面談があります。

5. Kanji matching (answers)

横	よこ
化	か
病	びょう
意	い
第	だい
談	だん
平	へい
員	いん
次	じ
央	おう

Kanji Lessons 31-33:

Super Review 7

From the teacher...

Test your knowledge of the kanji learned in the last 3 lessons.

● 1. Build-a-Kanji 漢字の組み合わせ

Combine the left and right parts to make seven of the kanji learned in lessons 31-33.

RULES
1. You can use the radical and kanji parts as many times as you want.
2. Some kanji can use two kanji parts.

部首 (Radical)		
匕	言	金
扌	木	亻
立	口	艹
心	疒	氵

Other Kanji Parts		
立	口	失
黄	日	田
火	丙	旨
亻	力	自

SAMPLE	1	2	3	4	5	6	7
意							

● 2. Okurigana drill 送り仮名ドリル

Circle the correct 漢字 + 送り仮名 combination.

1. ばける	・化ける	・化る
2. あたためる	・温る	・温める
3. くるしむ	・苦む	・苦しむ

● 3. Kanji selection 漢字の選択

Select the best kanji to replace the underlined section of the sentence.

1. うちの子は＿＿意しても、ぜんぜん聞きません。
   A. 用　B. 同　C. 注　D. 合

2. 田中先生は、どちらの出＿＿ですか。
   A. 身　B. 国　C. 所　D. 県

3. みかんの＿＿をむいて、食べましょう。
   A. 実　B. 葉　C. 根　D. 皮

4. わたしは地下＿＿で会社に行っています。
   A. 銀　B. 道　C. 鉄　D. 路

● 4. Kanji reading selection 読みの選択

Select the best reading for the underlined kanji.

1. 次回にお会いできるのを楽しみにしています。
   A. つぎ　B. つ　C. じ　D. し

2. このケーキを平等に分けられますか。
   A. びょう　B. へい　C. たい　D. ひら

3. 十分に休息を取ってください。
   A. いき　B. けい　C. そく　D. か

4. わたしたちは宮田さんを代表に指名しました。
   A. し　B. さ　C. ゆび　D. せん

● 5. Compound kanji word puzzle 熟語パズル

Fill in the correct kanji based on the list below the puzzle.

	1)		2)
3)	4)	5)	
	6)		7)
8)		9)	

Down ↓	
English meaning	**Hiragana**
2) face in profile	よこがお
3) hospital director	いんちょう
Left to Right →	
1) railroad, railway	てつどう
5) round face	まるがお
8) bleeding	しゅっけつ
9) nasal mucus, dripping nose	はなみず

← Right to Left	
English meaning	**Hiragana**
1) railway (iron) bridge	てっきょう
2) side street, wrong way	よこみち
4) hospital	びょういん
6) station master	えきちょう
7) central station	ちゅうおうえき
9) nosebleed	はなぢ

SR7 Answer Key 答え合わせ

1. Build-a-Kanji (answers) (order can vary)

SAMPLE 意 1) 鉄 2) 指 3) 息 4) 横 5) 病 6) 化 7) 談

2. Okurigana drill (answers)

1. ばける	**・化ける**	・化る
2. あたためる	・温る	**・温める**
3. くるしむ	・苦む	**・苦しむ**

3. Kanji selection (answers)

1. C – 注意(ちゅうい) Even if I warn my child they don't listen.
2. A – 出身(しゅっしん) Where were you born Mr. / Mrs. Tanaka (teacher)?
3. D – 皮(かわ) Let's peel the tangerine skin and eat it.
4. C – 地下鉄(ちかてつ) I'm going (I go) to work on the subway.

4. Kanji reading selection (answers)

1. C – 次回(じかい) I'm looking forward to the next time I see you.
2. A – 平等(びょうどう) Can you divide this cake evenly?
3. C – 休息(きゅうそく) Please take adequate rests. (じゅうぶん not じっぷん)
4. A – 指名(しめい) We nominated Miyata-san as a (our) representative.

5. Compound kanji word puzzle (answers)

橋	鉄	道	横
院	病	丸	顔
長	駅	央	中
出	血	鼻	水

Glossary A: Search by Reading

あ

あ(く)	開	68
あ(ける)	開	68
あ(る)	有	156
あい	相	168
あきな(う)	商	339
あく	悪	20
あじ	味	362
あじ(わう)	味	362
あそ(ぶ)	遊	156
あたた(か)	温	21
あたた(かい)	温	21
あたた(まる)	温	21
あたた(める)	温	21
あつ(い)	暑	21
あつ(まる)	集	95
あつ(める)	集	95
あぶら	油	387
あらわ(す)	表	145
あらわ(れる)	表	145
あん	安	20
あん	暗	20

い

い	医	189
い	委	270
い	意	402
いき	息	415
いく	育	57
いそ(ぐ)	急	106
いた	板	289
いのち	命	351
いん	員	271
いん	院	189
いん	飲	57

う

う	有	156
う(える)	植	56
う(かる)	受	94
う(ける)	受	94
う(つ)	打	117
う(わる)	植	56
うご(かす)	動	130
うご(く)	動	130
うつ(す)	写	84
うつ(る)	写	84
うつく(しい)	美	45
うん	運	68

え

え	重	33
えい	泳	57
えき	役	178
えき	駅	189

お

お	和	374
お	悪	20
お(う)	負	146
お(う)	追	129
お(える)	終	84
お(きる)	起	83
お(こす)	起	83
お(こる)	起	83
お(ちる)	落	157
お(とす)	落	157
お(わる)	終	84
おう	央	427
おう	横	426
おく	屋	190
おく(る)	送	117
おも	主	167
おも	面	351
おも(い)	重	33
おもて	表	145
おもて	面	351
およ(ぐ)	泳	57
おん	温	21

か

か	化	426
か	荷	362
か(える)	代	118
か(つ)	勝	145
か(わる)	代	118
かい	開	68
かい	階	254
かえ(す)	返	146
かえ(る)	返	146
かか(る)	係	168
かかり	係	168
かく	客	168
かさ(なる)	重	33
かさ(ねる)	重	33
かな(しい)	悲	45
かな(しむ)	悲	45
かみ	神	179
かる(い)	軽	34
かろ(やか)	軽	34
かわ	皮	415
かん	寒	21
かん	感	69
かん	漢	311
かん	神	179
かん	館	190

が

がん	岸	216

き

き	期	254
き	起	83
き(える)	消	46
き(せる)	着	118
き(まる)	決	68
き(める)	決	68
き(る)	着	118
きし	岸	216
きみ	君	167
きゃく	客	168
きゅう	宮	204
きゅう	急	106
きゅう	球	340
きゅう	究	271
きゅう	級	254
きょ	去	107
きょう	橋	216
きょく	局	204
きょく	曲	46
きわ(める)	究	271

ぎ

ぎょう	業	339
ぎん	銀	402

く

く	区	205
く	宮	204
く	庫	229
く	苦	33
くすり	薬	300
くば(る)	配	145
くら(い)	暗	20
くる(しい)	苦	33
くる(しむ)	苦	33
くる(しめる)	苦	33
くん	君	167

ぐ

ぐ	具	363
ぐう	宮	204

け

け	化	426
け(す)	消	46
けい	係	168
けい	軽	34
けつ	決	68
けつ	血	414
けん	県	205
けん	研	271

こ

こ	去	107
こ	庫	229
こ	湖	216
こう	向	106
こう	幸	45
こう	港	217
こう	神	179
こおり	氷	386
こと	事	270
ころ(がす)	転	129
ころ(がる)	転	129
ころ(げる)	転	129
ころ(ぶ)	転	129
こん	根	324

ご

ご	期	254
ごう	号	255
ごう	業	339

さ

さ(す)	指	414
さ(る)	去	107
さい	祭	373
さいわ(い)	幸	45
さか	坂	228
さか	酒	373
さけ	酒	373
さだ(か)	定	129
さだ(まる)	定	129
さだ(める)	定	129
さち	幸	45
さま	様	179
さむ(い)	寒	21
さら	皿	289

し

し	仕	270
し	使	83
し	始	83
し	指	414
し	次	426
し	歯	414
し	死	69
し	詩	311
し(ぬ)	死	69
しあわ(せ)	幸	45
しき	式	229
しな	品	299
しま	島	228
しゃ	写	84
しゃ	者	167
しゃく	昔	373
しゅ	主	167
しゅ	取	94
しゅ	守	84
しゅ	酒	373
しゅう	州	205
しゅう	拾	94
しゅう	終	84
しゅう	習	95
しゅう	集	95
しゅく	宿	190
しょ	所	204
しょ	暑	21
しょう	勝	145
しょう	商	339
しょう	昭	374
しょう	消	46
しょう	相	168
しょう	章	255
しょく	植	56
しら(べる)	調	118
しろ	代	118
しん	深	34
しん	申	56
しん	真	402
しん	神	179
しん	身	415
しん	進	107

じ

じ	事	270
じ	仕	270
じ	持	95
じ	次	426
じ	路	229
じつ	実	340
じゃく	着	118
じゅ	受	94
じゅう	住	106
じゅう	拾	94
じゅう	重	33
じょ	助	46
じょう	乗	56
じょう	定	129
じん	神	179

す

す	主	167
す	守	84
す	州	205
す(まっ)	住	106
す(む)	住	106
すけ	助	46
すす(む)	進	107
すす(める)	進	107
すべ(て)	全	350
すみ	炭	288
すみ(やか)	速	33

ず

ず	事	270
ず	豆	324

せ

せ	世	339
せい	世	339
せい	整	107
せき	昔	373

ぜ

ぜん	全	350

そ

そ	想	69
そ(らす)	反	350
そ(る)	反	350
そう	想	69
そう	相	168
そう	送	117
そく	息	415
そく	速	33
そそ(ぐ)	注	387
そだ(つ)	育	57
そだ(てる)	育	57

ぞ

ぞく	族	178

た

た	他	178
たい	代	118
たい	対	350
たい	待	117
たい(ら)	平	427
たく	度	241
たす(かる)	助	46
たす(ける)	助	46
たび	度	241
たび	旅	362
たま	球	340
たん	反	350
たん	炭	288
たん	短	34

だ

だ	打	117
だい	代	118
だい	第	403
だい	題	311
だん	談	427

ち

ち	血	414
ちゃく	着	118
ちゅう	柱	288
ちゅう	注	387
ちょう	丁	255
ちょう	帳	300
ちょう	調	118
ちょう	重	33

つ

つ	都	228
つ(く)	着	118
つ(ぐ)	次	426
つ(ける)	着	118
つい	対	350
つい	追	129
つか(う)	使	83
つか(える)	仕	270
つぎ	次	426
つど(う)	集	95
つら	面	351

て

てい	丁	255
てい	定	129
てい	庭	217
てき	笛	288
てつ	鉄	403
てん	転	129

と

と	度	241
と	登	130
と	都	228
と(い)	問	156
と(う)	問	156
と(ぐ)	研	271
と(る)	取	94
とう	島	228
とう	投	130
とう	湯	386
とう	登	130
とう	等	241
とう	豆	324
ところ	所	204
ととの(う)	整	107
ととの(う)	調	118
ととの(える)	整	107
ととの(える)	調	118
とん	問	156

ど

ど	度	241
どう	動	130
どう	童	179

な

な(げる)	投	130
なが(す)	流	157
なが(れる)	流	157
なご(む)	和	374
なご(やか)	和	374
なみ	波	386
なら(う)	習	95

に

に	荷	362
にが(い)	苦	33
にが(る)	苦	33
にわ	庭	217

ぬ

ぬし	主	167

ね

ね	根	324
ね(る)	練	157

の

の(せる)	乗	56
の(む)	飲	57
の(る)	乗	56
のう	農	323
のぼ(る)	登	130

は

は	歯	414
は	波	386
は	葉	324
はい	配	145
はぐく(む)	育	57
はこ	箱	300
はこ(ぶ)	運	68
はし	橋	216
はしら	柱	288
はじ(まる)	始	83
はじ(める)	始	83
はた	畑	217
はたけ	畑	217
はつ	発	363
はな	鼻	415
はな(す)	放	146
はな(つ)	放	146
はな(れる)	放	146
はや(い)	速	33
はや(まる)	速	33
はや(める)	速	33
はん	反	350
はん	坂	228
はん	板	289

ば

ば(かす)	化	426
ば(ける)	化	426
ばい	倍	241
ばん	板	289

ひ

ひ	悲	45
ひ	氷	386
ひ	皮	415
ひつ	筆	289
ひつじ	羊	323
ひと(しい)	等	241
ひょう	氷	386
ひょう	表	145
ひら	平	427
ひら(く)	開	68
ひら(ける)	開	68
ひろ(う)	拾	94
ひん	品	299

び

び	美	45
び	鼻	415
びょう	平	427
びょう	病	427
びょう	秒	242

ふ

ふ	負	146
ふえ	笛	288
ふか(い)	深	34
ふか(まる)	深	34
ふか(める)	深	34
ふく	服	299
ふく	福	374
ふで	筆	289

ぶ

ぶ	部	242
ぶつ	物	299

へ

へい	平	427
へい	病	427
へん	返	146

べ

べん	勉	312

ほ

ほう	放	146
ほう(る)	放	146
ほか	他	178
ほつ	発	363
ほん	反	350

ま

ま	真	402
ま(かす)	負	146
ま(がる)	曲	46
ま(ける)	負	146
ま(げる)	曲	46
ま(つ)	待	117
まさ(る)	勝	145
まった(く)	全	350
まつ(り)	祭	373
まつ(る)	祭	373
まめ	豆	324
まも(る)	守	84

み

み	味	362
み	実	340
み	身	415
みじか(い)	短	34
みずうみ	湖	216
みどり	緑	323
みなと	港	217
みの(る)	実	340
みや	宮	204
みやこ	都	228
みょう	命	351

む

む(かう)	向	106
む(く)	向	106
む(ける)	向	106
む(こう)	向	106
むかし	昔	373

め

めい	命	351
めん	面	351

も

も(つ)	持	95
もう(す)	申	56
もつ	物	299
もの	物	299
もの	者	167
もり	守	84
もん	問	156

や

や	屋	190
や(む)	病	427
やかた	館	190
やく	役	178
やく	薬	300
やす(い)	安	20
やど	宿	190
やど(す)	宿	190
やど(る)	宿	190
やまい	病	427
やわ(らぐ)	和	374
やわ(らげる)	和	374

ゆ

ゆ	油	387
ゆ	湯	386
ゆ	由	363
ゆ	遊	156
ゆい	由	363
ゆう	有	156
ゆう	由	363
ゆう	遊	156
ゆだ(ねる)	委	270
ゆび	指	414

よ

よ	世	339
よ	予	312
よ	代	118
よう	様	179
よう	洋	387
よう	羊	323
よう	葉	324
よう	陽	403
よこ	横	426
よし	由	363

ら

らい	礼	312
らく	落	157

り

りゅう 流 157
りょ 旅 362
りょう 両 351
りょく 緑 323

る

る 流 157

れ

れい 礼 312
れつ 列 242
れん 練 157

ろ

ろ 路 229
ろく 緑 323

わ

わ 和 374
わざ 業 339
わらべ 童 179
わる(い) 悪 20

-

-ization 化 426

Glossary B: Search by English Meaning

A

a long time ago 昔 373
a sink 流 157
abandon 投 130
accept 受 94
account book 帳 300
admit 服 299
advance 進 107
agree upon 決 68
agriculture 農 323
album 帳 300
alcohol 酒 373
all 全 350
another 他 178
answer 返 146
anti- 反 350
anti- 対 350
appoint 決 68
arranging 整 107
arrive 着 118
article 品 299
arts 業 339
ascend 登 130
ask 問 156
aspect 相 168
aspect 面 351
assemble 集 95
assist 助 46
attend 仕 270
attitude 度 241

B

bad 悪 20
badge 章 255
baggage 荷 362
ball 球 340
bank 岸 216
basis 根 324
bath 湯 386
be blinded 暗 20
be photographed 写 84
beans 豆 324
beautiful 美 45
beforehand 予 312
begin 始 83
bend 曲 46
benefit 薬 300
beyond 向 106
billows 波 386
bin 箱 300
bitter 苦 33
blessing 福 374
blood 血 414
board 板 289
body 身 415
both 両 351
boundary 世 339
bow 礼 312
box 箱 300
breath 息 415
bridge 橋 216
bright 昭 374
building 館 190
bureau 局 204
business 事 270
business 業 339

C

call 号 255
campaign 役 178
capital 都 228
cargo 荷 362
carry 持 95
carry 運 68
case 箱 300
center 央 427
ceremony 式 229
ceremony 礼 312
chain 列 242
change into 化 426
change 代 118
change 動 130
change 化 426
channel 局 204
chapter 章 255
charcoal 炭 288
chart 表 145
chase 追 129
chemical 薬 300
chest 箱 300
chief 主 167
child 童 179
China 漢 311
circularize 配 145
clarinet 笛 288
class 等 241
class 級 254
class 部 242
clear 昭 374
client 客 168
climb up 登 130
clothing 服 299
coal 炭 288
cold 寒 21
column 列 242
command 命 351
comment 注 387
committee 委 270
compare 対 350
complete 全 350
composition 章 255
concept 想 69
confront 向 106
confusion 動 130
connection 係 168
constellations 宮 204
convert 代 118
copy 写 84
copy 部 242
counter for carriages 両 351
counter for sheets 丁 255
counter for suits of clothing 着 118
county 区 205
courtyard 庭 217
cover 守 84
current 流 157
curve 曲 46
customer 客 168
cylinder 柱 288

D

dark 暗 20
date 期 254
daytime 陽 403
deal 配 145
dealer 屋 190
dealing 商 339
death 死 69
decide 定 129
decide 決 68
decree 命 351
deep 深 34
defeat 負 146
defy 向 106
degrees 度 241
department 局 204
departure 発 363
depend on 待 117
dept 部 242
describe 写 84
desire 意 402
destiny 命 351
determine 定 129
determine 決 68
devote 委 270
diagram 表 145
die 死 69
dignity 品 299
diligent 勉 312

disappear	暗	20
discard	投	130
discharge	服	299
discharge	発	363
discuss	談	427
disease	病	427
dish	皿	289
distance	路	229
district	区	205
doctor	医	189
doing	仕	270
double	倍	241
drill	練	157
drink	飲	57
drive away	追	129
duty	係	168
duty	役	178
dwell	住	106
dwell	宿	190

E

eliminate	去	107
emergency	急	106
emotion	感	69
employee	員	271
enchant	化	426
encourage	勉	312
end	終	84
endeavor	勉	312
entire	全	350
entrust to	委	270
envoy	使	83
equal	等	241
eras	代	118
erase	消	46
escort	送	117
established	定	129
etc.	等	241
even	対	350
even	平	427
evil	悪	20
excel	勝	145
exist	有	156
extent	度	241
exterior	表	145
extinguish	消	46

F

face	面	351
facing	向	106
fact	事	270
fade	返	146
fall down	転	129
fall	落	157
false	悪	20
family	族	178
farmers	農	323
fast	速	33
fat	油	387
fate	命	351
feast	祭	373
feeling	感	69
festival	祭	373
fetch	取	94
field	畑	217
find	拾	94
finger	指	414
finish	終	84
flat	平	427
flavor	味	362
floor	階	254
flow into	注	387
flow	流	157
flute	笛	288
fold	倍	241
follow	守	84
follow	追	129
foreign	洋	387
fortune	福	374
fortune	運	68
freeze	氷	386
freight	荷	362
fruit	実	340

G

garden	庭	217
gather	拾	94
gather	集	95
get	受	94
gloss	練	157
gods	神	179
gone	去	107
goods	品	299
grade	級	254
green	緑	323
group together	集	95
grow	育	57
guard	守	84
guest	客	168
gunshot counter	発	363

H

hail	氷	386
Han	漢	311
hand out	配	145
handwriting	筆	289
happen	有	156
happen	起	83
happiness	幸	45
harbor	港	217
harmonize	調	118
harmony	和	374
have	持	95
have	有	156
heart	意	402
heavy	重	33
help	助	46
hide	皮	415
hill	坂	228
hit	打	117
hold	持	95
home	宿	190
horizontal	横	426
hot spring	湯	386
hot water	湯	386
hot	暑	21
house	屋	190
hurry	急	106

I

ice	氷	386
idea	想	69
idea	意	402
illness	病	427
incline	坂	228
indicate	指	414
inexpensive	安	20
influence	化	426
ingredients	具	363
inhabit	住	106
inn	宿	190
institution	院	189
inter-	相	168
invest in	投	130
investigate	調	118
iron	鉄	403
island	島	228
item	号	255

J

Japanese style	和	374
journey	旅	362
juvenile	童	179

K

knock	打	117

L

lake 湖 216
land 畑 217
large building 館 190
leaf 葉 324
learn 習 95
leather 皮 415
leave to 委 270
leave 去 107
let go 放 146
life 命 351
light 軽 34
lightweight 軽 34
line 列 242
live 住 106
load 荷 362
lobe 葉 324
lodging 宿 190
lord 主 167
luck 福 374
luck 運 68

M

main thing 主 167
make a deal 商 339
male name suffix 君 167
manner 様 179
mansion 院 189
mansion 館 190
mask 面 351
master 主 167
matter 事 270
matter 物 299
means 具 363
medical 医 189
medicine 薬 300
meet 集 95
member 員 271
merchant 商 339
messenger 使 83
method 式 229
metropolis 都 228
middle 央 427
midget 豆 324
mind 意 402
mind 神 179
minus 負 146
mister 君 167
motion 動 130
move 動 130
mutual 相 168
myself 予 312

N

name 号 255
needle 葉 324
negative 負 146
next to 横 426
next 次 426
nose 鼻 415
notebook 帳 300
number- 第 403
number 号 255
number 員 271
nut 実 340

O

obey 服 299
object 物 299
occur 有 156
occurrence 度 241
ocean 洋 387
offer prayers 祭 373
offer 申 56
office 局 204
office 役 178
official 仕 270
oil 油 387
old times 昔 373
once upon a time 昔 373
oneself 身 415
open 開 68
opposite 反 350
opposite 対 350
order 次 426
ordinal 第 403
organize 整 107
other 他 178
owe 負 146

P

pages 丁 255
painful 苦 33
painting brush 筆 289
palace 宮 204
palace 館 190
past 去 107
path 路 229
pea 豆 324
peace 和 374
peace 平 427
peaceful 安 20
pelt 皮 415
performance 業 339
period 期 254
person in charge 係 168
person 者 167
person 身 415
phase 相 168
pick up 拾 94
pile up 重 33
pillar 柱 288
pipe 笛 288
place 所 204
plane 葉 324
plank 板 289
plant 植 56
plate 板 289
plate 皿 289
play 遊 156
poem 章 255
poem 詩 311
poetry 詩 311
point to 指 414
polish 研 271
polish 練 157
polite suffix (Mr. Mrs. etc.) 様 179
port 港 217
portion 部 242
positive 陽 403
possess 有 156
post 柱 288
pound 打 117
pour 注 387
practice 練 157
prefecture 県 205
prepare 調 118
previous 予 312
principal 主 167
problem 問 156
proceed 進 107
progress 進 107
progress 運 68
promote 進 107
protect 守 84
province 州 205
publish 発 363
pursue 追 129

Q

question 問 156
quit 去 107

R

raise 育 57
rank 列 242

rank	級	254
reality	実	340
reality	真	402
reason	事	270
reason	由	363
receive	受	94
refine	練	157
refinement	品	299
region	区	205
relax	安	20
release	放	146
repay	返	146
replace	代	118
rescue	助	46
research	究	271
reside	住	106
respiration	息	415
rested	安	20
return	返	146
ride	乗	56
ripen	実	340
ritual	祭	373
road	路	229
role	役	178
roof	屋	190
root	根	324
route	路	229
row	列	242

S

sad	悲	45
sake	酒	373
salute	礼	312
say	申	56
school	院	189
scissors	丁	255
sea	洋	387
second (1/60 minute)	秒	242
section	部	242
seller	屋	190
selling	商	339
send	送	117
sensation	感	69
sequence	次	426
seriousness	真	402
serve	仕	270
service	役	178
set	定	129
shade	暗	20
sharpen	研	271
sheep	羊	323
shift	動	130
shining	昭	374
Shinto shrine	宮	204
shop	屋	190
shore	岸	216
short	短	34
sick	病	427
side	横	426
side	面	351
silver	銀	402
situation	様	179
skin	皮	415
slope	坂	228
snout	鼻	415
someone	者	167
son	息	415
song	曲	46
sorrowful	悲	45
soul	神	179
source	根	324
sphere	球	340
stage	板	289
stair	階	254
start from	発	363
start	始	83
state	州	205
station	駅	189
steep	急	106
storehouse	庫	229
story	階	254
strand	岸	216
strike	打	117
strive	勉	312
study of	研	271
study	究	271
style	式	229
subject	題	311
submit	申	56
substitute	代	118
sudden	急	106
suffer	苦	33
sunshine	陽	403
support	柱	288
surface	表	145
surface	面	351
swim	泳	57
system	式	229

T

table	表	145
take place	起	83
take up	取	94
take	取	94
take	受	94
talk	談	427
taste	味	362
temple	院	189
ten	拾	94
tend toward	向	106
term	期	254
thanks	礼	312
the others	他	178
thing	事	270
thing	物	299
thought	想	69
thought	意	402
throw	投	130
time	期	254
times	倍	241
times	度	241
title	号	255
together	相	168
tone	整	107
tone	調	118
tool	具	363
tooth	歯	414
topic	題	311
train	練	157
transcribe	写	84
transport	運	68
travel	旅	362
tribe	族	178
trip over	転	129
trip	旅	362
true	真	402
truth	実	340
tune	整	107
tune	調	118
turn off	消	46
turn	曲	46
twice	倍	241

U

undergo	受	94
unfold	開	68
unseal	開	68
use	使	83
utensil	具	363

V

variable measure of fabric	反	350
versus	対	350
vice	悪	20
victory	勝	145
visitor	客	168
vocation	業	339

W

wait	待	117

wake up 起 83
war 役 178
warehouse 庫 229
warm 温 21
waves 波 386
way 様 179
wealth 福 374
wear 着 118
Western-style 洋 387
wherefore 由 363
whistle 笛 288
whole 全 350
width 横 426
win 勝 145
world 世 339
writing brush 筆 289
wrong 悪 20

Y

yard 庭 217
you 君 167

Glossary C:

Search by Parts

1 stroke parts

丨	消 (#258) 申 (#259)
丶	主 (#315) 州 (#334) 祭 (#410) 氷 (#415) 血 (#427)
し	礼 (#384)
亅	事 (#362)
ノ	乗 (#260) 向 (#284) 着 (#293) 追 (#295) 者 (#314) 係 (#318) 第 (#425)
一	定 (#296) 表 (#302) 事 (#362) 題 (#381) 業 (#392) 両 (#400) 命 (#402) 具 (#406) 昔 (#411) 福 (#412) 平 (#439)

2 stroke parts

了	予 (#382)
川	曲 (#256) 乗 (#260)
𠂉	遊 (#309) 族 (#319) 旅 (#403)
辶	速 (#248) 運 (#265) 進 (#287) 送 (#289) 追 (#295) 返 (#305) 遊 (#309)
阝	院 (#326) 都 (#343) 部 (#353) 階 (#355) 陽 (#426)
⺀	寒 (#246)
ソ	美 (#254) 幸 (#255) 消 (#258) 着 (#293) 商 (#391) 業 (#392) 平 (#439)
亠	商 (#391)
亻	使 (#272) 住 (#283) 代 (#292) 係 (#318) 他 (#320) 宿 (#330) 倍 (#351) 仕 (#361) 荷 (#404) 化 (#436)
儿	発 (#408)
冂	向 (#284) 両 (#400)
冖	写 (#275) 受 (#278)
冫	次 (#435)
几	投 (#298) 役 (#321)
刂	列 (#354)
匚	医 (#325) 区 (#336)
卩	服 (#374)

厂	岸 (#337) 炭 (#367)
ク	急 (#285) 負 (#304)
ナ	有 (#308)
マ	予 (#382)
ム	去 (#286)
丁	打 (#290) 丁 (#360)
九	究 (#366)
二	乗 (#260) 発 (#408)
人	実 (#395) 命 (#402)
入	全 (#399)
刀	昭 (#413)
力	助 (#257) 動 (#300) 勝 (#303) 勉 (#383)
ヒ	死 (#269) 指 (#428) 化 (#436)
十	表 (#302) 真 (#421) 平 (#439)
又	取 (#277) 受 (#278) 投 (#298) 役 (#321) 度 (#349) 服 (#374) 祭 (#410)
子	遊 (#309)

3 stroke parts

艹	苦 (#247) 落 (#310) 薬 (#376) 漢 (#380) 葉 (#389) 荷 (#404)
丂	号 (#358)
与	写 (#275)
凵	歯 (#429)
宀	安 (#242) 寒 (#246) 守 (#276) 定 (#296) 客 (#317) 宿 (#330) 宮 (#331) 実 (#395)
广	庭 (#341) 庫 (#347) 度 (#349)
廴	庭 (#341)
廾	鼻 (#431)
廿	度 (#349)

弋	代 (#292) 式 (#348)
ヨ	緑 (#387)
彳	待 (#291) 役 (#321)
扌	拾 (#279) 持 (#280) 打 (#290) 投 (#298) 指 (#428)
氵	温 (#244) 深 (#251) 消 (#258) 泳 (#264) 決 (#267) 落 (#310) 流 (#311) 湖 (#339) 港 (#340) 漢 (#380) 酒 (#409) 波 (#416) 湯 (#417) 油 (#418) 注 (#419) 洋 (#420)
ヨ	急 (#285)
三	実 (#395)
也	他 (#320)
八	具 (#406)
千	重 (#249)
卄	昔 (#411)
口	向 (#284) 問 (#307) 君 (#313) 号 (#358) 事 (#362) 員 (#363) 品 (#373) 品 (#373) 品 (#373) 漢 (#380) 味 (#405) 福 (#412) 昭 (#413) 和 (#414)
土	幸 (#255) 去 (#286) 者 (#314) 坂 (#345)
士	仕 (#361)
夕	祭 (#410)
大	美 (#254)
女	安 (#242) 始 (#273) 委 (#364)
寸	守 (#276) 対 (#398)
小	県 (#335)
尸	屋 (#328) 局 (#332)
山	岸 (#337) 島 (#344) 炭 (#367) 両 (#400)
川	流 (#311) 州 (#334)
工	式 (#348)
己	起 (#271) 配 (#301) 港 (#340)
巾	帳 (#378)

干	幸 (#255)　岸 (#337)

4 stroke parts

⺅	旅 (#403)
𠫓	育 (#262)　流 (#311)
龰	定 (#296)　題 (#381)
𠀍	事 (#362)
爫	受 (#278)
月	育 (#262)　有 (#308)　湖 (#339)
开	開 (#266)　研 (#365)
戸	所 (#333)
攵	整 (#288)　放 (#306)
歹	死 (#269)　列 (#354)
牜	物 (#375)
ネ	神 (#323)　礼 (#384)　福 (#412)
云	転 (#297)
介	世 (#393)
勿	物 (#375)
及	級 (#356)
反	返 (#305)　坂 (#345)　板 (#370)　反 (#397)
壬	庭 (#341)
夫	漢 (#380)
少	秒 (#352)
尹	君 (#313)
尺	駅 (#327)
弔	第 (#425)
心	悪 (#241)　悲 (#253)　想 (#268)　感 (#270)　急 (#285) 意 (#422)　息 (#433)
文	対 (#398)
斤	所 (#333)

方	放 (#306) 遊 (#309) 族 (#319) 旅 (#403)
日	暗 (#243) 温 (#244) 暑 (#245) 者 (#314) 題 (#381) 昔 (#411) 昭 (#413) 指 (#428)
曰	曲 (#256)
月	消 (#258) 勝 (#303) 期 (#357) 服 (#374)
木	深 (#251) 乗 (#260) 植 (#261) 想 (#268) 集 (#282) 相 (#316) 様 (#324) 橋 (#338) 柱 (#368) 板 (#370) 箱 (#377) 葉 (#389) 根 (#390) 横 (#434)
欠	飲 (#263) 次 (#435)
止	歯 (#429)
水	氷 (#415)
火	畑 (#342) 炭 (#367)
王	美 (#254) 着 (#293) 主 (#315) 球 (#396) 全 (#399)

5 stroke parts

𠂤	追 (#295)
业	業 (#392)
圣	軽 (#250)
夬	決 (#267)
氺	様 (#324) 緑 (#387)
疒	病 (#438)
癶	登 (#299) 発 (#408)
且	助 (#257)
世	葉 (#389)
丙	病 (#438)
主	住 (#283) 柱 (#368) 注 (#419)
冬	終 (#274)
古	苦 (#247) 湖 (#339)
句	局 (#332)
叩	命 (#402)

可	荷 (#404)
台	始 (#273)
失	鉄 (#424)
未	業 (#392) 味 (#405)
正	整 (#288)
永	泳 (#264)
田	申 (#259) 畑 (#342) 世 (#393) 福 (#412) 鼻 (#431)
由	笛 (#369) 由 (#407) 油 (#418)
申	神 (#323)
白	習 (#281)
皮	波 (#416) 皮 (#432)
皿	温 (#244) 皿 (#372) 血 (#427)
目	想 (#268) 着 (#293) 相 (#316) 県 (#335) 箱 (#377) 具 (#406)
矢	短 (#252) 族 (#319) 医 (#325)
石	研 (#365)
示	祭 (#410)
禾	秒 (#352) 委 (#364) 和 (#414)
穴	深 (#251) 究 (#366)
立	童 (#322) 章 (#359)

6 stroke parts

关	送 (#289) 勝 (#303)
糸	終 (#274) 練 (#312) 係 (#318) 級 (#356) 緑 (#387)
共	港 (#340)
各	落 (#310) 客 (#317) 路 (#346)
合	拾 (#279)
吏	使 (#272)
央	央 (#437)
寺	持 (#280) 待 (#291) 等 (#350) 詩 (#379)

早	章 (#359)
曲	農 (#385)
百	宿 (#330)
竹	等 (#350) 笛 (#369) 筆 (#371) 箱 (#377) 第 (#425)
米	歯 (#429)
羊	様 (#324) 羊 (#386) 洋 (#420)
羽	習 (#281)
耳	取 (#277)
聿	筆 (#371)
自	鼻 (#431) 息 (#433)
至	屋 (#328)
衣	表 (#302)
走	起 (#271)

7 stroke parts

亜	悪 (#241)
冏	商 (#391)
呂	宮 (#331)
完	院 (#326)
束	速 (#248) 整 (#288)
求	球 (#396)
艮	根 (#390) 銀 (#423)
言	調 (#294) 詩 (#379) 談 (#440)
豆	短 (#252) 登 (#299) 豆 (#388)
貝	負 (#304) 員 (#363)
足	路 (#346)
身	身 (#430)
車	軽 (#250) 転 (#297) 庫 (#347)
辰	農 (#385)

酉	配 (#301) 酒 (#409)
里	重 (#249) 童 (#322)

8 stroke parts

食	館 (#329)
隹	集 (#282) 進 (#287)
咅	倍 (#351) 部 (#353)
免	勉 (#383)
其	寒 (#246) 期 (#357)
具	真 (#421)
周	調 (#294)
官	館 (#329)
東	練 (#312)
炎	談 (#440)
者	暑 (#245) 都 (#343)
金	銀 (#423) 鉄 (#424)
長	帳 (#378)
門	開 (#266) 問 (#307)
非	悲 (#253)

9 stroke parts

昜	湯 (#417) 陽 (#426)
咸	感 (#270)
直	植 (#261)
軍	運 (#265)
重	動 (#300)
面	面 (#401)
音	暗 (#243) 意 (#422)
頁	題 (#381)
食	飲 (#263)

10 stroke parts

皆	階 (#355)
馬	駅 (#327)
鳥	島 (#344)

11 stroke parts

黄	横 (#434)

12 stroke parts

喬	橋 (#338)

13 stroke parts

楽	薬 (#376)

Glossary D: Search by Stroke Count

2 strokes

丁 255

4 strokes

予 312
化 426
区 205
反 350

5 strokes

世 339
主 167
仕 270
他 178
代 118
写 84
去 107
号 255
央 427
平 427
打 117
氷 386
由 363
申 56
皮 415
皿 289
礼 312

6 strokes

両 351
全 350
列 242
向 106
守 84
安 20
州 205
式 229
曲 46
有 156
次 426
死 69
羊 323
血 414

7 strokes

住 106
助 46
医 189
君 167
坂 228
対 350
局 204
役 178
投 130
決 68
究 271
豆 324
身 415
返 146

8 strokes

事 270
使 83
具 363
取 94
受 94
味 362
命 351
和 374
始 83
委 270
定 129
実 340
岸 216
幸 45
所 204
放 146
昔 373
服 299
板 289
油 387
波 386
注 387
泳 57
物 299
者 167
育 57
苦 33
表 145

9 strokes

乗 56
係 168
品 299
客 168
屋 190
度 241
待 117
急 106
拾 94
持 95
指 414
昭 374
柱 288
洋 387
炭 288
畑 217
発 363
相 168
県 205
研 271
神 179
秒 242
級 254
美 45
負 146
追 129
送 117
重 33
面 351

10 strokes

倍 241
勉 312
員 271
宮 204
島 228
庫 229
庭 217
息 415
旅 362
根 324
流 157
消 46
病 427
真 402
荷 362
起 83
速 33
配 145
酒 373
院 189

11 strokes

動 130
商 339
問 156
宿 190
帳 300
悪 20
族 178
深 34
球 340
祭 373
章 255
笛 288
第 403
終 84

習	95
転	129
進	107
部	242
都	228

12 strokes

勝	145
寒	21
悲	45
暑	21
期	254
植	56
歯	414
温	21
港	217
湖	216
湯	386
登	130
着	118
短	34
童	179
筆	289
等	241
落	157
葉	324
軽	34
遊	156
運	68
開	68
陽	403
階	254
集	95
飲	57

13 strokes

想	69
意	402
感	69
暗	20
業	339
漢	311
福	374
詩	311
路	229
農	323
鉄	403

14 strokes

様	179
緑	323
練	157
銀	402
駅	189
鼻	415

15 strokes

横	426
箱	300
調	118
談	427

16 strokes

整	107
橋	216
薬	300
館	190

18 strokes

題	311

Other From Zero! Books

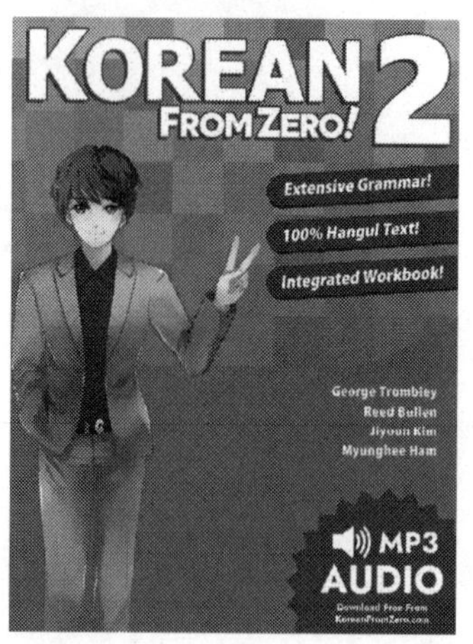

出力日： 2022-05-31

更新版： 1.1

Made in the USA
Columbia, SC
24 April 2024